CHICAGO'S IRISH LEGION

Colonel Timothy O'Meara, born in Tipperary, served in the U.S. Mounted Riflemen and as captain of Company E, 42nd New York Volunteer Infantry, before commanding Chicago's Irish Legion until his death at Missionary Ridge in November 1863. (Courtesy of the Abraham Lincoln Presidential Library, Springfield, Ill.)

CHICAGO'S IRISH LEGION
THE 90TH ILLINOIS VOLUNTEERS IN THE CIVIL WAR

JAMES B. SWAN

Southern Illinois University Press
Carbondale

Printed in the United States of America

27 26 25 24 5 4 3 2

Jacket illustrations: Captain Patrick Sarsfield Real, who led Company K, June 1863–September 1864 (private collection); and map of march of the 90th Illinois during campaigns at Vicksburg and Jackson, Mississippi.

Library of Congress Cataloging-in-Publication Data
Swan, James B.
Chicago's Irish Legion : the 90th Illinois Volunteers in the Civil War / James B. Swan.
p. cm.
Includes bibliographical references and index.
ISBN-13: 978-0-8093-2890-1 (cloth : alk. paper)
ISBN-10: 0-8093-2890-9 (cloth : alk. paper)
1. United States. Army. Illinois Infantry Regiment, 90th (1862–1865) 2. United States—History—Civil War, 1861–1865—Regimental histories. 3. United States—History—Civil War, 1861–1865—Participation, Irish American. 4. United States—History—Civil War, 1861–1865—Campaigns. 5. Irish American soldiers—Illinois—Chicago—History—19th century. 6. Chicago (Ill.)—History—Civil War, 1861–1865. I. Title.
E505.590th .S93 2009
973.7'473—dc22 2008026838

Printed on recycled paper ♻

SIU
Southern Illinois University System

To the officers and men of the 90th Illinois

CONTENTS

ILLUSTRATIONS

Frontispiece

Maps

Figures

Photographs (following page 116)

ACKNOWLEDGMENTS

In writing the history of Chicago's Irish Legion, I have benefited from a wealth of information contained in official records and in engrossing personal accounts and observations of the Legion's actions as well as those of its members. Official reports, including those recorded in *The War of the Rebellion: A Compilation of the Official Records of the Union and Confederate Armies*, volume 5 of the *Report of the Adjutant General of the State of Illinois*, the 90th Illinois files contained in Record Group 94 of the National Archives, and the Illinois State Archives, provided a wealth of detail on the Legion's Civil War military experiences. In his 1876 county history, *Fifteen Years Ago or the Patriotism of Will County*, George H. Woodruff provided a brief account of the formation and early adventures of the Irish Legion, told with the skill of an experienced raconteur. He also included a short narrative by an unidentified officer of the regiment describing the regiment's first year of service.

The staffs of the National Archives (Washington, D.C.), Illinois State Archives and Abraham Lincoln Presidential Library (Springfield), and Newberry Library and Chicago History Museum (Chicago) were most helpful in obtaining information pertaining to the 90th Illinois from their files. Special thanks are due the Abraham Lincoln Presidential Library for preserving and giving permission to quote from the Owen Stuart letters, the Newberry Library for preserving issues of the *Chicago Post*, and the Chicago History Museum for preserving and granting permission to quote from the letters of Peter Casey. The Chickamauga and Chattanooga National Military Park's maps and files on the 90th Illinois and the 100th Indiana and the insight of the park's historian, James Ogden, assisted in locating the Legion's positions and actions during its attack on Missionary Ridge. The history is enriched by the Chicago History Museum's permission to publish the photograph of Captain Peter Casey and by the Abraham Lincoln Presidential Library's permission to publish the rare photograph of Colonel Timothy O'Meara.

I am indebted to the families of William White, Patrick Real, Patrick Sloan, and Redmond Sheridan for providing photographs of their Irish Legion ancestors.

Special thanks and recognition are due to Marguerite Main, Julia Fulton, the Sheridan family, and Chuck Real for providing letters from their respective Irish Legion ancestors, which added greatly to the history. I am indebted to Marguerite Main for the many excellent accounts and keen observations of Lieutenant William White contained in his letters and papers; to Julia Fulton for the Civil War letters of Corporal Patrick Sloan, who was a keen observer of the passing scene and gave insight into the enlisted man's view of the war; to the Sheridan family for the letters of Quartermaster Redmond Sheridan, the regiment's philosopher and gifted raconteur, who provided insight into the war and the regiment and was a source of memorable stories of wartime encounters; and to Chuck Real for information regarding one of the stalwarts of the Legion, "Cap" Real, and of Cap's brother James, who died a hero's death in the Confederate cause bearing the flag of the 154th Tennessee (Senior) on the second day at Shiloh. Thanks are also due to Sharon Moore and Frank Campo for their help in describing Private Alexander Moore's wartime experiences. Special thanks go to Bobby Joe Mitchell of Holly Springs for his patience and graciousness in giving me a personal tour of the site occupied by the 90th Illinois at Coldwater Station and identifying locations mentioned by members of the 90th Illinois in their letters.

I wish to thank Ellen Skerrett, Edwin C. Bearss, Hubert McAlexander, and Bobby Joe Mitchell for reading and commenting on portions of a draft manuscript. Terry Johnson and Michael Kane provided valuable newspaper articles dealing with the 90th Illinois.

The Illinois State Archives' files on the 90th Illinois, the Newberry Library's collection of the *Chicago Post*, the Yates Family Papers of the Abraham Lincoln Presidential Library, Theodore J. Karamanski's *Rally 'Round the Flag: Chicago and the Civil War*, and Ellen Skerrett's *At the Crossroads: Old Saint Patrick's and the Chicago Irish* provided valuable insights into the role of Chicago's Irish in the regiment's formation and actions.

Edwin C. Bearss's definitive three-volume study *The Campaign for Vicksburg* and also his *The Siege of Jackson* along with Warren E. Grabau's *Ninety-Eight Days: A Geographer's View of the Vicksburg Campaign* defined the geographical setting and military actions in which the 90th Illinois took part during the Vicksburg and Jackson campaigns.

This book would never have appeared without the intensive research of, encouragement of, advice from, and corrections of multiple versions by my wife, Patricia Swan. Her discovery and subsequent comments regarding Theodore Upson's description of the Irish Legion's tumultuous attempt to establish camp at the Big Black River outside Vicksburg provided the inspiration for this history of Chicago's Irish Legion.

CHICAGO'S IRISH LEGION

INTRODUCTION

The 90th Illinois Volunteer Infantry, known locally as the "Irish Legion," was a special Civil War outfit, distinguished from other Illinois regiments by its formation, composition, and behavior. As Chicago's second Irish regiment, it existed directly as a result of the efforts of the Reverend Denis Dunne, pastor of Chicago's St. Patrick's Church. Father Dunne promoted the regiment's formation not only out of patriotism but also out of the desire to refute criticism that Irish Catholics were not supportive of the Union's war effort. Enlisted primarily in August and September of 1862, the regiment's members were mainly foreign-born and somewhat older than most Illinois soldiers. They marched more than 2,600 miles, mostly as members of Major General William T. Sherman's XV Army Corps, and in the process traversed seven Southern states, participating in major battles at Chattanooga, Tennessee, and Resaca and Dallas, Georgia, and in three major battles around Atlanta. They were instrumental in the capture of Fort McAllister at Savannah, Georgia, following the march to the sea. After the grueling march through the Carolinas, they took part in the Grand Review in Washington, D.C. Although 356 soldiers reportedly deserted, mostly before the regiment left Chicago, the 626 remaining troops suffered in excess of 400 casualties and disabilities on behalf of the Union.[1]

Since the 90th Illinois was a largely Irish regiment, a few brief comments on the status and makeup of the Irish in mid-nineteenth-century America will aid in understanding some of the special challenges faced in forming the regiment. Much as today, being unskilled in the 1860s had drawbacks. This was especially true for an unskilled Irish Catholic immigrant who faced prejudice because of his faith, his numbers, and his presence as a significant voting block for the Democratic

Party. The Irish potato famine and associated clearances of Irish families from large estates by their landlords resulted in a flood of such immigrants. From 1841 to 1850, some 780,000 emigrated from Ireland to the United States, and 914,000 more arrived during the next ten years. Most settled in the industrial cities and towns of the Northeast, where they found employment in ports, mills, canal and railroad construction, and other businesses employing unskilled laborers. As the most recent group to immigrate to America, they occupied the lowest rung on the 1860s socioeconomic ladder. In 1860, the 87,000 Irish were the second largest immigrant group in Illinois, outnumbered only by Germans. Irish immigrants concentrated in and around the rapidly expanding city of Chicago, where the demand for unskilled workers was high. As a result, immigrants outnumbered native-born in Chicago in 1860, with associated economic and political ramifications.[2]

The concentration of immigrants in large cities and newly formed western states led to a significant percentage of the volunteer soldiers from these areas being foreign-born. Some 177,000 German-born and 144,000 Irish-born volunteers served in the Union army. Foreign-born made up 22 percent of the volunteer soldiers in Illinois. Of Illinois's 217,000 volunteer white soldiers, the most numerous foreign-born were the more than 18,000 from Germany and 12,000 from Ireland. Black volunteers from Illinois numbered 2,500. Since only two Illinois regiments, the 23rd and 90th, are recognized as entirely or largely made up of "ethnic Irish," the remaining 10,000 volunteers of Irish birth were dispersed throughout a number of Illinois regiments in which other nationalities predominated.[3]

In one of the paradoxes of the Civil War, white males of military age in the older northeastern states of New York and Massachusetts supported the war less strongly than their counterparts in the relatively recently formed states of Illinois and Indiana. The number of individual white soldiers from Illinois and Indiana represented an amazing 58 and 59 percent, respectively, of their states' military-age white male population reported in the 1860 census, whereas comparable figures for the states of New York and Massachusetts were 42 and 41 percent, respectively. Irish-born soldiers formed a greater percentage of soldiers from the states of New York, Illinois, and Indiana than the percentage of Irish-born of their states' 1860 population. However, the situation was reversed for the state of Massachusetts, leading to the conclusion that along with their neighbors, the Irish-born residents of Illinois and Indiana demonstrated equal if not greater patriotism than their compatriots in these two eastern states.[4]

Compared to many of their eastern counterparts, the Irish immigrants who made up the bulk of the 90th Illinois differed by possessing the means and will to leave the eastern seaboard and migrate to the relatively recently settled, rapidly growing state of Illinois. Some, especially single, unskilled laborers, had come to Illinois to benefit from the higher wages paid for work on western farms and cities. The Irish soldiers of the 90th Illinois entered a regiment that differed from most eastern Irish regiments in its method of formation, the nature of the military campaigns in which it took part, its relative isolation from other Irish regiments during its field service, the smaller size of the Irish community in its home state, and associated lesser newspaper coverage of its actions. Whereas the charismatic Irish nationalists Thomas Francis Meagher and Michael Corcoran recruited their respective Irish Brigade and Irish Legion of Irish Catholic soldiers, Father Denis Dunne directed the formation of the Catholic Irish 90th Illinois and selected its colonel. Nine Irish regiments served in Meagher's and Corcoran's brigades along with three other Irish regiments in the Army of the Potomac during the war. In contrast, from the time the 90th Illinois joined the XV Corps, it was the sole Irish regiment in Sherman's own XV Corps, and together with the partly Irish 17th Wisconsin of the XVII Corps, they constituted the only Irish regiments on the march to the sea and through the Carolinas. They were two of the three Irish regiments that served throughout the Atlanta campaign in the Army of the Tennessee. The greater concentration of Irish in the East assured eastern Irish regiments of greater newspaper coverage than western Irish regiments. The state of New York contained five times as many Irish-born residents as Illinois, while Massachusetts and Pennsylvania both had more than twice as many Irish-born residents as Illinois. Meagher's and Corcoran's fiery natures attracted press coverage as they fitted the popular image of Irish military prowess described by G. K. Chesterton as "the men that God made mad. For all their wars are merry and all their songs are sad." All these factors contributed to the relative obscurity of western Irish regiments during the war.[5]

Raising a state regiment involved many factors beyond a simple response to a call to the colors. In reality, the formation of a state regiment in the Civil War required considerable political and economic input, while raising an Irish regiment, by definition, had strong ethnic and religious connotations. To further complicate things, membership in the Fenian Brotherhood, a secret organization of militant Irish Nationalists who advocated the violent overthrow of British power in Ireland, was severely frowned on by the Catholic Church. It can be argued that during this war, nothing was ever simple for a recent Irish immigrant. He could easily find himself forced to choose his own path among his loyalties to the cause of Irish Nationalism, his recently adopted country, the Democratic Party, the church, and his family, if he was fortunate enough to have acquired one.[6]

To avoid littering quotations with corrections, I have left unchanged the original spellings—including misspellings—and terminology in use at that time except where confusion was likely to occur; corrected spellings and clarifications are enclosed in brackets. The following convention is used to identify Union army units: Union corps are designated by roman numerals, Union division names are spelled out, and Union state volunteer regiments are designated numerically. In quotations, however, unit designations are left unchanged and may not follow this convention. Confederate corps, divisions, and brigades generally took the name of their commander, with brigades also identified by state in some cases. From the start of the war, Union and Confederate forces often chose different names for the same battle, and this trend continued more or less unabated throughout the war. To minimize confusion, both Confederate and Union names for a battle are given initially, but thereafter its Union name is used.

The basic unit for recruitment was the regiment composed of about a thousand men, commanded by a colonel. Four or more regiments were combined into a brigade, commanded by a brigadier general or a colonel. Two or three brigades were combined into a division, commanded by a major general or brigadier general. An army corps contained two, three, or sometimes four divisions. Major generals commanded Union army corps, while lieutenant generals commanded Confederate army corps.[7]

Politics were heavily involved in the appointment of officers in state regiments. The colonel of a state volunteer regiment was appointed by that state's governor, while members of a company commonly elected their own officers, usually from within their own ranks. Due to the scarcity of trained military personnel in most state regiments, inexperienced officers and enlisted men were forced to learn soldiering together the hard way. Those officers and noncommissioned officers unable to function effectively in their new roles were eventually weeded out.[8]

The following history describes the formation, battles, and movements of the Irish Catholic 90th Illinois Volunteer Infantry regiment from its organization to its return to Chicago after the close of the Civil War.

{1}

THE RAISING OF THE IRISH LEGION

The story of Chicago's Irish Legion, the 90th Illinois Volunteer Infantry, begins with a meeting of the area's Irish leaders in the heat and humidity of an 1862 summer evening in a crowded schoolroom of St. Patrick's parish, a few blocks west of downtown. The chairman of this August 8 meeting, the Very Reverend Father Denis Dunne, looked out over the rapidly filling room, recognizing many members of his St. Patrick's parish and other nearby parishes. The meeting's secretary, James Washington Sheahan, a Stephen Douglas Democrat and editor of the *Chicago Post*, like most in the room strongly supported the war to preserve the Union. Other prominent members of the Irish community included J. J. Kinsella and Aldermen Redmond Sheridan and James Conlan. Several of those present were actively conducting disparate recruiting efforts to raise individual companies, but they faced fierce competition from some forty captains currently recruiting in Chicago. Despite their expenditure of time and money, none present at the meeting had enlisted enough men to form a complete company, let alone one of the several Irish regiments proposed as part of the state's quota under the call of President Abraham Lincoln for 300,000 additional troops. Current attempts by two of Chicago's Irish leaders, Smith McCleavy and Colonel William B. Snowhook, to raise Irish regiments also made only limited progress. Against this background, Father Dunne sought to raise the Irish Legion.

They met amid an atmosphere of unrest in Chicago. The previous day, the governor of Illinois, Richard Yates, had requested authority from the secretary of war, Edwin Stanton, to again declare martial law and had suggested suppressing the main Democratic newspaper, the *Chicago Times*, for being disloyal. Dunne saw and understood the growing dissatisfaction of the Irish with their own plight as well as with federal policies, but he also understood that some publicly questioned the patriotism of Irish Catholics, and failure in the current efforts to raise at least one Irish regiment would only reinforce such questioning. Bishop James Duggan's absence abroad left Father Dunne, as vicar-general, in charge of the diocese with the power to unite the Irish community and bring order out of the current chaos surrounding the formation of Chicago's second Irish regiment. A missionary priest in northern Illinois before directing the building of St. Patrick's Church, Dunne had proven to be a man of action, but before taking the steps necessary to recruit and form an Irish Catholic regiment, he wisely sought the support of his parishioners. That such a large number of Chicago's Irish responded on short notice provided reassurance that his efforts would succeed.

Calling the meeting to order, Father Dunne carefully explained that its purpose was to "take the views of the Catholic people respecting the proper manner in which they should join the military forces of the country, called for by the Government to protect the Union." He pointed out that the lack of a clergyman of their own faith in a regiment deterred enlistment by Catholics. Father Dunne had discussed the matter with Governor Yates, obtaining broad written authority from the governor "that as soon as the companies were raised he [Yates] would commission the officers and that he would authorize the regiments to select their own Colonel and officers and chaplains." The governor's willingness to make good on his promise would prove to be a key factor in the formation and leadership of the Irish Legion.[1]

After several in attendance spoke in favor of organizing an Irish regiment, the discussion concluded with a fiery speech "urging the duty of every man, and particularly of the Irish Catholics, to rally in all their strength for the defense of the Government, the Union and the Constitution." Acknowledging the moment for action had arrived, Father Dunne, as chairman, declared "the sense of the meeting to be that the regiment should be raised. He and the clergy of the diocese would use every exertion to have it filled up without delay." He then "called upon those presently engaged in recruiting, or intending to do so, to give their names and the number of companies." Fourteen responded, including Sheridan and several others who became officers of the 90th Illinois. Elected by acclamation, Father Dunne became the temporary colonel of the regiment and chairman of the executive committee in charge of organizing the regiment and expediting its recruitment, making Dunne truly the father of the regiment. The meeting concluded with a resolution from Kinsella, who as a loyal Irishman simply could not resist an opportunity to pull the lion's tail: "Resolved that this meeting view with contempt, abhorrence, and detestation those unfortunate Irishmen who have sought, or who are now seeking, the protection of the blood stained felon flag of Great Britain to escape their duty to the United States; and that such men deserve if not hanging, at least to be put out of the country." The motion, aimed to stir the conscience of the hundreds of draft dodgers or "skedaddlers" seeking rail or boat passage through Chicago to Canada in August 1862, passed unanimously.[2]

In forming the Irish Legion, Father Dunne's committee faced the challenge of overseeing the recruitment of nearly a thousand men, but of equal or even greater concern, they needed to fill company and regimental officer and staff positions with reliable personnel who could function efficiently. The sheer number and diversity of personnel required in a regiment was impressive. As initially recruited, a regiment included ten companies, each with a captain, a first lieutenant, a second lieutenant, a first sergeant, four sergeants, eight corporals, two musicians, one wagoner, and sixty-four to eighty-two privates. The regimental officer and staff positions of colonel, lieutenant colonel, major, adjutant, regimental quartermaster, surgeon, assistant surgeon, chaplain, sergeant major, regimental quartermaster sergeant, regimental commissary sergeant, hospital steward, and two or three principal musicians also had to be filled.

Formation of the Legion did not proceed smoothly, and the first impediment occurred almost immediately. A dispatch from Illinois adjutant general Allan Fuller, apparently declaring that Illinois's quota had been met, led to the suspension of recruiting at the ten stations opened following the August 8 meeting. Another dispatch from Fuller quickly followed, however, allowing recruitment to resume. To resolve the resulting confusion and rekindle enthusiasm necessary to get recruitment moving again, an even larger war meeting was held on the evening of August 12. The expected attendance exceeded the capacity of the parish's schoolroom, requiring the use of the recently completed Bryan Hall, located on the east side of Clark Street, between Washington and Randolph, and described by the *Chicago Tribune* as the "leading concert hall" and "principle assembly room of the city." Complete with fiery speeches by Chicago politicians and influential citizens, including former mayor John C. Haines's and Alderman Redmond Sheridan's resolutions of support for the Constitution and Union that passed unanimously, the meeting accomplished its objective of furthering the organization of the Irish Legion. A number of those present at the meeting either became members of the regiment or were influential in its formation. Sheridan called the meeting to order, which again chose the editor of the *Post*, James Sheahan, as secretary. Vice presidents chosen included Sheridan, Alderman Conlan, Smith McCleavy, and Captain Owen Stuart, part owner and a printer at the *Post*. Electing an editor as secretary assured accurate reporting of the meeting. Under the banner "The War Meeting at Bryan Hall: Irish Element Aroused," the next day's *Post* described the meeting as "large and enthusiastic."[3]

Father Dunne received a supportive letter from Colonel James Mulligan, located at the Virginia camp of Chicago's first Irish regiment, the 23rd Illinois. Mulligan began in humorous fashion by congratulating Dunne on his promotion to the colonelcy of the "Dunne Legion" and proceeded in a similar fashion: "I bid you welcome to the new vocation. I hail your conversion from the breviary to the bayonet; from the canon law to the law of the cannons; from 'taking heaven by violence' to taking towns by storm. It is meet and just. . . . I need not tell you, Father Dunne, how intimately in all ecclesiastical history St. Peter and saltpeter are blended, shedding luster upon many a mitre." Mulligan concluded by wishing Dunne success in rousing "our countrymen to their duty."[4]

By the summer of 1862, enthusiasm of potential recruits in Chicago for the war required some rousing, differing greatly from the early days of the war when torchlight parades and massed meetings brought swarms of recruits seeking military glory. In the spring of 1861, Mulligan—Irish Nationalist, prominent Chicago Democrat politician, and soon to be colonel—had recruited some 1,200 Irishmen within a week to form Chicago's first Irish regiment, which he grandly termed the "Irish Brigade."[5]

In contrast, the formation of Chicago's second Irish regiment took nearly four months and tested the patience of all involved, including both the Illinois adjutant general and the governor. By August 1862, much of the initial wave of enthusiasm for military glory had receded when the true nature of the war became apparent through lengthy casualty lists from such battles as Shiloh. The continuing series of Union defeats in the East, including the Seven Days' campaign around Richmond, Virginia, and the just-concluded Second Bull Run campaign, combined with the Confederate invasion of Kentucky, provided little assurance of ultimate Union triumph. Why, then, in the summer of 1862, when it was clear that it would be a long and bloody war, would any recent immigrant volunteer? In addition to patriotism, including the desire to preserve the Union, other more practical reasons also motivated enlistment.[6]

A story attributed to a Union officer in the Army of the Potomac during the siege of Petersburg illustrates the mixed views some soldiers held as to why a recent immigrant would serve in the Union army.

> One moonlight evening, when both sides were top of the trenches, the other side was particularly noisy. That day, or the day before, the enemy had captured a large herd of our beef cattle . . . and there was hilarity over it. . . . They were vociferously noisy, when an Irishman shouted with a distinct "old sod" accent: "Say, you Johnnies, stop yer hollerin' so soldiers can slape!" Back came, "Hello, Pat! How long you been over? Suppose you are soldiering for the Yankees'—beautiful greenbacks."
>
> "Well," said the Irishman, "yees is fightin' for money that has nayther beauty nor value."
>
> Laughter followed from both sides with cheers on our side for the Irishman's rejoinder.

Then from the other side: "Come over with us, Pat; we are fighting for honor and you are fighting for money."

"Thin we is both fightin' for what we most nade."[7]

Their motivation also involved other factors. The words "one nation indivisible, with liberty and justice for all," are repeated now without objection in every recitation of the Pledge of Allegiance, but the basic principles behind these words were not always so accepted. In 1861, disagreement over just such concepts was a major cause of our great civil war. Practical reasons for enlistment included the expectation that wartime service would translate into improved economic opportunity, increased social stature, and greater acceptance by other Americans for them and for the Irish in general, or at least less open hostility by the successors to the "Know-Nothings" and other such nativists. Stated another way, the Irish volunteer believed wartime service would improve his chances of being included as part of the "for all." Besides patriotic fervor and a sense of duty, bounties, unemployment, social pressure, the promise of adventure, the threat of being drafted, Irish nationalism and hatred of England, an appeal to the martial traits of the Irish, and the need to exploit the war for political advantage all have been suggested as explanations why an Irish immigrant would join a Union Civil War regiment.[8]

The quartermaster of the 90th Illinois, forty-three-year-old Redmond Sheridan, former Chicago alderman and staunch Democrat, summed up the reasons for enlistment as he saw them: "The Legion had not enlisted for any but the purest and noblest motives; not to carry out any partisan ends; not to fight for sectional purposes, but to strike a blow for freedom with the recollection of the wrongs of their own native Erin still living in their memory; not to enforce political dogmas; not to promulgate abolition or secession, but to fight for the constitution as it is and the Union as it was." It should be apparent that the causes of the American Civil War and an individual's reason or reasons for enlistment often differed markedly, especially for a recent Irish immigrant.[9]

By the time Father Dunne's regiment began recruiting, any volunteers, including Irishmen, were difficult to obtain, and the federal government and local authorities were forced to offer substantial cash bounties to spur enlistment. The federal government resorted to paying advanced bounties of twenty-five dollars and a month's pay of thirteen dollars for each soldier of a new regiment "when their companies are organized, muster-in rolls made out, and the mustering officer's certificate given thereto." Upon discharge, the soldier received an additional seventy-five dollars. Local groups provided additional bounties to spur enlistment and meet county quotas. In Chicago, the Board of Trade subscribed $10,000 for bounties of fifty dollars each, the Cook County Board of Supervisors voted $200,000 for bounties of sixty dollars each, and prominent individuals also provided bounties. Other counties, including Will and La Salle located south of Chicago and Joe Daviess in the northwestern corner of Illinois, similarly offered bounties.[10]

Recruitment and training of the Irish Legion progressed slowly during the late summer and fall of 1862, partly because, as described by Secretary of War Stanton, this was "one of those periods of despondency which occur in every national struggle." Support for the war was in decline in the Irish community even before the government's emancipation policy raised the threat of increased competition for employment in jobs requiring unskilled labor. Moreover, the fourteen other regiments actively recruiting in northern Illinois provided strong competition for recruits. Formation of the 23rd Illinois in 1861 and its subsequent re-formation during the spring and summer of 1862 had reduced the number of potential Irish volunteers in the Chicago area. Both farms and factories provided readily available better-paying jobs, with less risk than soldiering. The large number of previous enlistments decreased the supply of farm laborers to the extent that they received attractive wages of two dollars a day to cut and harvest the crops in many counties in northern Illinois during the summer of 1862, dwarfing soldiers' pay of thirteen dollars a month.[11]

A temporary spur to enlistment occurred with the Illinois adjutant general's August 1 instructions to county clerks to begin enrolling men prior to drafting. Non-citizens were subject only to enrollment and not to a draft, but some newspaper accounts did not make such a clarification. The threat quickly subsided, for by August 11 it became apparent that no draft was required to meet Illinois's quota of troops.[12]

Thus in the summer of 1862, recruitment of Chicago's second Irish regiment required the leadership of the Catholic Church with assistance from the press, local Democratic politicians, and prominent individuals within Irish communities in northern Illinois. The key person in organizing the recruitment of the regiment was Father Dunne, the diocese of Chicago's thirty-six-year-old vicar-general, perhaps the city's best-known Catholic clergyman. Although born in Queens County, Ireland, his family had moved to Chatham, New Brunswick, when he was young. There, the family practiced ship-building trades, and Denis attended school. After preparing for the priesthood in Quebec, he was ordained in Detroit in 1848 and migrated with his brothers to Chicago, a city with jobs for shipbuilders. Appointed a member of the faculty of the University of St. Mary of the Lake, he then served briefly as a parish priest in Galena and Ottawa, Illinois. He returned to Chicago in 1854 to serve as pastor of St. Patrick's parish, where he oversaw the building of the striking Romanesque yellow brick church that stands today at the corner of Adams and Desplaines Streets. Working tirelessly for the parish, as well as for the welfare of Chicago's burgeoning Catholic population and other newly arrived immigrants, Dunne became not only a religious leader but also a popular community leader who encouraged the establishment of some of Chicago's first charitable organizations. Moreover, as a practical man aware of the city's much larger number of Irish males as compared with Irish females of marriageable age, he had arranged for the immigration of twenty-four young women from Ireland under his care. In October 1862, he received the title of Doctor of Divinity, a measure of the high regard in which the Catholic Church at Rome and Chicago's Bishop Duggan held Father Dunne's work in Illinois. Father Dunne's earlier service as a missionary priest across the northern tier of Illinois counties closely acquainted him with the major areas of recruitment for the Legion. These factors could be expected to aid recruitment efforts for the Legion.[13]

Following the organizational meetings, recruitment of troops for the second Irish regiment proceeded apace. Richard C. Kelly, who at the end of July was reported to be recruiting the first company of Colonel Snowhook's Irish regiment in a vacant lot behind the post office, switched his allegiance to Father Dunne and raised Company F of the Irish Legion with himself as captain. Captain Owen Stuart recruited at Eighty-two South Dearborn Street and would become the regiment's major. Born in Armagh in County Tyrone, Ireland, Stuart immigrated to the United States in 1847 and lived in a number of eastern cities before coming to Chicago in 1854 with James Sheahan. There, Stuart ran the press department of the *Chicago Times*, a newspaper started in 1854 by Sheahan at the request of Senator Stephen A. Douglas. In 1860, Sheahan sold the *Times* and began publication of the *Chicago Morning Post*. Stuart promptly left the *Times* and "united" with the owners of the *Post*. The Emmet Guards, an Irish volunteer company in Chicago, elected Stuart their captain in 1856, and he continued to command the company until the outbreak of the Civil War. Black-haired and gray-eyed, with a high forehead and a bit of a florid complexion, the thirty-four-year-old Stuart married Margaret Cameron three days before the departure of the regiment for the field. In his numerous letters to her, he is revealed as a gentleman who loved his wife, fine horses, and his creature comforts including good whiskey, cigars, and a small portable ten-inch stove, but not necessarily always in that order. In 1861, when an aggrieved colonel, whose conduct had been criticized in the *Post*, had made an unprovoked attack on its editor, Sheahan, striking him in the back, Stuart had immediately dealt the attacker "a powerful blow behind the ear, felling him into the gutter." Anticipating trouble, Stuart had followed closely behind the colonel as he stalked Sheahan. Stuart's actions in this matter demonstrated his ability to think ahead and act decisively when necessary, useful traits for a future officer in the Irish Legion.[14]

In an August 12 telegram to Governor Yates, Father Dunne requested the key appointment of Alderman Sheridan as quartermaster of "Our Irish Legion," the name by which the regiment came to be known. Promptly appointed by the governor, Quartermaster Sheridan became the senior officer in the regiment. In choosing Sheridan, Father Dunne obtained an officer with mature judgment who was skilled in dealing with people, was honest, did not strive or conspire for higher military rank, and avoided involvement in regimental politics, all highly desirable attributes for the quartermaster of a volunteer regiment. Sheridan had demonstrated his political skills by being elected alderman of the Eighth Ward in 1860 and again in 1862. Giving up his influential positions of alderman and member of the Chicago's Common Council and leaving his successful business in order to serve in the army entailed considerable sacrifice on Sheridan's part. This evidence of devotion to the Union totally agreed with Father Dunne's vision of the regiment. In addition, Sheridan had been the first president of the Saint Vincent de Paul Society started in Chicago by Father Dunne, which would have made Dunne aware of Sheridan's leadership ability and strong moral character. Sheridan was one of a number of uniquely interesting individuals with which the regiment seemed to be particularly blessed. Born in Bristol, England, in 1820, two weeks after his parents emigrated from Cork, he grew up in London and learned the family trade of boot-making, which he later wrote he detested. Married in 1844, he and his wife, Agnes, immigrated to New York City in 1850, subsequently moving to Chicago in about 1855, where they quickly became established members of Chicago's Irish Catholic community while adding four sons to their family number. An early member and highly respected lay leader in the Jesuit parish of Holy Family, he had a successful shoe business downtown at 105 Clark Street. His letters revealed him to be an able communicator and a good judge of people, as might be expected of a successful politician in Chicago. He showed a keen if somewhat ironic sense of humor, possessed a definite philosophic bent, and had a knack for describing events in an interesting way. His appointment to the position of quartermaster was timely; there was a need for all deliberate speed as the War Department had set a deadline of August 22 for each new regiment to reach the required levels of enlistment. After that date, "incompleted regiments will be consolidated and superfluous officers mustered out," clearly something no prospective officer desired.[15]

Based on Chicago's rapid population growth from 109,000 in 1861 to 178,000 in 1865, one might expect it to have been fertile ground for troop recruitment. However, recruiting efforts in Chicago for the Irish Legion supplied less than four of the required ten companies of seventy-eight to ninety-six officers and men aged eighteen to forty-five. It soon became apparent that instead of raising three Irish regiments, it would be difficult to raise even one and that a great deal of effort and money would be required in the process. The remaining six companies of the Irish Legion were recruited throughout central and northern Illinois and into southwestern Wisconsin. Much of this recruiting occurred in cities and towns served by the Chicago and Rock Island Railroad, the Illinois Central Railroad, and the Galena and Chicago Union Railroad. Due to the slow pace of recruitment in Cook County, the first four companies of the 90th Illinois came from counties outside Chicago, demonstrating the importance of strong local leadership in obtaining volunteers. The varied composition of these companies represented the diversity of the pool of local recruits and of the dominant economic activities of the various areas.[16]

As time progressed during the summer and fall of 1862, the recruitment of Irish volunteers in New York also became increasingly difficult as opposition to the war increased in eastern Irish communities. In spite of his eloquence, Brigadier General Thomas Meagher raised only some 250 recruits during July and August, far too few to fill the depleted ranks of his Irish Brigade. Increasing "divisiveness" in the Irish communities also complicated Brigadier General Michael Corcoran's recruitment efforts for his new Irish Legion, as noted by Susannah Bruce.[17]

Company A of the 90th Illinois came not from Chicago but from Rockford, eighty-four miles northwest of Chicago in Winnebago County. Years later, its red-haired captain, Patrick Flynn, described his company's formation in a paper read before a campfire of the local Grand Army of the Republic post. Prior to the war, Flynn had engaged in a mercantile business in Rockford since his arrival there in 1858. The genesis of Company A began on July 14, 1862, when local leaders in Rockford persuaded Flynn, then thirty years old, to assist in raising an Irish regiment of volunteers. He demonstrated a knack for this sort of thing, having previously raised some 160 volunteers from Winnebago and surrounding counties. Flynn outdid himself obtaining 140 volunteers in only sixteen days, but he did not arrive in Chicago with what the *Chicago Morning Post* called his "seventy stout and hardy Irishmen" until August 20. Before proceeding south of the city to Camp Douglas, the men of Flynn's company stopped by the *Post* to pay their respects to editor Sheahan. They had adopted the name Mulligan Guards in honor of the colonel of the 23rd Illinois, to which they expected to be attached. Instead, they became Company A of the 90th Illinois on August 31. Flynn's recruiting activities continued as he toured towns and cities in northern Illinois seeking recruits to fill up the regiment.[18]

Company B, the Ryan Guards, recruited mainly from Galena in Jo Daviess County and from Grant and adjoining counties in southwestern Wisconsin, had the twenty-four-year-old blue-eyed and dark-haired clerk Michael W. Murphy as captain. The company's name honored William Ryan of Galena for his dominant role in its recruitment. He also funded the celebration that sent the Ryan Guards off to war, or at least to Camp Douglas in Chicago. The "Departure of the Ryan Guards" filled most of two columns in the local newspaper's September 4 issue, describing in some detail the presentation of "the Green Flag of Ireland and the immortal Stars and Stripes" to the assembled members of the outfit accompanied by the obligatory lengthy addresses made more bearable as they were delivered by Miss Katie Riely and Miss Lizzie Powers. Ryan generously sponsored a presentation of swords to the officers, army blankets to the men, and a most welcome dinner for all.[19]

Both Companies C and D were recruited in Will County at cities located on the Illinois-Michigan Canal south and west of Chicago. Patrick O'Marah, a thirty-five-year-old Lockport merchant, recruited Company C, the Lockport Guards. As the second company mustered into the 90th Illinois, the unit should have been Company B, but the men instead chose to be the color company, Company C, gaining the honor of bearing the regiment's flags. Private citizens of Lockport spent considerable money for expenses and extra bounties required to form the company. Blue-eyed and brown-haired Captain Daniel O'Connor, a thirty-year-old merchant and sometime law student in Chicago, began recruiting troops at Joliet for what became Company D, the Casey Guards, soon after the July 1862 request for volunteers by the governor of Illinois. O'Connor's habit of wearing a flower in his lapel earned him the nickname "Posy Captain." The Honorable Sam K. Casey, a former governor, described by George Woodruff in a short regimental history as "a most generous godfather," gave "one thousand dollars as a bounty for recruits." The company received a "splendid banner" donated by the ladies of Joliet, along with the obligatory presentation speech.[20]

Chicago provided most recruits for Companies E, F, G, and H, but some came from small towns along the railroads throughout northern Illinois. As an example, six Company G recruits came from the small Woodford County town of Minonk, on the Illinois Central Railroad, some hundred miles southwest of Chicago. Mathew Leonard, a twenty-eight-year-old dealer in hides, recruited Company E, and John Murphy, a blue-eyed, dark-haired twenty-three-year-old machinist, recruited Company G. Murphy had recruited a company for the 67th Illinois, a three-month regiment raised June 13, 1862, which he left to join the 90th Illinois. Before the war, Murphy, like Owen Stuart, had been a member of the Emmet Guards. Company F, with Richard C. Kelly, a thirty-two-year-old butcher, as captain, included twenty-one members recruited from Springfield, the state capital, located on the St. Louis, Alton, and Chicago Railroad. Kelly had three months' military experience in 1861 as a private in Colonel Michael Corcoran's 69th New York Militia and had fought in the First Battle of Bull Run. Not the ideal person to train and lead new recruits, Kelly possessed a violent temper, and his actions demonstrated both questionable honesty and racial prejudice. Thirty-four-year-old blacksmith, saloon owner, and ex-foreman of a Chicago volunteer fire company Peter Casey recruited Company H. Born in Dublin, Ireland, he had lived most of his life in Chicago.

Following the muster of Company H into United States service on September 15, 1862, recruitment lagged, with the last two companies finally mustered in at the end of October. William Cunningham, a thirty-one-year-old drayman from Belvidere, thirteen miles east of Rockford on the Galena and Chicago Union

Railroad, recruited Company I. Thomas Barrett, the thirty-one-year-old editor of the *Democratic Standard*, raised Company K, the Jackson Guards, in La Salle County at Ottawa, a city on the Illinois-Michigan Canal. He had failed in an earlier attempt to raise a company for the 104th Illinois.[21]

More than eight out of ten enlisted men in the Irish Legion were foreign-born. Out of every one hundred, seventy were born in Ireland, seventeen in the United States (mostly first-generation Irish), four in Germany, and the balance in other countries. Two out of three of the company officers were born in Ireland. All officers serving in the rank of major or higher were born in Ireland. Seven out of ten enlisted men were single. The median age of twenty-seven years for the enlisted men of the 90th Illinois was four years greater than that of most Illinois regiments. The range in age of enlisted men from fourteen to an amazing fifty-nine indicated that the upper limit of forty-five years was not enforced. Their median height was five foot seven and one-half inches, about an inch less than the average for Illinois soldiers. The most common occupation was laborer, with farming a close second and sailor or boatman a distant third.[22]

The regiment officially mustered into United States service on September 7, 1862, at Camp Douglas, located just south of Chicago. Built during the late summer of 1861 on open prairie donated by the estate of Stephen A. Douglas as a camp of "instruction and rendezvous," Camp Douglas by February 1862 also housed Confederate prisoners following then brigadier general Ulysses S. Grant's conquest of Confederate forts Henry and Donelson. During the stay of the 90th Illinois at Camp Douglas, Prison Square contained up to nearly nine thousand Confederate prisoners who were later replaced by about the same number of less well behaved paroled Union soldiers awaiting exchange. Parole meant that soldiers gave their word not to take up arms against their captors until they were formally exchanged for an enemy captive of equal rank.

The Illinois Central Railroad tracks, located just east of the camp, provided easy access for arriving and departing troops. Lake Michigan, just to the east of the tracks, provided the water supply. The camp was surrounded by a ten-foot fence with the main gate on the east leading into the large rectangular Garrison Square in the northeast section of the camp. A similar fence separated the squares on the east from the rectangular-shaped Prison Square, which occupied the west half of the camp.[23]

Volunteer regiments undergoing training were housed in tents outside the walls of Camp Douglas, increasing the total camp area to about 114 acres. The men of the 90th Illinois were housed in tents at Camp Dunne, located about one mile south of Camp Douglas. The Irish Legion's regimental commander and his subalterns administered whatever military training the regiment experienced prior to leaving for military action in the field; the post commander, Colonel Joseph Tucker, issued only the briefest itinerary. The 90th Illinois presumably followed the daily training schedule at Camp Douglas described in Tucker's General Orders No. 8: sunrise—reveille and roll call; 7:30 A.M.—breakfast; 8:30 A.M.—surgeon's call; 9:30 A.M.—guard mounting; 10:30 A.M. to noon—drill and roll call; noon—dinner; 1 P.M.—fatigue call; 2 P.M.—drill and roll call; 3 P.M.—battalion drill; sunset—retreat and roll call; 9 P.M.—tattoo, roll call, and taps. This daily routine omits any mention of target practice. In fact, Colonel Tucker worried more about accidental wounding of recruits than about their proficiency with small arms. In General Orders No. 10, he forbade discharging muskets in camp, directing that "whenever arms are to be discharged the men should be sent to the Lake Shore." Tucker's worries included the tendency of officers and men to modify their training to include a daily visit to a nearby Chicago tavern or other facility without permission of a superior officer, as indicated by the five roll calls in his daily training schedule. His General Orders No. 18, dated September 10 and directed to Captain C. P. Bradley, Chicago's general superintendent of police, authorized and requested him "to arrest all Soldiers from this Camp found in the City of Chicago without written passes in proper form and report the same to me." He listed six infantry regiments, including the 90th Illinois and two artillery batteries, as being in camp. While at Camp Douglas, the regiment became proficient at standing for reviews and general inspections called on short notice.[24]

Besides learning basic military formations and maneuvers, members of the regiment stood guard over Confederate prisoners at Camp Douglas. Most prisoners had been exchanged by September, leaving only 150 or so sick prisoners in camp. They were soon replaced with nine thousand rather insubordinate paroled Union soldiers who found the camp thoroughly uninviting, with their barracks in awful shape and the area a virtual sea of mud. The paroled troops had not enlisted for this and did not take kindly to the situation, with the result that a number burned their barracks or committed other similar acts of destruction. On October 3, some four hundred parolees broke down the fence surrounding their compound and headed for town. Fed up with the situation, the editor of the *Post* wrote: "There are hundreds of these soldiers on the streets all day and night. . . . You see them on the streets and in houses, in whisky shops and in the gutter, in the police court, and in the bridewell [the city jail], in fact everywhere, but in camp." On October 17, members of a Vermont regiment set fire to their barracks and attacked the fire engine crew sent to put out the blaze. According to another newspaper account, the soldiers next attacked the hose-cart and would very quickly have demolished it "had not Lieutenant Harrington [first lieutenant of Company C] of the Irish Legion, stepped boldly forward and, drawing his revolver, threatened to shoot the first man that dared to move towards it." Harrington then escorted the engine crew safely back to the fire station, stopping another threatened attack on the way. A member of the Chicago Fire Department before the war, John C. Harrington took a personal interest in protecting his fellow firemen. Quartermaster Sheridan described him as "one of the most powerful of men physically that I ever knew." The undisciplined behavior of the paroled soldiers ran directly counter to efforts of officers of the 90th Illinois to instill discipline in their new recruits, making their job of training the troops that much harder.[25]

The cold reality of only one Irish regiment and thus only one colonel's commission to be awarded resulted in heated competition for leadership of the regiment between Captain Timothy J. O'Meara, backed by followers of Father Dunne, and Colonel William Snowhook, backed by influential Chicago Republicans. A lawyer, staunch Democrat, and successful businessman who had served nine years as the Collector of the Port of Chicago, Snowhook was a fifty-eight-year-old Irish immigrant, a Catholic with a Protestant wife. His military experience was confined to northern Illinois, where he had raised and equipped the 60th Regiment of Illinois Militia (Montgomery Guards), advancing in rank from fourth sergeant to first lieutenant in 1842 and to captain in 1847. His military title of colonel derived from the Mormon disturbances in 1846 at Nauvoo, Illinois, when he served on Governor Thomas Ford's staff.[26]

Wary of Snowhook's marked lack of military experience, Father Dunne and others involved in forming the regiment wanted it led by "a practical and experienced military man, who should at the same time be of Irish birth or descent, and of the Catholic faith," according to Woodruff. The disastrous consequences of trusting a newly formed regiment to a military amateur such as Snowhook had been clearly demonstrated earlier by the embarrassing capture of Mulligan's Irish Brigade, the 23rd Illinois, in its first action. They clearly wanted to avoid the possibility of a repeat of that performance. Dunne preferred the twenty-seven-year-old Tipperary-born Irishman Captain O'Meara of the 42nd New York (Tammany regiment) for colonel of the regiment. General Corcoran had recommended the handsome gray-eyed, dark-haired, fair-complexioned, five-foot-ten-inch-tall O'Meara to Father Dunne. O'Meara's prior military experience included his five-year enlistment beginning in 1855 at the age of twenty-one as a private in the regular army. He served in the Regiment of Mounted Riflemen in Texas and New Mexico, rising to the rank of sergeant. He then served in Benito Juárez's Mexican army as a major of cavalry. With the coming of the Civil War, he returned to his adopted state of New York and enrolled on May 3, 1861, for three years' service at Great Neck, Long Island, as an adjutant in the 42nd New York. Rapidly promoted to captain of Company E, he demonstrated leadership ability under fire, acquitting himself with honor at the Battle of Ball's Bluff on October 21, 1861. Arriving at the battlefield when the Union troops were in retreat, his company fought well. With the battle hopelessly lost, he directed the use of a rowboat to save several boatloads of wounded. Although he could have escaped capture, he chose to remain with his troops.

While in a Confederate prison at Salisbury, North Carolina, O'Meara became acquainted with, and obviously favorably impressed, the then colonel and fellow captive Michael Corcoran. O'Meara had been one of two captains selected by lot and kept under close confinement as hostages, or as "subjects of retaliation" in General Robert E. Lee's terminology, in case the Union executed two captured partisan officers, whom Lee described as members "of the Ranger Service of the State of Virginia."[27]

After the settlement of the hostage situation and the formalities involved in being properly exchanged, Captain O'Meara arrived in Chicago by September 8, 1862, on leave from his regiment and accompanied by a strong letter of endorsement from now Brigadier General Michael Corcoran to Father Dunne. In the letter, published in the September 9 *Chicago Morning Post*, Corcoran recommended O'Meara "as qualified in every respect to command the regiment now being raised." Corcoran described O'Meara's devotion to the Union, while they were fellow prisoners of the Confederates, and then concluded the letter with this clincher: "I know no man better qualified, nor none in whom I have more implicit confidence and trust that he will [be] acceptable to you." This was high praise indeed, and coming from such a respected Irish military leader, O'Meara obviously met Father Dunne's criteria. Furthermore, O'Meara made a fine impression. The *Post* described him in glowing terms: "Col. O'Meara, since he has been here, has won the respect and confidence of the officers and men of the regiment. His military experience and knowledge renders him far more acceptable than any mere civilian would have been. In addition to his military acquirements, Col. O'Meara is a gentleman of high personal character, and will be a popular as well as skillful officer."[28]

Having served in the prewar American army, although clearly Irish and wholly Catholic, O'Meara had adopted his new country fully, as shown by his "lion like" demeanor when declaring unflinching support of his government's policy in the presence of his captors while a Confederate prisoner and his later outspoken public support of President Lincoln's Emancipation Proclamation. O'Meara's loyalty seemed to lie entirely with the United States and not divided between his old home and his new.[29]

Selection of the regiment's colonel created something of a dilemma for Governor Yates, a Republican, who had to choose between the candidate backed by fellow Republicans in Chicago and the one backed by prominent Catholic clergy. In this matter he received plenty of unsolicited advice, including several letters of endorsement of Snowhook's candidacy. Some letters included vicious personal attacks on Snowhook's competition in a bold attempt to swing the selection in his favor. In a letter to Yates dated August 25, a Republican politician made the unsubstantiated, potentially dangerous charges that "Father Dunne & Co." had discouraged enlistment, were "creating division and ill feeling in our ranks," and had unfairly "told the men that if they went with Snowhook they could have no

Catholic Chaplain." He concluded by requesting appointment as the regiment's surgeon, which he did not receive. Another equally partisan letter, this time addressed to Adjutant General Fuller, attacked Dunne and asked that the governor specify that the election of the colonel be by "a secret vote by ballot of the Entire regt. rank & file." Neither letter showed much knowledge about the election process used to elect field officers in the regiment, which was by vote of company officers.[30]

A dispatch from Springfield in the August 29 Chicago papers indicating Colonel Snowhook would be the likely choice for colonel of the Irish Legion galvanized Father Dunne's supporters into action. Former mayor John C. Haines promptly sent a sharply worded letter of protest to Governor Yates defending Father Dunne's interests, integrity, and plans: "I need hardly remind you that in the authority given by you to Father Dunne to raise the Irish Legion it is promised & provided that the Rev. Father shall have the naming of the officers of the regiment including the Chaplain & it would be in bad faith now to name officers for the regiment contrary to his wishes, and besides the Father Dunne is acting bishop of the Diocese of Illinois & as such is certainly entitled to fair consideration." Haines added: "The Rev. Father is now in communication with Genl. Corcoran & will I think indicate a man for the Colonelcy of the regiment with whom you & all hands will be pleased." In conclusion, Haines thought Snowhook would have no trouble raising a regiment of his own and supposed that he might do so. To drive the point home, on August 30 Father Dunne telegraphed Governor Yates: "Beware of misrepresentation. Snowhook had nothing to do with the Irish Legion. He has had no companies to consolidate with it. I will see you next week about the Colonelcy." About this time, the Springfield authorities received a supporting letter from nine company officers and two field officers of the "Irish Legion 90th Regiment" certifying that they and their command "have enlisted not for Col. Snowhook's regiment but for that of Father Dunne." The letters and telegram achieved their goal as someone in Yates's office sent Haines's letter to Adjutant General Fuller with the notation, "Read carefully—such dispatch if any was not authorized by me, wasn't by Yates. Cant you fix this thing some way?"[31]

Following Captain O'Meara's arrival in Chicago, Father Dunne wasted no time. On September 10, he wrote Governor Yates that in spite of the diversion of one company from Peoria to another regiment, the Irish Legion had eight full companies and that a colonel should now be appointed. Dunne sought to hold the governor to his promise that Dunne could select the regiment's colonel. "The Gentleman is now here. . . . His name is Timothy O'Meara. . . . He is both a soldier and a gentleman and it is my desire and that of the Irish Legion that you send him his commission as Colonel of the Regiment. An informal election was held and both officers and men, without exception, voted for him." Dunne further justified his request with the admonition: "The appointment of the Colonel is besides necessary in order to fill up the Regiment & to keep order & discipline amongst so many men." Clearly, Dunne thought it was time for the governor to act, but recruitment of the last two companies lagged, with the prospect that the Irish Legion would have to be combined with another regiment as the August 22 deadline for filling up the regiment had long since passed. Haines, well aware of the problem, wrote Governor Yates on September 17 to try to head off such a fate for the regiment. He pointed out to the governor that "the regiment as you know is wholly Irish Catholic & it would raise a row on both sides to consolidate with it any other companies not Irish & Catholic—the only alternative which seems to be left is to give him [Rev. Dunne] time to fill up or give him men from elsewhere who are in sentiment & nationality like his regiment." He warned Yates: "I very much fear it will do you & him much harm if he is not now supported in such a way as to ensure an immediate filling up of the regiment under the field officers elected today by the line officers of the regiment. . . . The only reward he now seeks is that you will commission the field officers elected this day." According to a line officer, "Col. O'Meara was the choice, not one vote being cast against him." Quartermaster Sheridan described O'Meara's selection by the regiment to his brother: "There were so many Flunkey La[w]yers and politicians aiming at the Colonelcy that we resolved to apply to Col. Corcharan now B[rigadi]er G[ener]al who sent us O'Meara. He is a soldier in truth." In contrast, he characterized Snowhook unfavorably as an "adventurer of a lawyer."[32]

The unanimous vote for O'Meara drew an angry response from Snowhook, now an eagle without a perch. In a letter to the acting governor, Francis Hoffman, he vented his indignation. A notification and pass from the post adjutant at Camp Douglas to attend the election of field officers of the 90th Regiment had arrived ten minutes after the election was underway, not two days before the election, as promised by Governor Yates and the adjutant general. As a consequence, he had been unable to attend the election, and that infuriated him. He inferred that the election had been for lieutenant colonel and urged Hoffman to readily commission him the colonel and O'Meara the lieutenant colonel, which would settle the matter to his satisfaction. He also promised to quickly fill the regiment with any available troops.[33]

Yates was in a box: the regiment could not rapidly—and might never—be filled up, as few Irish Catholics recruits were currently available, but neither could he commission a colonel without violating his stated policy of granting such a commission only when the regiment completed its recruitment. He resorted to delaying tactics by appointing O'Meara as lieutenant colonel; Owen Stuart as major; the thirty-three-year-old printer at the *Post*, Edwin S. Davis, as adjutant; and Redmond Sheridan as quartermaster to date from September 23, 1862, thus leaving the position of colonel open to future negotiation.[34]

After his arrival, Lieutenant Colonel O'Meara improved the appearance of Camp Dunne as well as that of the soldiers. An article in the October 3 *Chicago*

Morning Post described the camp as "by far the most pleasant and the finest appearing camping ground in the vicinity of Camp Douglas. Although the ground is flat, and might be expected during this muddy weather to be in a cheerless and muddy condition, yet the grounds are dry and perfectly clean." O'Meara's past military experience paid dividends for the regiment. "By the aid of ditching the water has all been carried away, and instead of wading through sticky mud six inches deep, as in some of the other camps, the men have dry ground about their tents." The article complimented O'Meara on strictly enforcing discipline in the camp. The writer observed the regiment during dress parade and reported that the troops skillfully performed their "evolutions" and promptly obeyed commands so that "any one can see that they have no ordinary commander over them." All was not perfect, however, as the article concluded with an announcement titled "Absentees": "There are a large number of the members of this regiment at present absent without leave. The Colonel desires it to be published that, unless these absentees report at camp within two days from this time, they will be considered and dealt with as deserters."[35]

While recruitment slowly proceeded during October, numerous officers of the Irish Legion received presentations of swords, sashes, and belts at Camp Dunne from friends and relatives—or admirers, if they were young and single. The separate events invariably involved lengthy and sometimes witty speeches and responses. As reported in the *Post*, some two thousand citizens of Rockford and Belvidere, Illinois, arrived at Camp Dunne via the Galena and Chicago Union Railroad, bringing with them a veritable feast of "chickens, turkeys, pies, cakes, and good things without mention, to which the entire Legion paid their respects without standing on ceremony." Former parishioners from Bridgeport and Carville, Illinois, presented Chaplain Thomas Kelly with "a sum sufficient to purchase a splendid horse, saddle and bridle." Some of Second Lieutenant William White's lady friends from Springfield presented him with a sword, sash, and revolver, while Lieutenant John C. Harrington received a "very beautiful sash presented to him by several of his lady friends of this city [Chicago]." Such presentations became so numerous that the writer for the *Post*, apparently fed up reporting such events, wrote: "For the past three months nearly every captain, lieutenant, sergeant and minor officer has been honored with some symbol of the position which he holds as a testimonial from his appreciative friends and persons who are in the habit of patronizing the morning papers have well nigh come to the conclusion that military life is made up of 'entertaining occasions,' 'lively times,' 'sword presentations from dear friends,' 'spontaneous dinners,' etc. instead of laborious military service, while many a sighing individual wishes himself a 'soger.'"[36]

While the 90th Illinois remained at Camp Douglas, fourteen other northern Illinois regiments formed, mustered into service, and departed for the field. Twelve of the fourteen left for the field within thirty-six days of their muster. Five left within eleven days, an indication of the urgent demand for troops in the field during August and early September. Two other regiments, which like the 90th Illinois left for the field in November, required up to sixty-four days. The unusually long eighty-one days the men of the 90th Illinois required between their muster into service and departure for the field reflected the greater difficulty experienced in obtaining and retaining recruits.[37]

Progress on filling up the regiment continued to be slow with a count of 831 enlisted men on October 19; however, recruitment did not keep up with losses. Captain Barrett's Company K, for example, claimed to have eighty recruits at Ottawa by August 23. However, by mid-September, his company numbered only forty-two in spite of his August 30 "Last Notice" to absentees "Positively" requiring them to report to Camp Dunne. Company K added only thirteen men in September and eleven in October but had fifty-four absent without leave, deserted, or enlisted in other regiments as of October 19, related in part to dissension over the election of company officers. By November 25, the Legion numbered only 769 men. As the time at Camp Douglas dragged on, losses continued to mount, making the decision to wait for more volunteers a losing game. Aware of the situation, in a November 13 letter to Adjutant General Fuller, Father Dunne requested that "if you cannot fill up the regiment without interfering with its peculiar & distinctive organization. . . . Permit it to enter the ranks as it is." He then proceeded to back up his request: "I feel confident the authorities at Springfield will not ignore what I have done or treat me in any way unbecoming my rank & my position. We have now a fine body of men, & if they are as yet deficient in number, you will find they will compensate for that deficiency in true soldierly qualifications." The letter and a trip by O'Meara to Springfield did the trick. Following another unanimous regimental vote taken November 19, Governor Yates acquiesced, if not to divine intervention at least to intervention by the divine, naming O'Meara colonel of the 90th Illinois to date from November 22, 1862. One day later, Irish-born local merchant and prominent recruiter for the Legion Smith McCleavy became the lieutenant colonel. Colonel Snowhook apparently accepted defeat gracefully, becoming president of the prestigious Chicago Literary Union. Sheahan, also a member of the society, reported Snowhook's election in his November 23 edition of the *Post*.[38]

O'Meara's past experience in the army explained his no-nonsense approach to commanding the men of the Legion. The *Post* characterized O'Meara as "a good disciplinarian and indefatigable worker, and a thorough go-ahead man, possessing the necessary qualities to Command the brave boys of which the Legion is composed." Quartermaster Sheridan described him as "a soldier, in truth a handsome person [of] gentlemanly bearing with a command that will ever compel obedience." O'Meara's imposition of proper military discipline, his unavoidably delayed arrival, and the long interval before his appointment to command all contributed to the difficulties he faced upon assuming command, which included desertions and officers unversed in military matters who had been selected prior to his arrival. Upon reaching the field, Colonel O'Meara would find it necessary to continue the training of both officers and men.[39]

The difficulty of obtaining accurate personal identification and the relative ease with which the rather perfunctory physical examination could be circumvented was proven by Eliza Miller, who passed for a soldier until her gender was discovered. Soon after joining the regiment, O'Meara observed a sentinel who seemed younger than regulations permitted. Upon advancing toward the guard, he became suspicious that the sentinel was female. The *Post* described the clever way O'Meara resolved the matter:

> "Sir," said the colonel, "I think I have seen you before, but where or under what circumstances I cannot now recall to mind."
>
> "I think not colonel," was the reply of the soldier, in a respectful manner. "Before I came here I never saw you, to my knowledge, in my life."
>
> The colonel turned again. With a well feigned look of interest on his countenance, he spoke slowly and impressively; "I had a near and dear friend once, much younger than myself, and, if you be not he, I never saw a more striking resemblance. But if, as I suspect you are the person, though I cannot divine why you should seek to conceal the fact from me, there is a mark—a red mark—upon your left breast, by which I shall be able to identify you. Open your coat, sir!"
>
> The soldier hesitated, "Colonel," said he, "I am sure you are mistaken, for, believe me, sir, I never saw you before I enlisted in your regiment."
>
> Suspicion now grew to firm conviction in the colonel's mind, and he was determined in his purpose of discovery. With a manner which admitted of no hesitation, he said, "Sir, I tell you to unbutton your coat, and I wish you to obey me."
>
> Slowly the guard unbuttoned the garment, and threw it back from his breast. Beneath it was a white ribbed shirt, and the lapels of the coat were thickly padded with cotton to hide, when buttoned, a certain rotundity of form, which was now plainly visible beneath the folds of the shirt. But the colonel was not satisfied. "How, sir," said he, "can I discover whether the mark is present through the folds of your shirt? Unbutton it sir; you are not ashamed that I should see your breast, are you?"
>
> There was a brief silence. The colonel was implacable, and in his countenance the soldier read suspicion of the correct state of affairs and a determination to know the truth. There was no help for it, and slowly and hesitatingly these words came forth;
>
> "Colonel, rather than expose my person I will reveal my sex. *I am a woman!*"

> The colonel immediately relieved the soldier from guard duty.
>
> Subsequent inquiry has led the commanding officer to believe that she is a chaste girl, of pure motives, but who, with a mistaken zeal and patriotism enrolled herself in the service of her country.
>
> The sequel of this strange discovery will probably be her adoption as Daughter of the Irish Legion.[40]

Removal from the ranks did not end Eliza Miller's association with the Irish Legion. Medical records of the Adjutant General's Office for the 90th Illinois and press accounts written during and after the war indicate the presence of a woman in the ranks of the 90th Illinois known by the name of Frank or Francis Miller, or Francis Hook, who at times may have acted as a soldier. However, none of these names appears in the reports for the 90th Illinois, the Illinois adjutant general's report, the Book Records of the Volunteer Union Organizations of the Adjutant General's Office in the National Archives, or the Muster and Descriptive Rolls in the Illinois State Archives, so it is not possible to state with certainty that such an enlistment took place. Only the army's medical records confirm "Frank" Miller as a soldier in the 90th Illinois.[41]

A different sort of identity problem occurred in early November when some fifty-three soldiers of the Legion, from companies raised outside Chicago, voted illegally in a local town election in the Fourth Ward. Illinois adjutant general Fuller received a request from those investigating possible fraud for the muster rolls of Companies C and K "to aid in contesting Mr. W. Fuller's seat in the legislature, their votes having defeated him."[42]

Retention presented an even greater challenge than recruitment. In an attempt to identify each enlistee clearly, regimental descriptive books recorded by company the age, height, complexion, color of eyes and hair, country of birth, and occupation for each soldier. False identities could be easily assumed by unscrupulous individuals, as modern means of identification, including photo IDs, did not exist. Lacking some identifying feature, a man was who he said he was until proven otherwise. The relative ease of assuming a new identity allowed the practice of fraudulent enlistment and bounty jumping to flourish.[43]

According to the Illinois adjutant general's report, of the 928 enlisted men (omitting four unassigned recruits) who served in the 90th Illinois, 356 deserted during the war, a desertion rate for enlisted men of 38 percent. A comparable figure for the Union army would be around 8 percent. Other Irish units recruiting in Illinois in 1862 also had high rates of desertion. Chicago's first Irish regiment, the 23rd Illinois, had a desertion rate of 26 percent among recruits as it attempted to bring itself back up to strength, most having been enrolled in 1862 before the 90th Illinois began recruiting. The "lost company" from Peoria, Illinois, which had been expected to join the 90th Illinois but instead became Company I of the

108th Illinois, lost thirty-one of ninety-three enlisted men through desertion while in camp or soon after departing for the field.[44]

In his brief history of the regiment, Woodruff attributed the high level of desertion in the Irish Legion to "restlessness." He explained the behavior thusly: "As may be imagined, a thousand Irishmen could not be got together without having some restive ones; and to bring so many men, who heretofore regulated their movements by their own sweet will alone, into proper regard for the discipline of the camp, was not an easy task. Under this restlessness many deserted." He commented that while the regiment was at Camp Douglas, an officer was sent each day to Chicago to "hunt up the missing ones." This indicates an apparent lack of control of movement of individual soldiers to and from their camp area. Following O'Meara's arrival, his imposition of a higher level of discipline on the regiment may have caused some to desert. Such a possibility is supported by Quartermaster Sheridan's description of O'Meara as "rather too strict a discipl[in]arian for a volunteer corps. he having served in the regular service from boyhood. Less could not be expected of him. He was unpopular with both men and officers until he had them as he wanted them." To complicate matters further, the War Department allowed ten men from an individual volunteer regiment to leave their regiment and enlist in a regular army regiment and gave a two-dollar premium for each recruit. The premium increased to three dollars if the recruit joined a preexisting regiment rather than a newly forming one. To recover their substantial investment, Captain Patrick O'Marah and five others from Company C had the task of retrieving three Company D men from the clutches of the federal recruiting officer. According to Woodruff's account, the retrieval was accomplished "by force." The offended federal officer preferred charges, but the matter was dropped as the regiment soon left for service in the field.[45]

Desertions increased as the date of departure for the field approached, with 43 having deserted by September 7, 152 by October 31, and 289 by departure on November 27. A total of 304 deserted from the 90th Illinois by November 30, 1862, with the following losses by company: A—20, B—10, C—17, D—45, E—26, F—39, G—21, H—48, I—42, and K—36. Other than local bounty money, the soldiers received no pay from the federal government during the four months of their stay at Camp Dunne until just before their departure. The *Post* reported: "The men and officers have never been paid a cent since their enlistment. The money offered by the government of twenty-five dollars bounty, one month's pay in advance, and two dollars enlistment money, was withheld from the men until the last moment, and then, at a late hour running into night, they were only paid twenty-five dollars each. The other fifteen was not paid over. The reason given for this is, want of funds. . . . The result of this was considerable discontent and general dissatisfaction. The officers received no money." Obviously, failure of the government to meet its obligations encouraged desertion.[46]

No single cause appears to explain the regiment's high rate of desertion by enlisted men. Desertion rates differed much more among companies than among the various categories of age, marital status, nativity, and occupation. For example, Company H, raised in Chicago, had a desertion rate over four times that of Company B, raised in Galena and northwestern Illinois, even though the percentage of foreign-born in the two companies differed by only 4 percent. Clearly, all foreign-born did not behave identically. Company G had a desertion rate about half that of Company H, even though both were raised in Chicago. The average desertion rate of the first three companies formed was less than half that of the last three companies. The quality of leadership provided by company officers, community influences or the lack thereof, and attitude, background, and interaction of individual enlisted men with their officers and each other more likely determined their decision whether to desert or remain with the regiment.[47]

The high level of anonymity provided to deserters by large cities and the lack of family and community ties of recent immigrants to Illinois, whether from foreign countries or other states, favored desertion. Local bounties, especially those paid in full upon enlistment, may have encouraged the process of desertion and fraudulent reenlistment. However, the wide range in dates of departure by deserters after their respective companies were mustered, combined with the loss of forty-five to desertion prior to muster by Companies H and I, indicates that factors other than bounty jumping may have been more important in generating the regiment's high rate of desertion while at Camp Dunne. In a November 13 letter to Illinois adjutant general Fuller, Father Dunne blamed desertions and problems with recruitment on the failure of state leaders to appoint an officer with authority over the regiment, as he had requested from the start. The high rate of desertion may also reflect heavy recruitment of transient workers and sailors required to fill up some companies.[48]

Provost Marshal General James B. Fry noted that the process of election of company officers often produced a "dissatisfied and often highly intelligent minority," which contributed to desertion. Such dissatisfaction occurred in two companies of the 90th Illinois. The members of Company K elected Irish-born candidates to the positions of first and second lieutenant over the opposition of Captain Barrett, who had backed American-born Irish for those positions. As a result, "a bitter feeling" existed between Captain Barrett and his first lieutenant so that they were not on speaking terms when the regiment left Chicago, according to a sworn statement some twelve years later by Barrett. Significant dissatisfaction with the officers elected in Company F resulted in the letter of October 29, 1862, to Governor Yates from Camp Dunne signed by thirty-seven privates and by Lieutenant William White of Company F, "humbly" petitioning that Captain Richard C. Kelly and First Lieutenant Patrick Feeney "be relieved from the command of this company." The letter described the two as "intolerably tyrannical" and stated that neither had "the ability to fill their position." As evidence, the letter cited Kelly's racial prejudice and a "decrease in our number from about eighty five to fifty five men," mostly by desertion. An accompanying unsigned letter accused the two Company F officers of theft and deception. The letter claimed Captain Kelly and Lieutenant Feeney had drawn "bounties from the County for some men that was Rejected by your adjutant and the Mustering officer." On the day the company mustered in, the actual number present was only sixty-two. To meet the required number, "the balance to fill up the company was borrowed from another company for the occasion, our officers stating they had between Eighty and Nin[e]ty Men and that the balance were in town and would be fourth coming. But they have not come, nor no prospect of their coming."[49]

These charges should not be taken lightly, as both Lieutenant White and his brother Thomas had prior service before joining the 90th Illinois and knew what they were talking about. They had enlisted for short-term service in April 1861 and had been sent to Cairo, Illinois. Upon expiration of their enlistment, they returned to Springfield before joining the 90th Illinois. Furthermore, they were devoted to the cause of preserving the Union. White had delivered a ringing message of loyalty to the Union and a well-reasoned argument in support of its preservation at a meeting in Cook's Hall in Springfield on March 18, 1861, nearly a month before the attack upon Fort Sumter in Charleston harbor. He had concluded his speech with a quote from "one of Ireland's exiled patriots," indicating the likely presence of other Irish Americans in the audience.[50]

Issuance of the preliminary Emancipation Proclamation on September 22, 1862, five days after the bloody Battle of Antietam (Sharpsburg), was another divisive factor within the regiment and the Irish community, probably leading some to desert. Colonel O'Meara's public support of the proclamation during a standing-room-only meeting at Bryan Hall on September 27 conflicted with opposing views equally strongly held by certain of his officers, forming another possible source of dissension within the regiment. The widespread opposition in Illinois to the proclamation included the Illinois state legislature labeling of the Emancipation Proclamation as "unwarranted in military as in civil law; a gigantic usurpation" and "a total subversion of the Federal Union."[51]

The men of the Irish Legion represented a cross section of Illinois Irishmen in 1862. That they diverged significantly in their makeup and adjustment to military regimen merely demonstrated the futility of characterizing the Illinois Irish as homogenous and the impossibility of describing their behavior as conforming to a particular pattern of actions and responses. In 1862, they were far too intelligent and diverse—and some might add perverse—to ever fit such a description.

As the time for departure approached, Major Owen Stuart received a beautiful, small leather bound *Treasury of Prayer* inscribed "to Owen Stuart Major 90th

Illinois Volunteers, 'Irish Legion' Chicago, Nov. 25, 1862 by his friend and long time associate in business, James W. Sheahan," which Stuart treasured for the rest of his life. The gift was soon needed as the Legion staged a memorable hurrah and farewell to Chicago, testing everyone's patience. The *Post* reported the departure of the Irish Legion from Chicago: "On Thanksgiving night [November 27], at some hour beyond midnight, the 90th regiment of Illinois volunteers left this city for Cairo on the way to Memphis." The description of the regiment's departure sounded like the proverbial attempt at herding cats. Woodruff conceded that "it was no easy task to get one thousand Irishmen all aboard of a railway train, at the same time, and keep them there." That was especially true since they were paid their twenty-five-dollar federal bonus just before departure, causing a significant number of the "byes" to consider that a justifiable reason for celebration as it was the first money they had received from the government. They were to prove a highly spirited outfit that never lost their spirit or their love of spirits. During the confusion of leaving, two soldiers of the 90th "insulted a comrade" who "drew a revolver" that discharged, accidentally wounding First Lieutenant Patrick Sarsfield Real, Company K, in the thigh, thereby delaying his departure to the field.[52]

According to one less-than-friendly newspaper report of the outfit's departure, "The 90th regiment Illinois infantry, or rather about one half of it, left last night for Cairo via the Illinois Central. The others having been paid off gave thanks on such an immense scale that the police have had their hands full ever since noon yesterday in picking them up. These stragglers will be forwarded in squads as fast as they can be found." The *Post* reported the regiment's departure in somewhat more favorable terms: "Although ordered to move a week or more since, the time for their departure was postponed from day to day on account of the men not receiving their pay from the government." The unexpected nighttime departure further confused the situation. "The tents were not struck until night, and then it was hours before the regiment of dissatisfied men could get their traps in order and on board the cars. There seemed also to be much uncertainty as to the time for the departure of the train, and owing to this many were left behind." As a result, "Col. O'Meara, Adjutant Davis and perhaps some other officers remained behind to collect the stragglers, and in a day or two the entire regiment will be on its way to Dixie." Some stragglers evaded collection as Captain Daniel O'Connor, Company D, and First Lieutenant John C. Harrington, Company C, spent January and February 1863 on detached duty collecting deserters in and around Chicago.[53]

Once on the train, losses decreased, but an additional 15 deserted by head-count time on November 30, the day after arrival in Cairo. Including men mustered in on November 27, 1862, the 90th Illinois recruited a total of 963 in 1862, but 304 deserted, 2 died, and 6 were discharged before the regiment left Camp Douglas, leaving 651 at the end of 1862.[54]

Upon arriving in the field, the 90th Illinois had some 220 to 290 fewer troops than four other regiments formed at the same time in northern Illinois. Whether restlessness, avarice, or some other factor, such as objection to the Emancipation Proclamation, caused the large number of the regiment's desertions in 1862, the result was that the 90th Illinois was and would remain significantly understrength throughout the war.[55]

As members of Major General William T. Sherman's XV Corps, the 90th Illinois was to see action at Missionary Ridge and during the Atlanta campaign, the march to the sea, the attack on Fort McAllister, and the march through the Carolinas. At those times, the men of the Irish Legion would fulfill Father Dunne's prediction that they would compensate for smaller numbers with "true soldierly qualifications."[56]

{2}

ATTENTION FROM TWO GENERALS

On November 29, 1862, after spending two days and nights on the train, the men of the 90th Illinois arrived in Cairo, Illinois, in amazingly good humor (Map 1). The *Chicago Times* reported their arrival at Cairo, describing them as "a gay, rollicking set, having on foot some sort of excitement continually." There would be no repeat of their chaotic departure from Chicago as "they were stationed on the levee during the day and close guard lines [were] thrown around them to keep them from scattering." The soldiers of the Irish Legion never quite succeeded in visiting the town, despite a number of highly creative individual appeals ranging from a sudden desire by one soldier to pay his taxes, another to collect rent, and a third to see about a horse he owned, to a final desperate plea by another that unless he got a particular brand of patent worm medicine he "would have spasms." In the evening they boarded the *Florence*, a 397-ton stern-wheeler, which anchored overnight in the Ohio River.[1]

Captain Peter Casey of Company H chose this time to write his wife, describing their trip and commenting that soldiering "was not what I thought it was.... We are laying in the center of the River opposite Cairo with a gunboat. Iron clad monsters with their guns frowning upon us." It had been an eventful trip from Chicago. Captain Daniel O'Connor had accidentally shot Casey's second lieutenant, George W. McDonald, in the leg above the knee. Casey considered that "it was partly accidental for he shot himself in the hand." He also reported that four "men fell overboard. Some say they were all saved & others say 2 were lost. Me and the Colonel saved one but I will carry the marks of his nales on my rist fore some time. He took a death grip on me."[2]

On November 30, the *Florence* steamed the short distance from Cairo to Columbus, Kentucky, on the Mississippi River, where the regiment disembarked. During

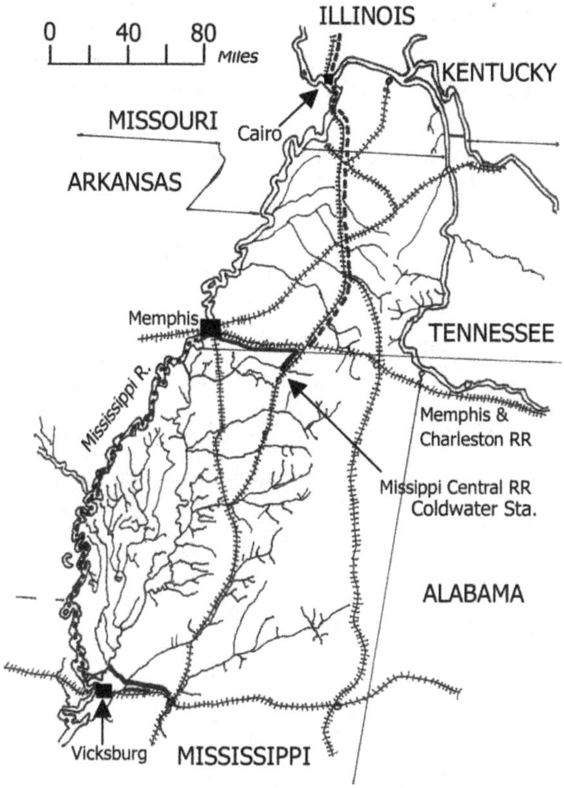

Map 1. Locations and routes traveled by the 90th Illinois from November 1862 to October 1863. Solid line indicates march route; dashed line indicates rail route; and dotted line indicates boat route.

the previous three weeks, some 40,000 soldiers had passed through the busy port and railroad terminal heading south. Major Owen Stuart's bride, Margaret, accompanied him from Chicago to Columbus, apparently none the worse for the lengthy trip. The *Chicago Post* printed a report from Columbus that the 90th Illinois arrived "from Cairo in good order, and when drawn up before headquarters, to be inspected by Gen. [Thomas A.] Davies, commanding the district, made a good impression. Col. O'Meara made a very good impression on the military men here, as in fact did the whole regiment." On December 2, the Legion left by train and arrived that night in La Grange, Tennessee, remaining on the railroad cars overnight (Map 2). Strategically located on the Memphis and Charleston Railroad almost fifty miles east of Memphis, La Grange had been occupied alternately by Confederate and federal forces until reoccupied by Major General William T. Sherman's troops in early November 1862. A town of about two thousand inhabitants in 1861, La Grange was located on a high bluff over 150 feet above the Wolf

River, where wealthy citizens from Memphis owned elegant homes with good views south across the river and into Mississippi. An educational center, the city housed the La Grange Female College and the newly constructed Presbyterian College for Men. The Legion proceeded to pitch tents on even higher ground one mile east of La Grange at Camp Yates, named for the then governor of Illinois.[3]

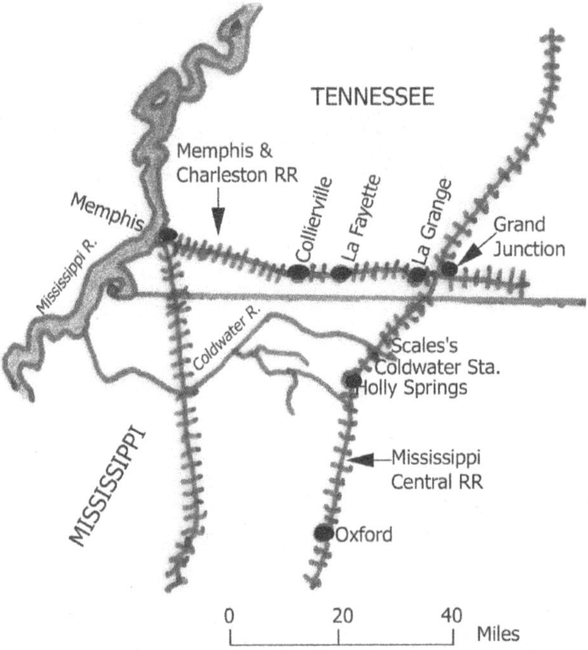

Map 2. Camps and railroads guarded by the 90th Illinois

The stay of the 90th Illinois at Camp Yates would be short but notable. A convalescent reported the conditions there as "mud . . . almost twelve inches deep" with the only firewood available consisting of rails from "neighboring fences, which are carefully guarded." Soon after the regiment's arrival, a major snowstorm hit the area. The officer in charge at La Grange, Colonel Addison S. Norton of the 17th Illinois Infantry, explained to Major General Ulysses S. Grant that following the snowstorm, none of the four regiments at La Grange nor the 1,200 convalescent soldiers in camp had any fuel. As the troops were suffering from the cold, he directed them to "procure rails sufficient for the emergency." As he carefully phrased it, the 90th Illinois "took a portion of the fence from the inclosure around your former headquarters." It could be argued that the 90th just gave the orders a liberal interpretation and built fires to keep warm using whatever rails were handy. Grant's response is not recorded. By the time he received Norton's communication, much larger problems due to the Mississippi mud, which bogged down his overland offensive against Vicksburg, and securing his supply line occupied his attention. The Mississippi Central Railroad served as the chief line of communication and supply route for Grant's army. Only three days after arriving at La Grange, the 90th Illinois received orders to proceed south to Coldwater Station, four miles north of Holly Springs, Mississippi, Grant's main supply depot, to guard bridges on that railroad.[4]

The success of Grant's overland operations against Vicksburg required that his supply line, including the Mississippi Central Railroad through Holly Springs, be protected from disruption by Confederate raiders. On December 3, Grant warned commanding officers at posts up and down the railroad, including those at Grand Junction, La Grange, Davis's Mill, and Coldwater, of "guerrilla bands" intent on "burning railroad stations, tanks and bridges." He ordered them to exercise "great vigilance." The order continued: "Guarding railroads and keeping communication open to the army is now the vitally important duty of troops in this district. . . . The attacking party must be repulsed and annihilated. Disloyal persons are to understand that destruction of their property will follow a guerrilla raid." Just to make sure his officers got the point, the order concluded: "Disgrace will inevitably follow a defeat."[5]

The area between Holly Springs and the Tennessee border was disputed territory, with Union and Confederate forces alternating in its control. In late June and early July 1862, troops under Sherman went down to the Holly Springs area to try to suppress local guerrilla activity. Sherman quickly received orders to retire north into Tennessee and by about July 8 had left Holly Springs and the surrounding territory to be reoccupied by the Confederates, who remained there into November. During this time, several cavalry encounters occurred in northern Mississippi, including some with local groups such as Mitchell's Partisan Rangers, which the Union termed "guerillas."[6]

Although the 90th Illinois would have to be on guard against hit-and-run attacks by local guerrillas, the troops' relations with the local population proved quite congenial. While in Tennessee and Mississippi, a number of the members of the regiment received true Southern hospitality granted to friend and foe alike. Captain Peter Casey remained behind in La Grange, sick with a cold he blamed on having to visit sentinels hourly in the rain while serving as officer of the day. He lamented to his wife that the soldier detailed "to attend to me . . . went off and got drunk and neglected me." Fortunately for Casey, "one friend turned up in the shape of a planter's wife that owned the shanty [where he was quartered]. . . . She made me tea and toast" and waited "on me as soon as she found out that I was here." Casey clearly had not yet adjusted to the rough and tumble existence of active duty.[7]

On December 5 and 6, the Legion, minus Casey, marched about twenty miles from La Grange to a point on the Mississippi Central Railroad some four miles north of Holly Springs. The regiment camped nearby on a ridge in a grove on

Wall's plantation next to "Sunnyside," the McPherson house, approximately at the location designated Wall's Valley Station or simply as Wall on an 1863 map of the region, located at the eastern edge of a much larger elevated area some two miles in extent known as Coldwater and variously reported as four to six miles north of Holly Springs. Alternately occupied by both Confederate and Union troops, the adjacent springs and small tributaries of the Coldwater River provided an abundant source of water, making the area a suitable camp for large numbers of soldiers. General Sherman thought Coldwater to be a "most agreeable and defensible" campsite, a judgment the 90th Illinois would prove correct. In June and July 1862, Sherman found water scarce in Holly Springs and considered Coldwater "the first and only point where water can be had between the Wolf River [across the border in Tennessee] and Holly Springs."[8]

The Legion more or less adopted Sherman's terminology and referred to the camp as Coldwater or Coldwater Station. Unfortunately, numerous official military dispatches used the same names to refer to the town of Coldwater, Mississippi, located directly south of Memphis on the Mississippi and Tennessee Railroad and some thirty miles west of Holly Springs. However, none of the actions of the 90th Illinois involved the western Coldwater. Therefore, the camp of the 90th Illinois four miles north of Holly Springs is referred to as Coldwater Station in this book to emphasize its proximity to the Mississippi Central Railroad and the fact that the main Coldwater camping area lay a mile or so to the west of the regiment's camp (see Map 2).

Colonel Timothy O'Meara promptly divided his forces, keeping seven companies at his Coldwater Station camp to guard the bridges and railroad north toward Hudsonville Station, also known as Scales's Station. From December 7, the three other companies, A, I, and K, under the command of Major Stuart, were posted at Hudsonville Station some three miles northeast of the regiment's main camp, guarding nearby railroad bridges. That these four or five miles of track required the protection of a regiment of some six hundred soldiers indicates the seriousness of the threat to the railroad by Confederate raiders.[9]

The 90th Illinois left La Grange with rations for only two days and quickly ran out of food. The task of obtaining supplies fell to Captain Patrick O'Marah of Company C. In command of a group of thirteen army wagons with their teamsters, he moved supplies from their old camp at La Grange through three and a half miles of guerrilla-infested country to the railroad station at Grand Junction. The railroad then moved the supplies to their new camps at Hudsonville (Scales's) Station and Coldwater (Wall's Valley) Station. The first trip was successful, but with night approaching, one driver from an Ohio regiment refused to go on a second trip and started jettisoning his load of supplies. According to George Woodruff, this had a "bad effect" on the other drivers, but O'Marah, equal to the situation, ordered the driver to move into line. The driver refused with "oaths and threats," whereupon O'Marah drew one of his very large navy pistols and fired, just clipping the driver's ear. This action produced the "desired effect" resulting in the prompt delivery and unloading of the supplies at the railroad station. The recalcitrant driver got nowhere with his subsequent complaints to higher authorities.[10]

On December 11, apparently still on short rations, the 90th Illinois requisitioned 875 pounds of ham from a local farmer, Joseph H. Brooks, whose eighty-acre farm had the misfortune to be conveniently located between the Legion's two camps. The troops seemed to prefer some succulent home-cured ham to their rather monotonous army ration.[11]

Quartermaster Redmond Sheridan described their Coldwater Station campsite as "admirably adapted for Shelter and defense with fair water in easy distance. It was located on an extensive plantation immediately South of the owners Residence on an elevation Commanding a view of the Country on all Sides. A valey on three Sides, east, South, and west [with] the R.R. on the north." Sheridan readily approved of their campsite: "Beyond the valey was rolling land so that a continuation of hills and valley made up the Scene here in this beautiful spot which was at This time of the year was rendered almost enchanting. The weather being Salubrious a regular groth of fine trees Shading the grove in the heat of the day added to its importance in this Sunny Spot."[12]

The area surrounding the Coldwater Station camp, and also Holly Springs in Marshall County, consisted of a mixture of cultivated land interspersed with woodland and low wet areas. The cultivated land provided good crops of cotton before the war, and large numbers of cotton bales remained in local storage. Many of the planters in the region surrounding the camp of the 90th Illinois had large farms with four to five hundred acres under cultivation and even larger acreages in woodland or otherwise unimproved land. Their pleasant plantation homes signified the prosperity of the region. The planters who settled in the Hudsonville and Coldwater areas were primarily from Virginia and the Carolinas. Successful farmers in their home areas, they were drawn to Mississippi by the attraction of large acreages of cotton-growing land newly opened by the federal government through an 1832 agreement with the Chickasaw Indians. The assignment of the Legion thus placed the regiment in one of the Confederacy's more prosperous areas populated with families representative of the well-developed culture of the areas from which they had emigrated.[13]

On December 4, Major Stuart's twenty-four-year-old wife, Margaret, and the wives of Lieutenants John Kelly and John McAssey all received railroad passes to proceed to Coldwater Station. Margaret's exact date of arrival is uncertain, since the 90th Illinois did not arrive there until December 6, but by the seventeenth she had become well adjusted to keeping house, not in an army tent, but in a part of the impressive plantation home, Oakland, owned by the Scales family at Hudsonville Station. This was as close as the Stuarts would get to a honeymoon, having been married only three days before the regiment left Chicago. In a mid-December letter to her sisters and brother, she described life at Oakland as "keeping house in a kind of a way but we enjoy it and so do the others as we are never without company for dinner and tea. I get presents from all the planters in the neighborhood of butter, milk, and preserves. It comes to the commander of the post, which is the Major, and as there are no women along here but me they all try to make me feel comfortable, both officers and men." The officers of the 90th Illinois had to purchase their own food supplies, which were likely to be army rations, so they obviously preferred the convivial atmosphere of dining in a Southern mansion on the bounty of the country. Margaret wrote: "We had the Col. O'Meara, Doctor, Capt. Casey, Capt. Murphy, Capt. O'Connor, Capt. Flynn and the Sutler to dinner. We had a very pleasant time indeed. Captain Flynn boards with us but indeed we have a table full every day. We have two cotton buyers stay with us also." Margaret also served as a banker for some of the officers: "I have two hundred dollars of Captain Flynn's and I must say he is the nicest man I ever met." The location was quite agreeable: "The weather here is beautiful, the windows are never closed all day. Flowers are in bloom and birds are singing."[14]

The high-spirited daughter of plantation owner Peter Scales, sixteen-year-old Cordelia Scales—Delia to her family—became well acquainted with Margaret Stuart and Captain Patrick Flynn while they stayed in her home. The three companies of the 90th Illinois camped in the grove next to Oakland. Delia loved to walk around wearing a pistol and taunt visiting, admiring Union soldiers with blatantly pro-Confederate sentiments. In a letter to a school friend, she gave an interesting insight into how members of the Legion related to a local Southern family. Delia wrote that the Legion, being all Democrats, "treated us a great deal better" than the Republican 26th Illinois, which previously occupied the grounds around her plantation home. She considered Major Stuart's wife, Margaret, who "staid here" to be "a very nice lady . . . almost a Secesh." Margaret appreciated the "Rebel songs" that Delia played for her and had her "write them off" so she could take them back to Chicago.[15]

Delia's letter indicated the state of near-destitution to which her family had been subjected due to depredations by successive waves of Union troops. After initially refusing Captain Flynn's request for her to "sing 'My Maryland' for him," she relented when her father told her she "must" because Flynn "had kept us from almost starving." Pleased with the song, Flynn had Delia write the words on a sheet of paper to which she added a "little <u>Confederate</u> flag at the top" with an expression of sympathy for the Confederacy below it. Flynn sent it "North to his wife." Some members of the Legion admired her spunk, referring to her as the "right bower [the highest trump in the card game euchre] of the <u>Rebel</u> army."[16]

During their first two weeks in the field, the men of the 90th Illinois experienced the usual period of adjustment and nervousness typical of raw troops. Company

K reported being constantly menaced and under arms for nearly a week and that pickets were "actually attacked," but no major engagement occurred. By way of contrast, Quartermaster Sheridan considered the first three weeks at the Coldwater Station camp as relatively uneventful while the regiment guarded four bridges on the railroad. Captain Casey claimed that a false alarm occurred almost every night, as the threat of local guerrilla activity had to be taken seriously. A sentry, a native of Ireland, belonging to the regiment relieved by the 90th Illinois had his throat cut the night of December 6, according to Casey. The 90th Illinois properly marked his grave with a cross. The grave obviously bothered Casey, now reported fit for duty and detailed officer of the day for December 15. Rain poured down in torrents later in the day, which did nothing at all to improve Casey's disposition. He complained to his wife: "It is a job to be officer of the day here. It is not much like Camp Dunne. Our lines take in 8 miles and the officer must keep on the move for 24 hours without any sleep and it is up and down hill and woods all the way. I can ride a horse in daytime but at night I have to go on foot and alone at least once after 12 o'clock at night, and that grave I have to pass by it every time." However, Casey found his quarters quite acceptable as they were nearby "in a splendid mansion" (probably Robert and Martha Wall's palatial plantation home, Cloverland). Casey particularly enjoyed the food there, adding "we have good board."[17]

The Company K report contained a complaint about their armament with the cryptic comment: "Discipline very good, arms and equipment very inferior." At this time, the Legion had 457 Austrian rifle-muskets, having left 100 considered unserviceable with the ordnance officer at La Grange. The remaining muskets were only marginally better. While at Coldwater Station, Colonel O'Meara wrote Illinois adjutant general Allan Fuller that "a board of examination on the Austrian Rifled Muskets" found them "utterly worthless." He requested Fuller to "kindly use your influence to have them immediately replaced by efficient weapons." He also pleaded with his superior to replace the Austrian rifles with an "efficient weapon." O'Meara termed the rifles "unserviceable and utterly worthless even for guard work." Historian Woodruff clearly did not like that particular model of Austrian musket either: "They were a very inferior arm, almost more dangerous to those who carried them as to those against whom they were aimed. Many would not go off at all, and those that would got heated, and went off prematurely, often taking off a finger, a cap-visor, or a piece of an ear. The stocks were of soft wood and easily broken; and the bayonets were also easily broken. In fact the ramrod was the only reliable part of the Austrians [musket]." During their stay at Coldwater Station, two Company C men accidentally shot off one or more fingers on their right hands while on picket duty. One died at La Grange, Tennessee, on February 8, 1863, from "ill treatment. Inflammation consequent to loss of 2 fingers by accidental discharge of musket." Colonel O'Meara concluded what amounted to his year-end report for 1862 with the following summary: "Camp and garrison equipage very poor, transportation none. Hospital accommodations and supplies very inefficient and arms inefficient." Along with many other regiments, the Legion found that the Union could enroll regiments more rapidly than they could properly equip them.[18]

Since Coldwater Station was their first experience in the field, the troops of the 90th Illinois were still adjusting to the realities of life as soldiers. Woodruff recounts several amusing and "absurd occurrences as would be expected from new troops." One such incident dealt with the incompetence of a lonely sentry of the 90th Illinois posted on a wagon road near a bridge. Upon hearing the noise of approaching horsemen, he suddenly realized that although his rifle was loaded, he had forgotten to put in place the cap required for it to fire. The approaching group, fortunately men from his regiment, quickly dissolved in laughter upon receiving "from the dark recesses of the trestle work" the following challenge delivered in a squeaky voice: "Wait till I cap! Wait till I cap!" Called before the colonel, the sentry's explanation was even more unique: "Kernel, when I thought it was the inimy, I was as wake as wather, but whin I knew it was our own min, I was bould as a lion." The other extreme of behavior occurred when Major Stuart, after devoting much time and labor instructing the men in proper behavior on picket duty, returned from Coldwater Station to his command at Hudsonville Station. As he approached one of his pickets in the dark, he received the correct challenge, "Halt," followed by "Dismount." A most awkward pause for both the sentry and the major then followed while the sentry desperately tried to remember the rest of the challenge. "Determined to have no foolishness, the sentry drew his gun to his shoulder, took steady aim at the portly figure of his commanding officer and roared out. 'Throw your hands over your head, and declare your intinshuns!'" The major complied.[19]

Quartermaster Sheridan adapted well to his life as a soldier, as shown in a letter to his brother: "I must confess there has been nothing at which I drove in previous life so adapted to my natural, or seemingly so, disposition. I really never felt so lively or healthy notwithstanding the variety of diversity to which in Tennessee and Mississippi we were exposed." O'Meara was also adjusting to his role as colonel, as implied by Sheridan's description of their professional relationship: "I was independent of an appointment from the Colonel, who however made no objections to me. thus we worked together. but he wanted to be both Q.M. and Colonel, but that would not do for me, and I took pains to let him know it. We were therefore Civil and in our places." Sheridan and O'Meara had come to understand and respect each other.[20]

Colonel O'Meara also continued the work of bringing the regiment to what he considered a proper state of discipline and order. Two days after arriving at Coldwater Station, he issued orders prohibiting both the discharge of firearms "in and around the camp" and also "straying outside the limits of the camp." He instructed pickets "to arrest all persons who attempt to break through their lines" and immediately send them under guard to camp headquarters. Finally: "The unnecessary destruction of property by this command is emphatically prohibited and officers are commanded to enforce strict military law in the government of their respective commands." At this time of the war, commanders still attempted to protect civilian property.[21]

In a letter to his brother, Sheridan described the Legion's first real action: "The Irish Legion spent three weeks of Comparitive happiness for with the exception of an occasional alarm of guerillas nothing interupted us until the 20th day of December the Rebble Gen. Van Dorn paid a running visit to Holly Springs." With the bulk of General Grant's army located well to the south in the Oxford area, keeping Confederate lieutenant general John C. Pemberton's army pinned down along the Yalobusha River, Confederate major general Earl Van Dorn with his 3,500 raiders paid an unexpected early morning call on Grant's supply depot at Holly Springs, quickly capturing most of the garrison. Van Dorn's troops were firmly in control of Holly Springs and had begun the plunder and destruction of Union supplies by 7 A.M. According to one of Van Dorn's soldiers, J. G. Dupree, a private in Company G, 1st Mississippi Cavalry, the morning was frosty, and most of the Confederates were "thinly-clad and hungry," so while they equipped themselves with captured pistols, carbines, sabers, and ammunition, they also made the best use possible of captured Union "rations, blankets, shirts, hats, boots, and overcoats." He added: "With our new overcoats on, it was difficult to tell us from Federals." Van Dorn posted Colonel William Hicks "Red" Jackson's troopers to the north of Holly Springs to prevent Union reinforcement from that direction, and probably they were the troops that made contact with the 90th Illinois about 10 or 11 A.M. By 4 P.M., Van Dorn's men had destroyed whatever they could not carry away and headed north to further disrupt Union communications.[22]

Colonel O'Meara reported General Van Dorn's visit: "On December 20 at daybreak brisk firing was heard in the direction of Holly Springs. At 9 o'clock A.M. about 100 of 2nd [Illinois] Cavalry arrived at this post having cut their way through Van Dorn's forces at Holly Springs and were followed in about an hour by four companies of the 101st Ill. Inf. falling back on us from their station between me and Holly Springs."[23]

Woodruff described the initial phase of the encounter. Smoke from the burning of supplies at Holly Springs alerted the 90th Illinois of approaching trouble, allowing O'Meara to take down the regiment's tents, thereby hiding his strength. The remaining seven companies were formed in a small ravine "nearly midway between the railroad and wagon road," where they awaited attack. Kelly's Company F was on the extreme right of the regiment's line. Twelve Company F men under Second Lieutenant William White formed an advanced skirmishing party. The 2nd Illinois Cavalry troopers and infantry from the 101st Illinois were placed behind the railroad as a reserve. O'Meara politely declined a request for surrender.[24]

O'Meara put up a brave front, which stopped the Confederate approach. He wrote: "Being in command I immediately posted my little forces as advantageously as circumstances would permit and found the enemy in force 5000 or above strong on my front and left." O'Meara then made a demonstration that "evidently disconcerted the enemy, who after the exchange of a few shots fell back for reinforcements, & I accordingly prepared for a renewal of the attack, which I subsequently ascertained was only prevented by continued heavy explosions of ammunition at Holly Springs being mistaken by him for the artillery of General Grant's army in pursuit. The enemy was repulsed with some loss. Our only casualty was the capture of the Q. Master, now paroled and awaiting exchange." The next day, December 21, Colonel O'Meara ordered Major John Mudd, 2nd Illinois Cavalry, to Holly Springs under a flag of truce. Finding the Confederates gone, Mudd took possession of the town and held it until the arrival of other Union forces at about 10 A.M.[25]

Lieutenant Charles Dickey, native of Ottawa, Illinois, and son of T. Lyle Dickey, the colonel of the 4th Illinois Cavalry, arrived at Holly Springs sometime after noon on the twenty-first. He "found the depot in ruins—together with other buildings containing Government stores. One whole square near the court-house was destroyed and the explosion of the ammunition shattered a large number of buildings in the vicinity—amongst them several fine churches and some splendid residences. The loss by the Government is immense." Dickey then commented on the actions of the 90th Illinois: "After taking Holly Springs with 1500 prisoners he [Van Dorn] sent a detachment to Cold Water—four miles this side—to take that point and destroy the Rail Road but the Irish Legion from Ill. were too much for them & they were repulsed. All honor to the Irishmen. They always fight well for the Union."[26]

In his December 20, 1862, report to Confederate general Pemberton of his capture of Holly Springs and destruction of $1,500,000 in stores, Van Dorn failed to mention any contact with the 90th Illinois. J. G. Dupree later blamed Van Dorn's raiders' lack of artillery for the failure to capture other points on the Mississippi Central Railroad: "With but a single piece of artillery, this garrison [Middleburg], as well as those of Davis' Mill and Cold Water, might have been easily captured." He wrote that "at Cold Water we also found the garrison too strongly posted to admit of capture without excessive loss." In effect, Dupree complimented O'Meara on the way he directed the 90th Illinois. In his history of the Vicksburg campaign, Edwin Cole Bearss similarly concluded that although the Confederates greatly outnumbered O'Meara's troops, Van Dorn was deep in Union-held territory and could not afford the time required to capture the Union forces, so he withdrew after a brief skirmish.[27]

Three soldiers of the 90th Illinois wrote of Van Dorn's attack in their letters home. In one way or another, all praised their colonel for his leadership, tactics, and the way he handled the regiment in their first encounter with the Confederates.

Patrick Sloan, a blue-eyed, dark-haired, dark-complexioned twenty-eight-year-old corporal in Company C, described the action from his location at the 90th Illinois camp four miles north of Holly Springs: "When we heard the firing at daylight we were all out and formed in the line of battle in a hollow and in a little wood so that for them to see us they would be within hitting distance." Confederate troops arrived "about eleven o'clock and our Col. sent out the 240 cavalry that came to us so as to lead the rebels around to our front and where some of us were in ambuscade. Pretty soon the firing began and the ball[s] began to whistle but they would not come any nearer. The firing continued for some time with but little damage to our side." Finally, with O'Meara "at their head," the cavalry advanced "and the rebels fell back but kept hovering around for 24 hours trying to find out how strong we were. We learned by prisoners we took that they thought we had about 7,000 men by the way the Col. placed us." Sloan added: "For 48 hours we were within sight of our tents and had to lay flat on the ground without moving or sleep or anything to eat accept a dry cracker." Sloan claimed the 90th Illinois captured "8 prisoners and about 20 horses." He praised O'Meara's leadership: "Oh, our Col. is a cuss in a fight. We all believe that the way he had us placed the way he was going to fight us, that we would have whipped the whole seven thousand at once and at our ease." According to Sloan, O'Meara was rewarded "for the bravery shown and the way he handled the troops here" by being "appointed Post Commander and is over all the troops in Holly Springs and around here for 5 or 6 miles, about 8,000 men now. . . . Father Kelly gave us all his blessing and we recited an act of Contrition just before the enemy fired on us and when we were in the line of battle each and every company separately." Sloan summarized their losses as three men wounded and one private and the quartermaster captured.[28]

In a letter to his brother, Quartermaster Sheridan described O'Meara's troop dispositions and his own capture at the start of the action. O'Meara had carefully arranged his troops to best utilize the defensive cover of their location and to deceive the Confederates as to his true numbers. Sheridan wrote that O'Meara placed his seven companies and the four companies of the 102nd Illinois "off on the brow of the hill beyond the Camp laying on their bellies. they could not be seen, but he rose them by Squads and in single file marched and countermarched them so that in the distance it would appear as though our force was formidable. The Cavalry were thrown out on picket and the infantry called in. this state of things could not last long. Eagerly the boys looked for a chance to pick out one or two with decent Saddles and empty them at a Short distance. The pickets exchanged compliments." O'Meara then used to good effect his experience as a Mounted Rifleman as well as that gained commanding cavalry in Benito Juárez's army in Mexico. Sheridan wrote: "After I was taken, the Rebs became rather too close neighbors to our boys. They gave them a few volleys and the Col. [O'Meara] at the head of only 200 [of the 2nd] Cavalry made a sortie and dashed at them.

I suppose they imagined he had a Division for they turned round and flew for dear life amid the shouts and yells of a handful of men hid behind the hills." Sheridan estimated that "about twenty-five hundred" of Van Dorn's troops attacked the 90th Illinois at Coldwater Station.[29]

Captain Peter Casey, Company H, wrote his wife an emotional letter, emphasizing his part in repulsing Van Dorn's attack beginning with the return of their pickets, "firing on the enemy as they came." Casey added, "But, oh, what a suspense. we were in line of battle laying down upon our arms below a low ridge and as they came from the woods out into a large cornfield within shooting distance of us the Colonel motioned to me with his Sword to show them to me." In response, Casey mounted the ridge and, "for the first time Beheld the enemy in battle array and thirsting for our blood and, oh what a feeling came over me. My heart sunk and swelled within me. It sunk for feere that the live of the Brave men that I com'ed. Many of them from comfortable homes and loving families were about to be slain." Casey wrote his heart "swelled as it never sweld before as I saw the Rebble rag flounting in the breese and turned and saw the glorious Stars and the green flag of Erin with the harp in its center and a rieth [wreath] of Shamrocks intertwined around it planted in its left." At this sight, it seemed to Casey "as though the blood of the Casey's, O'Briens and the Quenns for the last Seven Generations were coursing threw my veins that moment and I Resolved that I would leve my dead body upon that field before them flags Should be torn from our grasp."

As Casey described the action, Colonel O'Meara rode along the lines, instructed the troops to keep cool, and gave them a brief pep talk. In response, "The boys gave him three cheers that would do your heart good." The Confederates "formed a half circle in front of us and gave us a volley which came near killing the Colonel and Lieutenant [Colonel] McCleavy and the Quartermaster as they were between us and the enemy. The balls flew very close to them and over our heads." O'Meara had concealed most of his regiment from view by the Confederates, and according to Casey the Confederates "thought the cavalry and the 4 companies of the 101st Ill Vols. and Kelley's Company were all the numbers we had, but when they came around the hill and got sight of our regiment laying down they thought we had more men than we had for the Colonel had us 3 feet apart and in single file so we made a big show. . . . They were afraid to attack us so they left us alone."[30]

Their narrow escape definitely got the troops' attention. Company G reported they "repulsed the enemy and lay on [our] arms expecting an attack every moment until the 23rd [of December], when news came of Van Dorn's retreat." Three miles farther up the railroad at Hudsonville Station, Major Stuart's three companies of the 90th Illinois formed line of battle and awaited the arrival of Van Dorn's cavalry. Captain Thomas Barrett, Company K, proudly claimed his "brave Ottawa boys were assigned the position of danger . . . the exposed entrance to the camp." Stuart's new bride, Margaret, excitedly wrote her sisters: "I have seen great times since I saw you. We are only a few miles from Holly Springs and we heard them fighting as plain as day we were under arms for four nights and days never went to bed. We saw Van Dorn's army pass us about 1 mile from us. Our pickets skirmished with their pickets all night." Margaret described her husband's actions: "We have two companies of cavalry under the Major [Stuart] scouting the country all round. . . . My husband threw up breast works and fortified us with cotton [bales]. I do not think they can take us very easy."[31]

Greatly embarrassed at the destruction of his base of supplies, which ended his overland attempt to capture Vicksburg, Grant seemed relieved that someone had stood up to the raiders. Generously overlooking the Legion's past transgressions regarding his headquarters fence, he issued congratulatory orders to the 90th Illinois for its defense of the Coldwater River Bridge and to the two other units farther up the railroad line that also repulsed Van Dorn's attacks. As a reward, the order granted the 90th Illinois soldiers the right to inscribe the name Coldwater on their regimental flag to commemorate their battle with Van Dorn.[32]

The men of the Legion had performed very well in their first encounter with only a couple of minor glitches. Woodruff related one that occurred just before the engagement: "Lieut. Col. McCleavy, while riding along the line, saw the rebs advancing, when he gave the following order to the 90th: 'Get up into rows, boys they are coming again.' There was not much 'West Point' about that order but it answered for the occasion. The bye's got up into 'rows' to some purpose!"[33]

In his own inimitable style, Woodruff gave his version of the capture of Quartermaster Sheridan: "During the skirmishing with the enemy, the military arder [ardor] of the Quartermaster impelled him to leave his stores and books with a subordinate, while he sallied forth to join the fray." Woodruff describes Sheridan's appearance: "Now, it happened that the quartermaster, while he was a man of undoubted valor, was, like Zacheus of old, 'little of stature.' To counterbalance this deficiency he had recourse to an expedient somewhat like that of his prototype,—he mounted a very tall horse. Being in full uniform, and sporting in his hat a long green plume, emblematic of the land of his birth, he presented a novel, if not a formidable figure." Woodruff explained Sheridan's choice of weapons: "At the last moment he bethought himself that he was not armed. To be sure he was the happy possessor of a sword, but past experience had convinced the quartermaster that a conflict between his sword and his legs was an irrepressible one, and that it was more ornamental than useful. Appealing to a friend, he was supplied with a small, a very small pistol, and with this armament he sallied forth to annihilate the enemy." Then disaster struck: "It happened just at this moment that the squads of the 2nd Ill. Cavalry were coming in, as we have related, and the quartermaster having constituted himself a volunteer aid-de-camp, assigned them their positions." Sheridan unfortunately mistook a squad of approaching Confederate troopers dressed in Union overcoats for Union horsemen, resulting in his capture. Woodruff concludes: "This terminated 'Sheridan's ride' and the only consolation he ever got out of the affair, was given him by Col. O'Meara, who suggested, that the reason why Van Dorn did not press the assault any longer, was undoubtedly the fact that the quartermaster's size and equipments had convinced him of the utter helplessness of the attack!" Besides being a strong leader and firm disciplinarian, O'Meara also knew how to use his keen sense of humor to everyone's advantage.[34]

After waiting at Benton Barracks in St. Louis, Missouri, some six weeks to be exchanged, Sheridan wrote to his brother and described in detail his capture and subsequent meeting with Confederate general Earl Van Dorn:

> The Lt. Col. and myself were standing on the brow of the hill just over where the boys were laying when I suggested to him that it would be well to know where the shots were exchanged to be the better on our guard in that direction and volunteered to ride over. Go ahead Said he. I rode to a spot where a minute before one of our Cavalry were. when I made the inquiry not doubting but he was our picket, he made no answer, his carbine lay across his Saddle as harmless as a stick. I rode closer to repeat the question entirely off my guard when to my inexpressible horror and Surprise a Squad Surrounded me from the road and from behind the hedge. They put on some of our overcoats that morning which proved an admirable disguise. I was gobbled and marched off to Holly Springs here in the midst of all those who were made prisoners in the morning. I was ordered to dismount and give my parole. Not understanding the nature of the parole, the Cartel never having come under my notice and thinking [it] dishonorable I peremptorably [peremptorily] refused to accept it. I must then be taken to the General, away with said I. on our way a pup with the assurance of a Napoleon dismounted and ordered me to do in like manner. No choice I obeyed when he coolly unsaddled my beautiful horse and presented me with a bag of bones. The fortunes of war said he. I took it cool but I think I would know that fellow again. after an hours Search we discovered the incendiary Van Dorn.
>
> "What do you do here?" said he.
>
> "I came here to assist in preventing you pulling to pieces a fabrick the fairest and finest handiwork of man."
>
> "He refused to [be] parolled," said the Lt. of the guard, "what shall we do with him?"
>
> "Hang him," said he, "I don't know what else to do with him."
>
> "Detail a file of men, and if the enemy attack us see he is shot." said he.
>
> "Are you Gen. Van Dorn?" said I.
>
> "Yes," he answered angrily.

"Thank you," I answered.

He waived his hand and I was driven some little distance from him. I had a revolver and a double barrel pistol both of which were taken from me but my sword etc. which were presented to me by the Common Council of Chicago of which you know I am a member I fortunately left in camp. After marching about untill eve when he was about to evacuate the place for he feared the approach of Grant, the Major of the 62nd Ill. was at that moment found and paroled. he called me; requested to speak with me. I dismounted, when he explained the conditions of the Cartel which set me straight on that subject. I then consented to take the parole. I have reason to believe since it is well I did for he certainly would not have allowed me to escape and he could not take me along. I was however introduced to Genl. the 2nd time.

"Then," said he, "you have wisely altered your mind."

"The Major whom you just paroled done that" said I "and wish you to understand that it was not the threat you made to hang me this morning that intimidated me."

"Well," said he," I don't wish you to go away impressed with the idea that I intended to carry it out, except your people attacked me in which case rather than you should escape I would shoot you."

"That is understood," said I, when he extended his hand to me which I took. he shook mine cordially, and said he hoped the next time we met it would be under more favorable circumstances.

"If during this war, I hope so" I answered, and I quit.[35]

Civilian and military affairs commingled while the 90th Illinois remained into early 1863 at the Coldwater Station camp. Between December 27 and 30, 1862, the Legion's adjutant, Edwin S. Davis, administered an oath of allegiance to the Union to more than 140 local citizens, mostly from Marshall and Tippah counties in Mississippi, in which they swore "to support and protect the Constitution of the United States against all their enemies whether domestic or foreign." The regiment's order book contains the names of those who took the oath, including most neighbors of the 90th Illinois who lived between the Legion's two campsites. Delia's father, Peter Scales, J. R. Daniel, J. H. Brooks, J. W. Gray, William Wall Jr., and Martha Wall were among the seventeen Marshall County residents who signed the oath. Colonel O'Meara doubted the sincerity of some taking the oath and documented his suspicions in his January 4, 1863, letter to his brigade commander, Colonel John Mason Loomis: "A large number of able bodied men from Tippah Co. Miss.—a very hot bed of rebeldom—have presented themselves the past two days at this post for the purpose of taking the Oath of Allegiance [to] the U.S; actually for the purpose of taking a small quantity of cotton to Memphis, which I have reason to believe is often exchanged for Salt and other commodities which finds it way to the Rebels." He suspected that "the unusually large number presenting themselves the past few days is significant, and the careless manner in which the oath has been taken by many impresses me with the belief that they are working collectively in the matter, and I beg to refer to you for instructions in the promises [oaths]."[36]

The Union's need for cotton also intruded into the local area. According to General Sherman, a bale of cotton was worth up to three hundred dollars in gold, with the result that "hundreds of greedy speculators flocked down the Mississippi, and resorted to all sorts of measures to obtain cotton." At Coldwater Station, Colonel O'Meara wrote Colonel Loomis on January 4 describing the surrounding area as "overrun by a Swarm of Cotton thieves, who plunder the poor defenseless and almost starving people of the little that they may have succeeded in saving from the guerillas under the pretense of being employed by our Government to do so." Upon being apprehended, one of the offenders, a private in the 20th Illinois employed in the Quartermaster Department at Holly Springs as a saddler, offered a bribe of $150 to the arresting officer, who laughed at the offer and promptly brought the man under arrest to O'Meara. O'Meara reported that the private brazenly offered him "300 dollars with a promise that at least 600 dollars a week should be regularly paid by certain parties in Holly Springs—if, to use his own expression, I would let the present little matter slide, and promise not to see him in the future." O'Meara arrested the man and reported him as under the "charge of a Guard in my Camp. He had several Negroes with him to assist in plundering, two escaped in the darkness to the woods, and the others I hold." Colonel Loomis responded that the "Superintendent of Contrabands (Negroes) has by order of Maj. Gen. Grant entire control of such persons as at this post. Will you please return his three Negroes, two yoke of oxen, and the Cotton (the latter to be turned over to U.S.Q.M.). The soldier I desire to have sent me under guard for proper punishments. I particularly desire that the soldier should not escape and require any information in your possession to enable the Provost Marshal to round up the others connected with the transaction." Grant's headquarters took note of the affair as his adjutant, Lieutenant Colonel John Rawlins, promptly ordered Colonel O'Meara to send the cotton thief and Negroes arrested by him under close guard, with no communication allowed, "to these headquarters." O'Meara had demonstrated his honesty and courage in refusing to permit abusive cotton speculation that was known to be condoned, if not initiated, by some higher-ranking Union officers. In any case, O'Meara did not appear to suffer for his chosen way of dealing with cotton speculators.[37]

While the Legion camped at Coldwater Station, some of the troops of the 90th Illinois toured Holly Springs, a town well worth a visit. Centered in excellent cotton-growing land and connected to the Mississippi River by railroad, prewar Holly

Springs had enjoyed great prosperity from the cotton trade, and the number of large and beautiful homes that had been recently built reflected that prosperity. It also served as the educational center for the area, with the Holly Springs Female Institute, St. Thomas Hall (a military school), Chalmers Institute (for boys), and the Franklin Female College. Nearby at Sylvestria, close to where the 90th Illinois camped, the Cottrell family established both a female and a male academy.[38]

Lieutenant William White of Company F wrote a letter home describing the experiences he and two members of Company B, Second Lieutenant Charles Bellingale and drum major Henry Bell, had as they spent Sunday, December 28, touring Holly Springs. After describing the ruins of the depot, a large foundry, and railroad cars and wagons burned by Confederate raiders, White found several large intact buildings in use as hospitals and "many nice yards adorned with beautiful green trees." A sentinel at the gate of the most attractive house and yard identified it as General Grant's headquarters and allowed them to enter. As White's two friends were from Grant's home town of Galena, they decided to pay a call on the general. On the porch they met Colonel John Rawlins, of Grant's staff, also from Galena and with whom White's two friends were acquainted. Rawlins in turn took them to see the general, who "soon brought them [White's friends] to mind and reached his hand." White was formally introduced and shook hands with General Grant. White observed "several colonels there and many officers, besides a number of red tape gentlemen." Soon after leaving the headquarters, they met a doctor, an acquaintance of Lieutenant Bellingale's, who invited them to join him for a meal, which they all agreed "was the best dinner that fell to their lot since they left the United States." They returned to camp in time for dress parade, and after supper White eloquently described the scene: "The night was a beautiful one, the moon in all the loveliness of her refulgent light shone bright. The merry twinkling stars seemed conscious of the fact that it was Sunday. After tattoo the men assembled at Father Kelly's tent, as they do every night, and said the rosary with simple piety but seemed a solemn ceremony, beneath inspiration of such a night." And so ended "a Sunday in the South."[39]

Accurate reports of the action of the Irish Legion at Coldwater Station reached Chicago slowly, making the last days of the year a time of unease for relatives and friends of the 90th Illinois soldiers. The mail was not getting through, and the first newspaper reports of Van Dorn's capture of Holly Springs raised fears that the 90th Illinois had suffered the same fate as the 23rd Illinois and had been captured in their first encounter with the enemy. Finally on December 30, the *Chicago Times* received "reliable details of the raid," which briefly mentioned that a detachment of Confederates had attacked Coldwater and been repulsed. The next day, the *Times* reported the action at Coldwater in greater detail, concluding, "Our boys were on the lookout, and repulsed them handsomely. . . . No Federals were killed, and none seriously hurt." Father Denis Dunne had put his heart and soul into raising the 90th Illinois and had obtained the best soldier available to lead them. One can imagine his concern upon reading such tidings, but also his great sense of relief upon learning that the Irish Legion had survived their first test virtually unscathed and under Colonel O'Meara's direction had brought honor to the regiment. That their action had been recognized and praised by no less than General Grant was just frosting on the cake.[40]

Colonel O'Meara reported an aggregate of 669 officers and men on December 31, 1862. The 90th Illinois had 10 captains, 8 first lieutenants, 8 second lieutenants, 47 sergeants, 58 corporals, 16 musicians, 570 privates, and a field staff of 12. Several companies still carried on their rolls soldiers later listed as deserters, somewhat inflating their numbers. As the old year ended and the new began, halfway across Tennessee at a site thirty miles southeast of Nashville, Union and Confederate armies fought the bloody battle the Union named Stone's River and Confederates called Murfreesboro. Stymied on the overland route, Grant's army retired northward back toward La Grange and Grand Junction in Tennessee. The war would continue with no foreseeable end in sight for the Legion.[41]

{ 3 }

LIFE ON "ONE CRACKER A DAY"

Major General Earl Van Dorn's destruction of Major General Ulysses S. Grant's supply base at Holly Springs, combined with Brigadier General Nathan Bedford Forrest's thorough wrecking of the Mobile and Ohio Railroad from Jackson, Tennessee, north into Kentucky, severed the communications of Grant's army with the North for a week. Along with the rest of the Union army, the Irish Legion lived off the surrounding country for some two weeks before rations could be issued in anything approaching the normal way. Convinced of "the impossibility of maintaining so long a line of road over which to draw supplies for an army moving in an enemy's territory," Grant began a staged withdrawal back to La Grange and Grand Junction just over the border in Tennessee. During his subsequent campaign to capture Vicksburg, Grant made the Mississippi River his supply line, thereby assuring its virtually immunity to interruption by Confederate attacks.[1]

As part of the retreat, the seven companies of the 90th Illinois withdrew from their position at Coldwater Station on January 11, 1863, and on the next day made the twenty-mile march in pleasant weather back to Camp Yates, their old campground outside the once beautiful town of La Grange, Tennessee (see Map 2, in chapter 2). As the regiment closest to Holly Springs, the 90th held the post of honor as the rear guard of Major General James Birdseye McPherson's XVII Corps. Company K of the 90th Illinois had already arrived at Camp Yates on January 9 after leaving Hudsonville on January 8. A "large Rebel force" rumored to be a few miles behind them and "approaching" minimized straggling in Company K. The march took its toll on the health of Second Lieutenant Thomas Larkin, who took sick on January 11 with sciatic rheumatism and remained unable to perform duty until May 1863. A sleet storm on January 14 turned into a three-inch snowfall the next morning, making picket duty thoroughly unpleasant. Several days later, about the time the snow melted, the First Division, and thus the Legion, became part of the XVI Corps, headquartered in Memphis. The change meant that instead of heading downriver with Grant's army, the 90th would remain in Tennessee guarding the Memphis and Charleston Railroad.[2]

In what one would not exactly call a sober homecoming, George Woodruff recounted that upon their arrival in La Grange, some of the Legion's officers found the hotel full and secured lodging with considerable difficulty. However, their spirits rose when upon kindling a good fire, a local Irishman named Kelly appeared laden with two large bottles of gin. Aware that they were in enemy country, they prudently insisted their benefactor take the first drink. He did and survived without ill effects. After the officers and their new drinking companion finished his two bottles and several more like them, Woodruff wrote that they were convinced that "he was a true Irishman, and a good fellow besides."[3]

A letter printed in the *Chicago Post*, dated March 6, described a day with the Irish Legion at their encampment in Camp Yates, located about half a mile from La Grange, on the Memphis and Charleston Railroad. According to the author, its location on two small "not very picturesque" hills provided the camp the advantage of being "free from dampness and puddles of mud in wintry weather."

After the noon meal, the Legion's troops went to the nearby drill ground where the visitor observed their proficiency at drill. With the Legion drawn up in line of battle, Colonel Timothy O'Meara commenced battalion drill, making good use of his previous military experience as a sergeant in the Mounted Riflemen. The author described the scene: "He [O'Meara] rides in front of the line, and gracefully unsheathes his sword. A glance from the right to the left assures him that the men are in their proper places. For about two hours the regiment went through the various evolutions in a very creditable and excellent manner." Before executing each "movement the colonel would explain how it was to be done, in a comprehensive and succinct style. The drill was a good one, and the drill master is well qualified for his position. He is a thorough tactician, a good swordsman, and the best equestrian that I have met with in this army." O'Meara obviously impressed the visitor, who wrote: "The officers and men have a great regard for the colonel, and proudly boast that, 'there is nothing round here near him.'" He observed that "Father Kelly has the rosary every evening, and the spiritual wants of the 'Legion' on the Sabbath are impressive and ready to the minute, rain or shine." He added that the members of the Legion know "the importance and value of the Union" and "hope to win from the American people a recognition as beautiful as that which the unfortunate Marie Antoinette bestowed upon the Irish soldier—semper et ubique fidelis—'always and everywhere faithful.'" This report indicates that the men of the Legion had responded to O'Meara's leadership and were rapidly adapting to their new vocation.[4]

In the absence of Quartermaster Redmond Sheridan, not yet officially exchanged, O'Meara appointed First Lieutenant Thomas Murray, Company I, the acting quartermaster. The Legion remained at Camp Yates through February with only an occasional skirmish with small groups of Confederates to break the monotony of garrison duty. The nature of the war had changed, and Company F reported that on January 12–13, 1863, they "marched sixteen miles southeast into Tippah County, Mississippi, on a reconnoitering and foraging expedition. Returned with teams laden the next day." Sergeant Charles Woollett, Company H, wrote of "frequently having to depend for supplies on foraging over a country pretty well foraged already." The duties of the Legion's soldiers required "untiring vigilance demanded to keep the railroad in order through a country swarming with guerillas, and every hostile feature." Along with the rest of Grant's army, the men of the 90th Illinois improved their ability to provide for themselves, with the result that the war became increasingly hard on civilians and their possessions. Despite Colonel O'Meara's attempts to secure "efficient" weapons, the troops armament still consisted of 442 of those detested Austrian muskets, an indication of their current troop strength. On January 24, Second Lieutenant William White, Company F, transferred to the Signal Corps, where he would remain until May of the following year. With his transfer, the Legion temporarily lost a valuable officer and a gifted writer, for which its history remains all the poorer.[5]

In a February 4 letter from the camp of the 90th Illinois at La Grange, Tennessee, Corporal Patrick Sloan informed his wife, Jennie, that he was now the teamster for Company C, which involved "hauling company property when we are on the march and foraging and hauling commissary stores when encamped." The job also required him "to drive and take care of six mules." An attack, expected for the past ten days, kept the troops busily engaged "digging rifle pits, building breastworks, and stockades and embrasures for batteries, breastworks of cotton, etc." The men of the Legion did not consider the food ration to be the high point of their existence at La Grange, according to Sloan: "Our rations are pretty much the same all the time. Hard bread or shingles we call them. Coffee (we teamsters steal ours) and fat pork." His new position provided several advantages: "Our mess (teamsters) have plenty of these articles but I am sorry to say the companies do not have a plenty for this reason: our rations come from Memphis every day and but one day's rations at a time for fear that it would fall in the hands of the rebels. But as the Teamsters have the hauling of the stores from the depot here to the camp they always manage to have enough of said articles and then when we are out foraging we always pick up some extras for ourselves." There were additional compensations: "The sutler brought some whiskey from Memphis the other day. . . . I got . . . one mouth full for a half a dollar . . . and Lieut. [John] Harrington [Company C] promised to bring me a drink from Chicago when he came back so when I get it and two others then I will have had five drinks." Whiskey seemed to have been considered to possess medicinal value, possibly explaining frequent references in letters to the access to—or lack of—spirits.[6]

The paucity of the current food ration provided by the government disgusted the troops, and so in the fashion of soldiers from time immemorial, they made fun of their situation. One of the boys in the 90th Illinois made up a song expressing the soldiers' complaints, which Corporal Patrick Sloan sent to his wife with the admonition: "It is contraband down here and I suppose is there also but you can cut the leaf off and then I don't care who sees it." The name of the song was "One Cracker a Day," and it began:

> You friends of the soldiers I pray lend an ear
> A sad and a true story I will let you hear
> I'll sing you a song about our rations and pay
> And how we subsist on a cracker a day.
>
> To get such cruel treatment indeed it is a shame
> But the administration of course is to blame
> They've neglected to give us our rations or pay
> And compelled us to live on one cracker a day.
>
> Many of us long in the service have been
> And many a battle and skirmish have seen
> But it's sweeter to fight or to die in the fray
> Than to be compelled to subsist on one cracker a day.

The song continued through eleven more stanzas, "each worse than the first," at least from the standpoint of the administration, as they covered shortages of clothing and equipment and other gripes. The song also expressed the soldiers' disgust with the administration's emancipation policy, abolitionists, and slackers at home:

> . . . We enlisted to fight for a more glorious cause
> In defense of our flag, our union, and laws
>
> Old Abe's proclamation we soldiers do abhor
> It will do us no good but will prolong the war
> And while this war lasts, it is true what I say
> Each soldier must live on a cracker a day.
>
> All ye shoddy patriots who hang around home
> Who are howling for blood but they won't risk their own
> For them the poor soldier from home far away
> Half naked, half starved on a cracker a day.[7]

On February 5, another snowstorm hit the area, but by mid-February, in the midst of several days of rain, detachments of the 90th Illinois along with some nine hundred other soldiers dug entrenchments around a general hospital on top of a large hill half a mile from La Grange. Captain Peter Casey wrote that he "had charge of the pick and Shovel brigade as the Boys call it. There is 150 detailed from each regiment each morning." Casey's comments to his wife revealed much about himself. He was obviously expecting sympathy when he wrote of his willingness "to die for my adopted Country. A great many of the officers of this regiment and of other regiments around here are resigning. I thought some of doing it also, but in all the letters that you have written you have not in one instance Hinted a wish or a desire for my return." His comment on his relations with O'Meara was similarly revealing: "A planter's wife told the Col. That I was the best looking man she ever saw. He takes pride in letting [on] that there is family resemblance in us." According to Casey, the disruption of the Union's supply line by Confederate raiders reduced the Legion's daily food ration to "a few crackers and a little pork." Finding service in the army to be too much, Casey expressed a fear of sickness along with the desire to leave the army and return home, "if I can get out honorably with my life Which is doubtful for there is so many dying in our regiment that we have quite a little Graveyard. Now the night is so cold and damp and we have so much rain that the men take cold and they take a kind of a chill that is common in this country and it carries them off in a short time. I hope I will not take one of them."[8]

Indeed, sickness plagued Camp Yates as 36 of the Legion's 530 enlisted men present on February 28 were reported sick, and three died during their stay there. The level of sickness increased in March and April. Lacking sufficient sanitary supplies for the sick troops at Camp Yates, Second Assistant Surgeon Darwin Hinckley wrote the Sanitary Commission in Memphis that the 90th Illinois "has been in the field now nearly five months, and that we have quite a number sick in Hospital, and have never yet received any sanitary items, a supply of which would greatly relieve the wants, and add immensely to the comfort, and greatly relieve the necessities of those under my care." Gray-eyed with a light complexion, Hinckley was fifty-two years old. A graduate of a medical college in New York, he had left a good practice in Illinois to join the Legion in November 1862.[9]

Money, or rather the lack of it, created other problems. The men of the regiment had received only one month's pay since their enlistment the previous August or September, and letters from their families at home contained "urgent pressing calls for aid." In a long letter to his divisional commander, Brigadier General James Denver, dated March 18, O'Meara did his best to look out for his troops, appealing for Denver to intercede "with the Department Commander . . . for the payment of my Regiment up to 30th of December 1862."[10]

In a February 23 letter to his wife, Corporal Sloan commented on the nature of the skirmishing going on every day at La Grange: "They [Confederates] come up in small bodies and attack our pickets . . . and then when the pickets are reinforced they fall back or skedaddle on the double quick. This country is all a heavy woods and they keep a-prowling around in it . . . and when they see a good chance to make a dash on them, they do it. But they never attack openly for I don't think they are strong enough." The attacks kept the troops on edge with the result that on Washington's Birthday, when troops at one of the Union outposts fired their salute much earlier than ordered, the whole post turned out under arms, and scouts were sent to determine the cause of the commotion.[11]

On March 9, the 90th Illinois left La Grange by railroad for the small village of La Fayette, now called Rossville, where the regiment relieved the 99th Indiana. La Fayette was an important post on the Memphis and Charleston Railroad, located about eighteen miles west of La Grange, seven miles east of Collierville, and about thirty miles east of Memphis. The elevation at La Fayette is some two hundred feet lower than at La Grange, and the Wolf River spreads over a large area just to the north of the town. Woodruff referred to the site as "Camp Misery." Company D found the place rainy, muddy, and thoroughly disagreeable. The Legion now had the job of guarding railroad bridges, including the Wolf River Bridge, telegraph wires, and a large water tank that local guerrillas were constantly trying to destroy. Major Owen Stuart described the regiment's location as "a very unhealthy place on Wolf River bottom, but still a beautiful place and one of the most important Stations on the R.R." He added, "The health of the regt. is good."[12]

The relative good health of the 90th Illinois when compared to other regiments could be credited in no small measure to the care of Second Assistant Surgeon Hinckley, who had been without an assistant since the Legion left Coldwater. To show their appreciation of his efforts, the men of the Legion gave Hinckley a purse of $150 along with sword, sash, and belt. He gratefully declined the money and obtained a large hotel for a hospital at his regiment's location, paying the rent for it with $40 of his own money. The Irish Legion obtained a needed addition to the medical staff when Surgeon Henry Strong mustered on May 7. A native of Buffalo, New York, the fifty-one-year-old Strong had attended Louisville Medical College in Kentucky. Earlier in the war, he had been sent by Rockford folks to "look after their boys." He had been at the Battle of Bull Run and then served as the surgeon of the 74th Illinois before joining the Legion. Colonel O'Meara received the good news in a very friendly letter from Illinois adjutant general Allan Fuller dated May 8, 1863.[13]

Patrick Sloan expressed his thorough dislike of their new location in his March 12 letter to his wife: "We were afraid at first that it was for Vicksburg we were destined but as bad as Vicksburg is described to be it must be better than this place." They were situated "in as low and swampy a hole as there is in Tennessee. At present the water is so deep around and in the camps that the men have to get on to a mule to go from one place to another and posting the pickets outside of camp is all done with mules." By April 6, the health of the regiment was becoming a problem, according to Sloan: "This is a very sickly place. . . . At one time about one third of the Regt. is unable for duty." Sickness remained a problem as six of the Legion's soldiers died while at La Fayette.[14]

Alarms due to guerrillas occurred two or three times a week, with some in response to attempts to destroy the railroad bridge. Firing at pickets occurred nightly, but the 90th Illinois suffered few casualties. In March, the officers and men of Company A fell out and formed line of battle on three successive nights and slept on their arms another two nights. In addition to disrupting sleep, the minor alarms could be hazardous. During one such alarm in the middle of the night, Adjutant Edwin Davis's horse fell, throwing him and injuring his hip and leg.

To aid the Legion in obtaining replacements for those detested Austrian muskets, Colonel John Mason Loomis, commanding the First Brigade, wrote to the XVI Army Corps headquarters in Memphis pleading that the 90th Illinois be rearmed with "Enfield Rifled Muskets" presently on hand at that post. Loomis termed La Fayette "one of, if not the most exposed stations on the R.R." On March 31, a force of one hundred Confederate cavalry approached within two miles of La Fayette. In early April, Colonel O'Meara wrote to his brother that "my present position is a very hardshiping one. The Rebels keep annoying us all the time particularly at night." A letter to the editor of the *Chicago Post* dated April 20 and signed with the nom de plume "Veritas" assessed the regiment's situation more positively: "At first the guerrillas gave us some annoyance; but a gentle intimation that a recurrence of their visits toward our lines would necessitate the removal or demolition of every sheltering abode within five miles around here, rather tranquilizes them of late. We have also had advices of a rebel force of 6,000 with 19 pieces of artillery, being in our vicinity under Gen. Chalmers, and are under orders to be in readiness for them at a moment's notice." In another positive note, the men of the regiment received their pay due up to December 31, 1862, and sent home about $30,000, much to the relief of those on the home front.[15]

By the third week of March, spring began to arrive in La Fayette, the peach and plum trees were in full bloom, and the Illinois troops saw the first newly planted field of corn. Not surprisingly, at least one of the young men of the regiment found himself, as described by Tennyson, with his "fancy lightly" turned "to thoughts of love." In April, Lieutenant Lawrence S. McCarthy, Company E, married a local fifteen-year-old Southern belle with Father Brady of the 15th Michigan officiating. Years later, Corporal John Lyons, also of Company E, remembered putting up wedding decorations.[16]

In March 1863, the 90th Illinois left the Third Brigade, First Division, XVI Army Corps, and joined the 26th Illinois and 12th and 100th Indiana as the First Brigade, commanded by the thirty-eight-year-old Chicago lumber merchant Colonel Loomis. This brigade would remain intact for nearly the next year and a half.

A Confederate report placed the strength of the 90th Illinois at 600 effective men with a two-gun battery while at La Fayette. Actually, the 90th Illinois reported only 409 enlisted men present for duty out of a total of 541 enlisted men present and absent, indicating over one in five enlisted men as either sick, detached, or absent for other reasons. Colonel Loomis's March 28 letter apparently moved the ordnance officer at Memphis into action, for in early April the regiment got rid of all but twenty of the Austrian muskets, receiving 403 Enfield rifle muskets in exchange. According to Major Stuart: "The men have all the confidence in themselves and the new arms and I believe could fight 3 to one." Stuart also looked forward to promotion: "There is Several vacancies in the Regt. which will be filled soon. I expect to go up a step unless I am Euchred out of it, but I think not."[17]

Captain Casey, anxious for a twenty-day leave but reluctant to make the request, attempted strategy. In an April 13 letter, he wrote his wife, first expressing doubts about his safe return as "the hot weather is upon us here and we are surrounded by enemies. Our pickets is attacked almost every night and we expect to get it Every day." He added: "I cannot resign. The Colonel will not allow me. he thinks a great deal of me. We had a little fuss some time ago but we are the best of friends now." He then urged his wife to see Father Dunne and ask for his help: "I know that the Col. would give me one [leave] before July . . . if Father Dunne would make the request of the Colonel In Writing for the Col thinks every Thing of Father Dunne." As a second line of attack, he instructed his wife to appeal to former mayor John C. Haines to see if he might influence "Father Dunne and the Colonel" to grant Casey a leave. Possibly to convince his wife to act, he concluded his letter with a description of himself asleep: "Tell Mother I dream of her often at night when I am lying rapt up in my blanket upon the greene grass with my sword naked and grasped in my rite hand with my boys all around me and my revolvers pressing my ribs very uncomfortably and dream I am a boy again." Presumably, with their captain so armed, his "boys" all wished him a calm and peaceful sleep. His strategy failed, for nothing came of his request for a leave.[18]

Casey rode an emotional rollercoaster. Sick of war and ready to go home, he wrote: "I wish this unholy war was Brought to an end for my heart is not in it. It is heartrending to see the beautiful homes redused to ashes, fences burnent and the inhabitants, old men and old women and young women and children for there is none others left hiding from us when we happen to go outside of the lines." Casey especially felt compassion "for the little children. The poor little Things tell me their fathers are off to the war but they do not know that they are fighting us, would to god that I could stop it. I would do it tonight if it could be done honorable for All parties concerned."[19]

Major Stuart apparently felt the need to assure his wife's parents of her continued health and satisfactory adjustment to army life. In an April 12 letter to them, he described Margaret's health and activities: "She is well and in much better health than I have ever seen her. She ways about 125 lbs. She is happy, and enjoys her Self living in a tent and is a member of the Cols. mess and the only lady in it. I have a very nice pony for her to ride given to me by a Scotch Lady and Gent. in La Grange for her." Margaret wrote she was now keeping house in an army tent and was "very happy indeed." She planned to send her "beautiful pony" home to Illinois "as soon as I get transportation for her." In a May 20 letter, Stuart again reassured them regarding their daughter: "My wife is a favorite of the Regt. with both officers and men. This week she was the recipient of two presents." Colonel O'Meara gave her "a handsome set of Studs. But the one she thinks most about was presented her by two Sergts. belonging to Co. B that she never Spoke to before. It was a beautiful gold pencil Purchased by them in Memphis. Shortly after we arrived at this post [La Fayette] one of their men got Stabbed while on picket duty and Mrs. S. paid particular attention to [him] while sick. He is a fine young man and I believe a blood relation of mine but never knew it until his wounding."[20]

The Legion, in the midst of reshuffling its officer corps, experienced several adjustment problems. O'Meara expected his officers' performance to meet a standard based on his years of experience in the regular army. An example of the resistance he faced in instilling such a level of military discipline and efficiency occurred on January 26, 1863, when Captain Mathew Leonard, Company E, completely lost his temper in a most conspicuous manner and directly defied Colonel O'Meara in the presence of other members of the regiment. For this serious breach of military discipline, he was tried by court-martial for neglect of duty, disobedience of orders, breach of arrest, and insubordination and mutinous conduct. Found guilty by the court, he was promptly dismissed March 26 by order of General Grant.[21]

O'Meara's efforts to shape up his officers, dissatisfaction over the emancipation policies of the Lincoln administration, and disability and health issues led to the resignation of six company officers between February 1 and April 7, 1863. First Lieutenant Joseph Teahon and Second Lieutenant John J. O'Leary, both Company I officers, resigned February 1, 1863; Captain Richard C. Kelly, Company F, resigned February 11; Second Lieutenant Peter O'Brian, Company D, resigned on March 6 and was honorably discharged March 17; Second Lieutenant George W. McDonald, Company H, accidentally wounded in November 1862, resigned March 6 due to disability; and Second Lieutenant Charles Bellingale, Company B, resigned on April 7 for health reasons. In addition to the dismissal of Captain Leonard, Company E, on March 26, First Lieutenant Andrew Liddle, Company H, received a dishonorable discharge on April 28. The *Chicago Tribune* literally fulminated over the three officers who resigned in protest of the issuance of the Emancipation Proclamation. Two other officers unsuccessfully offered their resignations. Lieutenant Colonel Smith McCleavy resigned on March 6 due to health problems. One of the resigning officers, Captain Kelly, later served in the 9th Illinois Cavalry from March to October 1865.[22]

The spate of resignations in the officer corps provided Colonel O'Meara an opportunity to choose replacements who met his standards; however, filling the now numerous vacancies in the regiment's officer corps only added to his problems. In early May, Illinois adjutant general Fuller sent O'Meara the commissions for several 90th Illinois officers, including one promoting Captain Patrick Flynn of Company A to major. O'Meara considered several of his officers, including Flynn, as unqualified for higher-ranking positions and withheld their commissions. This produced a confrontation between Flynn and O'Meara, resulting in Flynn sending a blistering letter on May 13 to Fuller and appealing his case to the divisional commander, Brigadier General William Sooy Smith. Flynn's poorly written letter to Fuller probably did more harm than good to his case, as his bragging on his own accomplishments revealed more about himself than he probably intended. He accused O'Meara of dereliction of duty and of being "a Habitual drinker and from the Effects of whisky has been laying ill for one week." During the war, Flynn frequently wrote to Fuller, generally with a request or complaint of some sort. Residents of neighboring towns in northern Illinois, they may have been acquainted before the war. Flynn's disposition probably suffered from the fact that he was under arrest from May 13, the date of his letter to Fuller, until May 29, 1863. Flynn's protests proved fruitless as Major General Stephen A. Hurlbut, who had assumed command of the district of West Tennessee on February 11, 1863, strongly backed O'Meara in a May 15 letter to Governor Richard Yates. Hurlbut's support of O'Meara was doubly effective as Hurlbut and Fuller maintained friendly relations as lawyers from the same area of northern Illinois. Hurlbut explained to the governor that under an act of Congress, the small size of the 90th Illinois did not entitle it to three field officers, returned the commissions given him by O'Meara, and scolded the "authorities at home" for not consulting O'Meara before making out the commissions in question. O'Meara meanwhile had explained the matter to Yates and wrote Adjutant General Fuller on May 28 detailing his reasons for withholding the commissions. In the letter, O'Meara stated his objections to filling the commissions with the individuals named: "I could not consent to see them elevated to positions which their ignorance of military matters would be sure to jeopardise the honor of the State and Regiment." O'Meara offered to resign if overruled, which he was not. Consequently, Flynn remained a captain, though not an entirely happy one.[23]

At least one soldier advanced in April as Patrick Sloan became wagon master of the 90th Illinois. Sloan reported the good news in a letter to his wife. His bad news centered on pest problems. The warm weather had brought out "any amount of mosquitoes, flies of all kinds, gallinippers that will make a man jump a rod [16 2/3 feet] when he gets a bite from one of them." He added: "There is also an interesting variety of snakes of most any size you could want to look at and any amount of bats, lizards, scorpions and any amount of other varmint that I ever seen before or don't know their names, but there is a variety of them that gives us a great deal of trouble at night for some of them are very fond of sleeping with Federal soldiers at night and they will arrange to do it if he is not very careful of how he rolls his blanket about on going to bed." At least life continued to be interesting, if not restful. Likewise fed up with the surrounding animal life at La Fayette, by April 30 Captain Casey wanted to move on: "I am tired of this Swamp, Snakes, lizards, Frogs, musketoes, bugs, spiders as large as your Fist, and many other things that help to make Our Stay here miserable." He repeated the request for his wife to see Father Dunne and have him write Colonel O'Meara requesting a leave for Casey. He wanted to go home but felt he could not resign as O'Meara would not give his consent. The troops mustered for pay on April 30, which at least temporarily took their minds off the camp's pest problems.[24]

With the arrival of warmer weather, the health of the Legion appeared to improve as the number of present enlisted men (EM) reported as sick declined from forty-seven in April to thirty-eight on May 31. However, the number of sick EM absent from the regiment increased from nine in April to nineteen in May. By the end of June, the thirty-two EM reported absent sick nearly equaled the thirty-three sick EM present with the regiment. This trend would continue throughout 1863, with increasing numbers of EM reported as absent sick in hospitals or recuperating at home.[25]

By May 13, Captain Casey found the weather "as hot as hell." He needed new clothes, having worn out four pairs of uniform pants since leaving home; his shirt-tail was now exposed. He was not in a good mood due to being up all the previous night as officer of the day, which required him to be in the saddle for nearly twenty-four hours. He felt "Sick, Sore, and down harted." He wished that "every damn abolishinest in Chicago felt as I do this Morning." In their letters, Casey and others expressed little antipathy toward their Confederate foes, directing it instead toward their old antagonists, the abolitionists, whom they blamed for bringing on the war. In the years before the war, the reform and nativist anti-Catholic and anti-foreign movements in New England had fused to the disadvantage of recent immigrants. As a result, the abolitionist press and prominent abolitionist authors kept Irish Americans under what Timothy Meagher termed a "constant derisive barrage." In addition, prominent abolitionists opposed the labor movement and thus the aspirations of unskilled Irish immigrants to improve their lot. During the large immigration of Irish Catholics in the 1840s and 1850s, nativist movements were especially strong in the northeastern United States. One such group, the Know-Nothings, feared both immigrants and the power of slavery. As the Irish Catholics were staunch Democrats, the Know-Nothings and Republicans associated the political power of the Irish with that of Southern Democrat slaveholders.[26]

Numerous Irish American newspapers as well as New York archbishop John Hughes expressed their indignation at the Lincoln administration's Emancipation

Proclamation, denouncing it as an outrageous change in policy from that of preservation of the Union. Opinions of soldiers within the regiment reflected the division within the Irish community. In January, Sergeant Charles Woollett, Company H, a native of England, described the negative effect of the Lincoln administration's emancipation policy on the Legion: "The emancipation policy and proposed arming of negroes is causing deep dissatisfaction, which, I fear, will bear bitter fruits." In another letter, Captain Flynn denied allegations that he had resigned over the issuance of the proclamation and strongly defended the loyalty of the Irish soldiers to the Union, stating: "There is not one word of truth in it. I have raised no issue on that question, and I leave all such to the people at home to settle. It is none of my business, even if I did differ with the President. I will faithfully endeavor to do my duty to my country by fulfilling every obligation I owe as an officer and a soldier. Every Irish-American Soldier in the Army is animated by this thoroughly order-loving, law-abiding spirit."[27]

Colonel Reuben Williams of the 12th Indiana, a sister First Brigade regiment to the 90th Illinois, summed up the prevailing attitude during this gloomy period of the war: "There was a wide spirit of complaint not only among the people at home but also among the soldiery in the field . . . to the arming of the Negro and permitting him . . . to fight for his own freedom." In a letter to the editor of the *Chicago Post*, Flynn made the point that if a Black "wants to be free, why don't he fight for his freedom himself. He never had a better opportunity. . . . You can be assured that soldiers will never fight for one nor with one, who won't fight for himself." Whether Flynn recognized it or not, he had made a powerful argument for Adjutant General Lorenzo Thomas's current activity. Secretary of War Edwin Stanton had become so dissatisfied with Thomas's performance that, in orders dated March 25, 1863, Stanton sent him away from Washington with instructions to organize black regiments in the Union army. Now a big duck in a somewhat smaller puddle, Thomas took seriously Stanton's order "that any obstacle thrown in the way of these ends [creation of black regiments] is regarded by the President as a violation of the acts of Congress and the declared purposes of the Government in using every means to bring the war to an end." In an April 6 speech in Helena, Arkansas, Thomas, full of fire and bluster, declared: "The policy of the Administration must be carried out, and no opposition on the part of officers and soldiers will be allowed. Even the stars [general's rank] will be no protection to the officer, who by act or word opposes the policy of the Government."[28]

Given their differing views, it is hardly surprising that in spite of his rank and appearance in full military regalia, Adjutant General Thomas's May 16 speech before Colonel Loomis's First Brigade provoked a major confrontation with the Irish Legion. Intrepid scout Theodore Upson, Company C, 100th Indiana, described the scene: "Our Brigade was paraded and formed a hollow square in front of the depot platform. He [Adjutant General Thomas] came out dressed in the most gorgeous uniform I ever saw. After a short speech he read a general order from the President as Commander in Chief of all the Armies of the United States in regard to arming the Negros. Then drawing his splendid sword he said by the authority of the President he declared the order in force." Colonel Williams of the 12th Indiana then "called for three cheers for the President of the United States. They were given with a will. Then three for our distinguished visitor. Well given. Then three for the order. Very fair cheering; and the 90th Ill—the Irish Regiment—hissed. Then came confusion, worse confounded. We were hastily marched back to our parade grounds. The 90th Ill Regiment stacked arms and their officers were told they were under arrest." Upson added: "I don't know how it will turn out with the 90th Illinois, but the truth is none of our soldiers seem to like the idea of arming the Negros. Our boys say this [is] a white mans war and the Negro has no business in it, but a good many say they have stood [for] emancipation which came, of course, as fast as our armies occupied slave territory."[29]

The *Chicago Post* reported the action of the 90th Illinois and the adjutant general's reaction as less confrontational. When called upon to cheer the order, "the regiment remained silent, save a few persons who cried 'Never! Never!'" The adjutant general directed Major Stuart, who was in command of the regiment, to determine who the men were that refused to obey the order. After conferring with his men, Stuart reported "that the entire regiment refused. Nothing more was said upon the subject."[30]

Adjutant General Thomas's self-laudatory summary of raising black regiments in Louisiana and Tennessee, which appeared as a letter in the *New York Times*, includes an account of his encounter with the Irish Legion. Thomas reported that he spoke "some seven or eight times a day" to troops along the railroad and that "during my tour I met with an Irish regiment, the Ninetieth Illinois, from Chicago—men who read the *Chicago Times*, after talking to them a while I proposed three cheers for the President of the United States. They were given heartily. Three cheers were then proposed for the settled policy of the United States with regard to the negroes. This was met by cries of No! No!" Thomas wrote he "inquired what such conduct meant? The Lieutenant-Colonel endeavored to excuse the men by saying that they had had no opportunity to think over the matter. I replied, 'You are not telling the truth Sir: I know the fact if you do not.' The officer was considerably mortified." At this point, Thomas forced the issue by ordering "those who opposed this policy of the Government to step forward, and said I knew the regiment had seen considerable service and fought well; but I also knew that there was but little discipline observed among them; that I wanted a distinct recognition of this doctrine—that was the point with me. Several stepped forward. They were instantly seized and sent to the guardhouse." As he left, Thomas gave the regiment "a week to consider what they would do." Fortunately, at the next station Thomas "met the Colonel of the regiment, who begged that I would leave the matter in his hands, and he would see that the men were taught the duty of soldiers. I complied with his request."[31]

Thomas's account led to widespread criticism of his treatment of the 90th Illinois in newspapers both large and small. The *Chicago Times* described it as another attempt by the administration "to cram its party politics by force down the throats of the soldiers." Other newspapers expressed similar views. Although the *New York Sunday Mercury* supported the administration's policy of arming blacks, it objected to actions that compelled soldiers to express concurrence with a policy with which they did not agree, calling such actions "the despotism which converts the soldier into its slave." The *Mercury* then gave a resounding defense of the rights of soldiers to the free expression of their own opinions: "The Soldiers owe prompt obedience to their superiors in all military matters; but beyond that, the humblest private is as much entitled to exercise unrestrained and freely, according to his own judgment, the prerogatives of an American citizen as the Commander in Chief." Actions such as those of Thomas led the *Chicago Times* to ask, "Is it any wonder that volunteering has stopped?" Recruitment among Democrats, including the Irish, was now so difficult that despite numerous attempts to add to the Legion's numbers, the 90th Illinois would obtain only fifteen assigned recruits during the rest of the war.[32]

The only officer of the Legion known to give an account of Adjutant General Thomas's speech and the Legion's reaction, Captain Thomas Barrett of Company K, was in the hospital when Thomas spoke to his troops. Barrett soon recovered, however, and his scathingly derisive letter to the editor of the *Chicago Times* was prominently featured on the front page of its May 25, 1863, edition. Barrett titled his letter "Headquarters 90th Illinois Volunteers," making it appear to be an official regimental communication in which he cleverly mocked the adjutant general's appearance, speech, and actions as well as the Lincoln administration's emancipation policy. A Peoria, Illinois, newspaper reprinted much of his letter along with favorable editorial comments indicating that the letter had received considerable attention downstate. However, Barrett had clearly overstepped the bounds his commanding officers were willing to tolerate, and retribution was swift and final. Colonel Loomis, Barrett's brigade commander, promptly placed him under arrest and on May 29 sent a copy of the offending article to the XVI Corps headquarters along with a statement that "summary punishment alone can do the subject justice as I see it." Headquarters concurred, as did Adjutant General Thomas, who got his revenge in his own way on June 10 in Special Orders No. 34: "For a highly insubordinate statement respecting the Adjutant General of the Army, published in the *Chicago Times* over his official Signature, Capt. Thomas K. Barrett of the 90th Illinois Volunteers is hereby dishonorably dismissed from the service of the United States." The special orders were signed by none other than Thomas himself and with more intensity than usual, as his signature was uncharacteristically bold and legible. Barrett's prompt expulsion from the army demonstrated the ability of the War Department to react rapidly when motivated. Barrett's protest to Illinois adjutant general Fuller over his dismissal from the service without a trial by court-martial was to no avail.[33]

Thomas's form of summary justice did not quite end the matter, as Captain Barrett refused to go quietly into oblivion. An article in the *Boston Pilot* described Barrett as "a victim of the official injustice of this 'demagogue in epaulettes.'" The article defended the 90th Illinois as having been "most foully misrepresented by Adjutant General Thomas." The article also claimed that Captain Barrett gave a "complete, and very opportune vindication" of the Legion, whose only crime was a refusal to applaud Thomas's announcement.[34]

On May 25, the same day Barrett's letter appeared in print in Chicago, seven companies of the 90th Illinois moved to Collierville, leaving some 120 men of Companies C, E, and H under command of Captain Patrick O'Marah, Company C, at La Fayette swatting bugs and doing guard duty. Captain Casey, feeling lonesome after the other seven companies left, practiced his engineering skills, directing the construction of a breastwork and fortification dubbed "Fort Casey." The same seven companies remained at Collierville doing garrison duty until June 1, when they marched some ten miles east on the railroad to Grisson's Bridge on the Memphis and Charleston Railroad, about four miles east of La Fayette. Company D reported the men bivouacked there without tents. On June 1 or 2, the three companies at La Fayette rejoined the regiment at Grisson's Bridge. On June 3, Companies A, E, and F were detached and marched back to La Fayette. Amid all the shuffling back and forth, six men from Company C deserted on May 26, and three from Company K deserted on May 30. From January 1 to May 31, the regiment fought no battles but still lost sixty-three officers and men: six officers resigned, one was discharged for disability, and two were dismissed, and twenty-four men deserted, ten died, seventeen were discharged (of which thirteen were for disability and one for wounds), and three transferred to other units. The regimental muster rolls for May 31 showed 508 enlisted men present and absent.[35]

While the 90th Illinois battled mosquitoes, snakes, lizards, and partisan rangers—not necessarily in that order or with equal success—General Grant's army conducted a lightning campaign and placed Confederate lieutenant general John C. Pemberton's army under siege in Vicksburg, Mississippi. The winter of their discontent behind them, the men of the Irish Legion faced the prospect of leaving Tennessee and rejoining the war then underway in Mississippi.

{ 4 }

THE FATHER OF WATERS UNVEXED

Major General Ulysses S. Grant's army had Lieutenant General John C. Pemberton's Confederate army bottled up in Vicksburg, and regiment after regiment of Union troops steamed downriver to make sure things stayed that way. Summoned to Vicksburg as part of those reinforcements, the troops of the 90th Illinois left their camps at Grisson's Bridge and La Fayette and marched to Collierville on June 6, arriving at 11 P.M., fatigued by the rapid pace of the march. During the day, Wagoner Patrick Sloan endured the usual case of "hurry up and wait." With the other teams and teamsters of the regiment at Collierville, he observed the passing artillery and infantry units while rather impatiently awaiting the Legion's arrival. He described the busy scene to his wife, Jennie: "The road . . . [is] covered with troops going to Memphis, from there I suppose to Vicksburg. at sun rise this morning they began to go by and it has been thronged ever since. . . . We are packed up and ready to fall in as soon as they [90th Illinois] pass." Sloan commented on Colonel Timothy J. O'Meara's importance to the regiment: "Our Col. is very sick the last three or four days and the men are all down hearted about it. I hope he will soon be well for I am positive that this Regt. could not be handled or commanded in a fight to our advantage or safety by any one in it but himself. He is all fight and so is the men when he commands." Sloan added that the men lacked confidence in anyone else. "You can have no idea of the feelings of a soldier when he has to go into a battle under an officer whom he has no confidence in as a fighting man. Our Col. is beloved, respected, and obeyed by his Regt." What more Sloan might have written in praise of O'Meara will ever remain unknown as the order to move out promptly ended the letter. The men of the Legion well appreciated O'Meara's leadership ability.[1]

On June 7, the 90th Illinois marched about twenty-three miles to within one or two miles of Memphis, camping at the "Big Spring." Their march to the levee would go through the Irish section of Memphis, and the local Irish were rumored to be preparing a decidedly unfriendly welcome for their northern brethren. The Irish Legion intended to make a good impression on the citizens of Memphis, especially the local Irish. Historian George Woodruff described the regiment's entry into Memphis at 3 P.M. on June 8: "Never did the Legion make a better appearance. Its ranks full," their "guns and swords glistened in the sunlight," and their "army blue was fresh brushed and clean. The officers of the line were in new and bright uniform, and the field officers were well mounted. All the officers wore green plumes in their hats. The stars and stripes, and the green flag as well, floated gaily in the breeze. The regiment marched with the regularity of veterans. Their alignment on the march was as straight as an arrow." As it marched through Memphis, the Irish Legion "was an imposing sight—a sight calculated to awaken admiration, touch the Irish love of martial display, and at the same time to suggest that such an array it would be wise to let alone." However, the crowd was becoming unruly: "A few hisses and groans were heard, and many defiant scowls were seen. The band was ordered to strike up that grand old Irish air, 'Saint Patrick's Day,' and to continue with 'Garry Owen,' both of which were rendered with great spirit." The music had a magical effect on the crowd. "The Irish heart was reached by these appeals to the eye and ear, and in an instant the whole scene was changed. The contemplated assault became a perfect ovation. Cheer after cheer went up from those who had come to hiss—brick-bats were dropped and hats were swung; the feeling for the dear old green flag, and the stars and stripes returned, and wave after wave of acclamation followed the regiment down the street." Upon reaching the levee, "suddenly, as if by magic, baskets of nice lunch, hampers of wine, and cases of liquors, appeared upon the scene, and were pressed upon officers and men with the utmost cordiality. Nor did the good feeling abate until the regiment was safely aboard the steamer, and it loosened from her moorings. Indeed so overcome were some of the men and some of the officers with the hilarity of the scene and the hospitality shown them that they did not get aboard until the next day."[2]

Captain Peter Casey, among others, literally missed the boat and would eventually suffer the consequences. Two days later, in a June 10 letter, he told his wife that the Legion had left for Vicksburg the previous day and he would soon follow them. He explained that "the Col. and Gen Loomis" had detailed him to stay behind and "pick up Straglers belonging to the regiment and the brigade or I would be near Vicksburg now." The large number of Union casualties from Vicksburg in Memphis hospitals caused Casey to again question his chances of survival and seek sympathy from his wife: "Pray for me that we may meet in heaven for our chances of meeting here again is doubtful if all the stories they tell about Vicksburg is true, and I think they are." In a postscript he added the good news that Quartermaster

Redmond Sheridan, now officially exchanged, had arrived, bringing with him the package containing the pair of pants Casey had requested from his wife. The ability of officers of the Irish Legion to obtain needed supplies from home through such informal arrangements indicates that their families maintained some level of contact with each other during the war.[3]

Eleven men of the Irish Legion, including a private from Minonk, deserted in June before the regiment's departure from Memphis and never did make the trip to Vicksburg. The Legion, minus Casey and the eleven others, departed Memphis on June 9 aboard the transport boat *G. W. Graham*, part of a flotilla of fourteen steamboats. The scene impressed the Legion's chaplain, Thomas Kelly, who wrote: "I never saw a more glorious sight than the departure of the fleet from Memphis. Twenty-four vessels carrying eight thousand infantry, six batteries of artillery and the wagons and ammunition of the whole division; the flagship first, the second vessel carried the Commandant of the Brigade. The vessels kept about a hundred yards from each other. After sailing three days and three nights, we reached the Yazoo, a narrow, deep river, full of alligators" (see Map 1, in chapter 2; Map 3). The trip proved hazardous, as one man from Company B and one from Company F drowned on June 9.[4]

On June 10, during the trip to Vicksburg, O'Meara promoted First Lieutenant Patrick Sarsfield Real, who had replaced Captain Thomas Barrett in command of Company K on May 31, to the rank of captain; however, Real would have to wait until February 24, 1864, to receive his commission. Named for Patrick Sarsfield,

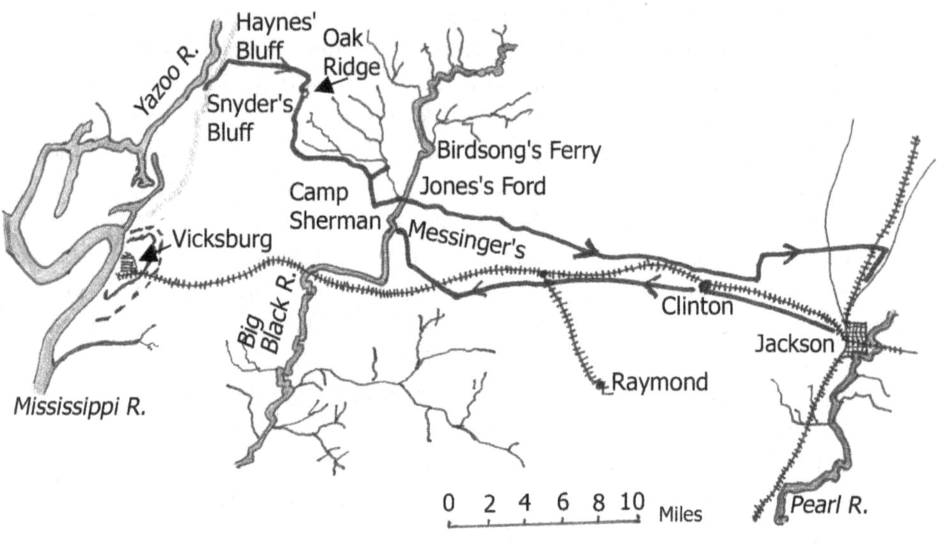

Map 3. Marches of the 90th Illinois during campaigns at Vicksburg and Jackson, Mississippi

Earl of Lucan, the redoubtable leader of Irish Catholic resistance to England's William III and of 20,000 Wild Geese who fought for France, Real had prior military experience, having enlisted and served for a year in Company E, 7th Missouri, before joining the 90th Illinois. While in Memphis, Real's thoughts must have been somber as his brother James, a prewar resident of that city, had entered the Confederate army and died a hero's death at Shiloh while bearing the flag of the 154th Tennessee (Senior).[5]

On June 11, the Legion, including the remaining four men from Minonk, disembarked at Snyder's Bluff on the Yazoo River some nine miles north of Vicksburg. Chaplain Thomas Kelly placed the regiment on Haynes' Bluff, some two miles farther north up the Yazoo River from Snyder's Bluff, which he described as "three hundred feet high, the prettiest place I ever saw, one little hill topping another, with many delicious springs of pure transparent water." After five months of inactivity, waiting to be exchanged, Quartermaster Sheridan rejoined the regiment just after the troops' arrival at Haynes' Bluff, or as he wrote, "before the Col. of my regiment quite finished pitching his tent." Before departing from Chicago on his way to Vicksburg, Sheridan had resigned his position as alderman of the Eighth Ward.[6]

Grant was deploying troops to protect against a possible attack by General Joseph E. Johnston's army from the northeast down the ridge between the Big Black and Yazoo Rivers, the so called Mechanicsburg Corridor (see Map 3). To guard against such an attack, strong Union defensive positions were built to protect the Snyder's Bluff area, including construction of extensive entrenchments behind Snyder's and Haynes' bluffs. The regiment remained in the area until June 22 doing fatigue duty, which included digging trenches. Although it involved hard labor, the duty of the 90th Illinois at the bluffs was much preferable to being in the lines around Vicksburg. In a June 19 letter to his wife, Corporal Patrick Sloan compared the troops conducting the siege to ants as "they lived entirely underground." At some point in their digging, the men of the Legion probably got better acquainted with their brigade commander, Connecticut-born thirty-eight-year-old Colonel John Mason Loomis. An experienced leader, having been elected captain of a Connecticut militia company at age eighteen, he later captained a clipper ship in the East India trade and headed a large lumber firm after moving to Chicago in 1853. He commanded the 26th Illinois from its formation in 1861 until assuming command of the First Brigade in May 1862.[7]

Their location on Snyder's Bluff provided the 90th Illinois troops a view of the bombardment of Vicksburg by Rear Admiral David D. Porter's mortar scows. Chaplain Kelly described the scene from his position on the heights: "I see every shell thrown. At one point, there are five one-hundred-twenty-pound mortar shells thrown into Vicksburg. At night the city is apparently burning from the light of the bursting shells. It is frightful to see them." Many years later, dark-haired, blue-eyed Private Simon Swan, Company G, told his sons of watching mortar shells, made visible at night by their burning fuse, as they rose in an arc and descended on the city. The sights and sounds of the "Bombardment of Vicksburg" were also described in detail by a *Chicago Tribune* reporter:

> The sight was one of the sublimest I have ever seen. The first intimation that a bomb was coming was a lurid flash, like summer lightning from a cloud beneath the horizon. A moment after a dim spark like a meteor half aglow, could be seen slowly climbing the sky, momentarily visible, and as often disappearing as the "globe of death" revolved in its upward career. Soon after the fuse of the shell began to ascend, the sound of the discharge would come swinging along the air with a sullen boom. Meanwhile the shell can be seen making its way upward, until it attains an immense altitude, where it hangs for a moment as if poised in the air, then begins to descend slowly at first, but accelerating its velocity till it shoots into the earth with the speed of lightning. At the same time you hear a rushing sound, broken somewhat like that of a locomotive in the distance, and ceasing with a sudden thump. Sometimes the shell explodes before reaching the earth, breaking into a puff of flame and smoke. Then follows a sharp crash that makes the earth shake again.[8]

Apart from jangled nerves and lost sleep, the 218-pound mortar shells caused relatively small damage unless they scored a direct hit. The federals fired large numbers of mortar shells during the siege, averaging one shell every five minutes. The crude fuses available could not be accurately timed to explode at the surface, where they would inflict the most damage. Consequently, most mortar shells either buried themselves up to thirty-seven feet into the deep loess soil underlying Vicksburg, detonating with a resounding but harmless burp, or exploded at some height, rather indiscriminately throwing potentially lethal shell fragments around the landscape. A Southern soldier on the receiving end inside Vicksburg described watching "the flying meteors" at night. If a mortar shell appeared to be falling directly on them, the soldiers sheltered "as close as possible" to a nearby hillside. Their "sweet slumber" was continually interrupted by a nearby "tremendous crash," temporarily ending any hope of sleep. While the viewers' location largely determined their attitude toward the bombardment, its main effect on those inside Vicksburg appeared to be loss of sleep.[9]

While the 90th Illinois waited for something to happen at Vicksburg, back in Chicago Mrs. Owen Stuart received a letter from one of her Southern acquaintances from La Fayette, Tennessee, regarding William, the Confederate soldier son of Mrs. Stuart's friend. William had been captured by Union forces, and Mrs. Stuart had earlier offered to visit him if he was sent to Camp Douglas in Chicago. The letter thanked her for her kind offer of assistance to William but informed her he was being held in an Ohio prison. The letter writer then named two young men at Camp Douglas, "both sons of respectable families of this vicinity who were taken prisoners about 6 weeks ago. In their behalf, I am requested by their friends to ask your kind offices. Any kindness you may be able to extend to them will be gratefully remembered."[10]

Like a bolt from the blue, Special Orders No. 260, dated June 12, 1863, from the Adjutant General's Office of the War Department, "dismissed the Service of the United States Major Owen Stuart, 90th Illinois Vol." The army may not have been able to pay the men on time, but for Captain Barrett, and now Major Stuart, it could and did dismiss an officer without delay. Late in June, in an apparent attempt to reinstate her husband, Mrs. Stuart visited Governor Richard Yates, accompanied by letters of introduction from prominent Chicago citizens supporting Major Stuart's promotion to lieutenant colonel. An early July article in the *Chicago Post* speculated that resistance by members of the regiment to the Emancipation Proclamation caused Stuart's dismissal. The War Department's prompt action probably represented Adjutant General Lorenzo Thomas's revenge following the disruption of his speech by the Legion.[11]

Governor Yates of Illinois wrote to Edwin Stanton, secretary of war, on June 30, inquiring as to the cause of Stuart's dismissal. Subsequently, War Department Special Orders No. 331 revoked the dismissal of Stuart on July 25, restoring him to his command. In a July 31 letter to Illinois adjutant general Allan Fuller, James Sheahan, editor of the *Chicago Post*, explained the War Department's sudden change of mind regarding his friend: "I was in Washington when Major Stuart came there, and was able to contribute to the exposure of the infamous forgery and fraud upon which he was dismissed. He was promptly restored the moment the facts were made known."[12]

As a consequence, from the time of Stuart's dismissal until his reinstatement and return to the 90th Illinois, Colonel O'Meara had neither a lieutenant colonel nor a major to assist him in running the regiment. The perpetrators of the fraud were never identified. Although dismissed, Stuart managed to obtain the following order from the Headquarters Division of Cairo: "Capt. Flange. Give permit to Major Stewart to ship his horse north, by order of Gen. [Napoleon B.] Buford." Stuart always took good care of his horses.[13]

For the Irish Legion, things started to heat up on June 22 when Confederate troops overran Union outposts at Bush's Ferry, near Birdsong's Ferry, on the Big Black River. To protect against a possible attack by Confederate general Johnston's Army of Relief, Grant assigned his friend and confidant, Major General William T. Sherman, command of a group of hastily assembled Union forces. These included the 90th Illinois, which along with the rest of Brigadier General William Sooy Smith's First Division of the XVI Corps was attached to Major General John G. Parke's IX Corps. This was the Legion's first service under Sherman, who was to be the Irishmen's commander, at one level or another, for the rest of their time in the army. Sherman directed Parke's forces "to move out on the Ridge road to the Oak-Ridge Post Office, leaving a reserve at Neeley's [plantation]," located a mile or so south of Oak Ridge (see Map 3). Parke's troops proceeded to fortify the area as part of a strong line from the Yazoo at Haynes' Bluff to the Big Black Bridge.[14]

General Smith's First Division moved rapidly, and the 90th Illinois left Snyder's Bluff at 3:30 A.M. on June 23 with three days' rations and fifty rounds of ammunition, marching ten miles to Oak Ridge, then continuing another nine miles to Bear Creek near the Big Black River. Quartermaster Sheridan described the trip for the 90th Illinois as marching "under a scorching sun—choked with dust—and a large number almost shoeless." Marching in hot weather on wind-deposited loess soil, which does not contain rocks, some soldiers may have marched barefoot by choice.[15]

The soldiers' frequent lack of definite information as to the location and probable actions of Confederate forces, and possibly Union as well, is apparent in a June 23 letter in which Wagoner Patrick Sloan described the march to Oak Ridge to his wife, Jennie: "This whole army of four Divisions or about thirty-two thousand men" left their camp "last night at twelve o'clock precisely." It was now midday and they were "laying in the woods resting," waiting for evening "to start again . . . if the enemy do not meet us before that time. We are somewhere about fifteen or twenty miles east of Vicksburg and going towards the Big Black [River] to fight Johnston who reached there yesterday coming to reinforce Vicksburg." Sloan expected to meet Johnston's army some time "tonight or tomorrow morning." Prisoners reported Johnston's force as "fifty-five thousand. If it is true there will be a bloody battle fought in this vicinity." Sloan had not "the least doubt as to the result. For we can be reinforced by forty thousand in a few hours after meeting Johnston if necessary. My Regt. I think is in the advance. I have not seen it since we started. I am with our train somewhere . . . about the middle of the crowd."

The heat, dust, and especially lack of safe drinking water made it a hard march for the troops. Sloan continued: "This is the most damnable place I ever seen for the want of water. . . . There is no water within ten miles of us that we care to taste. Although we passed several sloughs that there was a guard put on to keep the men from drinking as a drink of it would kill them." Sloan suffered from the effects of dysentery as he wrote that "I am pretty near dying since my last letter for drinking bad water. I am hardly able yet to sit in the saddle now and only for two canteens of coffee I brought with me I could not stand it. You can consider how valuable it is to me when I refuse three dollars for one of them." Sloan explained he "was taken very sick last week with something like cholera brought on by drinking water. I was in great agony for fourteen hours with cramps and pains. I am not able to be about yet only I did not want to be left in the hospital. I will get all right again in a few days. Weakness is all I complain of just now." He added: "The weather is extremely warm. Men cannot march in the middle of the day so that movements all take place at night."[16]

Sloan later commented on the local water supplies and the scarcity of wells: "I don't think that I have seen a half dozen of wells on this side of Cairo and they were at a depth of from one to two hundred feet. You will ask what the inhabitants do for water. They use rain water entirely. . . . Good water is very scarce every place I have seen in the southern confederacy."[17]

Captain Casey claimed the dust was six inches deep on the road and described the movement as "a hard march in the sun without half water enuff." According to Casey, Colonel O'Meara and his orderly, Private Hugh O'Neil of Company C, crossed the river and scouted for signs of Confederate forces. Much as if he were back in his days as a Mounted Rifleman in the southwest, O'Meara "went some seven miles on to the other side but found no enemy but saw some deserted camp fires." After resting from noon to 4 P.M., the regiment continued the march to the Big Black River, arriving there at evening on June 23. They assisted in destroying one or more bridges over Bear Creek before starting their return march to Oak Ridge at 11:30 P.M. the same day. However, Company G did not reach Oak Ridge until the following morning due to "a terrific rainstorm which came, making the woods through which we marched too dark, as to make it utterly impossible to proceed."[18]

The Legion would remember that return march until a worse one came along, and Quartermaster Sheridan clearly recalled:

> Whilst on the return march one of those terrific storms to which this latitude is accustomed, raged with more than ordinary fury; the rain poured in torrents, drenching every man in less time than it takes me to write it. For a short time the lighting flashed with terrific grandeur, accompanying which the peals of deafening thunder shook the earth as with terror-stricken palsy, warning man of the insignificance of all the destructive miss[i]les of war when compared with Heaven's Artillery. . . . But the night was one of those dark and cheerless nights—rendered still more despondently cheerless by a dense forest of heavy timber and thick briar brush—on Bluffs of only sufficient width to secure safe marching to five or six men abreast from the yawning ravines of fearful depth on either side. Over these paths our boys had to grope their way until the unearthly dismalness rendered it an impossibility to make further progress; when, Col. O'Meara, our commander, who was in the front carving the way at the eminent peril of limb, cheered and encouraged his men.

O'Meara solved the problem of men "stumbling over stumps and running in contact with trees" by ordering fires "lighted at distances that enabled us to pass in comparative safety till we were again within the boundary of our brigade lines."[19]

Once again, O'Meara demonstrated experienced leadership at the head of his regiment. It was getting to be a pattern: the colonel led, and the "boys" followed. The Field and Staff Report of the 90th Illinois rather jauntily summed it all up: "Marched 9 miles east in quest of Johns[t]on, but found him not. Bivouacked at Oak Ridge, on the plantation of H. W. Hill." The term bivouac simply meant the regiment slept in the field without tents or other shelter except for some rudimentary cover improvised from branches or other local materials.[20]

Sherman's defensive line covered the approaches to Vicksburg from the east and north between the Yazoo and Big Black rivers. In the Oak Ridge area, the defensive line occupied by General Smith's First Division, which included the 90th Illinois, extended generally from northwest to southeast and conformed roughly to the line formed by the following sequence of locally named ridge-top roads: Austin Road, Ballground Road, Oak Ridge Road, and finally the Ridge Road. The area was well suited for defensive positions, and Smith described his line around Oak Ridge Post Office as having "strong intrenchments," constructed "in anticipation of the advance of the rebel army under General Joseph E. Johnston," reportedly "moving to the relief of Vicksburg." A visit to the region reinforced Grant's observation that the country "stands on edge" with numerous sharp ridges and intervening deep valleys. Geographer Warren Grabau described the landscape of the loess hills as "a maze of narrow serpentine plateaus separated by mini gorges" with "unbelievably steep" slopes. The slopes of the ravines "were mostly covered with tangled scrub," while "immense canebrakes" grew in the ravine bottoms. An Illinois soldier, Captain Charles Wills of the 103rd Illinois, obviously impressed with the precipitous nature of the land, commented, "They call it level here when the surface presents no greater angles than 45 degrees."[21]

Sloan sensed that a battle was imminent when he wrote his wife on June 30 that he was "going out with a [wagon] train to the front in a couple of hours. Its expected that Johns[t]on will attack us in force in a day or two."[22]

On July 4, the Confederate army at Vicksburg surrendered. The loss of Vicksburg and its garrison of more than 29,000 Confederates, coming as it did almost simultaneously with the Union victory in the July 1–3 Battle of Gettysburg, dealt a severe blow to the Confederacy's hopes. On the third, when it became apparent that Vicksburg would soon surrender, Grant, ever aggressive, notified Sherman to be ready to attack Johnston's army. Following the surrender on the fourth, three Union army corps commanded by Sherman advanced on Jackson, the capital of Mississippi, in pursuit of Johnston's forces. The only natural barrier between Sherman's army and Jackson was the Big Black River. To reduce congestion, each corps crossed the river at a different point. Sherman directed the XIII Corps to cross directly east of Vicksburg on the railroad bridge and the XV Corps to cross upriver at Messinger's Ford. He directed the IX Corps, which included the 90th

Illinois, to cross some four miles farther upriver in the vicinity of Birdsong's Ferry. This marked the start of the Jackson campaign, the first big offensive campaign in which the Legion had something to do besides guard railroad bridges or dig entrenchments. On the afternoon of the fourth, Parke moved his command toward Birdsong's Ferry as well as toward Jones' Ford some two miles farther downstream from Birdsong's. Smith's division had the lead, and when the troops arrived at Birdsong's Ferry the morning of the fifth, they found the Confederates defending the opposite bank (see Map 3). During the resulting standoff, the opposing skirmishers kept busy firing at each other across the intervening river but doing minimal damage in the process.[23]

The 90th Illinois left Oak Ridge at 4 P.M. on July 4 on a route over hills and through woods and canebrakes before arriving at Bear Creek at 10 P.M., where the troops bivouacked on its banks. Next day, the First Brigade, including the 90th Illinois, reached the nearby Big Black River and supported the Second Brigade. After skirmishing during the day, the Second Brigade attempted to cross the river two miles farther south at Jones' Ford but found the water too deep to cross. The next day, July 6, the Second Brigade constructed a floating bridge and by 7 P.M. had crossed the river. Not to be outdone, the Third Brigade raised an old sunken ferryboat discovered some three miles south of Birdsong's Ferry and on the sixth towed it upriver some distance above Jones' Ford. By 3 P.M., they had crossed the Big Black River on the ferry, and the Fourth Brigade soon followed. Loomis's First Brigade then started crossing, and toward evening the 90th Illinois began to cross using the same ferryboat, which the troops referred to as a "scow." The First Brigade completed crossing on the next day, July 7, and marched to Queen's Hill, where the men bivouacked in a heavy rain. Although the rain temporarily relieved the heat, it resulted in soaked troops marching through deep mud and mired mule teams. The next day they continued their march, reaching Hall's Plantation. According to General Smith, their division commander, it took two days, the seventh and eighth, to ferry over his infantry, artillery, and ammunition train. Wagoner Sloan, still with the division's trains, crossed the Big Black River at Messinger's Ford, located two miles to the south of Jones' Ford.[24]

The march started out badly for Quartermaster Sheridan as he had taken sick earlier while at Oak Ridge with probably the same illness that Patrick Sloan had suffered. In a letter written well after the march, Sheridan described his condition on July 4 as so poor that he "barely had strength to superintend the striking of camp, I was in and out of my tent till all was set in column, 'They were going to Jackson' I could not sit in my saddle, everybody knew it, except my Col, Come Q.M. said he. All right Said I." Sheridan wrote that the doctor had urged him to remain: "'But they were going to Jackson' if I died on the Road I resolved to attempt the journey, but as soon as I got the baggage in motion I had to Submit to Nature. I then insisted on occupying one of the ambulances. our Surgeon told me it might wind me up, So it did, but like a clock. I was in good running order in two days, indeed when we moved the next day I mounted my horse and up to this date [August 11] have enjoyed good health."[25]

Sheridan favorably described the area through which the men of the Legion marched on their way to Jackson: "On the evening of the 4th of July we left Oak Ridge, light and cheerful, on our way to Jackson, when after marching, countermarching, and skirmishing over hills, through ravines, and fording streams, traversing dense forests and highly cultivated plantations that on all sides, between Big Black river and Jackson, adorn this fertile and beautiful corner of Mississippi." He became almost lyrical in describing what he saw on the way: "Indeed, it may be said to be the best of the States, abounding as it does with corn, vegetables and fruits of every variety, interspersed with flower gardens, decorated with artistic skill and refined taste. The magnolias soaring with a delicate elegance, spreading its large verdant leaves, shading as it were, to protect from the scorching sun the tender plants underneath."[26]

In contrast, Captain Casey described the impressive sight of the Union and Confederate armies on the march from the Big Black: "Our regiment was in the advance after we crossed the Big Black and it was a splendid sight to see the three columns moving." The 90th Illinois moved "in column of companies the ten companies moving one after the other." Regiment after regiment followed, "moving in the same way and on our right a trane of artillery moving two abreast. as far in the rear as the eye could extend and on the other side of the artillery another column of infantry moving the same as our column of infantry. They moved like three big snakes fifteen miles long each and hundred feet thick." Casey described the appearance of Johnston's rear guard: "His cavalry covering his retreat all dressed in white shirts mounted on splendid horses falling back slow, sometimes some of them would Get into a corn field and could not get out thru any opening so they would have to jump the fense, and they would do it in grand stile. They have splendid horses and they are good riders." Heavily outnumbered, Johnston's rear guard could not make a stand and so "fell back and we swept on. This thing lasted for some twenty miles and took us all of one day until twelve at night and part of next day before we drove them into their works here at Jackson."[27]

Not all the companies had their full complement of officers. Second Lieutenant Lawrence McCarthy, twenty-two years old, commanded Company E from June 18 through August 1863 as First Lieutenant John McAssey, sick with "chronic diarrhea, ague, and pain in his spine," could not accompany his command to Jackson.[28]

Another twenty-two-year-old, First Lieutenant James Conway, commanded Company A on the march to Jackson as Captain Patrick Flynn remained behind. Even the prospect of imminent military action could not abate the friction between Colonel O'Meara and Captain Flynn. Colonel Reuben Williams of the 12th Indiana wrote that, denied promotion to major, "Flynn grew sulky and had refused to accompany the expedition we were then making unless it could be in the rank to which he had been promoted." This produced the following conversation between men of the 90th Illinois, overheard by Williams:

> "Jamie, did you know we have a new major?"
> "I do not," said Jamie. "Who is the lucky man?"
> "Pat Flynn," was the response.
> "I don't know of a man that deserves the promotion more," said Jamie, "he minds his place so well in the rear!"

Reuben concluded that as "the proper place of the Major is in the rear of his regiment, and Pat Flynn was then thirty miles behind, the ready wit of Jamie can easily be perceived."[29]

Sherman's three corps advanced toward Jackson on separate roads with the route of the XIII Corps on the main Vicksburg-Clinton-Jackson road, which paralleled the railroad. The XV Corps marched on the Bridgeport road through Bolton and Clinton some three miles or so north of the XIII Corps' route. Sherman's orders instructed Parke's IX Corps to march on a nonexistent third road north of and parallel to the others. Parke's advance quickly ran into trouble on July 8 when the men of his corps found the XV Corps using the only available road. That route blocked, Parke's troops took a detour on a side road and camped a few miles from Clinton as instructed. The next day, their route again blocked by the XV Corps, Parke improvised: "Finding that there was but one main road for us north of the railroad leading to Jackson, we diverged, and, after a good deal of labor, cutting through timber, we succeeded in opening a road through the plantations, nearly parallel with the main road. Toward sundown we came upon the enemy's cavalry, when some skirmishing ensued, in which both the enemy and ourselves used artillery."[30]

This skirmishing involved the 90th Illinois, as reported by Colonel O'Meara in his best matter-of-fact style: "Nothing of importance to my regiment took place on the march until the evening of the 9th instant, it [90th Illinois] being in advance, and within about 4 miles of the city of Jackson. The two companies (C and I), thrown forward as skirmishers, engaged the enemy on [Robert Eduard] Lee's plantation and drove them very handsomely." The skirmishing over, the 90th Illinois, along with the rest of Parke's corps, bivouacked for the night.[31]

General Smith summarized the division's march to Jackson, somehow getting his dates all one day late, while commenting favorably about the 90th Illinois: "On the 9th, we resumed our march, and reached Robertson's, near Queen's Hill and Jeff. Davis' [actually Joseph Davis's] plantation. On the 10th, we reached a point 4 miles northwest of Jackson, where we had a brisk skirmish with one of the enemy's outposts, in which the good conduct of Colonel O'Meara and the officers and men of his regiment, the Ninetieth Illinois, deserve especial mention." The next day, Smith's division arrived "in front of Jackson at about 2 P.M., moved up on the right of the Ninth Corps, driving the rebel pickets and skirmishers within their intrenchments, where they were closely held by a hot fire of our skirmishers, who were advanced to within effective rifle range of the rebel works and well supported."[32]

The arrival of summer in Mississippi brought oppressive midday heat and a shortage of drinking water. First Lieutenant James Conway, Company A, described the march to Jackson: "The weather is very hot there was a grate many men sun struck on the march and died but none out of our regt." Many of the ponds contained the carcasses of dead animals put there by the retreating Confederates so that often the only water available on the march was from cisterns. To a sister First Brigade regiment, the 100th Indiana, the march to Jackson consisted of either marching in very hot weather on dusty roads or slogging through deep mud following a heavy rain. The Hoosiers obtained water from "ponds and wagon ruts along the road." Confederate general Johnston thought the shortage of water outside Jackson would work to his advantage. He did not expect to have to withstand a protracted siege, writing that because of "scarcity of water" Sherman's troops "could not besiege, but would be compelled to make an immediate assault." According to historian Edwin Bearss, individual companies acquired mules and used them to transport water to help alleviate the shortage on the march and during the siege when water had to be transported long distances.[33]

In his memoirs, Sherman described the location of the three Union corps facing the Confederate defenses during the siege of Jackson. His XV Corps "held the centre, extending from the Clinton to the Raymond road; Ord's (Thirteenth) on the right, reaching Pearl River below the town; and Parke's (Ninth) the left, above town." Parke reported that his corps "started on the morning of the 10th over a plantation road that brought us out on the Livingston and Canton road, 5 miles north of Jackson." By dark, Parke's corps occupied Insane Asylum Ridge with a line at a right angle to the Canton road. On July 10, the Irish Legion formed line of battle and moved to within two miles of the city. That night the men slept on their arms, and the next day they, along with the rest of the IX Corps, drove the Confederate skirmishers back into their main fortified line. Parke reported his corps' action: "We found the enemy posted behind a continuous line of rifle-pits, with batteries at intervals, raking the road and approaches. Our men were covered and protected as much as possible, and epaulements [breastworks] thrown up for our batteries as rapidly as the limited supply of tools would admit. The enemy made several attempts to drive our skirmishers, but were as often repulsed." Sooy Smith's division was located on the right of the IX Army Corps line with the left of Loomis's First Brigade resting on the Canton road. Loomis wrote that his brigade spent July 12–16 constructing offensive works and "feeling the enemy."[34]

According to Colonel O'Meara, from July 11 until 3 P.M. on July 14, when they withdrew to the rear, the men of the Legion occupied their position "day and night on the line of battle, 800 yards distant from the batteries of the enemy, and about 400 from their advance [troops]." Their location in front of their own batteries supplied them a ringside seat for watching artillery duels. Woodruff wrote that "the reader can readily understand that to be under this cross-fire, when both sides were engaged firing as rapidly as possible, was one of the most terrific and grand sights in modern warfare." He cited a narrative of an unnamed officer of the 90th Illinois that described the regiment "suffering dreadfully from the terrible heat and scarcity of water" while in position in front of the Jackson fortifications. Even worse, the night Sherman's troops closed on Jackson, they received orders not to build fires, which deprived the soldiers of coffee, their "main dependence," according to Colonel Williams of the 12th Indiana.[35]

Captain E. J. Sherlock of the 100th Indiana, also of the First Brigade, described his regiment's experience under fire: "During the night of the 11th the 100th Indiana planted a sunk battery within short range of the Confederate fort in our front, and at about 7 A.M. on the 12th four batteries of the First Division opened fire on the enemy with twenty four guns. The 100th Indiana lay in line directly in front of these batteries, and every shot, including such replies as the enemy were able to make, passed only a few feet directly over their heads." To Sherlock, "the screech of those elongated shot and shell in such close proximity to our heads was simply indescribable. Fragments of shot and shell fell all around us." The bombardment referred to occurred on July 12 when some three thousand artillery rounds were fired from ten- and twenty-pound Parrotts and twelve-pounder Napoleons by Union gunners. The shelling also impressed General Johnston, who reported, "The missiles reached all parts of the town."[36]

In a letter to his invalid father, Lieutenant Conway, in command of Company A of the 90th Illinois, described his experience under fire on July 12: "We advanced within 20 rods [333 feet] of their works under a battery of 7 guns but were so near them they could not do much damage. In advancing I had some pretty close calls." He wrote that bullets knocked "splinters off the fence in my face. Still I never thought of being shot." At about "11 O'clock I had one man shot through the hart in the act of loading his gun all the rest came out without a scrach thank god and I can say the coolest and bravest company of men that ever went into a battle field." Conway commented on his health and the limited food supply during the siege: "I am as tough as a knot & can live on one cracker a day and fight to which we have done." He also noted the effect of battle on one of his men: "P. McLaughlin, tell him Pat Corcoran is well and in the hottest of the fight Pat was praying." Patrick Corcoran's prayers were answered as he made it through the war. The 90th Illinois suffered another casualty on the twelfth when Assistant Surgeon Darwin Hinckley's horse threw him.[37]

With the exception of Conway, most of the 90th Illinois and 100th Indiana were still getting accustomed to the sounds and sights of battle. The cannon fire impressed Captain Casey, Company H, who directed 150 men involved in digging four large pits for siege guns in front of the Union position. Supporting troops drove the Confederate skirmishers back on their own fortifications, allowing digging to begin. However, attacks by Confederate skirmishers and cannon fire slowed the rate of construction. After seven hours under fire, Casey's command returned to the regiment, having lost one man, killed as described by Conway, one slightly wounded, and one severely wounded, the only casualties the Legion suffered at Jackson. Casey wrote, "The Col. gave me great creddit for the manner in which I saved the men." Casey was impressed with his accomplishments, writing his wife that "all the officers and men of the regiment, and other regts. they call me bloocher," a reference to the Prussian field marshal Gebhard Leberecht Blucher von Wahlstatt, who contributed greatly to Napoleon's defeat at Waterloo.[38]

The next day, General Johnston abandoned Jackson, saving Casey and the regiment any further exposure to enemy fire. Johnston considered abandonment necessary because, in his words, the enemy "was evidently preparing to concentrate upon us the fire of about two hundred pieces of ordnance." Colonel O'Meara gave his professional analysis of why Johnston's army escaped capture at Jackson: "It is my opinion that his clearing out was winked at by some of our Generals. . . . We all expected to have a hard fight for numbers were nearly equal, and we could have had one any time during the ten or twelve days that we were surrounding the place. But it seemed that we were in no hurry so we commenced our old work of cutting, digging, and slashing down the country around the doomed town." O'Meara was pleased with his regiment's performance as indicated by the concluding sentence of his report to Colonel Loomis: "The firmness and determination exhibited by Officers and Enlisted men under very trying circumstances have proven them worthy of the hopes that I entertained of them, as worthy defenders of the glorious cause they are battling for."[39]

General Sooy Smith commended "you [O'Meara] and the gallant Regiment you command, for your patience, good conduct, and heroism, exhibited during the advance upon Jackson. Men that will march in their bare feet and fight as bravely as the officers and men of the 90th have, cannot be too highly praised. Accept my warmest thanks and tender them to your command."[40]

The Confederates abandoned Jackson the night of July 16, and the Union troops entered the city the next morning, ending the brief siege. Quartermaster Sheridan described his regiment's entry into Jackson: "None of our regiment were permitted by the Colonel to enter the city except by his permission, nor was there evinced any disposition to do so. On Sunday, July 19, he accompanied them in regular marching order through the city to the river, where a regimental bath was indulged in—and much needed—after which they marched back to the camp ground in the same order as they went."[41]

With Johnston's army gone, Sherman now conducted the type of destruction that would make him famous, or infamous, depending on one's perspective. He reported to Grant on July 18: "We have made fine progress today in the work of destruction. Jackson will no longer be a point of danger." They had destroyed the captured cotton; thrown heavy artillery, shot, and shell in the river; and torn up railroads to the east, north, and south. "The land is devastated for 30 miles around."[42]

Captain Casey's description of the destruction and looting of buildings in Jackson indicated Colonel O'Meara's lack of success in his attempt to keep his men out of the city. "The boys had been in all day and a part of the evening of the 18th of July and in the morning when I woak up there was a barricade of china ware, silverware, mahogany rose wood chairs, and mirrors six feet high all around me." According to Casey, Jackson had suffered severely: "The houses were all destroyed, Statehouse and all. I do not think there is six houses left standing in Jackson which I think was wrong. I pittied the poor women & children. There was thousands of them in the woods for several days afrade to come in to the city."[43]

The city of Jackson definitely had not escaped unscathed. In his diary, the bishop of Natchez, Henry Elder, wrote of his July 20 visit to Jackson, commenting on the "crowds of Federal Soldiers on foot or horse & mules," the "Melancholy desolation" with "warm ashes— & ruins at every step." Things had pretty clearly gotten out of hand, for the priest that Bishop Elder visited subsisted on army rations as his clothes and provisions had been stolen. However, a Catholic soldier had returned a chalice and crucifix that had been stolen from the priest's chapel.[44]

On July 19, the 90th Illinois began a closer association with Sherman. His General Orders No. 60 attached the First Division to his XV Army Corps and ordered the troops to "move by the direct Clinton and Bolton road, crossing Big Black River, and taking post for the present near Black River and Bear Creek." By this order, the Irish Legion would become and remain the sole Irish regiment in the XV Corps throughout the rest of the war. The Legion's brigade, which still included the 12th and 100th Indiana and the 26th Illinois, became the First Brigade of the Fourth Division of the XV Corps and received a new division commander as Brigadier General Hugh Ewing replaced Sooy Smith. Ewing was Sherman's brother-in-law as well as foster brother, and the two had practiced law together at Leavenworth, Kansas, in 1857. A West Point drop-out, Ewing had participated in the Battle of Rich Mountain, led the assault at South Mountain, and commanded a brigade in Burnside's IX Corps at Antietam. In January 1863, together with his brigade, he had been transferred to Sherman's command and during the siege led an assault on the Vicksburg defenses. Following the fall of Vicksburg, he participated in the capture of Jackson, taking command of the Fourth Division, XV Army Corps, on July 20, 1863.[45]

On July 23, the Irish Legion left Jackson and marched some ten miles to Clinton (see Map 3). The next day, the troops reached Champion Hill after a march of fifteen miles, and the following day they marched the remaining ten miles to Messinger's Ford on the Big Black River. Wagon trains soon left, bound for their former camp on the bluffs to bring back personal and camp equipment. The regiment crossed the Big Black River and by July 27 started to settle in at Camp Sherman. The troops' arrival at Camp Sherman was matter-of-factly recorded by reliable scout Theodore Upson, Company C, of the 100th Indiana: "The 90th Ill, the Irish Regiment, came into camp just back of us this morning. And such a time as those fellows did have. They had got into a row about putting up thier [their] tents and had a free for all fight and were knocking each other over the head with pick handles, tent poles, or any thing they got hold of." The ruckus ended abruptly when Colonel O'Meara "came out of his tent with a great wide bladed broadsword that is said to have belonged to some of his ancestors. And the way he did blast those Irish fellows with the flat of it was a caution. He stopped the row, and they settled down. His Regiment adore him." The arrival of the trains from Haynes' Bluff on the twenty-seventh with only part of the regiment's knapsacks and camping equipage probably explains the dustup. The violent storm the regiment endured without shelter the previous afternoon and night probably disposed the men of the Legion to choose the method described by Upson to achieve a mutually agreeable distribution of the limited portion of the camp equipment that arrived with the train. Or perhaps the "byes" were still a wee bit keyed up after their experience at Jackson and chose this occasion to let off some steam.[46]

Opinions about Camp Sherman were divided; its beauty was deceptive. Quartermaster Sheridan described their camp on the Big Black River as "on Messenger's plantation, a spot of romantic beauty, being well wooded with heavy timber on rolling ground with ravines on all sides." However beautiful it was, the campsite was also deadly, according to Sheridan: "From the first week of our arrival, sickness has been steadily on the increase; strong, heavy-framed men are suddenly transformed into walking shadows by attacks of congestive fever, chills and fever and other malaria, a great deal of which, I think, is produced by bathing in the swampy cesspool. . . . Some days, one half of our entire regiment has been reported sick. . . . We too have lost by death, up to this date, five by sickness." Patrick Sloan confirmed Sheridan's assessment: "The health of the regiment does not improve any. I think there is a great many sick and burial parties are going by continually. Some more of our men are going home on sick furloughs and some discharged."[47]

Indeed, camping on the Big Black did not improve the health of the regiment, as the number of sick enlisted men reported present with the regiment increased dramatically from thirty-eight on July 31 to ninety-one on August 31, which accounted for most of the ninety-seven fewer enlisted men reported as present for duty in August than in July. The sick, including both those present and absent, amounted to 26 percent of the regiment in August. Companies A and B had a combined total of forty-three enlisted men sick. Nine of the 90th Illinois died while the regiment remained at Camp Sherman. Disease, described by Corporal Sloan as "fevers and diarrhea" or "fever and ague," was the main reason for sickness in the regiment.[48]

Of the health problems that occurred, one in particular saddened the regiment. The chaplain of the 90th Illinois, Father Kelly, contracted a disease while in the line of duty near the Yazoo River, which forced him to resign. Colonel O'Meara wrote on August 5 that "Father Kelly poor man has been and is at present very sick. He has resigned and it has been accepted. He is at present with me waiting and trying to gain sufficient strength before he starts for Chicago. I am just completing a subscription for him. We raised $400 which will be a great service to him when he goes back. He never had as much money at one time in his life and the only thing that puzzles him now is to know what he is going to do with it."

Sloan described the touching scene at Father Kelly's leave-taking: "This morning we heard the last Mass that Father Kelly will ever say to this Regt. as chaplain. On account of ill health he resigned and started for home this morning after saying Mass. The regt. went out on the parade ground and Father Kelly went out and delivered a farewell address." Parting with Father Kelly deeply affected the soldiers of the Legion. Sloan wrote: "When he bid them good bye more than half of the Regt. were in tears. To say that he was beloved by the Regt. would be but a lukewarm expression for I have never seen any person so dearly beloved, respected and obeyed as was Father Kelly by this Regt. The Col. was more attached to him I think ever his wife will receive and he is the only man that can or could control the Col." According to Sloan, the entire regiment wished for Father Kelly a speedy recovery and that he have a long life. Father Kelly promised to send a substitute if he could, but Sloan doubted they would have another chaplain unless Father Dunne would "interest himself in the matter." Four captains going home on furlough—Patrick O'Marah, Peter Casey, John Murphy, and Michael Murphy—accompanied Father Kelly to Illinois.[49]

Unfortunately, Father Kelly died a few weeks after his return to Chicago. A resolution strongly praising him and his services to the regiment and sincerely lamenting his loss was subsequently drafted by Colonel O'Meara. The officers of the regiment unanimously adopted the resolution, which was published in Chicago and Boston papers. Major Stuart began the first of several unsuccessful attempts to obtain a replacement for Father Kelly by writing Father Dunne on September 25, emphasizing the regiment's need for a chaplain.[50]

Due to the extended stay at Camp Sherman, some twenty-eight soldiers of the Legion received furloughs by early August, including Captain Casey, whose twenty-day leave began August 11. Since his arrival at Camp Sherman, Casey had been so unwell he could barely stand alone due to a very bad case of diarrhea. However, his leave application citing "sickness" in his family and "other business matters" requiring his "immediate presence" accomplished his objective. Casey wrote that he obtained the leave upon the advice of the regiment's colonel and surgeon with the usual provision that the leave "would be extended from time to time if his health did not permit him to return provided he should report his condition every twenty days" accompanied by a physician's certificate. Evidently his health did not improve, but given the uncertainty in delivery of the mail, it seems hardly surprising that Colonel O'Meara did not receive such notification, which resulted in Casey being reported absent without leave. But there was more to it than that, for earlier in June 1863 and again on November 20, O'Meara submitted letters to the adjutant general of the Army of the Tennessee requesting the dishonorable dismissal of Captain Casey from the military service of the United States, citing Casey's absence without leave at Memphis from June 9 to June 20, 1863, unspecified conduct unbecoming of an officer, and his unexplained absence from August 31 to date. O'Meara regarded Casey less highly than Casey indicated in his letters. His replacement was newly promoted First Lieutenant Lawrence McCarthy, formerly of Company E, who assumed command of Company H on October 21, 1863, and continued in command until July 31, 1864.[51]

Not all the officers granted twenty-days' leave returned on time, requiring issuance of a special order dated September 20 restoring Captains John Murphy and Michael Murphy and Adjutant Edwin Davis to duty. Second Lieutenant Thomas Murray was in command of Company I as of August 11 but was not mustered as first lieutenant until October 19. During his return trip to the Legion, Captain Patrick O'Marah was a passenger on the steamer *Robert Campbell, Jr.* at Milliken's Bend when it was set on fire by a Confederate secret agent. Another passenger, General Sooy Smith, writing some time after the war, lauded O'Marah for his part in rescuing women and children from the burning transport. Smith considered O'Marah "a brave and unselfish man" and added, "His gallantry in action was always conspicuous."[52]

To assure that the 90th Illinois received proper recognition for past service, in early August, Colonel O'Meara wrote to the board of officers examining claims of regiments for services rendered and presented his regiment's claim to inscribe on their banner the names "Coldwater," "Vicksburg," and "Jackson." O'Meara wrote Illinois adjutant general Fuller, carefully explaining why he no longer had the officers' commissions previously issued by Fuller. He had prepared a list "of men who have distinguished themselves and done credit to the state, during the late campaign," but would not send the list until instructed by Fuller on how to proceed in submitting names for promotion. O'Meara wanted to fill up the gaps in his officer corps now that he had found individuals who met his standards. He received the requested instructions as Fuller received a list from the headquarters of the 90th Illinois, dated September 2, containing the names of nine officers and seven noncommissioned officers of the 90th Illinois recommended for promotion. Seven of the officers and two of the noncommissioned officers received promotions as requested. Interestingly, O'Meara recommended Captain Michael Murphy, Company B, and not Captain Patrick Flynn, Company A, for promotion to major; however, Murphy remained a captain.[53]

The promotion process within Illinois volunteer regiments involved state authorities Governor Yates and Illinois Adjutant General Fuller, who were subject to political pressure. Some officers of the 90th Illinois pleaded their case directly with these officials and used the assistance of others within as well as without the regiment to support their quest for promotion. During the course of the war, Fuller continued to receive unsolicited advice on promotion and reinstatement of officers within the 90th Illinois and similarly on promotion of noncommissioned officers.[54]

In a letter to his brother John, Colonel O'Meara requested advice on whether he should take a thirty-day leave and travel to New York. From O'Meara's letters, he appears to have been a major source of support for his mother, brother, and sister. Thus, the four- to five-hundred-dollar cost of the round-trip to New York and governmental policy that officers on leave received only half pay would be a drain on family resources and had to be discussed.[55]

From June 11 to September 30, the time the 90th Illinois was in the general vicinity of Vicksburg, the regiment had a total of sixteen men die, only one of whom was killed in battle; six deserted; and four were discharged. Three transferred, including First Lieutenant William White's brother, Sergeant Thomas White of Company F, who transferred to the Signal Corps. By this time, the Legion had only a handful of the detested Austrian muskets. The September 30 report listed 311 enlisted men present for duty out of a total of 393 reported present. Sickness remained a problem, as the report listed forty-eight as present sick and forty-five as absent sick, which together represented 20 percent of the 465 enlisted men in the regiment. Camp Sherman on the Big Black River had not been a healthy location for the troops.[56]

At Camp Sherman, the 90th Illinois kept busy soldiering while General Ewing "occupied some weeks in restoring discipline and drill" in his Fourth Division. Wagoner Patrick Sloan described the drill routine as "two heavy drills in the day, morning and night for one hour each time." He found drill at night to be "the most disagreeable part of the day . . . though the coolest." Quartermaster Sheridan declared the summer weather "intolerable" as the air temperature reached 113 degrees in the shade. Understandably, he "kept awful quiet . . . when in camp it was hard to get me outside of my tent except by Some unavoidable cause, but we lived tolerably well." On September 27, Owen Stuart, now back with the Legion, could celebrate as he was officially promoted from major to lieutenant colonel. Stuart had learned of his impending promotion and other news when his wife wrote him on September 26. Major General William S. Rosecrans's army had suffered heavy casualties in the Battle of Chickamauga on September 19–20, 1863, and she was greatly disturbed by "a rumor in town that Sherman has reinforced Rosecrans and I am almost wild to think of it. I pray God it is not so. I think I would go crazy if you were there. . . . There are a great many Chicago men killed in the past battle with Rosecrans. Oh! How I do hope you will not go to join him." She had some good news, though: "I have got you a gallon of whiskey which [First Lieutenant Patrick] Campion [Company G] will take down."[57]

There was no need for the folks at home to send most major newspapers to the men of the 90th Illinois as they were available in camp, restoring contact with the outside world for those who remained. By September 23, Corporal Sloan had managed to protect himself against the elements through his ability to "confiscate a new wagon cover and with it build as pretty a little house as you ever seen." Unfortunately, the Legion departed Camp Sherman four days later, cutting short his residency in the new abode. Sloan had suspected something was up after learning that two divisions of their army were going to Vicksburg to embark on boats. He thought they probably would be going to assist Rosecrans.[58]

The Jackson campaign had given Quartermaster Sheridan another chance to evaluate the regiment and their colonel. Sheridan wrote: "We have got a bully lot of boys . . . good fighting material." He was equally impressed with O'Meara, "who has filled our expectations to the brim. He is young, intelligent, prepossessing with commanding air even to imperiousness. This last is assumed to command respect. He is a Soldier a practical one of good talents [and] is esteemed so by all the commanding officers of his acquaintance. Knows enough to command respect from them. he never appears to attach much importance to their opinions and generally contradicts his guests giving his own opinion with emphasis, which in a majority of cases, if they don't believe they don't contradict." Sheridan though that O'Meara had more social conversation with him "than any other officer in the Reg. I find his mind pretty well balanced. He knows more of military than anything else. [He] evidently contradicts to obtain information which is proven in the fact of his using his competitor's language after with another when in conversation."[59]

Many, probably most, of the 90th Illinois volunteers went into the field as Irishmen first and soldiers second, but Colonel Timothy O'Meara had by now reversed that order, even though he was clearly Irish. His service from the rank of private in 1855 to his current rank as colonel demonstrated O'Meara's dedication to his adopted country.

Situated in Camp Sherman, the "byes" of the 90th Illinois presumably knew they had marched almost 120 miles during the current campaign and that they could expect longer marches in the future. However, they might have been surprised to know that as members of the XV Corps, they were in for a journey through seven Confederate states, which would involve marching more than

2,400 additional miles, and that they would do it all under the command of a general—Sherman—who preferred to maneuver rather than simply fight battles. In moving from Chicago to La Grange and from Memphis to and from Vicksburg, the 90th Illinois was a small part of a much larger demonstration of the use of rail and steamship transportation to rapidly move troops and equipment between and within military theaters of operation. More important, the Legion had played a part, however small, in restoring to the Union the control of the Mississippi River, an achievement celebrated in President Lincoln's words: "The Father of Waters again goes unvexed to the sea."[60]

{ 5 }

THE MARCH TO CHATTANOOGA

On September 25, 1863, the men of the 90th Illinois, along with the rest of the Fourth Division of Major General William T. Sherman's XV Army Corps, learned they would be going to Chattanooga, Tennessee, for the relief of the Army of the Cumberland, just as Patrick Sloan had suspected and Margaret Stuart had feared. Confederate general Braxton Bragg held Major General William Rosecrans's Union army under siege at Chattanooga following its defeat in the September 19–21 Battle of Chickamauga just south of Chattanooga. The XV Corps would take only three of its four divisions: the First Division under Brigadier General Peter Osterhaus, the Second Division under Brigadier General Morgan L. Smith, and the Fourth, Brigadier General Hugh Ewing's, temporarily under Brigadier General John M. Corse. Sherman received Brigadier General John E. Smith's Second Division of the XVII Corps, which he referred to as his "Third" Division, giving Sherman a total of four divisions during the Chattanooga-Ringgold campaign. The Third Division of the XV Corps remained at Vicksburg, producing the somewhat confusing situation of two Third Divisions in the XV Corps. The 90th Illinois would serve alongside or under all these officers at one time or another in future campaigns.[1]

Moving the XV Corps, and thus the 90th Illinois, to Chattanooga involved transporting the troops by steamboat from Vicksburg to Memphis, followed by a difficult march across nearly the length of Tennessee, a distance of 317 miles by current highway maps (Map 4; see also Map 1, in chapter 2). As the Irish Legion would find out, Tennessee's east-west roads in 1863 were abominable. The route Sherman chose for the Fourth Division, and thus for the 90th Illinois, crossed the Cumberland Plateau in eastern Tennessee, making it a much longer and more difficult march for the troops and especially challenging for their accompanying wagon train. The men of the 90th Illinois left Camp Sherman on September 28 and marched to Bear Creek. The next day, they continued on to Vicksburg and boarded the 238-ton stern-wheel steamer *Norman* on September 30 for the slow upriver trip to Memphis. Sherman blamed the "unprecedented low water in the Mississippi and the scarcity of coal and wood" for the slow progress in moving troops from Vicksburg to Memphis. The *Norman* stopped periodically to refuel. Company A reported a three-day delay at Griffith's Landing where they were detailed to obtain forage and wood. The seemingly interminable upriver trip to Memphis finally ended at 11 P.M. on October 8. In contrast, the Legion's earlier trip downriver had required only a little over two days. The troops remained onboard until the next morning, when they disembarked and marched to a camp two miles outside Memphis. George Woodruff reported that the Irish Legion was "visited by a great many people from Memphis, mostly Irish, and treated hospitably and kindly as before." This time there were no desertions.[2]

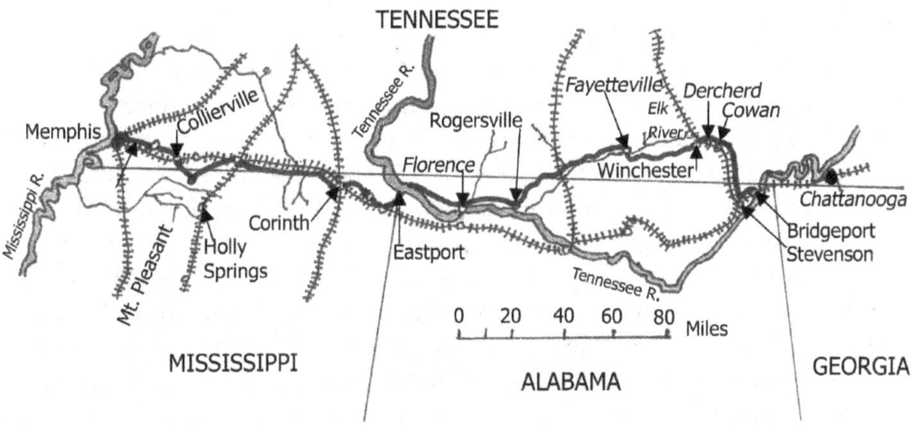

Map 4. March of the 90th Illinois from Memphis to Chattanooga, Tennessee

As Major Owen Stuart and the rest of the regiment steamed slowly upriver, Mrs. Margaret Stuart wrote in an October 3 letter to her husband, "I want to be the first to congratulate you on your promotion." She had heard the good news directly from Colonel Timothy O'Meara, who had stopped in Chicago on his way to visit his mother and brother in New York. The colonel had spoken highly of Major Stuart to Margaret, convincing her that "he is your friend." As proof, she added that she had planned to send a pair of shoulder straps to the soon-to-be Lieutenant Colonel Stuart, "but the Col. says no as he intends to give you his." She added that the colonel meant to give Captain Patrick Flynn his long-sought commission as major "if he proves himself worthy of it in a week or two" and that the colonel "told me he always intended to give you your commission but wanted to get it himself for you." Margaret added that Captain David Duffy of Company E had married a few days before and pointedly wrote that the new Mrs. Duffy "would like to go down when you get settled and so would I, my dear Husband." The experience of keeping house in a tent had apparently not diminished her love of adventure.[3]

Inevitably, logistics intervened. Since Rosecrans's army remained under siege at Chattanooga, enduring shortages of nearly everything including food, forage, and ammunition, Sherman would have to provide his own provender. Orders to Sherman made that quite plain. Sherman wrote that he had "to repair the Memphis & Charleston Railroad eastward . . . as far as Athens, Alabama, to draw supplies by that route, so that, on reaching Athens, we should not be dependent on the roads back to Nashville, already overtaxed by the demand of Rosecrans' army." They could "in no event . . . depend on General Rosecrans for supplies." According to Sherman, "The railroad was in fair condition, as far as Corinth, ninety-six miles," but with rolling-stock in short supply, the Fourth Division had to walk those ninety-six miles to Corinth, Mississippi, while earlier arriving divisions rode the trains.[4]

Things got more exciting on Sunday, October 11, when the Legion left Memphis, leading the Fourth Division's march to Corinth (see Map 4). General Sherman started for Corinth in a special train, accompanied by his brother-in-law, General Ewing, Sherman's staff and their horses, some clerks, a few officers going to their commands, and some 240 of the 13th U.S. Regulars for escort. They did not go far, as about noon their train abruptly stopped at the Collierville depot where they hurriedly prepared to resist an attack by a large Confederate cavalry force approaching from the southeast. Before the raiders could cut the wires, Sherman quickly sent a telegram to Germantown and Memphis calling for help. He then deployed his escort, and under his direction, they and the five hundred or so troops of the 66th Indiana Infantry stationed at Collierville proceeded to fight off over two thousand attackers led by Confederate brigadier general James Ronald Chalmers, previously a lawyer in Holly Springs.[5]

To First Sergeant P. J. Carmody, Company E, 13th U.S. Infantry, an Irishman defending a post in what he called the "dismantled" fort at Collierville, "It was hammer and tongs until about four o'clock in the afternoon." The most interesting thing to watch throughout the fight was General Sherman. Carmody related: "He was Sherman all the time that afternoon. I could not help studying this remarkable man whenever I got the opportunity. . . . The general with his hat off in the broiling sun was a marvel to look at. When a man was shot he would get one of these headquarters' employees and say to him: 'Don't you see that man is killed? Take his cartridge box and his gun and load it. Fight for your country, sir.'" The fort was a hot place as the three men with Carmody at his post were either killed or wounded. Sometime during the attack, Carmody tried to convince Sherman to keep under cover but received a brusque response: "Sergeant, said the General, attend to your business, sir; attend to your business, I will take care of myself, sir."[6]

According to Woodruff, the 90th Illinois found out about General Sherman's difficulties at Germantown, about nine miles from Collierville, through a telegram "ordering the regiment forward as rapidly as possible" to reinforce Sherman. The telegram also alerted the Legion's sister regiment, the 100th Indiana, who, according to Captain E. J. Sherlock, "double quicked nearly all the way from the former place to Collierville." The 90th, more fortunate, rode the train five miles, then marched the last four miles on the double-quick with Companies B and C flanked on either side of the railroad as skirmishers. The skirmishers forced their way through "woods, thickets, over fences, through fields and swamps" with only one or two stragglers from each company, according to Woodruff. Quartermaster Redmond Sheridan similarly described the regiment's trip to Collierville: "My Reg. was run to the Scene, but the dogs tore up the road, thus they had to double quick it to Collierville a distance of 4 miles."[7]

When the two regiments reached Collierville, they found Sherman safe and the Confederates just leaving. Sergeant Carmody, still at his post, described the regiment's arrival at "about four o'clock. The first man to reach the fort and report to General Sherman was Col. Tim O'Meara and his orderly bearing a green Irish flag of the 90th Volunteer Irish regiment. The advance of reinforcements caused the rebels to fall back." Carmody concluded, "Being an Irishman myself, I naturally felt proud that the flag of the Emerald Isle had led the way to help save Sherman." Quartermaster Sheridan wrote that the Legion "got there in time to See the Rebs in full gallop leaving a few to be buried having Killed and Wounded Some 60 of the 13th U.S. Inft. and Captured amongst others the horse rode by Major Gen. Sherman. We gave them chase but they were Smart enough not to reappear." Sheridan, ever the philosopher, concluded, "Thus it is not only necessary to whip them but [to] occupy the ground permanently."[8]

With the approach of the Irish Legion, the Confederates prudently retired to the south with their captured booty, which included "135 prisoners, 13 wagons and teams, 1 ambulance, and a number of horses and mules," according to General Chalmers's after-action report. Chalmers missed a chance to alter the course and conduct of the war, for without Sherman there could have been no "march to the sea" or through the Carolinas.[9]

Sherman reacted quickly to the Confederate attack at Collierville, sending his nearest troops, the Fourth Division, including the 90th Illinois, on a march to Mount Pleasant, Mississippi, in pursuit of the attackers, hoping that together with other Union forces in the area they could catch Chalmers's mounted troops. To Sherman's disappointment, Chalmers's cavalry easily escaped and remained a force to be reckoned with. Sherman's close call at Collierville brought down his wrath on the farmers of northern Mississippi. The Confederate force besieging Collierville included local guerrillas, some of whom had taken the oath of allegiance to the Union. One captured Confederate, who worked at a nearby gristmill, had a copy of the oath in his pocket, and several dead Confederates at Collierville likewise had the federal oath of allegiance and various passes "on their persons." Convinced that sterner measures were necessary to stop such activity, Sherman instructed the commander at Memphis, Major General Stephen Hurlbut, "to take all horses and mules between the railroad and the Tallahatchie, burn all mills and corn-fields, and let them feel that to attack our road will be surely followed by vengeance." Hurlbut broadened Sherman's instructions, ordering his cavalry to "drive in all stock that can be available."[10]

Along with the rest of the First Brigade, the 90th Illinois left Collierville on October 12 and marched the eleven miles to Mount Pleasant. The men had a late start as their brigade brought up the rear, guarding the division's wagon train. Some of the troops tested their marksmanship, indiscriminately firing at random targets as they marched, which thoroughly kindled the ire of their commanding officer, General Corse. The next day, some thirty minutes after daylight, the now properly chastened First Brigade, including the 90th Illinois, changed direction and marched northeast toward La Grange, behind the Second Brigade, which had the advance. The Third Brigade brought up the rear and guarded the division's trains. This daily rotation in the order of march by brigades would be a common feature of future marches.[11]

From La Grange, the line of march of the Fourth Division, and thus the 90th Illinois, paralleled the Memphis and Charleston Railroad toward Corinth. However, rain made the roads very slippery, delaying the troops' arrival at Corinth until October 17. Colonel John Loomis's First Brigade again slogged along at the rear of the division, guarding the trains. Also on the sixteenth, General Ewing officially assumed command of the Fourth Division. The brigade arrived at Burnsville on October 19, where they had a four-day wait due to stiffening Confederate resistance and to Major General Henry "Old Brains" Halleck's requirement that Sherman repair the railroad as he proceeded. The 90th Illinois followed the railroad to Burnsville and Iuka and thence to Eastport, Mississippi, where on October 28 the regiment crossed the Tennessee River on Gunboat No. 32, part of the fleet of riverboats requested by Sherman. On October 17, orders from Major General Ulysses S. Grant arrived, directing Sherman to "drop all work on the railroad east of Bear Creek: push your command toward Bridgeport." That got things moving again, and the Legion arrived at Florence, Alabama, on October 31, where the troops mustered for pay in the evening. So far, their march from Memphis had covered about 175 miles.[12]

On November 1, the 90th Illinois marched east to Rogersville, Alabama, probably along much of what is now US Highway 72 and State Highway 2, until the men reached the Elk River, a few miles past Rogersville, where nature intervened. Sherman found the "Elk 200 yards wide, 4½ feet deep, and running very swift" and impassable for artillery and wagons. Attempting to save time, Sherman marched his "Third" and Fourth Divisions, including the 90th Illinois, up the Elk River through Gilbertsborough, Prospect, and Elkton, searching for a crossing. On November 8, they finally crossed the Elk River at Fayetteville, Tennessee, some fifty miles by air from Rogersville and eleven miles into Tennessee, after a difficult eighty-six mile march from Florence, Alabama. Sherman's aide, Major Joseph Audenried, described the roads as "exceedingly hilly, rocky, and in some places very muddy; marching very difficult with wagons." At Fayetteville, Sherman declared, "All roads leading east and west in Tennessee are execrable."[13]

Quartermaster Sheridan also found road conditions in Tennessee challenging, and the reoccurrence of an old political rivalry with his brigade commander, Colonel Loomis, didn't help matters any. In a letter written to his brother in March 1864, Sheridan explained how O'Meara came to his rescue:

> Myself and our Brigade Commander are not on terms of the Strictest intimacy. He don't like me from some cause, I recon it is because on one occasion whilst crossing a Swamp in Tennessee one of my wagons amongst dozens of others was deep fastened in the mud. Some of my men were working under Some instructions given by me when he rode up to me and told me to turn the Wagon over to let some more favored Q.M. proceed. I politely but firmly requested him to reduce his order to writing.
>
> He Said he had no pen ink and paper. I quickly produced them from my Saddle bag. It Staggered him. He refused and all around laughed at him.
>
> He then Said "I premtorily order you Sir to over turn that Waggon."
>
> "Please deliver that order to Col. O'Meara" Said I.
>
> "Turn over that Waggon or I will put you under arrest" Said he.
>
> I lost all patience and told him to go to hell.
>
> He brought a squad to arrest me, meanwhile I Sent an orderly to the Col. explaining. When he [O'Meara] came as wrathy as a lion and dared his [Loomis's] men to lay a finger. I winked at the gentleman that made him worse, and in very rage he rode away.

Sheridan wrote that "previous to him [Loomis] going Recruiting we had 2 or 3 Spats. When he returns I think it will be hard to put up with him. He is a Chicago man with whom I differed often in discussions; he is a Natural Tyrant which he has cultivated to perfection in the army. He may be the cause of me resigning. . . . It is in his power to annoy me greatly on the march. I can't stand too much."

Sheridan then discussed his relationship with other officers and his approach to his work: "I know my bis [business], attend to it, don't mix in their drinking sprees. don't know any favorite in or out of the Regiment. I don't permit the commanding officer to interfere in my official business. I permit no horse swindle to exist, too Commonly done. indeed since I have been in the Service to this moment not one cents worth of governmental property has been willfully lost destroyed or used in my Regiment." Sheridan wrote that he could if he were so "disposed when in Mississippi have illegally made money but since I have thus far lived in the world on honest earned wages it would not be worth my while in the army to risk the forfeiture of all that in future life I hope to adorn my brow." Sheridan philosophically discussed his future: "My Salary keeps me in the field and my family at home comfortable but I have to be cautious, as it is; up to date I am just as I entered not a dollar ahead and don't expect to be and don't care for if I have my health. I can get my living Some way without working too hard." Sheridan "detested" shoe-making and did not intend to return to it. He added: "I have not given it a thought yet perhaps shall not until it becomes necessary to do so as I might never be Spared to return in which case if I bothered my mind about Such matters it would be So much waste of thought."[14]

Understandably, the Legion found the march difficult. Woodruff quotes a narrative by one of the Legion's officers that described the march to Fayetteville, Tennessee, in graphic terms: "The men were very tired, and many sick. Had hardly anything to eat for a few days past, but hard-tack and water. Shoes and clothes are wearing out, and much dissatisfaction prevailed." It was "raining heavily, roads muddy and marching bad, the men cold and hungry, obliged to sleep out without tents or covering. . . . Heavy dew and night very cold. . . . Roads very bad and broken. Resumed the march the next day, passing through a hilly and mountainous country, roads rocky and bad." Sherman reported the local food supply as plentiful but in the next paragraph requested "200,000 rations of bread, salt, sugar, and coffee at Decherd."[15]

From Fayetteville, the 90th Illinois reached Winchester on November 11 and moved on to Decherd. At Winchester, Sherman received the shoes he had requested to cross the mountain: some 20,000 mule-shoes and 10,000 horse-shoes. The troops would have to make do with the worn-out shoes they wore. They faced more serious trouble, for their detour north meant they now would encounter steep ascents and descents in traversing the Cumberland Plateau to reach Bridgeport, Alabama, on their route to Chattanooga. Equal to the challenge, on November 12 the 90th Illinois resumed the march from Cowan, Tennessee, located at the base of the Cumberland Plateau, crossed the mountains with the Fourth Division by following the general line of the railroad for about a hundred miles from Decherd, Tennessee, to Stevenson, Alabama, and reached Bridgeport three days later.[16]

According to Captain Charles Wills, 103rd Illinois, the route traveled by the 90th Illinois from Stevenson along the Tennessee River toward Chattanooga was definitely less than scenic due to "the conglomeration of dead mules and mud that fills the ditches on the roadside between Stevenson and Chattanooga" (Map 5). Dead mules were particularly numerous along the road near Bridgeport, the terminus of the makeshift sixty-mile Union supply route over Walden's Ridge to Chattanooga. Confederate troops had controlled all other supply routes until the arrival of Major General Joseph Hooker's XX Corps, combined with Brigadier General William B. Hazen's amphibious attack that captured Brown's Ferry, reopened a direct route to the supply base at Bridgeport. By that time, the appalling road conditions and resulting overwork, in addition to the lack of forage and outright starvation, had taken a terrible toll on draft animals at Chattanooga.[17]

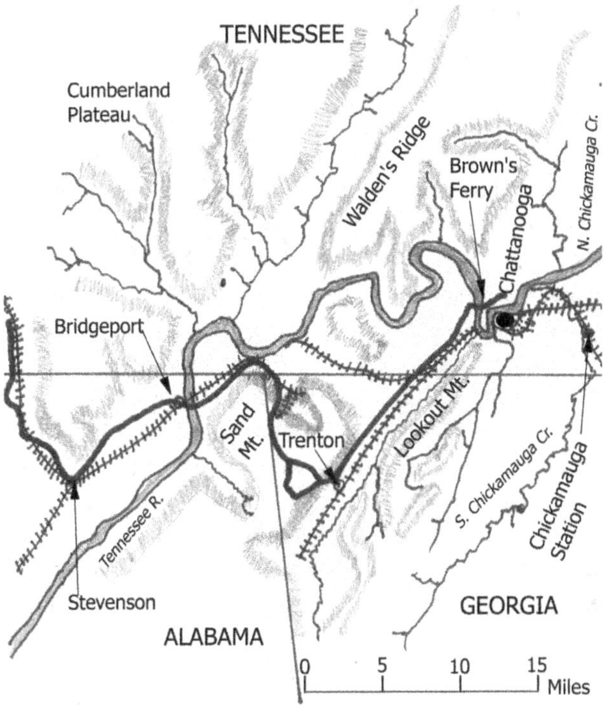

Map 5. Approach to Chattanooga by the 90th Illinois

Sherman's friend General Grant, now in charge of the various Union commands at Chattanooga, wanted to end the Confederate siege quickly. This was partly due to his own concern but more specifically to President Abraham Lincoln's and Secretary of War Edwin Stanton's knowledge that Union major general Ambrose E. Burnside's army in Knoxville, Tennessee, would soon run out of supplies, as well as to their doubts about Burnside's ability to withstand a threatened attack by Confederate lieutenant general James Longstreet's army. Understandably, Lincoln expressed a high level of concern, since Burnside, after notable early successes, had thoroughly demonstrated the validity of the "Peter Principle" by being promoted to his own particular level of incompetence.[18]

Sherman ordered his leading division, the Fourth, to make a planned demonstration against Lookout Mountain intended to mislead the Confederates into diverting forces to that area and away from intended points of attack by Union forces. On November 17, the 90th Illinois crossed the Tennessee River on the pontoon bridge at Bridgeport with the rest of the Fourth Division and, as Ewing reported, "moved by Shellmound and Gordon's Mines, over the Raccoon [Sand] Mountain by a trail to the summit overlooking the town [Trenton, Georgia] and camped concealing our fires" (see Map 5). The troops recalled it as a memorable ascent up a steep, narrow road blasted out of the face of Sand Mountain. The harrowing climb may have been worth it, for upon reaching the mountaintop, a breathtaking sight awaited the soldiers of the Irish Legion accustomed to the flatlands of Illinois. Even the normally reticent scribe of Company C felt called upon to comment on the splendor of the view. From their perch at the Sand Mountain gaps above Trenton, the men of the 90th Illinois had a panoramic view of Lookout Valley some eight hundred feet below and of the west side of equally high Lookout Mountain. Both mountains trailed off as far as the eye could see to the northeast and southwest. On November 18, Loomis's brigade halted at the summit above Trenton, sent a detachment south to Wimm's Gap, and built extensive campfires at night atop the mountain. The next day, while part of the Fourth Division made a demonstration against nearby Lookout Mountain, Loomis's brigade descended Sand Mountain from Wimm's Gap and marched up the valley. The 90th Illinois remained behind to build extensive fires at night at the two gaps above Trenton. Adjutant Edwin Davis reported seeing "the enemy's campfires . . . distinctly visible on the opposite range of Lookout Mountain." The Fourth Division's demonstrations had caused the Confederates to shift troops to counter a possible Union flanking movement south of Chattanooga.[19]

On November 21, after two days and nights of lighting fires on the mountain, the 90th Illinois descended to the valley and, with the rest of the First Brigade, passed through Trenton. There the regiment joined the Fourth Division and promptly marched down Lookout Valley and camped. The demonstration had ended, but a long line of campfires visible from the valley below indicated that Confederate troops remained camped for some distance along the crest of Lookout Mountain. Before leaving Lookout Valley, Sherman ordered, "Each man will carry a blanket or overcoat, three days' cooked rations and as near 100 rounds of ammunition as possible, including that in cartridge boxes." Unmistakably, a battle was imminent.[20]

The 90th Illinois reported that after marching along the base of Lookout Mountain, the men crossed "the Tennessee River on a pontoon [at Brown's Ferry] under fire of Rebel artillery from the top of 'Lookout.'" As Brown's Ferry lies nearly three miles from the Confederate artillery position on Lookout Mountain, the long-distance cannon fire did not hurt anyone in the Legion but likely discouraged straggling. However, during construction of the pontoon bridge at Brown's Ferry, a Confederate artillery shell had holed one of the pontoon boats. After crossing, to remain hidden from the view of the Confederates, the Legion, along with the rest of the Fourth Division, camped behind hills about two and a half miles west of the mouth of South Chickamauga Creek and an equal distance north of and across the river from Chattanooga. The march from Camp Sherman on the Big Black River outside Vicksburg to this jumping-off point above Chattanooga covered some 375 miles and took fifty-five days. Sherman now had his troops, including the 90th Illinois, in position to make a surprise crossing of the Tennessee River and seize the north end of Missionary Ridge. He wrote that before crossing the river, his troops were issued two days' rations and were "without a change of clothing, stripped for the fight, with but a single blanket or coat per man." Obviously, something big was up.[21]

Thus forewarned, the soldiers of the Irish Legion prepared themselves for the trials of the next day in their own separate ways, as soldiers have always done. Seated in front of a log fire, their colonel, Timothy O'Meara, composed the following letter to his brother in New York:

> Headquarters 90th Ill Vol's
> Chattanooga, Nov. 23, 1863
>
> Dear John,
>
> After a march of two months length find us situated & enc[amped] in front of the Rebels. We arrived here yesterday after making one of the longest [marches] made during the war. It would be very interesting & entertaining to you if I could describe the incidences that transpired during our very long journey. Time, however, will not permit a detailed account at present. Over more, I have to communicate this intelligence that on the morrow we meet the enemy to fight the great battle of the war. Tonight we cross to the East bank of the Tenn. Be no alarmed about me. If it is my lot [to] fall I cannot [have] avoided it. If I am spared, it will be another proof of Almighty God's goodness and mercy to me. If the former should take place, I appoint you in behalf of my family to look after my affairs. Tell Mother and Mary to pray for me. If I am killed I want at least a dozen masses offered up for the welfare of my soul. Poor Mother will feel worried over this. I wish you could keep it still until after you ascertain the result. If I live I will write in a very short time after the fight. I write this by the light of a log fire. I cannot say much more. I was never in better health, thank God.
>
> To my poor dear Mother and my affectionate sister I send my warmest love. Say to them that my hopes are high. I am proud of being a

Union soldier. Victory must crown with God's assistance tomorrow's labours and if the sacrifice of my life is necessary to gain it, It will be offered freely for after that victory the Union is saved and a lasting peace is sure to follow. To all my friends and acquaintances I send kind regards. If I have enemies I send them defiance in life, foregivenances in death only—

To you my brother everything
Tim O'Meara
Col. Comd. 90th Regt. Illinois.[22]

{ 6 }

THE BATTLE OF CHATTANOOGA

"General Grant you are besieged." Major General William T. Sherman's surprised comment to his friend nicely summed up the situation at Chattanooga on November 15, 1863. From his vantage point in the Union defenses, Sherman viewed the encircling Confederate positions extending "from the river, below the town, to the river above," confining the Union forces within the "town and its immediate defenses." To break the Confederate stranglehold on Chattanooga, Major General Ulysses S. Grant developed his plan of attack, modifying it as circumstances required. In the final iteration of his plan, Grant intended to attack General Braxton Bragg's army on both flanks while holding his center relatively immobile. On November 24, Sherman's army, and thus the Irish Legion, would cross the Tennessee River and conduct the main attack against the north end of Missionary Ridge, in the process turning the northern flank of the Confederate defenses. Major General Joseph Hooker would probe Confederate defenses at Lookout Mountain. The Army of the Cumberland would occupy Bragg's attention along the center of Missionary Ridge. However, battles seldom work out as planned, and this one was no exception.[1]

A lot of things went wrong for Sherman, and therefore for the 90th Illinois, at Chattanooga, but crossing the Tennessee River went off almost like clockwork under the direction of Brigadier General W. F. "Baldy" Smith, who repeated the amphibious tactics used to secure a bridgehead on the Confederate side of the Tennessee River crossing at Brown's Ferry (see Map 5, in chapter 5). Between about 1:30 A.M. and daylight on November 24, some 116 pontoon boats ferried across two divisions of about eight thousand men, who rapidly entrenched to protect the bridgehead. Sherman did not intend to be surprised again on the banks of the Tennessee River. The resurrected ex-Confederate "commodious" side-wheel steamboat *Dunbar*, complete with barges in tow, showed up at 8 A.M. under the direction of Brigadier General James Wilson of Grant's staff, and by noon, Wilson had ferried Brigadier General Hugh Ewing's Fourth Division, including the 90th Illinois, over the Tennessee River, more or less dry-shod. Not everyone got to ride on the *Dunbar*; Company D reported crossing in pontoon boats. According to Company C's report, the Legion formed in line of battle at 11 A.M. A little after noon, other troops completed a pontoon bridge nearly 1,400 feet in length spanning the Tennessee River at the landing site.[2]

As the topography of Missionary Ridge would largely determine the nature of the forthcoming battle involving the 90th Illinois and strongly affect its outcome, a brief description of the area is in order. From the location of the 90th Illinois on the east bank of the Tennessee River, a relatively level valley extended from the river terminating in a number of cleared fields at the foot of Missionary Ridge, looming some one and a half miles to the east. A little over half a mile to the north of the Legion's landing site, the valley was bounded by South Chattanooga Creek, which ran in a predominantly east-west direction. At this location, both the Tennessee River and Missionary Ridge ran in a generally north-south direction.

Clearly in no hurry, Sherman waited until 1 P.M. before moving Morgan L. Smith's, John E. Smith's, and Hugh Ewing's divisions toward the northern end of Missionary Ridge. The 90th Illinois formed line of battle, awaiting the signal to advance. Finally, the bugles of the multiple units sounded the advance, and the men of the Legion stepped out toward their objective under drizzling rain and low clouds. The three divisions moved cautiously in echelon, arranged in a series of parallel stair-steps, with skirmishers in front. On the right as the bottom step, General Ewing's Fourth Division, including the 90th Illinois, brought up the rear, prepared to deploy toward Chattanooga to meet an attack from that direction. By 3:30 P.M., Sherman's troops had captured their objective, the steep hill Sherman thought formed the north end of Missionary Ridge. Company C of the 90th Illinois, in line of battle on the hill by 5 P.M., reported heavy firing as Confederate cannon welcomed the arriving Union troops and other Union units repelled a probe by Confederate skirmishers.[3]

To secure the capture, General Ewing got some cannon up the steep hill with the assistance of the 90th Illinois, who, according to George Woodruff, "helped to haul two pieces to the top." Unfortunately, Sherman's maps were faulty. The captured high hill, aptly named Billy Goat Hill, did not form part of Missionary Ridge proper (Map 6). In Sherman's words, it stood apart, separated by "a deep depression" from Tunnel Hill, his true objective. With little daylight remaining, Sherman fortified what he had gained, and the army settled in for the night. Sherman's delayed start from the bridgehead and his slow rate of advance, combined with faulty maps, the short period of daylight in late November, and his reluctance to take risks, was enough to keep him from reaching his true objective on Missionary Ridge on November 24. The Irish Legion would pay dearly for this failure.[4]

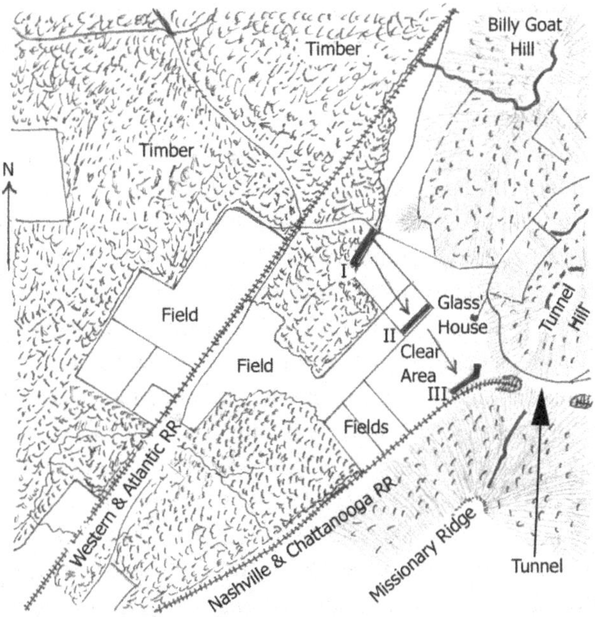

Map 6. Positions occupied by Loomis's brigade on November 25, 1863, during Union attack on Tunnel Hill

That night, Colonel John Loomis's brigade, including the 90th Illinois, remained in reserve camped on a bluff next to Billy Goat Hill. The ominous sounds issuing from Confederate positions on Missionary Ridge provided little comfort to the soldiers of the Irish Legion. During that night, they could hear the Confederate troops building fortifications and the rumble of cannon being put in place on the ridge. By delaying his assault, Sherman lost the advantage of surprise, and Confederate major general Patrick Ronayne Cleburne's veterans took full advantage of the opportunity to prepare a warm reception for Sherman's troops when they advanced the next day.[5]

From their perch at the north end of Missionary Ridge, the men of the 90th Illinois could distinguish little of Lookout Mountain, which rises 1,500 feet above the Tennessee River, some seven to eight miles to the southwest. This was a pity, as what became popularly known as the "Battle above the Clouds" was still underway. Closer to the action, at Grant's headquarters on Orchard Knob, Union quartermaster general Montgomery C. Meigs viewed his first battle, and what a view it was. In his battle report, he unintentionally gave General Hooker's attack its name: "The day had been one of driving mists and rains, and much of Hooker's battle was fought above the clouds, which concealed him from our view, but from which musketry was heard." At nightfall it got even better: "The sky cleared, and the full moon, the 'hunter's moon,' shone upon the beautiful scene. Till 1 A.M. twinkling sparks upon the mountainside showed that picket skirmishing was still going on." Some of Sherman's veterans, including Corporal Simon Swan, Company G, preferred to talk about the "Battle above the Clouds," however little they had seen of it, rather than recount their next day's experience. Or maybe they just liked the song, as "The Battle above the Clouds" was eventually set to music.[6]

The soldiers of the 90th Illinois might have viewed the outcome of the battle for Lookout Mountain less enthusiastically had they known that two Confederate brigades of Major General Carter L. Stevenson's Division, released from defensive positions on Lookout Mountain by its capture, would shift to the defense of Missionary Ridge and be in position to oppose the Legion's attack the next day, November 25. What Colonel Timothy O'Meara called the "great battle of the war" was imminent, and his Irish Legion would be in the thick of it.[7]

Sherman commanded the seemingly overwhelming force of three divisions of the XV Corps, Brigadier General J. C. Davis's division of the XIV Corps, and the rest of Major General Oliver O. Howard's XI Corps by late morning. His challenge was how best to use the large numbers of troops at his disposal. Early on November 25, in the "dim light of morning," Sherman obtained "as accurate an idea of the ground as possible" and determined that the "line of attack [from his army's positions on Billy Goat Hill] was in the direction of Missionary Ridge, with wings supporting on either flank." Sherman observed that "quite a valley lay between" the Union positions on Billy Goat Hill and his objective, steep-sided Tunnel Hill. Its western side had been partly cleared, but its northern side remained forested (see Map 6). Attacking the "breastwork of logs and fresh earth, filled with men and two guns" located on the "farther point" of its narrow wooded crest, presented difficulties. In addition, "the enemy was also seen in great force on a still higher hill beyond [south of] the tunnel, from which he had a fair plunging fire on the hill in dispute. The gorge between, through which several roads and the railroad tunnel pass, could not be seen from our position, but formed the natural *place d'armes*, where the enemy covered his masses to resist our contemplated movement of turning his right flank and endangering his communications with his depot at Chickamauga."[8]

The fear of unseen enemy masses cited in the last sentence may explain Sherman's failure to mount a turning movement around the Confederate right flank. Instead, Sherman's troops mainly attacked head-on against entrenched Confederate positions on Tunnel Hill. The railroad tunnel mentioned by Sherman pierced the ridge about 250 yards south of Tunnel Hill.[9]

Confederate major general Cleburne, whom the troops of the Legion could claim as a fellow Irish immigrant, commanded the defense of the northern end of Missionary Ridge. In the limited time available, he used the natural strengths of the topography to create a truly formidable defensive position, as the 90th Illinois and the rest of Sherman's troops would soon discover.[10]

Sherman planned that Brigadier General John M. Corse's Second Brigade should attack Tunnel Hill with support on both flanks. Loomis's brigade, including the 90th Illinois, would support Corse's right flank. Sherman intended Loomis's brigade "to move along the west base [of Missionary Ridge], supported by the two reserve brigades of General John E. Smith." Colonel Adolphus Buschbeck's brigade of the XI Corps, minus two regiments, also supported Loomis's brigade.[11]

For the 90th Illinois, the battle proceeded by fits and starts. In compliance with orders, the 1,200 or so men of Loomis's brigade made three separate advances, which for convenience are described as three phases. This disjointed forward progress subjected the 90th Illinois to long periods of immobility under Confederate fire with little opportunity to reply effectively.

The first phase began on Wednesday, November 25, when the 325 or so enlisted men and twenty-two officers of the Irish Legion ate an early breakfast and prepared to march by 4:30 A.M. Members of both the 90th Illinois and 100th Indiana reported their regiments in action by 8 A.M.; however, other reports place the time somewhat later. Company C of the Legion simply reported, "Moved our line down the hill and formed again at the bottom." The brigade then marched a short distance toward Chattanooga, concealed from view in the timber, before advancing toward Missionary Ridge until the men reached the edge of the trees (see Map 6, position I). Across the open ground, they could see the railroad tunnel directly in their front.[12]

Orderly Sergeant Eli Sherlock of the 100th Indiana noted the brigade's alignment in line of battle: "The 90th Illinois, Colonel O'Meara, the Irish Legion was on the left, nearest to the tunnel, then the 100th Indiana the left center, the 12th Indiana and the 26th Illinois on the right of the brigade." He described the effect of ground fog on the brigade's early action: "About 8:30 or 9 A.M. it was still foggy on the low land, where we were formed, but it was clear and the sun shone brightly on the top of Missionary Ridge so that the Confederates could not look down into the fog and see us, but we could look up through it and see one long column of rebels after another moving from the Confederate center to their right and being massed directly in our front." According to Sherlock, Loomis's brigade became involved in the battle about 9 or 9:30 A.M. when they advanced a strong skirmish line across the level ground toward the tunnel, with the result that "the Confederates being above us were compelled to fire downward upon us at an angle of 20 to 40 degrees, and we fired upward at them at the same angle."[13]

While waiting for the order to advance, and protected from view by timber, Colonel O'Meara could survey the half mile or so of open fields and pasture lying between the brigade front and the imposing bulk of Missionary Ridge looming to the east. What he saw would not have been pleasing. The relatively level ground directly in his front gradually sloped upward but rose more steeply near the railroad, which crossed from his right and entered a tunnel in what resembled a cul-de-sac in the ridge. The elevation at that point was some sixty to eighty feet higher than his present location. Recently constructed Confederate earthworks sprouting cannon crowned the dominant hills on either side of the open area to his front. Other cannon loomed menacingly on the ridge directly over the tunnel. The railroad embankment to his front and right and the group of farm buildings to the front and left of his line of advance both provided ready-made defensive positions for Confederate infantry. Several fences in the fields directly in his front presented no problem, but one, more substantial than the rest, surrounding an enclosure for livestock or corral, offered a more serious obstruction likely to slow troop movement. No protective cover existed between his present position and the tunnel other than the occasional dead tree, tree stump, or fence row, and these would provide minimal protection from plunging fire. Some in his regiment, farmers from the level, poorly drained land in northern Illinois, could have guessed, given the nature of the land and climate, that somewhere in their front they would encounter drainage ditches across their path of advance, which might provide some protection.[14]

As an experienced professional soldier, O'Meara could, if he so chose, make a reasonably accurately estimate of the losses his regiment would sustain in crossing the half mile of open fields between them and the railroad. They would have to move rapidly to minimize casualties, if they were to have any chance of continuing the attack against Confederate positions on the ridge. Whatever O'Meara's thoughts, about 9 or 9:30 A.M. Loomis advanced his First Brigade, with two lines of skirmishers in the lead, from the edge of the timber into the open fields. As the troops of the 90th Illinois advanced, the double line of skirmishers in their front under Lieutenant John C. Harrington, Company C, quickly came under fire. The left of the 90th Illinois hugged the base of the hill alongside which the regiment had formed. As the men emerged from the timber, a rain of solid shot and shell erupted from Confederate artillery. Under a cross fire from artillery on both sides of the ridge and over the tunnel, they did not go far before Loomis called a halt and "placed the brigade under the best cover afforded," the timber from which they had just emerged. In deciding not to advance into the open fields toward Tunnel Hill, Loomis was presumably guided by his understanding of General Ewing's orders "to push the enemy's skirmishers, but under no circumstances to bring on a general engagement." The Irish Legion, along with the rest of Loomis's brigade, now occupied an exposed position with no possibility of replying to Confederate fire, a truly uncomfortable situation. Fortunately, most of the fire from Confederate cannon was high. Confederate cannon on Missionary Ridge "could not be depressed sufficiently to make them effective," according to Colonel Reuben Williams of the 12th Indiana, located two regiments to the right of the 90th Illinois. Williams thought Loomis's order for the troops to "lie down" with solid shot and shells shrieking and screaming over their heads to be the most difficult as well as dangerous to carry out that he received during the war.[15]

After the war, Confederate colonel Roger Q. Mills of Smith's Brigade, Cleburne's Division, commented on Loomis's calm demeanor while under fire. Mills's position on Tunnel Hill overlooked the large open field and the woods beyond. He remembered that "a Federal brigade came through the woods and out into the open field. There the troops reformed their lines. This officer in command [Loomis] was perfectly cool. He took his time, and the troops formed as if they were on dress parade. They were within easy range and we fired into them. They broke and went back into the woods." Mills wrote that a few minutes later, "they came back and formed again in the same deliberate way. When the officer in command had got them formed to suit him, he made them lie down, while he rode up and down in front as if waiting for orders. Gen. Hardee came up to my brigade while we were firing on them and said: 'Stop shooting at those men. It's murder.' We stopped." Some time during the battle, Colonel Loomis's horse was severely wounded by a cannon ball; fortunately, the colonel was not injured.[16]

In addition to cannon fire from Missionary Ridge, the men of Loomis's brigade faced stiff opposition from Confederate infantry occupying positions on their left flank as well as in their immediate front. Not exactly a happy prospect for the Irishmen of the Legion, who formed that exposed left flank. Loomis described the location of the Confederates on his left as "resting on Tunnel Hill road, and occupying with skirmishers the house, log barns, and negro quarters on the Glass place." The Confederate positions extended "along the railroad, to and including the log house beyond the right of my line." Directly to his front, "three lines of skirmishers or sharpshooters" occupied the "abrupt hill-sides" behind the railroad. To relieve some of the pressure on his troops, Loomis ordered a section of artillery into position on his left and "opened their fire upon the enemy in the vicinity of Mr. Glass' house, where he [Confederates] appeared in force. . . . I succeeded in dislodging him from some of the buildings by artillery fire."[17]

Phase two began about 10:30 A.M., when Loomis received General Ewing's order to advance simultaneously with the attack of Corse's brigade on Tunnel Hill. Unfortunately, Loomis's location prevented him from closely supporting Corse's attack, as Sherman intended. To reach Corse's position, Loomis's brigade would have had to execute a left oblique and march around the hill on their immediate left and across a half mile of open fields to the western base of Tunnel Hill while under cross fire from Confederate positions on the surrounding hills and over the tunnel. Instead, Loomis's brigade attacked straight ahead toward the tunnel; consequently, Corse attacked without direct support from Loomis. This pattern of piecemeal uncoordinated Union attacks by Sherman's troops on Tunnel Hill continued throughout the day.

After hugging the ground at the edge of the timber and dodging falling tree branches for an hour or so, an order from Ewing got Loomis's brigade moving again, with Colonel Buschbeck's brigade in support. Severe skirmishing broke out as Loomis's brigade marched in line of battle over open ground directly toward the railroad tunnel under Missionary Ridge. As described by Sergeant Sherlock of the 100th Indiana, located on the right of the 90th Illinois, Loomis's brigade attacked across an area "almost perfectly level, with nothing whatever to protect our line from the plunging shot and shell of the Confederates, delivered at short range by several batteries and lines of infantry." Consequently, as Loomis's brigade advanced, "a great many men [were] killed and wounded from the fire of the Confederates, who literally swarmed on summit and slopes of the hills."[18]

An account by an unnamed officer of the 90th Illinois, cited by Woodruff, describes what the Legion faced as the troops advanced. "The mountains lapped each other and all formed a kind of half circle. The railroad . . . embankment formed a protection or breastwork for the enemy, where they had double lines of skirmishers posted. The mountain from base to crown was swarming with the enemy. They had rifle intrenchments at the base, and midway up the sides. Every tree, log and crag, and everything that would afford the least protection to them, was used by the enemy's sharpshooters." On top of Missionary Ridge, the Confederates had constructed "heavy works, bristling with cannon and guns of every description. The valley beneath afforded no shelter for the Union forces, but left them within easy range of the enemy's guns, both large and small, and from every direction."[19]

According to Loomis's report, his brigade advanced partway across the open ground, suffering "considerable loss" from "heavy direct and cross fire of artillery and the infantry and sharpshooters of the enemy." Although "hotly engaged," his skirmishers failed to "carry the railroad" anywhere except on the extreme right of his line. At "the termination of General Corse's assault," Loomis "ordered a halt, placing the brigade under such cover as the low ground afforded" (see Map 6, position II).[20]

As O'Meara moved his regiment across the open fields at the double-quick, they outpaced the rest of the brigade. To preserve proper alignment, the 90th Illinois stopped to allow troops on the right to catch up. After this first advance, Captain David Duffy of Company E placed the 90th Illinois about six to eight hundred feet from and a little to the right of the Glass family's buildings that occupied the "low ground near [the] railroad on [the] side farthest from Missionary ridge." Through the "smoke of bursting shells aimed at these buildings by a battery in our rear," he observed "two or three women, some youngsters and a dog or two, were getting away from the place and hurrying toward our lines."[21]

According to Woodruff, to maintain their alignment with the brigade, the men of the 90th Illinois had to pass through a large, well-constructed square two-acre livestock corral "fenced with rails, and staked and ridered on top." Advancing on the double-quick, the troops "could not stop to let down fences; therefore, [they] passed through as best they could. The 90th took the position and held it. It was at this corral, that the brave Col. O'Meara and many others were shot. The enemy's fire was so severe that our skirmishers did not advance far before they were ordered back to the regiment. This, many of them were unable to do." The 90th Illinois lost thirteen men as prisoners.[22]

This high and sturdy corral fence interfered with the advance of the 90th Illinois's skirmishers, including Privates Alexander Moore, Ulick Howard, Alexander

Mathews, and Jeremiah Quirk, all members of Company F from Springfield, Illinois. Moore wrote that as he climbed over the corral fence, "a portion of a shell struck the fence and completely demolished it and something struck me on the cheek bone below the left eye, breaking the bone." He was thrown violently to the ground, causing other internal injuries. About noon, he was helped off the field to the hospital. Mathews was killed on the field, and Howard received a severe leg wound. Moore recovered sufficiently to rejoin the regiment the next day.[23]

In a letter to Father Dunne, Quartermaster Redmond Sheridan described the wounding of Colonel O'Meara as he led his men into battle in the vicinity of the cattle pens: "Colonel T. O'Meara, who, when his horse was shot from under him, grasped a musket in one hand, and with his cap uplifted in the other, roared defiance to the foe, and bid his brave followers imitate his example. . . . The enemy's sharpshooters had already marked their man. Whilst in the act of charging up the ridge in front of the heaviest fire that your mind can picture, and fraught with as much destruction at that point as the rebels could desire, our brave Colonel fell, mortally wounded." O'Meara told "those who ran to his assistance . . . to avenge his death and render all the service they could to their country and waved them from him. Our men were driven back at that point. [First] Lieutenants [John C.] Harrington [Company C] and [Thomas] Murray [commanding Company I] leaped the fence and rallied the men to another charge." During the charge, Lieutenant Harrington went down with a severe gunshot wound to his right arm near the shoulder, putting him out of the fight. It could have been even worse as Captain John Murphy, Company G, "miraculously" escaped injury while dashing "with headlong bravery up the hill" when his canteen deflected a bullet meant for him, according to Quartermaster Sheridan.[24]

Colonel O'Meara's wounding effectively wiped out the Legion's command structure. Early in the fight, Lieutenant Colonel Owen Stuart, shot through the body, had fallen from his horse, and the position of major was vacant. During the battle, three captains and the sergeant major of the Legion were severely wounded and put out of action. Confederate sharpshooters had done their work exceptionally well. Captain Patrick O'Marah, Company C, commanded the regiment during the remainder of the battle.[25]

Figure 1 depicts the initial stages of Sherman's assault on Missionary Ridge. Corse's Second Brigade is shown attacking on the western slope of Tunnel Hill in the upper left. In the foreground and center, the 90th Illinois and 100th Indiana are maneuvering in front of the railroad tunnel with the Glass house in flames. Since Corse's attack took place on the northern slope of Tunnel Hill, the gap between the 90th Illinois and Corse's right flank was greater than shown in the sketch. Well out in front of the main body, the brigade's line of skirmishers approach the railroad cut. The skirmishers on the left have moved past the burning house and are to the right of the tunnel. The tunnel is hidden by the smoke above the house. The almost complete lack of cover in the cleared area in front of the ridge made the brigade's solid formations an inviting target for Confederate batteries, shown located on the hills on either side of and over the tunnel.[26]

Confederates positioned on Tunnel Hill and above the tunnel had a clear view of Loomis's brigade as the men advanced toward them. About 9:30 A.M., Confederate brigadier general Alfred Cumming's Brigade of General Stevenson's Division got in position on Missionary Ridge with the brigade's right resting over the tunnel. The Glass house and its surrounding buildings were about two hundred yards in front of Cumming's line. From his location on the ridge, he saw a long

Fig. 1. Attack on Missionary Ridge by the 100th Indiana on the right and the 90th Illinois on the left. Their skirmishers are at the railroad to the right of the burning house. To the left, other Union troops are assaulting Confederate positions atop Tunnel Hill. (Sherlock, *Memorabilia*, 69)

line of skirmishers followed by the main body of Loomis's brigade emerge into open ground and advance toward him. Lieutenant General William J. Hardee, in command of Bragg's right, ordered Cumming to send two regiments, the 39th and 56th Georgia, to hold the ground around the houses but to burn the houses if forced to retreat. The two regiments descended the ridge, one regiment going to the right of the railroad and the other to the left. A brisk long-distance skirmish then broke out between Loomis's troops and the Georgians, which Cumming thought resulted in few casualties because of the considerable distance involved.

The Georgians eventually withdrew without burning the house. However, a little before 1 P.M., four companies of the 39th Georgia returned and completed burning the houses, capturing nine prisoners in the process.[27]

General Cleburne observed Loomis's advance from his position on the crest of Tunnel Hill some three hundred feet above the elevation of Glass's house and outbuildings: "At 11 A.M., the first serious fight of the day commenced. It was heavy along Smith's whole line [Confederate positions on Tunnel Hill], and extended some distance south of the tunnel." Cleburne's description indicates that Loomis's advance was not a single forward movement but involved backward movement as well. "The right of the enemy's line [Loomis's brigade, with the 90th Illinois on the left flank], exposed to the fire of several pieces of artillery planted over the tunnel, and met by a brigade sent by General Hardee at the foot of the ridge, swayed backward and forward for some time, but did not dare to advance nearer than 400 yards, and finally lay down, contenting itself with sending forward a large body of skirmishers and sending to the rear a much larger number of stragglers."[28]

While the 90th Illinois and the rest of Loomis's troops moved from cover to a fencerow midway across the open fields and there struggled to survive, Corse's brigade had advanced up the steep, wooded northern slope of Tunnel Hill and given Cleburne's troops a severe struggle before being driven back to the base of Tunnel Hill. This setback ended the initial phase of Sherman's attack on the Confederate positions on Tunnel Hill but left the 90th Illinois and the rest of Loomis's troops exposed in the open fields, a very uncomfortable location. According to accounts written over forty years after the battle, the brigade remained in this position for no longer than twenty minutes.[29]

Phase three began when, spurred on by Grant, Sherman through Ewing ordered Loomis, at 12:30 P.M., in Loomis's words, "to advance and place my left on the Tunnel Hill road, and hold the ground. The advance was promptly made, and the position taken under heavy fire and with severe loss. At the same time the skirmishers carried the railroad, driving the enemy from it, Glass's house, and adjacent buildings, which were burned by the enemy." The 90th Illinois skirmishers reached the vicinity of Glass's house and buildings only to be repulsed when Confederates emerged from behind the buildings and charged into their left flank. One of the skirmishers, Sergeant Lawrence Morrissey, Company H, placed the location of the main line of the 90th Illinois in an orchard in the rear of the buildings. Some of the skirmish line of the 100th Indiana crossed the railroad track near their junction with the 90th Illinois but were soon driven back by Confederate skirmishers posted behind cover on the hillside. Beside fencerows, three drainage ditches in the open fields that the brigade crossed afforded some cover, particularly to the wounded. One ditch, some two hundred yards west of the remaining log houses and outbuildings of the Glass farmstead, deeper than the others, provided at least partial cover.[30]

Irving S. Buck, assistant adjutant general of Cleburne's Division, had a good view of Loomis's final advance toward the railroad and the punishment his brigade, including the 90th Illinois, received: "About the middle of the afternoon a strong Federal brigade, Gen. [Colonel] J. Mason Loomis commanding, approached Cleburne's left front, through an open field under heavy fire of artillery and musketry. The Napoleon guns, posted over the tunnels, and rapidly served, were turned upon this brigade with deadly precision. Every discharge plowed huge gaps through the lines, which were promptly closed up as these brave troops moved forward with a steadiness and order which drew exclamations of admiration from those who witnessed it." Buck commented that Loomis's brigade "advanced to an old fence row, where, planting their colors and laying down, they opened and kept up a damaging fire and held their position with a tenacity which was proof against all efforts to dislodge them." However, some of Loomis's troops questioned the effectiveness of their regiment's return fire.[31]

After their final advance, Loomis's line of battle stretched along the railroad from the tunnel to the right, with the 90th Illinois in front of and closest to the tunnel. The main line of the 100th Indiana and the two regiments on its right, the 12th Indiana and 26th Illinois, was located on the west or downhill side of the bed of the railroad track, which provided some protection from Confederate fire. Colonel Loomis described the scene: "I saw the enemy resting their rifles upon the iron rail on the other side, and our men do the same on our side of the track, each burnt by the fire from the other side, until our men with a cheer bounded over and won, and—proudly I say it—held all they won." The right of the 90th Illinois connected with the left of the 100th Indiana near the railroad. However, Captain Duffy's estimate that the railroad was some seventy-five feet in front of his position at the center of the 90th Illinois line implies that the left of the 90th was refused, or bent away from the line of the railroad. Such an orientation provided some protection against a flank attack by Confederate troops at the Glass farmstead, some six to seven hundred feet to the north (see Map 6, position III).[32]

With his brigade in place near the base of Missionary Ridge, Loomis justifiably worried about his unprotected left flank, which was "in the air" and thus vulnerable to attack. The 90th Illinois, on that left flank, had a right to be worried also. To solve the problem, Loomis ordered two of Colonel Buschbeck's regiments forward to strengthen his left. Things didn't work out quite as Loomis intended, as after Buschbeck's two regiments drove the Confederate infantry back up the hill, the men of the 27th Pennsylvania continued their assault up Tunnel Hill. The 73rd Pennsylvania troops remained in the position assigned them near the Glass house. At the time of the 27th and 73rd Pennsylvania's advance, Captain David Duffy, Company E, placed the 90th Illinois not far from the mouth of the tunnel. His company was near the center of the regiment, "within easy musket range of Confederate troops that were opposing [the] advance of" other Union regiments (the 27th Pennsylvania and another regiment) "on tunnel hill some distance back from [the] mouth of the tunnel."[33]

Loomis remained worried: "While this assault was in progress the enemy made an attack on my left with a strong column down Tunnel Hill road, I at once requested General Matthies, commanding a brigade of General John E. Smith's division, sent to my support, to stop them, which he most promptly did, driving them up the hill in confusion. General Matthies then joined in the assault upon Tunnel Hill in a most spirited manner." Surprised and none too pleased at seeing his Third Brigade, commanded by Charles L. Matthies, attacking up Tunnel Hill, General Smith promptly sent his Second Brigade, commanded by Colonel Green Raum, to Matthies's support. Loomis's concern about his left flank resulted in successive piecemeal attacks on Tunnel Hill by part of Buschbeck's brigade, then Matthies's brigade, and finally Raum's brigade. Colonel Loomis, rather than his superiors General Ewing and General Sherman, appeared to be directing this stage of the battle for Tunnel Hill.[34]

After the arrival and subsequent departure of the 90th Illinois skirmishers at Glass's buildings, other Union forces occupied the site. Called to assist Loomis's brigade, the men of the 73rd Pennsylvania of Buschbeck's brigade made a bayonet charge, driving a strong Confederate force from the log huts at Glass's farmstead, which they then occupied. They twice repulsed Confederate attempts to outflank their position at the foot of Tunnel Hill. Later, four companies of the 5th Iowa of Matthies's brigade took possession of the Glass farmstead, including what they termed the outhouses near the burning house.[35]

At this critical point of the battle, Cleburne's forces boldly seized the initiative, demonstrating one of the reasons why he was a Confederate major general. His troops charged against the front and flanks of the attacking Union troops on Tunnel Hill, capturing 500 Union prisoners and eight battle flags, according to Cleburne's report, or some 250, according to Union casualty returns. The charge cleared the hill of Union troops, effectively ending the action for the day. Confederates also recaptured the Glass farmstead, threatening Loomis's brigade by penetrating to his left and rear.[36]

Withdrawing the 90th Illinois required some heroics from Loomis's staff. About 4:30 P.M., Ewing gave the job of recalling Loomis's troops to Captain Ira Bloomfield, assistant adjutant general of Loomis's brigade. Bloomfield, mounted on his horse, reached Loomis's brigade after crossing three ditches and four fences in the open field and gave the order to recall the troops. Bloomfield wrote that he had started "to the 90th Illinois on the extreme left when Colonel Williams of the 12th Indiana said it was useless for me to attempt reaching it on horse back and he said he would send an officer to give the order to that regiment." Two officers were sent in succession on foot on the hazardous mission, and both were shot before reaching the Irishmen. A third, however, succeeded in delivering the message. Bloomfield had a harrowing return ride but arrived safely, much to Ewing's obvious relief and amazement. About half an hour before the 90th Illinois soldiers received the order to retreat, volleys of fire were heard well off to their right that grew in intensity into a steady roar. Something big was underway much nearer to Chattanooga, but the men of the Irish Legion would have to wait to find out how it might affect them.[37]

With the recall of the 90th Illinois, the battle at the northern end of Missionary Ridge essentially ended with Confederates in control of much of the battlefield, including most of Sherman's objective, Tunnel Hill. Except for Corse's brigade, Sherman's forces were now about where they had started the day, and unless something unexpected happened, Sherman, like Sisyphus, would face the prospect of doing it all over again the next day. It had not been one of Sherman's better days or efforts, and his direction of the battle, or lack of it, came in for some harsh criticism after the war.[38]

Fortunately for the Union, about 2:30 P.M., General Grant could stand it no longer and ordered the four divisions of the Army of the Cumberland to storm the rifle pits at the foot of Missionary Ridge, thereby hoping to aid Sherman's attack by drawing the attention of Confederate forces to the center of their line on Missionary Ridge. Against all odds and without orders, Major General George H. Thomas's troops continued to charge straight up Missionary Ridge, breaking through the center of the Confederate line, winning both the Battle of Chattanooga and subsequent promotion for Grant to lieutenant general and general-in-chief of the Union army. Sherman advanced to Grant's old command, the Military Division of the Mississippi. Even though Thomas's troops won the victory, he did not advance in rank but remained in command of the Army of the Cumberland. Just before dark, Cleburne was informed of the breakthrough and received orders to withdraw. Sherman had to wait until just after dark to receive word that despite his marked lack of success at Tunnel Hill, he would unexpectedly be conducting a pursuit in the morning.[39]

At the conclusion of the long, bloody day, the 90th Illinois next faced the work of tending for the many dead and wounded. Colonel O'Meara was found where he had fallen, near the cattle pen, and was carried in a stretcher or blanket to the hospital. During the night, large parties from the brigade brought off the dead and wounded. The next morning, another detail completed burying the dead and collecting equipment.[40]

Theodore Upson, a scout of the 100th Indiana, described Colonel O'Meara going "into the battle dressed in his best uniform, his famous sword at his side, his crimson sash across his breast, a foreign medal won in some other war above it, and last but not least a little amulet or charm hung by a chord around his neck. This, he said, would keep him from all harm. But the bright sash was his undoing. Some sharp shooter's ball pierced his body; and after a few hours of suffering, while faithfully attended by the Catholic Chaplain of his Regiment, he gave his life for the country he called his own." Ira Bloomfield of the 26th Illinois wrote that Colonel Loomis "warned him of the danger saying: 'Colonel, we have to go down over that open field, and the hill on the other side is full of sharpshooters. Your sash will furnish a good mark for them!' But the gallant colonel only smiled and held up a picture of the Virgin Mary that he always wore suspended by a cord around his neck, replying: 'They cannot hurt me while I have this.' A few minutes later he lay weltering in his blood, mortally wounded by a rifle ball through his left side, just below the heart."[41]

Both General Ewing and Sergeant Upson spoke of the "Brave" O'Meara. However, both the *Chicago Tribune* and *New York Times* misspelled his name in their casualty reports, conveying on Colonel Timothy O'Meara Sherman's definition of military fame, quoted by historian Burke Davis: "To be killed on the field of battle and have our names spelled wrong in the newspapers." A slightly more lasting memorial, an eight-gun lunette in the Union fortifications at Chattanooga, carried O'Meara's name in recognition of his service to his adopted country. Colonel Loomis considered O'Meara's death to be "a severe loss to his country, to his companions, and to his command. The illuminated memory of a brave man and gallant soldier remains." When they finally had time, the officers of the 90th Illinois adopted resolutions praising Colonel O'Meara and his service to his country and expressing deep sympathy to his mother and brother and had them sent to the colonel's mother and published in the *Boston Pilot*, the *Irish American*, and in Chicago newspapers.[42]

Colonel O'Meara's death deeply saddened Father Denis Dunne. His letter to the colonel's brother, John, informing him of O'Meara's death seems almost a cry of pain: "May God have mercy on his soul! I cannot describe to you my feelings. I loved him as a brother and a nobler man never lived. . . . I cannot offer you any consolation. May God console you." In a second letter to O'Meara's brother and family, Father Dunne wrote that when informed by his attending doctor that he could not live, "O'Meara merely said, 'My poor Mother.' She, next to his God, occupied his thoughts the last moments of his life. Lieut. Col. Stuart, Capts. Murphy, O'Connor, & Cunningham—all of whom were wounded . . . arrived here in yesterday. They will all, I think, recover. They all Speak of your Dear Brother with sentiments almost of veneration. They tell me that when his body was brought from where he died on its way to you, General Grant ordered the coffin to be opened that he might look upon the face of the gallant hero." Father Dunne's letter shows a human side of Grant that rarely appears in Civil War accounts.[43]

Quartermaster Sheridan had been with Colonel O'Meara when he died at 6:30 A.M. on the morning following the battle. He then had the difficult duty of returning the colonel's body to his family. Two days after the battle, he wrote to the colonel's brother, John: "It becomes my painful duty to pay to my late lamented Brave young colonel the last tribute of respect by forwarding his remains to you for burial with two Horses and two Valises all the property he possessed to my knowledge at the time of his death except a little box he used to keep a little refreshments in. This I thought unnecessary to send. I also kept his gilt tassel as a momento. His papers I destroyed as useless being all military matter." Sheridan sent O'Meara's "faithful orderly," Private Hugh O'Neil, Company C, to New York in charge of his body and his horses, adding that "the expenses were defrayed only as far as Nashville and this by special order of Maj. Gen. Grant. I hope in your distress of mind you will judge my conduct as lenient as possible. If I have not done as well as I ought I assure you it was because the means was not at my disposal." Sheridan expressed his grief at the loss of O'Meara. "Receive my sincere expression of sympathy for your loss and be assured there is not an officer of his grade in the U.S.A. died more wholly regretted by his Regiment or more universally —— by his superior officers from Gen. Grant to the Col. Commanding his Brigade. . . . Here in conclusion let me state for the consolation of your poor Mother that the Iron grey Horse 'Frank' was his favorite." Sheridan briefly described the circumstances of O'Meara's wounding and death, adding: "He received the last rights of his Church."[44]

O'Meara's body arrived in New York on December 15. His family declined the honors offered by the Common Council of New York City of a public funeral and that O'Meara's body lie in state in the Governor's Room. Instead, they chose a "Solemn Mass of Requiem" at St. Mary's Church on the following Saturday, December 19, followed by interment at Calvary Cemetery in Queens, New York. The tall marble monument marking Colonel O'Meara's gravesite stands near the large Civil War Soldiers Monument in that cemetery.[45]

The report of Lieutenant Colonel Owen Stuart's death in the December 1 issue of the *Chicago Post* understandably distressed Margaret Stuart's parents, the Camerons. The resulting gloom persisted throughout the day as friends called to express their sympathy until it suddenly dissipated with the arrival of a telegram from Owen Stuart himself informing Margaret of his wounding and instructing her to come immediately to Chattanooga by way of Nashville. A second dispatch contained a permit from General Grant for Margaret to go to Chattanooga; however, Margaret had already left on her way. Following the November 25 evening newspaper report of the wounding of Colonel O'Meara and Lieutenant Colonel Stuart, Margaret and the newly married Mrs. Captain David Duffy left Chicago on November 27, one year to the day of the departure of the 90th Illinois from Chicago. Anticipating the worst, they reached Nashville three days later, and from there Margaret proceeded to Chattanooga. Under the heading "Death of Colonel Owen Stuart," the December 3 *Chicago Post* proceeded to give his obituary while posthumously promoting him to colonel. The article stated that upon reaching Chattanooga, Mrs. Stuart received word that she had arrived too late, and she then set out to the field to obtain and bring home his body. Stuart would have understood Mark Twain's much later comment that "the report of my death was an exaggeration." Margaret eventually found her husband recovering in the field hospital from a severe gunshot wound through the loin and pelvis by a musket ball, which he retained as a souvenir. Upon returning to Chicago to convalesce,

Stuart, if he so chose, would have had the rare privilege of holding the minié ball that wounded him while reading glowing compliments from his obituary such as: "He was honorable, frank and manly, a devoted friend, and a generous hearted man in the fullest sense of the term."[46]

Margaret's December 7 telegram from Chattanooga somewhat reassured Captain Duffy's wife, as it implied he remained with the Legion: "The Lt. Col. is here and doing well, you had better go home as the regt. is not there." On December 21, Stuart was sent to the Officers' Hospital at Chattanooga, moved three days later to the General Field Hospital, Army of the Cumberland, at Bridgeport, Alabama, and then to the General Hospital at Nashville on Christmas Day. On December 27, accompanied by the regimental surgeon Henry Strong, Margaret, and the other wounded officers of the 90th Illinois, Stuart was admitted to Officer's General Hospital in Louisville, Kentucky. Discharged from that hospital on December 28 on "Surgeons Certificate of wounds received in battle," he received a twenty-day leave of absence. But even earlier, by December 24, Stuart had obviously recovered his sense of economics, if not his health, as he requested and received General Sherman's permission to take his two horses to Illinois at government expense.[47]

The 90th Illinois lost one officer killed in action, First Lieutenant James Conway of Company A. Colonel Loomis wrote that "Conway (of Freeport, Ill.) fell as the sun went down, kneeling as if at evening prayer. We found him as daylight broke, frozen stiff, but gracefully among the tall weeds, resting on his right knee and left wrist, his sword firmly grasped in his right hand, extended as at salute, his pistol in his left, his head bowed low. Peace to his gallant soul." First Sergeant Andrew Phinney replaced Conway as first lieutenant of Company A but was not officially mustered first lieutenant until February 27, 1864.[48]

At Chattanooga, Loomis's First Brigade had the honor, if it could be called that, of having the greatest loss of any brigade in the entire Army of the Tennessee, with 37 killed, 331 wounded, and 18 missing for a total of 386 casualties out of some 1,200 engaged. In contrast, in attacking Tunnel Hill, Corse's Second Brigade had 246 casualties, Raum's brigade had 204, and Matthies's brigade had 315 casualties.[49]

It had been the first battle in which the Irish Legion had a major role in an attack against an entrenched enemy position, and the regimental casualties list showed it. Now they truly were veterans. The surgeon of the 90th Illinois, Henry Strong, worked seventy-two hours dressing wounds and in the process wore out every other surgeon. In addition to the loss of Conway, the 90th Illinois had nine enlisted men killed; six officers, including O'Meara, who died of his wounds, and Stuart, severely wounded, and eighty-eight enlisted men reported as wounded; and thirteen missing, for an official total of 117 casualties, not quite one-third of the brigade's losses. Companies A, B, C, and G each had over twelve casualties. Company G had four killed, eight wounded, and one missing. Two soldiers from Minonk were casualties: Private James Ryan had been shot in the right leg, and Private Jeremiah Cullen was among those killed in action. Surgeon Strong wrote that the 90th Illinois had a greater number of casualties than officially reported: "Out of Three Hundred and Seventy enlisted men that rose from a bed of rocks after a fast of 24 hours & formed in line on the 25th of Nov. last I had at dark One Hundred & forty lying dead or wounded on the ground at a field Hospital as defiantly patriotic as ever & many contrary to my wishes marched to Knoxville with their wounds the next day." Private Alexander Moore, who had been wounded at the corral fence, was one of the unrecorded wounded of the 90th Illinois who made the physically taxing march to Knoxville and back. Possibly he and the twenty-two other unreported wounded members of the Legion considered their chances of survival to be greater outside the hospital than in it and thus failed to be included in the official count.[50]

Although long-range cannon fire received frequent mention in reports and descriptions of the battle by members of the brigade, the seventy-seven gunshot wounds reported greatly outnumbered the five reported wounds from shells. Of the ninety-four wounds reported for the 90th Illinois, the single bayonet wound indicates little close combat occurred.[51]

The number of officers and noncommissioned officers seriously wounded testified to the aim of the Confederate sharpshooters. In addition to Stuart, the wounded included Captain Michael W. Murphy, Company B; Captain Daniel O'Connor, Company D; and Captain William Cunningham, Company I. Twenty-year-old Sergeant Major Thomas R. Lonergan received a severe wound in the right hand resulting in his subsequent discharge due to disability. Quartermaster Sergeant Thomas McDonald, also twenty years old, replaced Lonergan as sergeant major. Three officers of the 90th Illinois—Captain Patrick Feeney, Company F; Lieutenant Patrick Campion, Company G; and Lieutenant Lawrence McCarthy, Company H—emerged from the battle under a cloud, being among seven officers in his brigade that Colonel Loomis felt compelled to mention in his report as "found out of place, in positions too doubtful to admit of explanation." There is no record of action taken against the three officers above the regimental level, and they continued to serve in their respective companies. Colonel O'Meara's death and the severe wounding of Lieutenant Colonel Stuart left the then-ranking officer, Captain Patrick Flynn (or, as he preferred, Major Flynn) in command of the regiment and eventually earned him his long-sought promotion to major to date from November 26, 1863.[52]

The large number of casualties suffered by the 90th Illinois at Missionary Ridge reduced the number of enlisted men present for duty from 325 on October 31 to 194 on November 30. Over the same period, the number of EM reported as absent sick, which included those wounded, increased from 62 to 163, while the number of officers present for duty decreased from twenty-two to eleven.[53]

The 90th Illinois fortunately had a skilled surgeon, Henry Strong. According to Woodruff, he was "regarded as a surgeon of superior skill and ability, one of the best in the 15th A.C., and kind and courteous as well as skillful." Under Strong's treatment, Captain Michael Murphy, Company B, amazingly survived "a severe gunshot wound of the abdomen, the ball passing through the spleen." Following treatment at officers' hospitals in Bridgeport, Alabama; Nashville, Tennessee; and Louisville, Kentucky; Murphy was granted a leave of absence on December 28 by General Sherman. Rather amazingly, Murphy eventually returned to the regiment, although a pension examiner later rated him one-half incapacitated for manual labor.[54]

By today's standards, the regiment's ninety-four official wounded and the fewer unofficial wounded received relatively primitive medical care. Fortunately, reliable descriptions of medical care during the Civil War and a soldier's chances of survival are available. The *Medical and Surgical History of the War of the Rebellion (1861–1865)* contains a description of the nature of the wound or illness, surgical or other procedure used, and outcome for large numbers of Union troops, including eighteen members of the 90th Illinois, ten of whom received gunshot wounds during the November 25, 1863, battle for Missionary Ridge. Six had arm wounds, which resulted in five amputations, and one "excision of the shaft of the ulna," which left the resulting arm and hand useless; however, all six survived to be discharged from the army. Five of the six were treated by the 90th Illinois's regimental surgeon, Strong.[55]

Lack of proper sanitation was a major problem affecting the health of soldiers in camp as well as in the hospital. Some soldiers considered confinement in a hospital the equivalent of a death sentence and something to be avoided if at all possible. Wagoner and soon-to-be Principal Musician and Bugler Patrick Sloan was one such soldier. On at least two occasions, he remained in his quarters although ordered to the hospital. He wrote his wife: "I fear an Hospital more than I do the battle field and I fear that as much as any one. And so long as I can keep out of one I will."[56]

What the men of the 90th Illinois thought of their day's work is not recorded, but it may have been similar to the opinion of Henry Robinson of the 100th Indiana, who wrote: "We retreated from the field, as we thought badly whipped for the day." Perhaps Colonel Reuben Williams of the 12th Indiana best summed up the brigade's attitude upon being ordered to return to the timber from which they had departed in the morning. He considered they had menaced the Confederates and served as a target for a sufficiently long time. Following the repulse of Loomis's brigade at Missionary Ridge, Williams, along with other brigade members, understandably endured what he termed a "dreary night." Weighed down by even heavier losses, the 90th Illinois, no doubt, did much the same. However, the survivors of the battle for Tunnel Hill had little time to recover from their experiences. News of General Bragg's retreat arrived at 10 P.M., and at daybreak the next day the remaining 225 or so officers and men of the Irish Legion marched in pursuit of Bragg's retreating forces. O'Meara had trained them well.[57]

{7}

THE WINTER OF THEIR DISCONTENT

On Thursday, November 26, 1863, officially the first national Thanksgiving Day by presidential proclamation, the men of the Irish Legion received their rations at 5:30 A.M. while immersed in a river bottom fog so impenetrable that figures remained indiscernible at a distance of six feet. Thankful mainly to still be alive, they made no recorded comment on the irony of the situation. Following breakfast, the four regiments of Colonel John M. Loomis's brigade, some 386 fewer than they had been twenty-four hours earlier, groped their way into line and at 6 A.M. backtracked through the fog to the mouth of Chickamauga Creek, where they crossed on a pontoon bridge. As they proceeded up its right (north) bank toward Chickamauga Station in pursuit of General Braxton Bragg's Army of Tennessee, the fog suddenly ended, and the 90th Illinois literally stepped into bright sunshine. Bragg's retreating army had attempted to destroy the large amount of abandoned supplies stored at the station to keep them out of Union hands. A Confederate soldier, Sam Watkins, a member of the 1st Tennessee Regiment charged with their destruction, commented on the immense stacks of flour barrels, corn, bacon, crackers, and other edibles "all now to be given to the flames." In contrast, Major General William T. Sherman commented mainly on the nature of the abandoned Confederate military equipment destroyed at Chickamauga Station. The 90th Illinois marched past the station and continued in a southeasterly direction, reaching Graysville, Georgia, about 2 P.M. on November 27, where they waited for the supply train to deliver their rations (see Map 5, in chapter 5; Map 7). On the same day, Major General Patrick Cleburne bloodily repulsed Major General Joseph Hooker's troops at Taylor's Ridge near Ringgold, ending the Union's pursuit of Bragg's army.[1]

After two carloads of General Hooker's wounded passed from Ringgold about 5 P.M. on November 28, Loomis's brigade destroyed three miles of the Western

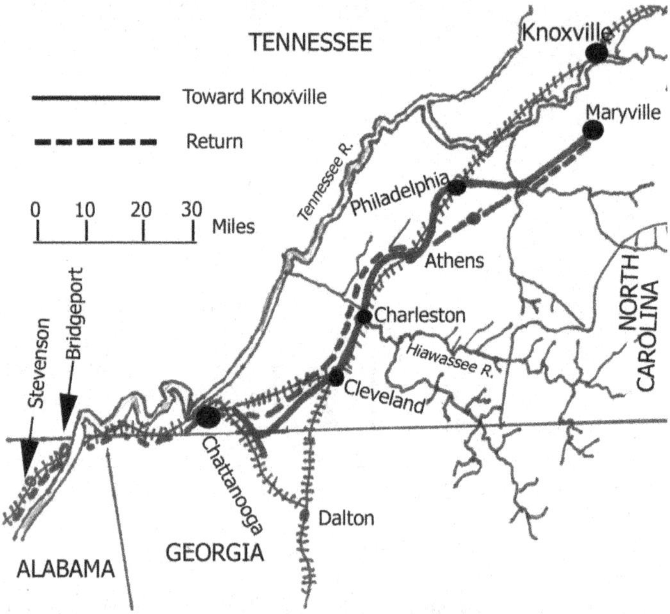

Map 7. March of the 90th Illinois during relief of Major General Ambrose E. Burnside at Knoxville, Tennessee

and Atlantic Railroad and burned two bridges over Chickamauga Creek before returning to Graysville and bivouacking for the night. Forage and food remained in short supply at Chattanooga, so Sherman sent back his artillery and wagons and marched his troops toward Cleveland and Charleston, Tennessee, where supplies could be obtained (see Map 7). After a twenty-five-mile march through Julien's Gap over difficult roads, the 90th Illinois reached Cleveland late at night on November 29 and bivouacked near the East Tennessee and Georgia Railroad. According to George Woodruff, the Irish Legion carried fence rails for more than a mile to build fires to "keep from freezing" in the bitter cold weather. The next day, after destroying part of the railroad, the 90th Illinois, along with the rest of Loomis's brigade, marched at the front of the division to the Hiawassee River at Charleston, where Sherman expected to find additional food and forage.[2]

There would be no time to rest for the 90th Illinois. Soon after reaching Charleston, Sherman received an order from Major General Ulysses S. Grant giving him command of troops moving to the relief of Major General Ambrose Burnside at Knoxville, Tennessee, some eighty-four miles away. Grant initially ordered Major General Gordon Granger with his IV Corps to relieve Burnside at Knoxville, but Granger's lack of progress caused Grant to place Sherman in charge of all troops moving to Burnside's relief. These included two divisions of the XV

Corps, Major General Oliver O. Howard's XI Corps, and General Granger's two divisions already underway toward Knoxville. The situation appeared critical as the Union forces under siege at Knoxville reportedly would run out of provisions on December 3.[3]

November 30 began what Woodruff called "that dreary march to the relief of General Burnside." It would be a difficult march for the Legion due to the lack of proper clothing, shelter, and food, the winter weather, and the troops' worn-out shoes. Only about half of the soldiers of the XV Corps had shoes. General Sherman admitted that his army was poorly prepared for the march to Knoxville. It had been a week since his troops left their camps and crossed the Tennessee River "with two days' rations, without a change of clothing, stripped for the fight, with but a single blanket or coat per man." The troops of the 90th Illinois could obtain provisions only by foraging, the military equivalent of the old frontier admonition "root hog or die."[4]

From Charleston, the 90th Illinois and Loomis's brigade advanced to Athens and Philadelphia, arriving on December 3 at the Little Tennessee River, opposite the small town of Morgantown, where Sherman's maps indicated a ford. They found the river three and a half feet deep, 240 yards wide, and quite swift, with an uneven bottom and a water temperature of 37 degrees. Ever resourceful, Brigadier General James Wilson, Sherman's chief engineer on the march, quickly built a bridge using locally available material (that is, the town). The men of the 90th Illinois did not wait for the bridge but ferried themselves across in a flatboat and camped a mile from the river. They arrived in Maryville, some fifteen miles from Knoxville, at 8 P.M. on December 5 at the head of the XV Corps. The previous night, Confederate lieutenant general James Longstreet's army had skedaddled to avoid contact with Sherman's relief force, ending the race to save Burnside.[5]

The Legion rested two days in Maryville, along with the rest of the XV Corps and Howard's corps. They had marched more than 100 miles from Chattanooga to Maryville (Company F claimed 120 miles), and now it had to be done in reverse. By this time, Sherman's troops had developed into pretty good scroungers. Company I of the 90th Illinois commented positively, almost cheerfully, on the food supply obtained during the march to Maryville: "Country fertile, grain and meal abundant." The food supply on the return march would be another matter.[6]

For the men of the Irish Legion, the return trip began on December 7 with Scottsboro, Alabama, as their final destination. They marched southwest through the Tellico valley, Madisonville, Athens, and Charleston, returning to Missionary Ridge on December 17 (see Map 7). The combination of bad and muddy roads; cold, rainy weather; an erratic food supply; a lack of tents; worn-out uniforms, blankets, and shoes (with many still barefoot); and the lack of a sense of urgency all made for a difficult march. The 90th Illinois troops had not had a change of shoes or clothing since they left their camp outside Vicksburg, almost exactly three months earlier, and their appearance showed it. Woodruff describes the ludicrous scene during a halt on the return march with the four regiments of the brigade, "one formed behind the other, and every man on his knees, or sitting, with his coat and shirt off; and many with their pants down, and all busy, taking advantage of the time allowed to rest, in destroying the vermin greybacks [lice], with which they were literally covered, the torture of which they could no longer endure." However, all was not misery as "the boys captured a fine lot of Linchburg tobacco . . . something they had not seen or used for a long time." Anyone that "used the weed" soon "forgot his suffering, and all moved on."[7]

The 90th Illinois reached Chattanooga on December 17, and, after marching in deep mud to reach the bridge over the mouth of Chickamauga Creek, the troops camped on the old Missionary Ridge battleground. Before leaving the next morning, some of the Legion looked around the area they had occupied during the battle and wondered how any had escaped from being slaughtered. An example of what they saw was recorded by Sergeant Eli Sherlock of the 100th Indiana: "Along the line occupied by the 100th Indiana, near the railroad track, between the old water tanks and the 90th Illinois on our left, there were spots of coagulated blood all along the short grass on the ground, and many holes were in the surface, where the plunging shells of the Confederates had entered the ground and exploded, leaving great holes."[8]

The next day, the Legion marched to Whiteside and crossed the Tennessee River to Bridgeport, Alabama, on the following day. On December 22 at Bridgeport, the men received pay for the months of September and October. They marched from Stevenson, Alabama, on December 24, reaching Scottsboro two days later. The 90th Illinois marched about 240 miles from Chattanooga to Maryville to Scottsboro. Combined with the march to Chattanooga, they had marched some 615 miles since leaving Memphis.[9]

Before reaching Scottsboro, the soldiers of the Irish Legion would have encountered some of General Hooker's eastern troops. Earlier in the war, each of the Union corps in the east adopted a badge that served as an identifying mark for the various units. The Union armies in the west had been slower to take such action. Of the several accounts purporting to describe how the XV Corps acquired its badge, about the only point of agreement is that the credit belongs to an Irishman. Woodruff's account, if not the most authentic, is certainly the most colorful.

> On the march, the Loomis brigade passed through a bivouac of the 11th army corps. It will be remembered that this corps with the 12th, had come from the Potomac army with Gen. Hooker. It will also be remembered that the record of the 11th army corps in the Chancellorsville fight, had been

an unfortunate one. Perhaps no stronger contrast could have been found in the army, than that presented by the Potomac boys, and the ragged, dirty, hungry 90th.

A soldier of the 90th—[Sergeant William] McGuffy, of Co. G—came straggling along by the headquarters of Gen. Butterfield. He was thinly and poorly clad; one foot was partly covered by an old army shoe, the other with an old blanket, tied on with strings, both feet cut and bleeding. He was plodding on, intent only upon overtaking his regiment, when he was halted by a sentinel in a clean uniform, paper collar, and trim rig, who said:

"Halt! What regiment is that?"

McG.—"The 90th Ill.—Irish Legion."

Sentinel—"What corps do you belong to?"

McG.—"Fifteenth."

Sentinel—"What's the badge of your corps?"

McG.—"Badge! What the blazes is that?"

Sentinel—"What do you wear to distinguish you from other troops? Our corps, the 11th wears a crescent—a half moon,—the 12th corps wears a star! What do you wear?"

McG. had halted, rested his chin upon the muzzle of his gun, and was taking a leisurely and contemptuous survey of the sleek and well dressed soldiers that were gathering around. Looking up at his interlocutor he says:

"Yes, I know what ye mane now; moon and stars! be jabbers! Ye needed them both to show ye the way back from Chancellorsville; badge is it!" and then executing a 'round about,' and giving his cartridge box a slap, "That's the badge of the 15th corps, forty rounds of cartridge!"[10]

Whatever version of the many iterations of the story is correct, the XV Corps commander, Major General John A. Logan, heard it and "thought it too good to be lost," according to Woodruff. A cartridge box marked "forty rounds" became the XV Corps badge as announced in Logan's General Orders No 10. Logan had replaced Major General Frank P. Blair as commander of the XV Corps on December 7, 1863. A lawyer and prominent Democratic politician in southern Illinois before the war, Logan was one of those rare species in the Civil War, a "War Democrat" politician who was also a capable general. When the war came, he raised a regiment, served under General Grant from the early battles of Belmont and Fort Donelson, and worked his way up the ladder to command a division in the Army of the Tennessee during the Vicksburg campaign. Over the winter and during the following spring and summer, the 90th Illinois would become better acquainted with "Black Jack," as he was known due to his swarthy complexion and coal-black hair. But first they needed some rest and relaxation in an Alabama winter camp. A few of the officers would even get leave to visit the folks back in Illinois.[11]

The 90th Illinois spent the winter in northern Alabama, where winter meant rain, and in 1863 rain meant mud and lots of it. For the next three months, the chorus "Mud, mud, glorious mud!" could have been the marching song of the Irish Legion. The four divisions of the XV Corps spread out along the railroad from Stevenson to Decatur, Alabama. In correspondence dated December 28, 1863, General Logan described the roads around Scottsboro, the Legion's location, as "almost impassible," and on January 4, 1864, he wrote, "The country roads are not in a condition to be used."[12]

With the troops still living in tents at Scottsboro on January 6, Adjutant Edwin Davis explained their lack of proper housing in a letter to his fellow printer, Lieutenant Colonel Owen Stuart, convalescing in Chicago: "It has either rained or been so cold it was impossible to do much work since we have been here, and having but few axes and other tools to work with (and they detailed to Brigade H.Q. nearly all the time) that we have not made very fast progress in fitting up winter quarters. We expect soon to get tools and then it will take but a few days to locate ourselves very comfortably." Davis commented that nearly all the regiment's officers had "good fireplaces in their tents, and the men are building them as fast as possible. I have a splendid one in my tent and am as comfortable as I could wish." Fireplace construction brought out the creative instincts of the troops, according to correspondent H. K. Smith: "The chimneys are surmounted by old barrels, boxes, or bits of stove pipe which they wear much as a New York rowdy wears his hat."[13]

Once in camp at Scottsboro, life for the 90th Illinois resumed a semblance of the normal order of days, and the regiment celebrated a Sunday Mass for the first time since leaving Camp Sherman outside Vicksburg. The Mass by Father Brady of the 15th Michigan took place in the morning with instructions and lecture in the afternoon. Patrick Sloan, now officially appointed Principal Musician and Bugler for the regiment, wrote of Father Brady, "He is a very fine man and is beloved by everyone that knows him. He often visits me, he being my nearest nei[gh]bor (the next tent to mine)." By January 11, the men of the 90th Illinois had constructed a comfortable camp. In a letter to his wife, Sloan described the process of creating their housing out of "very heavy timber. But we cut it all down and worked it into logs, boards, and shingles, &tc. for our houses and grubbed out all the stumps so the place looks pretty. Most all the houses are finished with fireplaces & chimneys so we will be pretty comfortable if we are allowed to stay here." They enjoyed their newly built houses exactly two more days. Under orders, they "struck tents" on January 13 and marched north some twelve miles through the mud to Fackler's Station on the Memphis and Charleston Railroad and began the process of constructing winter quarters all over again. Such was life in the army.[14]

In camp and firmly in command of the regiment, Major Patrick Flynn wasted no time before issuing a spate of general orders in an attempt to shape up his troops. He forbade leaving camp without papers countersigned by the brigade commander and held his officers "strictly accountable for the good conduct and discipline of their men." Straggling, random discharge of firearms, and "taking off accoutrements while on duty" were strictly forbidden. Order No. 3 on February 4 warned against straggling as "bands of guerillas and bushwhackers are in close proximity to this camp."[15]

Major Flynn also focused his attention on some unfinished business left over from the Battle of Missionary Ridge. On January 3, he prepared a list of "Charges and Specifications" against First Lieutenant Patrick Campion, Company G, for what he termed "Misbehaviour before the enemy" and "General Worthlessness," at the same time placing him under arrest and instructing him to deliver his sword to the adjutant. Flynn persisted in his attempt to have Fourth Division Headquarters file charges against three 90th Illinois officers: First Lieutenants Campion and Lawrence McCarthy and Captain Patrick Feeney, all "found out of place" during the Battle of Missionary Ridge. However, division headquarters failed to act, and all three remained in their positions with the regiment. To add insult to injury, McCarthy became a member of the brigade commander's staff. Flynn had greater success in reshuffling the noncommissioned officer ranks. He reduced two sergeants to the rank of private and promoted a private and corporal from his old Company A and a corporal from Company B to the rank of sergeant. He promoted Private James Cane, Company I, to sergeant and color sergeant of the regiment in recognition of his gallant and meritorious conduct. Sergeant Dennis Sullivan, Company C, and Corporal Henry Porter, Company C, also received praise for their actions at Missionary Ridge. Flynn replaced the regiment's sutler, or local camp vendor, with another of his choice. On January 8, Flynn, enjoying one of the privileges of his exalted rank of major, detailed private William Fitzgerald, Company A, as his cook.[16]

Somewhat understandably, Adjutant Davis eagerly awaited the return of his fellow printer, the lieutenant colonel, commenting in his January 6, 1864, letter to Owen Stuart: "The men have nearly all been fully clothed and blanketed, and only desire your presence to make them contented and satisfied." He added that the major was "running the machine heavy, and has a great opinion of his own abilities, much more, I am of the opinion, than any one would be willing to endorse for him. However, matters go as well as can be expected under the circumstances." Intending to encourage Stuart to speed up his return to the regiment, Davis added: "I believe he has opened correspondence with Adjutant General Fuller in regard to promotions to vacancies and intends having it arranged all to his own liking." Davis lamented the loss of "all my particular and intimate associates."[17]

Davis clearly preferred to have Stuart command the Legion; however, Stuart's recovery progressed slowly. On January 9, he remained confined to bed and unable to walk. An examining surgeon noted his "prospect of recovering so as to be fit for duty is distant and uncertain." But Davis's letter had the desired effect, spurring Stuart to action. In his January 27 letter to the Illinois adjutant general, Allan Fuller, Stuart spoke of his rapid recovery, indicating he hoped "soon to assume command of my Regt. 90th Illinois" and would very shortly furnish Fuller "with the names of those officers deserving promotion for their conduct in the field, in order to fill up the vacancies." Once again, Fuller received conflicting messages on promotion from the 90th Illinois. Flynn's promotion list apparently arrived before Stuart's, and Fuller promoted two sergeants selected by Flynn to the rank of second lieutenant. In another change, First Lieutenant John McAssey assumed command of Company I on February 4, replacing First Lieutenant Thomas Murray, assigned to three months' recruiting duty in Illinois. Stuart's estimate of the time required for his recovery was too optimistic, as on January 30 he received a twenty-day extension of his medical leave, and subsequent twenty-day extensions delayed his return to duty until mid-April. Stuart's loyalty to his regiment, his competition with Major Flynn over its command, and the urging by his friend Adjutant Davis secured his return to the Irish Legion.[18]

Fackler, Alabama, is located about ten miles north of Scottsboro, five miles south of Stevenson, and about two miles north of where the railroad crosses the prosaically named Mud Creek. Quartermaster Redmond Sheridan's letter to his brother contains his opinion of their location "between Stevenson and Bellefonte, Alabama. The Country around is very Swampy. I don't admire its Salubrity." He added ruefully, "But you know what I like amounts to." Things quickly settled into a routine with the regiment guarding bridges and trestle work, patrolling the railroad between Mud Creek Bridge and Stevenson, and sending occasional scouting parties into the adjacent country to search for guerrillas. According to Woodruff, Confederates "were just across the Tennessee river in strong force, and gave considerable annoyance by their constant raids on the railroad, and their many attempts to burn the bridges." Not all Confederates intended mischief, for by the end of January, from five to as many as thirty Confederate deserters daily surrendered to the brigade, according to Bugler Patrick Sloan. On April 11, a Confederate lieutenant and four privates surrendered to the 90th Illinois. Sloan wrote that the 90th Illinois sent out scouting parties "nearly every day picking up rebel deserters and chasing rebel cavalry who are sent out to hinder deserters from coming into our lines." The potential for attacks on the railroad remained, with an expected raid by Confederate cavalry causing the Legion to go on alert on February 27. The presence of Major Flynn's and Lieutenant McAssey's wives at Fackler's Station on April 3 may account for Flynn's high level of concern. Their presence was wryly noted by Sloan in a comment to his wife: "Wouldn't it be a devil of a Joke on them if a raid was made on the station while they were here and they had to tramp it through the mud with us."[19]

Flynn remained concerned and in early April reported in a letter to his new commanding officer, Brigadier General William Harrow, that "a party of 8 or 10 rebels, fully armed and equipped," had passed a local plantation and headed for the nearby mountain. Several local citizens had been robbed. Flynn sent a detachment "of 25 men to scout and reconnoiter at river crossings," but they found nothing. Another scout also failed to yield results. However, a "personal reconnaissance" convinced Flynn "that rebels—bushwhackers—are prowling around my camp." He thought they were crossing the Tennessee River "at the North end of Bellefonte Island." The letter came back with Harrow's cryptic instructions: "Maj. Keep close watch on guerrillas and shoot any one you take."[20]

Bugler Sloan wrote that on January 30, the Legion was "highly gratified . . . by six orders read to us containing the Thanks, Praise and Congratulations of the President" and Generals Grant, Sherman, Logan, and Ewing "for our conduct, bravery, & heroism at the Victory of Chattanooga and a very feeling address from Gen. Burnside on behalf of his men giving us great praise and thanks for our rapid and successful March against Longstreet . . . at Knoxville. It partly repays us for the hardships, privations and suffering that we endured. It does a soldier a great deal of good to have his Merits acknowledged by his Comd'g Gen'l."[21]

At dress parade on February 20, the men of the Irish Legion heard an order from General Grant authorizing them to inscribe the names "Coldwater," "Vicksburg," and "Jackson" on their regimental banner. This honor resulted from the "claim for services rendered" by the 90th Illinois, submitted nearly seven months earlier by Colonel Timothy O'Meara and, in a sense, his legacy to the regiment. Official recognition of the Legion's action at Missionary Ridge and in the relief of Knoxville would also be received in due time. The troops' response to official recognition of their past service is indicated by Sloan's reaction that Coldwater, Vicksburg, and Jackson, combined with Missionary Ridge and Knoxville, "will be considerable Glory for us [to have achieved] in 18 months." He then added: "and 300 men ready for the next fight."[22]

As the war progressed, comradeship, the desire to see the war to its conclusion, and a sense of duty and of obligation to their fellow soldiers of the 90th Illinois served as motivating factors for individual officers and men of the Irish Legion, sentiments that each would express in his own unique way. Although longing for his wife's company and unhappily complaining of "leading this miserable life" at Fackler's Station, Sloan wrote "that [in] enlisting I done a good act for myself and family."[23]

As in northern Mississippi, members of the 90th Illinois interacted with local inhabitants in several ways. Both Union and Confederate troops who previously occupied the area had supplemented their rations at the expense of local farmers, and the Legion logically continued the practice. One local farmer, whose farm lay within a mile and a half of the Legion's camp at Fackler's Station, filed a postwar claim for reimbursement from the government, asking for $105 for fifteen head of hogs taken by the 90th Illinois sometime in early 1864. At that time, he had complained to Major Flynn, who responded that "he did not allow his men to kill hogs."[24]

The alternate occupation of the area by Union and Confederate armies brought many of the citizens to a state of destitution. According to Sloan, "The inhabitants that come in and take the oath [of allegiance to the Union] can draw subsistence out of our commissary the same as we do and a great many do so and as the country is foraged and pilfered by both armies. They have to take the oath so as to draw their grub or else Leave." The low value of Confederate currency caused problems for the local citizens. Sloan included some Confederate bills in a letter to his wife: "It is worthless every where or I can buy all I want of it at from 7 to 10 cents on the dollar and I can get plenty of it for nothing. The inhabitants will give a dollar of it for every half teaspoon of either tea or coffee or a hat full of it for a pound of either of them."[25]

By January 1864, due to the loss of company officers through resignation, promotion, and battle wounds, only four Companies, C, E, F, and G, were commanded by captains. First lieutenants commanded Companies B, D, H, I, and K, while a second lieutenant commanded Company A. Company officers on leave due to wounds suffered at Chattanooga included Lieutenant John Harrington (Company C) and three captains, Michael Murphy (Company B), Daniel O'Connor (Company D), and William Cunningham (Company I). First Lieutenant John McAssey, on detached duty as acting provost marshal of Loomis's First Brigade since mid-November 1863, pleaded his case for promotion to both Colonel Loomis and Illinois adjutant general Fuller. The Legion also lost the services of Assistant Surgeon Darwin Hinckley, who was discharged at Scottsboro, Alabama, on February 13 due to health problems, leaving the Legion without a second assistant surgeon.[26]

The regimental numbers showed the effects of the 1863 campaigns. The January 1864 report lists only 225 enlisted men present for duty, while the aggregate total of 450 officers and enlisted men was some 245 less than a year earlier. Some 122 enlisted men were sick, of which 63 had been wounded at Chattanooga on November 25, 1863, with the rest scattered about in various army hospitals. Some twenty-seven enlisted men of the regiment remained on detached duty to brigade, division, and corps headquarters with one lucky private attached to General Sherman's headquarters. Ten enlisted men were listed as absent without leave. Bugler Sloan detected an increase in numbers in the Legion due to the return of sick and wounded and of deserters who had been caught and returned so that the Legion "begins to look like a Regt. instead of a Company." In February, fifteen enlisted men who had returned from desertion were restored to duty. Also in early February, a first sergeant and a first lieutenant were detached on recruiting duty in Illinois. However, at this time of the war, recruits were hard to find, and the Legion would add few to their numbers.[27]

Rail traffic flowed erratically on the railroad from Scottsboro past Fackler's Station to Stevenson. In a January 4, 1864, communication to General Grant's headquarters in Chattanooga, General Logan protested its undependability and poor service: "My quartermaster can never get satisfaction. . . . The railroad would be of little use were it not that we are able to push cars on the track by hand." After assuming command of the Military Division of the Mississippi on March 18, 1864, Sherman also took command of the railroads, and service improved somewhat. However, shortages persisted, as shown by a March 20 letter from Captain Charles Wills, 103rd Illinois, stationed at Scottsboro, in which Wills expressed some ambiguity as to who controlled the railroad: "'Our' railroad from Nashville via Decatur is about completed (will be finished tomorrow) and then we hope to have something to eat once more."[28]

Whether the 90th Illinois ever went without rations during the winter is not recorded, but by the spring of 1864, some of the troops likely suffered from a mild form of scurvy as few if any vegetables had been issued to the three divisions guarding the railroad between Huntsville and Stevenson, Alabama, which of course included Fackler. The medical inspector, Lieutenant Colonel E. D. Kittoe, commented on the health of the soldiers guarding the railroad: "For more than four months on short rations, but poorly housed and badly clothed, with no appreciable variation in diet, scurvy naturally prevailed to some extent in most regiments; in all a marked tendency to this disease was observable." Some members of the 90th Illinois received packages from home, but these were more likely to contain creature comforts such as cigars and whiskey than effective antiscorbutics unless such had been specifically requested. Whatever the deficiencies of their fare, the government's coffee ration remained highly regarded by the troops as a stimulant that enlivened them when worn out. Colonel Reuben Williams affirmed that "good strong coffee" did more to sustain a soldier during a march and to allow him to continue doing hard work than anything else he ate or drank.[29]

On February 8, 1864, the division received a new commander, Brigadier General William Harrow, from the II Corps of the Army of the Potomac and a veteran of Antietam and Gettysburg. Being from the Army of the Potomac was not necessarily in his favor, as western soldiers tended to be prejudiced against that army. A staunch Republican and an Indiana lawyer, Harrow had traveled the Eighth Judicial Circuit in Illinois with Lincoln earlier in his career. He knew something about how volunteer regiments behaved, having started as a captain in the 14th Indiana and worked his way up the ladder of promotion. The level of discipline shown by the troops in his new command did not impress Harrow, who considered them "an awful unruly lot." His attempts to instill discipline by methods common to the Army of the Potomac met strong resistance, proving an officer needed a pretty good sense of humor to command soldiers in the western army.[30]

In his March 2 letter, Quartermaster Sheridan commented to his brother on the state of the regiment and Owen Stuart's health: "We number 320 men for duty our aggregate is 450 we have no Colonel and under conscription act are not entitled to one. Our Lt. Col. who was Seriously wounded at the ridge is fast recovering he insists he will rejoin the Regmt but I differ with him I think he has led the Regmt for the last time in the field." Stuart would prove Sheridan wrong and return in time for the spring campaign. Captain Murphy, Company B, also planned to return to the company he had recruited and wrote Stuart on March 4, 1864, to inquire of his plans for "taking your departure for 'Dixie.'" Murphy admitted he still had "considerable soreness in my back. Rather too much to do duty yet. But I have got tired of civil life so will return to barbarism." Stuart also received a letter from Confederate captain Christopher Sherwin, a prisoner of war at Johnson's Island Barracks in Sandusky Bay on Lake Erie, who had learned from his parents of Stuart's wounding. He wrote: "When I say to you that I was very sorry indeed to hear it, it does not express half my sympathy or Sorrow for you. I have not now nor never can forget your many acts of kindness in days gone by. It is true this great national difficulty has placed us in arms & in opposing battle lines making us public enemies but I can see no reason why we should be personal enemies. For my part I still retain the same feelings of friendship & respect for you as in days of old." The letter concluded with a wish: "Hoping that this will find you able & strong enough to visit your old friends & that trouble and sorrow may ever be kept from your hearth shall ever be the wish of your old friend." The war had a strange way of reuniting old friends.[31]

Whether due to or in spite of their food and housing, the Legion slowly gained numbers, and by the end of April had 328 enlisted men present with 285 reported as present for duty. The difference of forty-three reflected the thirty-five on extra or daily duty, seven sick, and one under arrest. Even though the number of absent sick officers and men declined to sixty-five and some detached troops returned, the total aggregate officers and enlisted men continued its inexorable decline to 428. First Lieutenant Andrew Phinney from Company A temporarily commanded Company C as Captain Patrick O'Marah had been sick and on leave of absence since March 8. O'Marah's continued poor health lead to his discharge on June 15, 1864. Considering himself again fit for duty, Captain Peter Casey returned to his company March 20, but army paperwork dismissing him from the service effective January 11, 1864, finally caught up with him on April 25, ending his army career.[32]

While at Fackler, an unspecified number of the Irish Legion demonstrated their support of Irish Nationalism and the Fenian cause by sending $507 to the "Irish National Fair" to be held in Chicago on March 28 along with the statement: "The heartfelt wish of the Irish Legion is with every attempt that is or may be made to forward the work of regeneration in poor, downtrodden Ireland, when that work aims at the total overthrow and complete annihilation of British rule, that has cursed the sacred soil of our fathers for seven long centuries." Company F sent an additional $70 and warmly approved the stated objectives. Clearly the Irish Legion still had Fenians in the ranks, or at least a number who retained strong Fenian sympathies.[33]

However strong remained the ties of many in the regiment to old Ireland, the war had profoundly weakened their traditional loyalty to the Democratic Party for some, and probably many. News from home of violent Copperhead activity in two southern Illinois counties thoroughly infuriated Patrick Sloan. At Charleston, Illinois, in late March, a Copperhead mob had killed one officer and five soldiers of the 54th Illinois and wounded six other soldiers. Sloan wrote his wife: "I for one feel this morning as though I wanted to shoot a copperhead. This might have been a copperhead Regt. when it came out but I am sure its not one now and if this kind of Work continues at home I believe this Regt. will return a republican Regt. that will be eager to have every copperhead in the State Stretch a piece of rope from the limbs of a tree." Sloan blamed Copperheads for lengthening the war: "If it were not for the copperhead sympathy that the rebs receive and expect, this war would now be over and we would all be home instead of here in suffering & Hardship."[34]

In a letter to his uncle back in Illinois, Captain Patrick Feeney, Company F, similarly expressed his and, he believed, the army's lack of sympathy with "Copperheads," writing that "we believe in a thorough prosecution and speedy termination of this unholy warfare." He acknowledged slavery to be the cause of the war. They—he and the army—now favored the reelection of President Lincoln as it would "hasten the end of the war," and they "believe him to be honest and not to have ambitious views." This was quite a change for a man the *Chicago Tribune* considered to have been an influential Democratic politician before he joined the Legion.[35]

Spring came late to northern Alabama in 1864 due to an excess of cold, wet weather, including a foot of snow on March 22, which fortunately disappeared within two days. According to Captain Charles Wills, spring finally arrived in Scottsboro on April 22. A little farther north at Fackler, the 90th Illinois presumably enjoyed the scene described by Wills: "In the valleys, the poplars, the beeches and the black gums are nearly in full spring dress." He added, "Of the smaller trees the dogwood leads in assuming a spring costume." The troops of the 90th Illinois may not have been aware of the fact that they were enjoying, all at government expense, what General Sherman considered to be "one of the most beautiful parts of the United States," to quote Lee Kennett. In 1844, Sherman had spent time at the nearby town of Bellefonte, Alabama, and had been so attracted by the natural beauty of its surroundings and friendliness of the people that he later wrote his wife-to-be, Ellen, proposing they live in northern Alabama.[36]

The Irish Legion would not have much more time to enjoy the beauty of spring at Fackler as by April 28 they received orders to pack knapsacks and be prepared to move immediately. The Union's 1864 spring campaign had begun.[37]

{8}

THE ATLANTA CAMPAIGN: APPROACH TO ATLANTA

Along with the arrival of spring in northern Georgia came the renewal of active campaigning. The 298 officers and men of the Irish Legion, including those recovered from their wounds sustained at Missionary Ridge and returned to duty, found a number of changes in both the Union and the Confederate armies' command structures. General Joseph E. Johnston now commanded the Confederate Army of Tennessee. Ulysses S. Grant's promotion to lieutenant general and command of all Union armies produced a virtual cascade of command changes. Major General William T. Sherman replaced Grant in charge of the Military Division of the Mississippi, elevating Major General James B. McPherson to command of the Department and Army of the Tennessee and Major General John A. Logan to command of the XV Corps. What Logan thought of the Irish Legion is not recorded, but his biographer, James Pickett Jones, describes the XV Corps as "mischievous men" and "a colorful collection of western veterans," including the "rowdy Irishmen from the streets of Chicago." This probably referred to the Irish Legion, the only Irish regiment in the XV Corps.[1]

Lieutenant Colonel Owen Stuart, sufficiently recovered from his wound suffered at Missionary Ridge to return to the field, now commanded those Irish rowdies, much to the relief of his friend, Adjutant Edwin Davis. Colonel Reuben Williams of the 12th Indiana now commanded the First Brigade of the Fourth Division. The brigade's old commander, Colonel John Loomis, left the army after three arduous years of service, due in part to severe financial losses by his lumber business back in Chicago while he was in the service. Taking leave of their old commander who had led them at Vicksburg and Jackson and through the frustrating trial by fire at Missionary Ridge understandably became an emotionally touching event for both the men of the brigade and Loomis. Stuart described their final meeting: "Colonel Loomis, who feelingly took farewell of his old command; the kindest feelings of the regiment accompanied him." Williams also liked Loomis and described his parting from his troops as "quite affecting." As Loomis prepared to leave, "tears ran down the cheeks of the kind-hearted and thoroughly loyal old man as he shook hands with his fellow officers and bade them good-bye."[2]

An extrovert, Williams, the new brigade commander, promoted a convivial atmosphere with his brigade staff: "It was pretty well understood that when not on active duty my headquarters was generally a sociable and often a merry place." This may explain why he, a staunch Republican, got along so well with his fellow soldiers, and thorough Democrats, of what he called the "Ninetieth Ireland." A newspaper editor before and after the war, Williams wrote a series of accounts some forty years after the war that demonstrate his skill as a writer and provide a wealth of details to supplement his brief official reports. Upon assuming command of the brigade, he had already been captured and exchanged three times, often enough to have caused a moment of reflection by those of the 90th Illinois aware of that fact. The XV Corps now had only three divisions: the First Division, commanded by Brigadier General Peter Osterhaus; the Second Division, commanded by Brigadier General Morgan L. Smith; and the Fourth Division, to which the 90th Illinois belonged, commanded by Brigadier General William Harrow.[3]

By this time, the individual soldier of the 90th Illinois could be relied upon to appropriately equip himself for the coming campaign. The veteran reduced his equipment to the basics required for battle and survival: rifle, bayonet, cartridge box and cap pouch, canteen and tin cup, some container for cooking and to boil coffee, haversack and knapsack, blanket and shelter half, rubber sheet that could be worn as a poncho, and socks and underwear, according to historian Albert Castel. Many western troops wore a broad-brimmed hat, a much more practical headgear than the regulation kepi. The woolen uniform, when wet, combined with this amount of equipment created a heavy load for a soldier of the Legion to carry, especially when slogging along a muddy road in the heat and humidity of a Georgia summer.[4]

Possession of Chattanooga by the Union opened an invasion route into northwestern Georgia and the Confederacy's important transportation, supply, and manufacturing center of Atlanta. General Sherman knew the "Gate City" to be "too important a place in the hands of the enemy to be left undisturbed, with its magazines, stores, arsenals, workshops, foundries &c, and more especially its railroads, which converged from the four great cardinal points." Atlanta's railroad lines ran to Chattanooga, Tennessee; Macon and Augusta, Georgia; and Montgomery, Alabama. Obviously, the Confederacy would exert maximum effort to defend Atlanta.[5]

While the 90th Illinois rebuilt its strength at Fackler, Grant and Sherman together worked out the strategy for campaigns in 1864. Grant would see to it that the Army of the Potomac occupied the undivided attention of Confederate general Robert E. Lee, preventing him from sending troops elsewhere, and would attempt to defeat his Army of Northern Virginia. Meanwhile, Sherman would endeavor to do likewise to Confederate general Johnston and his Army of Tennessee and in the process devastate the Confederate heartland. Grant instructed Sherman "to move against Johnston's army, to break it up, and to get into the interior of the enemy's country as far as you can, inflicting all the damage you can against their war resources." Grant emphasized the destruction of Johnston's army with lesser attention paid to the destruction of Confederate resources. Fortunately for the soldiers of the Legion, Sherman chose to interpret Grant's instructions rather loosely, as their casualty list would likely have been much longer had he closely followed Grant's objective of destroying Johnston's Army of Tennessee.[6]

The campaign in Georgia would be a railroad war since only the railroad could transport the mass of supplies required by Sherman's more than 93,000 infantry, 12,000 cavalry, and 4,500 artillery officers and men as they advanced toward Atlanta. Of necessity, Sherman's southern incursion from Chattanooga advanced along the Western and Atlantic Railroad to Atlanta. The route of the XV Corps never extended more than twenty miles from the railroad during the advance on Atlanta (Maps 8 and 9). In order to provision his army adequately, Sherman restricted railroad transport to the movement of supplies only, cut off all civilian traffic, and required that beef cattle be driven on the hoof and that all troops other than train guards march rather than ride the railroad. From past experience, Sherman knew the vulnerability of his extended supply line and prepared accordingly for the inevitable interruptions. He recognized that "success might involve the necessity even of dropping all wagons, and to subsist on the chance food which the country was known to contain." He "had obtained not only the United States census-tables of 1860, but a compilation made by the Controller of the State of Georgia for the purpose of taxation, containing in considerable detail the 'population and statistics' of every county in Georgia." Sherman planned for the army to live off the country if necessary; the men of the 90th Illinois could be sure that they would not starve.[7]

General Johnston prepared a series of strong defensive positions along the obvious invasion route leading to Atlanta. The first of these, near Dalton at aptly named Rocky Face Ridge and Buzzards Roost, located a little over twenty-five miles southeast of Chattanooga, virtually defied attack. Fortunately for Sherman, Major General George Thomas knew the territory. Thomas proposed dislodging Johnston by moving his Army of the Cumberland south around the Confederate left flank and through the mountain barrier at Snake Creek Gap to cut Johnston's railroad supply line at Resaca, Georgia, about fifteen miles south of Johnston's fortified

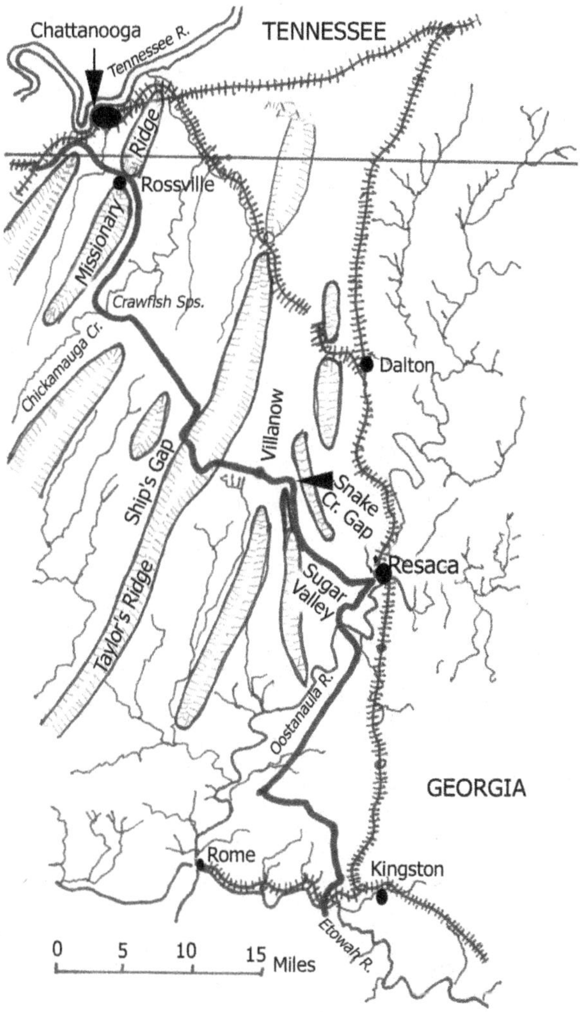

Map 8. Atlanta campaign: route of the 90th Illinois from Chattanooga to Etowah River

position around Dalton. If properly executed, such a move could spell disaster for Johnston's army, ending the campaign then and there. The 90th Illinois became involved because Sherman modified Thomas's plan, sending the much smaller Union Army of the Tennessee through undefended Snake Creek Gap to break the railroad at Resaca (see Map 8). The gap itself is about six miles in length, narrow in places, with steeply sloping, rocky side ridges. The execution of Thomas's plan, as modified by Sherman, brought on the Battle of Resaca.[8]

Map 9. Atlanta campaign: route of the 90th Illinois from May 23 to July 21, 1864

The concentration of the XV Corps near Chattanooga signaled the start of the Atlanta campaign and a return to war for the Irish Legion. The men broke camp and marched from Fackler's Station at 11 A.M. on May 1. That night, they bivouacked on a plantation within three miles of Stevenson, Alabama. The Legion marched at 8 A.M. the next day, but bad roads and high streams slowed the troops' movement as the winter weather and heavy traffic had not improved the wagon road to Chattanooga, which more or less paralleled the railroad from Stevenson to Bridgeport before it crossed the Tennessee River and continued east to Chattanooga. After joining their brigade at 10 A.M. on May 2, they took their final leave of their old brigade commander, Colonel Loomis, before camping at Crow Creek at noon, after marching only two miles. They made up for it the next day, with reveille at 3 A.M. followed by a march of thirteen miles, including crossing the Tennessee River at Bridgeport, before camping two miles beyond the river. At some point during the day, the Legion regained an officer when newlywed Second Lieutenant William White, detailed to the Signal Corps since January 24, 1863, returned to the 90th Illinois, possibly out of a sense of duty to the men of Company F he had led from Springfield to join the Legion. He arrived just in time to march with the Legion for twelve miles on a rough, mountainous road to Whiteside Station. The Legion took position in the rear of the Fourth Division at 10 A.M. on May 5 and marched across the foot of Lookout Mountain before turning south to camp near Rossville, Georgia, where the men sent tents and baggage to the rear. Being veterans, they knew things would get serious before long. While in camp at Rossville, Colonel Reuben Williams and his aide-de-camp, Lieutenant Lawrence McCarthy of the Irish Legion, climbed Missionary Ridge near what had been General Braxton Bragg's headquarters and marveled at the formidable nature of the Confederate position.[9]

The Irish Legion's march to Resaca shows that the phrase "Hurry up and wait" applied to moving troops in the Civil War just as in other conflicts. At Rossville, the Legion crossed to the east side of Missionary Ridge (see Map 8). At 10 A.M. on May 6, the troops marched south through Chattanooga Valley and bivouacked near Crawfish Springs on the west side of West Chickamauga Creek. The next day, the men marched at 8 A.M., crossing West Chickamauga Creek at Glass' Mill, but halted two hours later to wait for the XVI Army Corps and the Second Division of their own XV Corps to pass before resuming their march, which lasted until 11:30 P.M. On May 8, supply trains blocked the road, delaying the Legion's start until noon. Once on the road, the troops crossed Taylor's Ridge at 6 P.M. and bivouacked in Chestnut Valley. The 90th Illinois and Colonel Williams both reported crossing Taylor's Ridge at Ship's Gap, which conflicts with General Logan's report that the XV Corps crossed at Gordon Springs Gap some four miles to the northeast of Ship's Gap. Whichever route the 90th Illinois followed, on May 9 the Legion prepared to march at 4 A.M. but instead remained more or less in place, guarding a mountain pass until 9 A.M. when the troops marched to guard another "important" pass, presumably gaps on Taylor's Ridge, and bivouacked at noon. Roused at midnight, they rejoined their brigade only to countermarch at 8 A.M. to the position they occupied the night before.[10]

While the 90th Illinois rushed to and fro, the rest of Williams's brigade joined a brigade of the XVI Corps at the northwest entrance to Snake Creek Gap, where they guarded the bulk of the XV and XVI Corps' wagons and baggage while the two corps, minus impedimenta, passed through the gap on May 9. Once through the gap, the two Union corps failed to break the railroad at Resaca on May 9 and pulled back to a defensive position protecting their access to the gap. The failure to break the railroad at Resaca doomed Sherman's planned envelopment of Johnston's army, but by May 13 the Confederates abandoned their defenses about Dalton and prepared to defend Resaca.[11]

Soon after 5 A.M. on May 10, Colonel Williams began moving the XV Corps' wagons through the gap. The 90th Illinois men remained at their position on Taylor's Ridge until 4 P.M. on May 10, when they marched eight miles in a southeasterly direction through Villanow and Snake Creek Gap to Sugar Valley and rejoined their brigade. This late start guaranteed that instead of leading, the 90th Illinois marched through Snake Creek Gap in the wake of virtually all the animals of one and probably two army corps. Sometime during the evening, the rain poured down, adding to their travel woes. Such are the fortunes of war.[12]

On the evening of May 10, Colonel Williams secured lodging for his staff at the southern mouth of the gap in a nearby house, safely out of the rain. Williams remembered it as one of those "convivial" evenings, beginning with an excellent meal prepared by his "splendid" Paris-trained French cook, Private Theodore Susan, Company I, 90th Illinois, who lived up to his reputation of creating "really palatable dishes out of the most meager supplies." As the night progressed, things got more interesting with the discovery of six Confederate uniforms and three old large-caliber muskets in an adjoining room and closet. The house's lower floor soon became a "scene of merry-making. Larry McCarty of the 'Ninetieth Ireland' being a splendid singer" led off "with one of the late patriotic songs." Others donned Confederate uniforms and joined in "about one o'clock, and while Larry McCarty, who had a great number of songs at his command, was in the midst of a rollicking Irish ditty . . . a heavy knock came at the front door" interrupting the festivities. One of General Logan's staff officers entered and asked for Colonel Williams. When he finally recognized Williams, unexpectedly clad in Confederate gray, he laughed so hard he could hardly deliver his message. Leaving some ham and a plentiful supply of hardtack for the occupants of the house, Williams, who "was always willing to give away hard-tack," now back in Union blue and none the worse for the night's festivities, had the brigade ready to move out as ordered early on the next day.[13]

The 90th Illinois, along with the rest of Williams's brigade, did not go far as the XV Corps retreated back toward the mouth of Snake Creek Gap and formed a new defensive line on the left of the Resaca road. On May 11 and 12, the men of the Legion continued their back-and-forth movements. On May 11, they marched one mile and a half south to the junction of Snake Creek Gap and Sugar Valley, where they, along with the rest of the Fourth Division, firmly entrenched a position by nightfall. The next day the Legion advanced half a mile to the head of Snake Creek Gap and formed line of battle. Stuart reported that about 5 P.M., "General Sherman visited the position on a tour of inspection," apparently checking things out before the next day's advance on Resaca.[14]

Things got serious on May 13. After sending their knapsacks to the rear as ordered by General Logan, the men of the Legion went into battle "in light fighting trim, carrying their haversacks with three days' cooked rations, canteens filled, and one blanket rolled in their poncho and slung across the shoulder." Still suffering from the effects of his wound, Lieutenant Colonel Stuart turned over command of the Legion to Major Patrick Flynn. At 7 A.M., the troops left their camp at the mouth of Snake Creek Gap and marched eastward some four miles on the Resaca road to a crossroads about two miles west of Resaca. There they joined with the other regiments of Williams's First Brigade and formed facing east on the left or north side of the First Division, which straddled the Resaca road. This move placed Williams's brigade on the extreme left of the XV Corps line, where Williams's men connected with XVI Corps troops on their left. The Fourth Division's Second and Third Brigades remained in reserve behind the line. The 12th Indiana occupied the center of the brigade line with the 26th Illinois on its left and the 90th Illinois on the right. The 100th Indiana, at first held in reserve, moved to the First Division's left during the advance and conformed its movements to those of the First Division. Each regiment deployed a heavy line of skirmishers in front. The advance sounded about 1 P.M., and the line of battle moved forward against light resistance, with a few shots from Confederate batteries mixed in but doing little harm. The Legion advanced, along with the rest of Williams's brigade, over what General Logan described as "broken and irregular ground, with heavy growths of timber and underbrush, with occasional small cleared fields." After advancing three-quarters of a mile, they reached the edge of the timber and halted. To their front and left, they found Confederate infantry in rifle pits and behind small barricades on a ridge of hills that fringed the west side Camp Creek. After strengthening their skirmish lines and moving by their left flank for half a mile or more, the men of the brigade reformed their lines and advanced into and through woods and underbrush along the base of the occupied ridge of hills. This brought on a hot exchange of musketry with Confederates dug in on the ridge, which lasted, according to the 90th Illinois, for one hour and a half, until 6 P.M. By that time, Williams's soldiers had used up their ammunition, and the Second Brigade relieved them. At the close of the day, the XV Corps occupied the disputed hills bordering Camp Creek, a half mile or so from the main Confederate defenses east of Camp Creek.[15]

For the troops of the First Brigade, including the 90th Illinois, their part of the battle had nearly ended as they remained in reserve of the Fourth Division until 8 P.M. on May 14, when they moved to support of the Second Division where they suffered a few wounded. During the fighting on May 13 and 14, the 90th Illinois had 19 wounded, 2 mortally, while the First Brigade lost 15 killed, 106 wounded, and 3 missing, a total of 124 casualties, indicative of the intensity of the combat.[16]

None of the major Union attacks on Confederate prepared positions succeeded at Resaca except for the capture on May 14 of a series of low hills extending north from the Oostanaula River by XV Corps troops. Possession of these hills placed the vital Resaca railroad bridge in range of Union cannon. Also on May 14, at Lay's Ferry, five miles southwest of Resaca, Brigadier General Thomas Sweeny's Union forces threatened Confederate communications. A one-armed Mexican War veteran who had already been wounded twice in the current war, Sweeny sent his troops across to the south (Confederate) side of the Oostanaula River but immediately retreated back to the north shore; the next day, his men re-crossed the river to stay. Although the Union failed to exploit either opportunity, the dual threats to his communications caused General Johnston to abandon Resaca. His army quietly retreated south of the Oostanaula during the night of May 15, and on the next day the pursuit began. Again and again on the way to Atlanta, Sherman would use the pattern developed at Resaca: holding the Confederates in their defensive position with the Army of the Cumberland and maneuvering around the Confederates' flank with the Army of the Tennessee or the Army of the Ohio. It became something of a ritualized military dance with variations.[17]

At Resaca, the three hospitals of the XV Corps, located about a mile in rear of the battle line, received 794 wounded during the battle. One of the wounded, recently promoted Corporal Simon Swan, Company G, had been shot in the left forearm while on the skirmish line. His Civil War Carded Medical Record reads "flesh wound left forearm" by a "musket ball." The card lists his treatment as a "water dressing" and his condition as "convalescent." After three weeks, Simon returned to his regiment, having survived both the battle and the hospital stay. At Resaca, the wounded received prompt medical care by Civil War standards. The medical director of the Army of the Tennessee, Surgeon John Moore, commented that the uneven ground "offered protection to the ambulances very near to the front, and the stretcher-bearers were so prompt in bearing off the wounded, that there were very few instances of men remaining on the field more than an hour or two after being wounded." The wounded "were laid on very comfortable beds, made by strewing the tents thickly with pine leaves, and spreading blankets over these." Such extemporized facilities avoided some risks of disease transmission found in more permanent facilities.[18]

At 11 A.M. on May 16, 1864, the Fourth Division, including the First Brigade with the Irish Legion, began the pursuit of General Johnston's Army of Tennessee, going by way of Kingston and Van Wert to Dallas, where they arrived on May 26 (see Maps 8 and 9). Lieutenant Colonel Stuart described the high points of the march for the 90th Illinois, now numbering some nineteen fewer than before Resaca. The men crossed the Oostanaula River at Lay's Ferry, about four miles west of Resaca, and "continued the march, via Adairsville and Woodlawn plantation, to Kingston, arriving May 20, in rear of wagon trains of the Fifteenth Army Corps." After resting three days at Kingston, they marched to the Etowah River and crossed about five miles west of Kingston. While at Kingston, William White had something to celebrate, as he mustered in as a first lieutenant on May 21. According to Stuart's travelogue, the Legion passed through Van Wert and camped on Pumpkin Vine Creek west of Dallas on May 25.[19]

The formidable topography around Allatoona Pass caused Sherman's wide swing to the west. South of Kingston, the Western and Atlantic Railroad ran through Allatoona Pass, which Sherman knew "was very strong, would be hard to force, and resolved not even to attempt it, but to turn the position, by moving from Kingston to Marietta via Dallas." To minimize their dependence on the railroad, before crossing the Etowah River, General McPherson had his Army of the Tennessee obtain supplies sufficient to last twenty days. Until they returned to the railroad, additional supplies would have to be transported by wagon trains from the railroad to the various units.[20]

On May 23, Sherman's army left Kingston and moved through a densely wooded region with few roads toward the little but strategically important crossroads town of Dallas. Johnston anticipated Sherman's move, and the two armies met near Dallas in a series of disjointed battles. The potent combination of stiff Confederate resistance, awful weather, and miserable roads slowed Sherman's movements back toward his railroad lifeline so that his army did not secure Allatoona until June 3 and Big Shanty (now Kennesaw) on June 10. Sherman bemoaned the heavy rains that began "about the 1st of June, making the roads infamous."[21]

The few roads that existed were mostly of Georgia clay that when wet made the movement of wagon trains transporting supplies from the railroad a real challenge. The rule of "the worse the road, the less the load" now applied with a vengeance. On solid dirt roads, a six-mule team could haul 3,000 to 3,500 pounds, but only 1,800 to 2,500 pounds on poor roads. This also became the 90th Illinois's problem as the men guarded, assisted, loaded, and unloaded wagons for the rest of May, June, and well into July. Sherman started the Atlanta campaign with around 5,150 wagons and 860 ambulances pulled by some 12,000 horses and over 32,000 mules, more than enough wagons and mules to churn up the muddy roads while the troops of the 90th Illinois, and others, slogged alongside, prepared to assist the wagons up hills and to push them when the mud became too deep. Wagon trains made a tempting target for Confederate raiders, a fact recognized by General McPherson. On May 22, he instructed his corps commanders to carefully guard their trains "beyond the possibility of capture." That proved difficult, as two days later the commander at Kingston reported an attack on a wagon train near Cassville by General Joseph Wheeler's cavalry, who burned twenty wagons, captured an equal number, and killed and wounded some twenty men.[22]

The First Brigade served as XV Corps train guards on May 25 and 26, but according to Reuben Williams, the First's colonel, the men also guarded the wagons of the XVI and XVII Corps. The sheer size of his responsibility impressed

Williams. Parked west of Pumpkin Vine Creek, the wagons of the three corps occupied a square mile. In marching order on the road, the wagons and their accompanying mules would have formed an eleven-mile long procession. It was an anxious time for the Legion and for Williams as Union and Confederate armies actively skirmished only four miles from the wagon train park. Equally nervous, General Logan and other officers repeatedly sent messages prodding Williams to be "exceedingly vigilant and watchful." On May 27, the brigade, except for the 90th Illinois, which remained with the trains, marched through Dallas to the extreme right of the Fourth Division line.[23]

The Legion found protecting trains to be hard work. The men reported spending three days guarding XV Corps wagon trains, rather dryly recording: "May 26, guarding one of the flanks of the wagon trains. May 27, marched three miles, and took position on the right flank to prevent any attack on the trains. May 28, ordered to escort trains five miles east of Dallas." However, before they could leave, they literally had to fight a battle. The troops of the Irish Legion joined their brigade, sending Companies G and I to the skirmish line under Major Flynn, with the other companies in reserve. Their part in the Battle of Dallas erupted about 3:30 P.M. on May 28 when a spirited Confederate attack lasting two hours hit the Fourth Division, including the left of the First Brigade. It was hot work as Stuart, now back in command, wrote, "The lead whistled around our ears at a furious rate." The 90th Illinois had one man wounded severely and two officers slightly by spent balls. Flynn, by his account, "was much exposed . . . and received a slight wound in the thigh." Stuart described the officer's injuries somewhat differently in a letter to his wife: "The Maj. [Flynn] got Shot in a place I could not mention but it was not in the face, and Capt. Duffy in the leg all Slight from spent balls." Company G reported one man wounded, and Company I reported two officers and two men wounded. The discrepancy between company and regimental reports may reflect differing interpretations of what constituted a wound. Things quieted down after that little bit of excitement, and the Legion returned to guarding XV Corps trains. Ordered to the left at dark on May 29, the troops marched seven miles escorting wagon trains.[24]

The sudden Confederate attack at Dallas literally caught some First Brigade troops with their pants down. Some from each company were washing their mud-caked clothes and bathing in a small creek just behind their line when rapid artillery fire hit the brigade's line, followed quickly by the famous "rebel yell." According to Williams, these troops quickly ran for their works with some wearing only their shirts. All arrived before it was time to fire the first volley. Williams did not say how many of the Legion could claim to have "barely" repulsed the attack.[25]

To replenish his supplies, Sherman on May 29 ordered each of his three armies to send wagon trains with sick and wounded to the railroad at Kingston and return with needed supplies. Only a single regiment, the lucky Irish Legion, was detailed to accompany the trains of the Army of the Tennessee. Lieutenant Colonel Stuart reported that on "the 30th received orders from Maj. Gen. John A. Logan to report to Lt. Col. J. Condit Smith, chief quartermaster, Fifteenth Army Corps, as train guard." Apparently the Irishmen of the Legion were prized for their ability to do fatigue duty (load and unload wagons) as well as to guard wagon trains. On May 31, they took the direct route to Kingston "as guard to train for supplies; passed through Euharlee and crossed the Etowah River about four miles southwest of Kingston," arriving there at 6 P.M. (see Map 9). Including this trip, the 90th Illinois marched an estimated 206 miles in May.[26]

One of the wounded, Major E. C. Dawes, described his grueling experiences on the trip in a letter to his brother, Colonel Rufus Dawes of the 6th Wisconsin, part of the Army of the Potomac's Iron Brigade: "The wagon train unwound itself at midnight. I got into one of the wagons and sat on a bag of corn. . . . The road was very rough, much of the way through dark woods. . . . The misery of that night's ride was indescribable. Early next morning Major Patrick Flynn, of the ninetieth Illinois, who was commanding the train guard, saw me and brought up the only ambulance in the train. It was loaded with mail bags." Flynn threw some of the mail bags into one of the wagons to make room for Dawes in the ambulance and then fixed the mail bags so Dawes "could rest on them" for the rest of the trip to Kingston.[27]

While the Irish Legion guarded the supply train, the troops of the XV Corps finally extricated themselves from their position near Dallas on June 1 and moved some four miles closer to the railroad near New Hope Church. Also on that date, the men of the Legion began their return with the wagon train, arriving near New Hope Church about three and a half miles northeast of Dallas on June 3. McPherson notified Sherman of the wagon trains' safe return across Pumpkin Vine Creek at Russum's Mill in a message dated 6:30 P.M. on June 2. McPherson had good reason to be concerned, as a June 1 communication from Kingston characterized the roads as "being infested with small marauding parties. Three couriers were captured between here and Dallas last night, and mounted rebels picked up stragglers between here and Resaca to-day." By June 3, Sherman's troops held Allatoona, and he planned to move his army "across to the railroad as far east and south as I can without too heavy a loss." However, it would be slow going. Sherman noted that as of June 4, "it has been raining for three days, making roads bad and swelling all the small mountain creeks." The rain was also bad news for the 90th Illinois, as on June 4 Stuart reported that they escorted the wagon train four miles toward Acworth, located on the Western and Atlantic Railroad, some ten miles by road from New Hope Church. Adjutant Davis reported they arrived on June 6, the same date Harrow's and Logan's respective commands reached Acworth. Corporal Simon Swan rejoined Company G about this time, his arm sufficiently healed to return to duty.[28]

On June 7, the 90th Illinois escorted wagon trains to Cartersville on the north side of the Etowah River for supplies and returned the next day to Acworth. Stuart rather proudly described the Cartersville trip to his wife: "I had charge of a train of 1200 Wagons. Made a line of about 8 or nine miles. I had a Regt. of Cavalry Com. by a Junr [junior] officer." Stuart's health had improved, and to convince his wife he wrote, "I averaged 12 miles a day on horseback since the first of May."[29]

Worn down by arduous labor guarding trains, Stuart reported: "Marched [about six miles] to Big Shanty [now Kennesaw] on the 10th and remained guarding trains, doing fatigue duty for the commissary department at Big Shanty until July 3." The Army of the Tennessee drew its supplies from the Big Shanty depot until it moved away from the Kennesaw Mountain area. Much later, Stuart ascribed the Legion's posting at Big Shanty to the kindness of General Logan: "We had been on the march for a long time . . . and were in bad shape. My men were barefoot, ragged, and starved. We came up to where Logan was quartered at Big Shanty. I made our condition known to him. He at once arranged that we should be on duty there three or four days, and instructed General Beckwith, who had charge of the commissary stores, to supply our needs, it was done." Colonel Amos Beckwith served as Sherman's chief commissary during the Atlanta campaign. Stuart described the Legion's reaction to duty at Big Shanty: "The men are all glad of it as they have an easy time." He added, "We rest one day out of three." Later he wrote, "The whole Division are jealous of us because we have so good a time and tried their best to get us back but Genl. Logan would not hear of it." General Harrow and Colonel Williams had made several efforts to have the Legion rejoin the First Brigade, but they all failed. Stuart explained that "Genl. Logan Sent me an order Stating that no Col. or Genl. in the Corps had any power to relieve me from my present duty except himself." Stuart enjoyed excellent relations with the departmental quartermaster: "Col. Condit Smith has been a great friend of mine since I returned. I am now at his headquarters and I think will remain there until after this campaign." Stuart's health was still a problem, and he wrote that after they took Atlanta, he would resign if he did not get a leave of absence. "If I got my pay I would be home long ago, for if I had to do the Service of other Regt. I could not Stand it." Stuart added a reference to Major Flynn: "The Major is well but I have not seen him since morning. He straggles yet once in a while." Although the army was not known for possessing much of a heart, it is possible that the Legion's long stay at Big Shanty was simply Logan and Condit Smith "looking out" for the Legion and also for Stuart.[30]

On June 11, with the railroad bridge over the Etowah repaired, loaded trains began to arrive at Big Shanty. The 90th Illinois possibly saw, but certainly heard, the first train's engineer run his locomotive to the water tank under fire from Confederate guns on Kennesaw Mountain. He calmly filled his tender with water and returned safely, "answering the guns with the screams of his engine, heightened by the cheers and shouts of our men," according to Sherman.[31]

The weather remained abominable, severely restricting the movement of Sherman's armies. From his location with the wagon train three miles behind the lines, Stuart wrote on June 13 that "three days heavy rain have Stopped Sherman of Routing the enemy again." The weather also affected Stuart's movement but not his optimism, as he wrote his wife that "I feel a little Stif[f] and old, and would like to be home with you today, but it will not be long until I am." Stuart's other complaints were those of all soldiers: infrequent mail delivery and delay in receiving pay. He expected not to be paid until after the conclusion of the current campaign. In the midst of writing the letter, the war reasserted itself, leading Stuart to succinctly summarize the military situation and Sherman's eventual solution to the current stalemate: "This moment heavy cannonading and some musketry—Rebels well fortified on Kinasau [Kennesaw] Mountain. Must Flank them." Sherman's complaints during his operations around Kennesaw dealt understandably not of delay in pay but about delay due to the weather, which he characterized as "villainously bad, the rain fell almost continually for three weeks, rendering our narrow wooded roads mere mud gullies, so that a general movement would have been impossible."[32]

The Irish Legion remained with Condit Smith, the departmental quartermaster, and on June 25 Stuart described the scene: "This morning the cannonading is dreadful. We are four miles from the line of Battle but can see and hear everything that is going on. It is dreadful to witness the destruction of two powerful armies like these engaged. . . . The entire army have confidence in Sherman & McPherson and admire the cautiousness in which they move and the pains they take in Saving life. They are now fi[gh]ting by science and find it the best way." Stuart clearly wanted to return to his home and wife in Illinois. He wrote that Adjutant Davis "is very kind to me and feels bad at my talking about going home. He wants me to have him transferred before I leave and all the officers and men feels the same way and I fear there will be a row when I do leave." Stuart wrote that he would be very sorry "if anything of the kind should happen, for I must say I do like the Regt. and it is thought as much of by the high officers as any in the Service and I know I have my share of friends among them." He added a comment about Flynn: "The Maj. is about the Same as usual, getting dissatisfied." He also might have added that First Lieutenant John McAssey had relinquished command of Company I on June 9 and temporarily assumed command of Company K on June 25. On May 22, Captain Patrick Real had relinquished command of Company K and left for treatment of intermittent fever at the Officers' Hospital at Nashville. He returned to duty with the Legion on July 1. First Lieutenant Thomas Murray resumed command of Company I in July.[33]

The Legion's stay at Big Shanty wasn't at all bad, as it kept the men off the infamous dirt roads and out of the trenches where incessant day and night picket firing made life miserable as well as hazardous. It also kept the regiment out of the series of battles at and around Kennesaw Mountain, including the bloody repulse of the June 27 Union attack on the extensive Kennesaw fortifications.

On June 30, the regiment mustered for pay at Big Shanty, much sooner than expected by Stuart. In June, the 90th Illinois had a few more to pay as the number of enlisted men present, which included the combined four categories of for duty, on extra duty, sick, or in arrest, totaled a respectable 303, an increase of thirty-two over May. Some of the sick had returned, as the number absent sick decreased by eighteen to seventy-six. John Harrington, now a captain and recovered from his wounds, assumed command of Company C on June 15. Although it had taken him longer to "return to barbarism" than he had initially planned, Captain Michael Murphy, sufficiently recovered from his wounds received at Missionary Ridge, reported for duty to the regiment by June 25, as did Captain Daniel O'Connor. Worn out and in poor health, the fifty-two-year-old surgeon Henry Strong resigned from the service effective July 3.[34]

The stalemate around Kennesaw ended with a Confederate withdrawal on July 2, and the next day the 90th Illinois left Big Shanty as escort for the wagon train and marched about twelve miles southwest on the Sandtown Road to Powder Springs (see Map 9). From July 5 to July 7, various companies of the Legion either escorted trains from Powder Springs to Big Shanty or picketed roads and guarded trains somewhere along the route. On July 10, three companies guarded a train to Marietta, and on July 12 the rest of the regiment joined them there. The long, mutually agreeable association of the 90th Illinois with the Quartermaster Corps and Condit Smith ended on July 11, and after resting on July 13, the men of the Legion marched from Marietta at 4 A.M. the next day to rejoin their brigade at noon near the Chattahoochee River, about one and a half miles from Roswell. Colonel Williams certainly welcomed them back to the First Brigade after their prolonged absence because another of his regiments, the 100th Indiana, had been detailed to guard Marietta. Even with the return of the Legion, Williams's First Brigade would have only three regiments—Williams's 12th Indiana and the 26th and 90th Illinois—for the balance of the Atlanta campaign. The evening of July 14, the 90th Illinois crossed the Chattahoochee River, the last major river barrier before Atlanta, and camped about a mile and a half south of the river. The investment of Atlanta by Union forces would soon begin.[35]

{9}

THE ATLANTA CAMPAIGN: BATTLES AROUND ATLANTA

After the long stretch of time spent guarding trains, the Irish Legion at last neared the objective of the campaign, the fortified city of Atlanta. Atlanta's formidable main defensive lines encircled the city about one and a half miles from its center. Given Major General William T. Sherman's previous lack of success in attacking fortified positions at Kennesaw, Chattanooga, and Vicksburg and earlier at Chickasaw Bayou, taking Atlanta would require something other than blindly charging its ramparts. The contest for Atlanta turned on the control of its railroads. As Sherman clearly understood, cutting Atlanta's rail supply lines would force the Confederates to either abandon the city or come out and fight. Sherman planned to use Major General James B. McPherson's Army of the Tennessee to implement that strategy and conquer Atlanta (see Map 9, in chapter 8). Of Atlanta's four railroad links, Sherman controlled the Western and Atlantic from Chattanooga. Union raiders had wrecked thirty miles of the Montgomery and West Point Railroad connecting Atlanta with Montgomery, Alabama. It would remain out of service until nearly the end of August, depriving Atlanta of railroad contact with Selma's munitions factories and grain-producing regions in Alabama and Mississippi. Control of the remaining two Atlanta railroads—the Georgia Railroad, which ran east to Augusta, Georgia, and the Macon and Western Railroad, located south of Atlanta—would determine the fate of Atlanta.[1]

Sometime during the night of July 14, the 90th Illinois endured a terrific thunderstorm with an impressive display of lightning that tested everyone's nerves. Fortunately, the Legion escaped unscathed. Not all in the army shared the Irishmen's luck; in the XV Corps, casualties approached those from a major skirmish with four or five men killed and some thirty paralyzed. Lightning struck and destroyed several stacks of rifles. To those so disposed, the storm might have been seen as an omen of things to come. For the next two days, the men of the 90th Illinois remained in their camp south of the Chattahoochee River crossing at Roswell, some sixteen miles north of Atlanta (Map 10). Reunited with their brigade and south of the Chattahoochee River, they could logically expect to engage in something more exciting than picketing roads and guarding trains.[2]

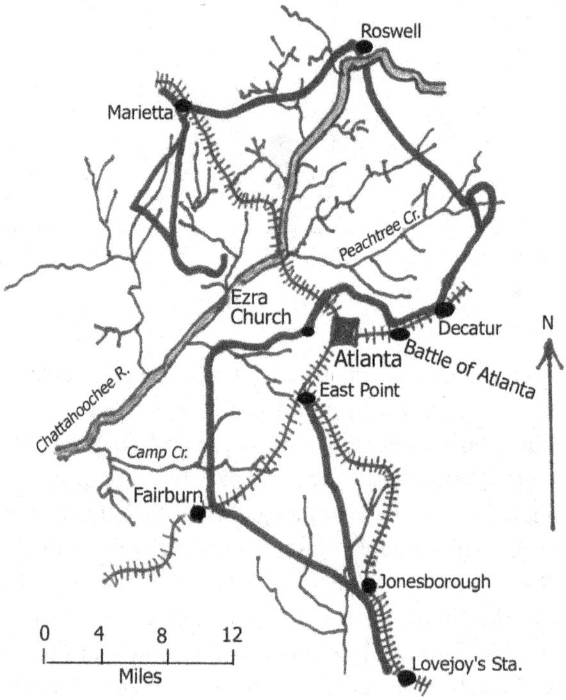

Map 10. Route of the 90th Illinois around Atlanta from July 4 to October 4, 1864

The next day, July 17, the 90th Illinois troops left their camp at 6 A.M. and, along with the rest of the XV Corps, marched south toward Stone Mountain and Decatur to tear up the railroad to Augusta. At some point in the march, they encountered enemy pickets and formed in line of battle. Farther to the west, Major General George Thomas's Army of the Cumberland crossed the Chattahoochee River in force with its skirmishers approaching Peachtree Creek only six or so miles from the center of Atlanta. With Sherman's army rapidly closing on the city from the north and east, the Confederate high command in Richmond relieved General Joseph E. Johnston from command of the Army of Tennessee by telegraph on July 17 because of his failure to "defeat and repel" the enemy and appointed General John Bell Hood to replace Johnston. The manner of his appointment left Hood little choice other than that of immediately going on the offensive to "defeat and repel" Sherman's army and save Atlanta. In the coming battles, Hood would attempt nothing less than the destruction of Sherman's army, while the capture of Atlanta remained Sherman's primarily goal.[3]

On July 18, the 90th Illinois started at 7 A.M. and marched to about four miles north of Stone Mountain, where the men halted and rested in the heat of the afternoon. In the evening, they resumed their march on the road to Decatur and continued until midnight. Meanwhile, Brigadier General Morgan L. Smith's Second Division of Major General John A. Logan's XV Corps struck the Augusta railroad near Stone Mountain and proceeded to tear it up for some distance. Hood immediately faced the necessity of stopping Sherman's advance in order to maintain Atlanta's two remaining railroad links with the Confederacy.[4]

On July 19 at 6 A.M., the 90th Illinois marched in what Logan termed "light fighting order" but progressed only six miles before camping one mile northeast of Decatur at 4 P.M. Beginning at Decatur, General Logan's XV Corps thoroughly destroyed the Augusta railroad as it moved west toward Atlanta. General Thomas's army began crossing Peachtree Creek but remained separated from the other two Union armies, the Army of the Tennessee and the Army of the Ohio. The next day, July 20, General Hood attempted to destroy Thomas's army before his men could entrench. Thomas's army withstood furious Confederate attacks that continued until sundown, when the Confederates retired back to their works around Atlanta. Starting at 5 A.M. on the same day, the XV Corps moved westward, with General Smith's Second Division in the lead, to within about two and a half miles of Atlanta. The 90th Illinois marched through Decatur and continued toward Atlanta for another two and a half to three miles before forming in line of battle. Confederate batteries then shelled the Irish troops but did no damage. The Legion advanced another half mile in line of battle, and the men fortified their line during the night. The brigade sent out skirmishers to prevent any nasty surprises.[5]

The next day, July 21, Logan moved his three XV Corps divisions into line facing Atlanta. Smith's Second Division remained straddling the railroad; Brigadier General William Harrow's Fourth Division, with the 90th Illinois, formed on Smith's left; and Brigadier General Charles R. Woods's First Division aligned on Smith's right. During the night, the men of the 90th Illinois strengthened their position, constructing earthworks and adding head-logs for additional protection. They would have heard fighting going on to the south of the XV Corps, where the XVII Corps took a commanding height alternately referred to as "Bald Hill," or after the battle as "Leggett's Hill." In the coming battle, this hill would anchor the southern end of the Army of the Tennessee's line.[6]

The failure of the July 20 attack on Thomas's army served only to spur Hood to attempt to crush McPherson's Army of the Tennessee, positioned east of Atlanta. Hood learned that McPherson's left was unprotected by cavalry and was open to attack. On July 21, Hood sent Lieutenant General William "Old Reliable" Hardee's Corps on a long, exhausting night march south of Atlanta intended to place them in position to attack McPherson's troops from the left flank and rear the next morning. This set the stage for what the Union called the Battle of Atlanta and Confederates called the Battle of Decatur on the next day, and the Legion would be right in the thick of it. The pickets kept up intense firing during the night of July 21; however, as it was summer, the soldiers of the Irish Legion slept rolled up in their blankets, not bothering to put up their two-man "dog tents."[7]

The next morning, July 22, the 90th Illinois troops found the Confederate line in their front abandoned, and about 7 A.M., they, along with other units of the XV Corps, advanced half a mile, occupied, and began to reverse the former Confederate positions using whatever shovels, picks, or improvised implements they could obtain. In the morning, the XV Corps occupied a nearly two-mile-long front facing west toward Atlanta along a gentle ridge that formed the northern half of the Army of the Tennessee line facing the city. The Fourth Division occupied the southern third of the XV Corps line. Colonel Reuben Williams's First Brigade, including the 90th Illinois, remained at the north end of the Fourth Division front with the brigade's right in contact with Colonel James A. Martin's First Brigade of Smith's Second Division. Colonel John M. Oliver's Third Brigade, in the center, connected with Colonel (soon to be Brigadier General) Charles C. Walcutt's Second Brigade, located on the southern end of the Fourth Division front, where Walcutt's left connected with the right of Brigadier General Mortimer Leggett's Third Division of the XVII Corps. The XVII Corps line extended about half a mile south of Leggett's Hill. Out of concern for his vulnerable southern flank, General McPherson held Major General Grenville Dodge's XVI Corps in reserve to the east behind the XVII Corps as protection against a flank attack, but a gap of half a mile yawned between these two corps. McPherson had virtually no cavalry to protect against a surprise attack on his exposed southern flank since Sherman had sent Brigadier General Kenner Garrard's division of cavalry to Covington, forty-two miles to the east, to burn bridges on the Augusta railroad. The lightly wooded land in front of the 90th Illinois provided little cover and thus little opportunity for a Confederate surprise attack. However, the heavily wooded left rear of the XVII Corps allowed General Hardee's troops to approach unobserved. About noon, they emerged from this area and attacked the southern flank and rear of the XVII Corps, immediately involving the Union XVI and XVII Corps in a desperate struggle. During the initial phase of this, the Battle of Atlanta, Confederate troops killed General McPherson, elevating General Logan to temporary command of the Army of the Tennessee.[8]

The men of the 90th Illinois must have felt increased anxiety as the heavy artillery and musketry fire far off on their left and rear drew closer with time. This was no squabble among feuding skirmishers but a sizable engagement underway with a large enemy force. As experienced troops, they listened for the cheers from the soldiers involved in the fighting for an indication of the battle's progress. Confederate troops cheered before their charges, while the Union men cheered after they had repelled the Confederates. The seriousness of the situation became obvious to the men of the Legion when to their left, Walcutt's Second Brigade pulled out of line, moved to the rear, and faced south to repel Confederate troops advancing to the north behind the XVII Corps line. Williams's First Brigade and Oliver's Third Brigade stretched their lines to occupy the space vacated by Walcutt's Second Brigade, requiring the 90th Illinois troops to extend their line to the left. The men of the Irish Legion soon had to extend their line again as their sister First Brigade regiment, the 26th Illinois, went to the left rear as reinforcement for Walcutt. The First Brigade, now down to only two regiments, the 12th Indiana on the right and the 90th Illinois on the left, deployed in a single line to defend about a quarter mile of earthworks.[9]

To the left rear of the 90th Illinois, the situation behind the XVII Corps rapidly became a cause for deep concern. Walcutt saw that Union "artillery and straggling men and wagons were coming through the timber to the rear of the Seventeenth Corps, followed closely by the enemy; so closely indeed, that 1 piece of artillery and several wagons had to be abandoned." With assistance from Oliver's Third Brigade and the 26th Illinois, Walcutt's troops succeeded in stopping the advancing Confederates, who then turned upon the rear of the XVII Corps line. This movement exposed the Confederates' flank to enfilading fire from Walcutt's troops, which aided in their repulse.[10]

While Oliver's troops assisted Walcutt, only four regiments—the 90th Illinois, 12th Indiana, 70th Ohio, and 26th Illinois—defended the entire Fourth Division line, initially occupied by three brigades. The troops of the 90th Illinois could hear the progress of the fighting to their south and to their rear, and the sounds of the battle indicated a Union retreat.[11]

Confused, intense action erupted just to the left of the 90th Illinois. After reporting to Walcutt, the 26th Illinois was placed on the front side of the works facing to the rear, where the troops alternately repulsed attacks from their rear and front by climbing over their works and fighting alternately from one side and then the other. About the time things died down a bit, Colonel Williams saw that some seventy-five to a hundred Confederates had broken through on the left of his line and sent two companies of the Legion to deal with them. The Confederates surrendered at Williams's command. Except for this single flurry of activity, up to now the 90th Illinois and the 12th Indiana had not been involved in the fighting. But about 3 P.M., Confederate troops formed to attack their section of the Union line. Fortunately, by then two of Oliver's regiments had returned to their place in line. In addition, the 70th Ohio remained in position across a ravine to Oliver's left, where Walcutt had placed it along with the 26th Illinois. Thus, at the time of the attack on the XV Corps from the direction of Atlanta, six regiments manned the Fourth Division's line.[12]

Union troops south of the railroad repulsed the attack by Confederate major general Carter L. Stevenson's Division. Things had gone very well for the 90th Illinois. The Confederate attack at 3:30 P.M. found the Legion deployed in single file occupying the left of Williams's First Brigade line, defending the length of line normally occupied by two regiments. Lieutenant Colonel Owen Stuart briefly described what happened: "The skirmishers in my front were driven in, and the enemy soon after appeared in heavy columns, advancing to attack. As soon as the skirmishers were all in, my command opened fire on the enemy and soon broke their line in my front, and held them in check. They reformed, but were soon broken and forced to fall back in disorder." At this point in the battle, the men of the Legion and the rest of their brigade felt pretty good about having turned back the initial Confederate attack.[13]

However, disaster loomed just to their north. Confederate brigadier general (soon to be major general) John C. Brown's Division attacked and broke through at a weak point where the railroad and wagon road intersected the federal line in front of the railroad cut. These Confederate troops poured through the railroad cut, emerging well behind Colonel Martin's First Brigade of the Second Division and the Fourth Division line. This changed everything. Without warning, Martin's brigade, on the right of the 12th Indiana, fell back from the line, astonishing Williams. Much worse, a heavy fire suddenly hit the 90th Illinois and 12th Indiana from their right flank and rear. Badly outnumbered, Williams directed these two regiments to fall back a quarter mile and form in the rear of a large tannery. As the 90th Illinois and 12th Indiana retreated past the advancing Confederates, they suffered from "friendly fire" from Union cannon on their right.[14]

Fire from Confederate forces to their right and rear, along with the renewed frontal attack by two Confederate brigades, forced first Williams's and then Oliver's brigades to retreat. Two Confederate brigades then broke through the Fourth Division line and moved as far as two hundred yards beyond. The tide of battle see-sawed back and forth, with neither side willing to yield. Stuart reported: "The right wing of the regiment fell back about sixty yards, but were reformed, and went forward to retake the line, when they were ordered to fall back to the lines occupied early in the morning. The regiment was reformed in this line and received orders to advance and reoccupy the line carried by the enemy, which they did, the enemy retiring in great disorder." In all the ebb and flow, Confederates captured the Irish Legion's flag bearer, Corporal Henry Porter of Company C, along with the Legion's flag. Imprisoned at Andersonville, Porter's weight decreased from 210 pounds to 120 pounds by the time of his exchange in March 1865.[15]

The back-and-forth attempts to reoccupy the First Brigade's works described by Williams, and by both the 12th Indiana and 90th Illinois, may be explained by orders Confederate brigadier general Arthur Manigault received to abandon the captured Union works and return to Atlanta, then very shortly to return again and occupy the Union works, and finally to retreat some two hours later after he had sent word to his commander that he could hold the Union works if reinforced.[16]

The Confederate attack forced all four Fourth Division regiments, located to the right of the 70th Ohio, to retire behind the Union line. The 70th Ohio reported that the entire line to its right (Oliver's and Williams's brigades) gave way so that the Confederate "advance reached a point some 200 yards to the rear of the works on our right." Two companies of the 70th Ohio formed at right angles to the line and fired into the flank of the advancing Confederates.[17]

Housed in the Cyclorama at Grant Park in Atlanta, the painting *The Battle of Atlanta* grippingly depicts the action as the soldiers of the XV Corps drive to retake their works following the Confederate breakthrough. The painting presents a scene of utter chaos centered on the railroad cut, the Troop Hurt house, and Captain Francis De Gress's abandoned battery. It shows the charge of the Fourth Division, with the 90th Illinois located in there somewhere on the division's right flank. Toward this maelstrom, the martial figure of General Logan is shown riding a large black horse at full gallop, intent on rallying the gathering troops of the XV Corps to repulse the Confederate incursion. Years later, Owen Stuart described the inspirational effect of General Logan's presence on his troops, including the Legion: "That was a day no man engaged on either side will ever forget. Logan seemed to be imbued with a determination to avenge the death of General McPherson. I doubt whether his equal in battle as on that occasion has ever been seen. The fight was raging at a furious rate; General Logan dashed to the front and galloped along the line waving his hat and cheering the boys on to renewed effort. His presence seemed to act like an electric battery." Stuart remembered that "bullets were flying like hail. Logan plunged ahead of his men into the thickest of the fight. He regained all the ground that had been lost and recaptured batteries taken by the enemy, among them the famous Chicago Board of Trade battery, which was guarding a deep railroad cut." In James Pickett Jones's biography of Logan, *Black Jack*, the general is described riding among the troops, "his black hair streaming, waving his hat in the air" crying, "McPherson and revenge boys." If one imagines the noise and smoke of battle and Logan's troops yelling, "Black Jack! Black Jack!" as they charged to retake their lines, one may get some hint of the passion and intensity displayed during the battle by the troops of both sides, including the Irish Legion.[18]

It had been a very near thing. The Union Army of the Tennessee had been near defeat, certainly nearer than the 90th Illinois probably knew. To the south of the 90th Illinois, the duration and intensity of the fighting on the XVI and XVII Corps front exceeded even the ferocious combat for the XV Corps line. Near the end of the day, General Hardee's Confederates finally broke the southern end of the XVII

Corps line and appeared to be driving for victory, but Union troops reformed in a line extending east from Leggett's Hill and held their position against successive attacks. Night ended the battle. Hood again had asked more than was humanly possible from his troops.[19]

The battle had been an exhausting experience for the men of the 90th Illinois and for the rest of the First Brigade. They passed the night near the old tannery amid the carnage from the battle, a truly awful scene. Casualties for the Irish Legion were listed as twelve wounded and twenty-three missing from the battle, with losses distributed throughout the regiment.[20]

The orders to the XV Corps for July 23 can be summed up in one word: entrench. The 90th Illinois troops returned to their position in the line, where they remained until the morning of July 27.[21]

Having disabled the railroad to Augusta, Sherman next turned his attention to breaking the Macon railroad, Atlanta's one remaining rail link "over which of necessity came the stores and ammunition that alone maintained the rebel army in Atlanta," to use his own words. He ordered his mobile striking force, the Army of the Tennessee, to move from the east of Atlanta to the west side of the city and march toward East Point and the Macon railroad south of Atlanta (see Map 10). His objective remained the capture of Atlanta rather than the destruction of General Hood's army.[22]

The Army of the Tennessee began its carefully planned movement around Atlanta the night of July 26. The First Brigade received orders to be ready to march at midnight, but after an early breakfast, it was almost daylight before the troops got in motion. The Legion's move to the extreme right of the army turned out to be another day of "hurry up and wait," so that it was well after dark before the brigade obtained a suitable camping place in the rear of the XVI Corps.[23]

Sherman appointed Major General Oliver O. Howard to command of the Army of the Tennessee late on July 26, and upon his assumption of command the next morning, General Logan returned to command of the XV Corps. Howard, the one-armed "Christian General," clearly wanted to avoid any more nasty surprises such as those his XI Corps had experienced at the Battle of Chancellorsville or the reverses they suffered during the first day at Gettysburg. Twice bitten, he cautiously moved his troops around the west side of Atlanta.[24]

During the night of July 27, Logan arranged his three divisions in a formation designed to protect the front and flank of his troops as they moved farther south the next day. The resulting formation looked something like an upside-down and reversed J pointed toward the south with the long leg facing Atlanta. Logan also didn't take any chances and ordered one hundred rounds of ammunition per man brought forward. General Harrow placed Colonel Oliver's Third Brigade in contact with and at a right angle to the south end of the First Division, with his

First Brigade, containing the 90th Illinois, behind the Third Brigade and with the Second Brigade in the rear.[25]

Hood countered Sherman's intention of wrecking the Macon railroad by ordering Lieutenant General Stephen D. Lee on July 28 to "hold the enemy in check on a line nearly parallel with the Lick Skillet road, running through to Ezra Church." Ezra Church was located some two and three-quarters miles west of the Atlanta train depot, while the town of Lick Skillet lay some three and a half miles farther west. Sherman's army had to cross the Lick Skillet road to reach East Point, the junction of the West Point and Macon railroads.[26]

Early on July 28, the 90th Illinois marched some three miles before stopping for breakfast. For some unexplained reason, it took some two hours to form in line of battle and make connections with the Third Brigade troops on the left. The 90th Illinois formed the left of the First Brigade line with the 26th Illinois to its right and the 12th Indiana on the right flank, where the 12th could reinforce the other two if required and also serve as flank guards. After quietly advancing in that formation for about a mile and a half, the brigade crossed a dense wood and finally emerged into an open field. Williams's First Brigade then moved to the right of the Third Brigade and occupied the crest of the hill immediately in Williams's front. The need for quiet no longer prevailed, which presumably gave Sergeant Major Thomas McDonald of the 90th Illinois an opportunity to use his full voice and whatever other encouragement he considered necessary to speed the regiment's realignment. Adjutant Edwin Davis reported that the 90th Illinois "advanced up a ridge about three miles [west] of Atlanta, driving the enemy's skirmishers before us," and occupied the ridge while under artillery fire. The imminent Confederate attack, which began the Battle of Ezra Church, or what Confederates called the Battle of Lick Skillet Road, fully justified Howard's and Logan's precautions.[27]

Once on the ridge, the troops of the 90th Illinois, along with the rest of the brigade, had about half an hour to throw up whatever minimal fortifications they could, mainly using fence rails from a field in their immediate front, before the first Confederate charge hit them. About 11:30 A.M., Confederates assaulted the right and center of the XV Corps line, quickly involving Williams's brigade and the 90th Illinois in the fray. Between attacks, the Irishmen improved their position, using their hands, tin plates, and bayonets to throw soil over the rails. Late in the fight, they obtained some shovels and willingly put them to work.[28]

During the battle, the Army of the Tennessee's line resembled a fishhook with a barb of twenty-six pieces of artillery placed to sweep the approaches to the right flank, another case of Howard taking no chances of another Chancellorsville surprise. The XVI Corps to the north and XVII on the south made up the shank. The XV Corps line formed the arc of the fishhook. The First Division on the left (east end) faced generally southeast, connecting on its left with the XVII Corps a little north of Ezra Church and on its right with the Fourth Division, which in turn connected with the Second Division, the right of the Union line. The Fourth and Second Divisions occupied a ridge facing generally southwest. The Fourth Division's Third Brigade on the left connected with the right of the First Division. Williams's First Brigade on the right connected with the left of the Second Division. The Second Brigade remained in reserve. At the start of the battle, the 90th Illinois formed the left of the First Brigade line, right in the middle of the fray. The 26th Illinois was on the Legion's right, and the 12th Indiana remained in reserve.[29]

After the second main assault, General Harrow ordered the 90th Illinois to support the Third Brigade. During the heavy fighting, some troops of the 48th Illinois had run out of ammunition for their Smith and Wesson rifles and could not be resupplied with the proper ammunition during the battle. The Legion moved the length of one regiment to the left to a position on the ridge crest directly above and behind the 48th Illinois, in the position the 48th occupied before moving forward from the crest to conform to the rest of the Third Brigade line. Lieutenant Colonel Stuart reported that the Legion first "occupied the temporary works thrown up by the Forty-eighth Illinois" before relieving the 48th on the front line about 1:30 P.M. The 90th Illinois remained on the front line for the rest of the battle.[30]

The Confederates attacked with determination for six hours. During the last of four attacks, Confederate troops reached a point only ten steps from the First Brigade line, where five stands of Confederate colors converged in front of the 26th Illinois. The 26th succeeded in capturing one of the five. At Ezra Church, Williams's brigade used more than the hundred rounds per man issued. According to Williams, the 26th Illinois fired some 70,000 rounds during the battle, and his other regiments fired similar amounts.[31]

The 90th Illinois lost one dead and twenty-two wounded in the fight. Major Patrick Flynn received a debilitating shoulder wound, ending his active service in the field. Company F was particularly hard hit: Captain Patrick Feeney received a severe leg wound, and a shell fragment wounded Lieutenant William White in the forehead, requiring treatment in the field hospital at Marietta. On August 6, the three wounded officers, Flynn, Feeney, and White, were granted the customary twenty days' leave "on Surgeons Certificate of disability from wounds received in action" and proceeded home to Illinois. Feeney and White would eventually return to the regiment. Company G reported one dead, and Company I reported three mortally wounded. The Legion reported roughly twice as many wounds in the upper body areas of head, arm, hand, and shoulder as in the lower body areas of leg, knee, and foot, an indication of the effectiveness of the protection provided by the temporary fortifications.[32]

The July report to the Illinois adjutant general showed the effects of the July battles on the 90th Illinois, as only 183 enlisted men were present for duty, a decrease of 71 from June. The 384 aggregate present and absent officers and enlisted men was 32 less than the June total. The 117 absent sick represented an increase of 39 from June. A letter dated August 1 written by Sergeant Charles Woollett, Company H, in the *Chicago Post* described the regiment's health: "Considerable sickness prevails consequent on an excessively arduous campaign." Woollett clearly knew what he was talking about as he received a discharge for disability on August 3, 1864.[33]

General Hood's aggressive attacks extracted a high price in casualties from his troops but achieved a stalemate in the battle for Atlanta, stopping Sherman's army well short of East Point. As a result of the battle, the men of the 90th Illinois would spend much of the month of August in the trenches, sweltering in their woolen uniforms under a broiling Georgia sun, besieging Atlanta.

After the Battle of Ezra Church, General Sherman extended his lines south of Atlanta in an attempt to reach and break General Hood's remaining lines of supply, the Macon and the West Point railroads. To protect Atlanta's railroad lifeline, Hood remained on the defensive, matching Sherman's extensions by rapidly constructing a series of forts to and beyond East Point (see Map 10). The Confederate defense line, shaped like an old fashioned dipper, eventually stretched some fifteen miles from near Decatur to below East Point. To break the stalemate, Sherman obtained large, 4½-inch rifled guns that fired into the city day and night starting August 10. The bombardment had no more success in compelling the surrender of Atlanta than had a similar effort at Vicksburg. General Howard wrote that during the siege, his Army of the Tennessee "was occupied in making approaches, digging rifle-pits, and erecting batteries, being subjected day and night to a galling fire of artillery and musketry." It was not exactly what one would call pleasant duty for troops of the Irish Legion.[34]

Immediately following the Battle of Ezra Church, the Fourth Division faced entrenched Confederate forces covering Lick Skillet road. When the fighting ended on July 28, the 90th Illinois soldiers fortified their line during the night, rejoining their First Brigade the next day. On July 30, the 90th Illinois "moved half a mile to the right and relieved troops that had taken position there the day before," according to Adjutant Davis. The Legion stayed in these works until August 2, when the men again advanced a quarter mile to another line. The next day, their skirmishers advanced and captured the Confederate picket line. About noon, the Confederates counterattacked and reoccupied their original picket line. The 90th Illinois reinforced its skirmishers, who attacked about 4 P.M., regaining the position, which they fortified overnight and held. This set the pattern for the next three weeks as fighting settled down to squabbling between the contending parties over some coveted and supposedly advantageous piece of real estate between the lines.[35]

Sherman's chief engineer, Captain Orlando Poe, described the tactics used by Sherman's troops, including the 90th Illinois, to close on the Confederate defense lines so that the distance between Union and Confederate lines was three hundred yards or less. "Successive advances . . . were made . . . by pushing forward, just before daylight, a strong line of skirmishers to the position chosen beforehand, which maintained its ground during the day, each man getting such cover as he could, generally by scooping out a rifle-pit at the foot of a tree, behind a log or stone, in which they could find shelter." As soon as night hid their movements, "working parties were thrown out to the skirmish line and connected by the ordinary rifle trenches the entire chain of rifle-pits. These lines were continually being strengthened until it was desired to make another advance, when the operation was repeated."[36]

The lingering effects of his wound at Missionary Ridge combined with the physical demands of the campaign completely wore out Lieutenant Colonel Stuart. He tendered the resignation of his commission, along with the required Surgeon's Certificate, dated August 11, declaring him unfit for duty. His request rapidly moved its way up the proper military channels, and on August 17 he received a twenty-day leave by order of General Logan. The order also contained a pass on the U.S. Military Railroad by order of General Howard. It wasn't what he had requested, but at least he got his way paid to go home to see his wife and beloved horses. By seniority, command of the 90th Illinois devolved to "Posy Captain" Daniel O'Connor of Company D.[37]

The Legion faced other changes. Wear and tear of the campaign had reduced the size of the Fourth Division's three brigades, requiring their consolidation. From May 13 to August 3, 1864, the 90th Illinois had suffered seventy-one casualties. The First Brigade alone reported a loss of nearly six hundred men killed, wounded, or missing since May 1. So on August 4, the 100th Indiana and 26th Illinois transferred to the Second Brigade, commanded by General Walcutt. The entire Third Brigade, consisting of the 48th Illinois, 97th and 99th Indiana, and 53rd and 70th Ohio, joined the 90th Illinois and 12th Indiana, forming the new First Brigade, commanded by Colonel John Oliver. Colonel Reuben Williams returned to the command of the 12th Indiana. But before he left command of the First Brigade, Williams commended his aide-de-camp Lawrence McCarthy, 90th Illinois, giving him "special attention for bravery in battles and strict attention" to duty "on all occasions."[38]

After the advance on August 3, the 90th Illinois remained in place until August 9, when the Irish Legion and the other regiments of the newly revised First Brigade advanced and fortified the line held by the skirmishers some eight hundred yards from the Confederate main line. Besides being uncomfortable, the siege became costly for the 90th Illinois. Enemy sharpshooters and raids on the opposing skirmish lines kept things lively. The Legion reported seven men wounded, including one fatally, in the action on August 3. Two days later, a private from Company F was killed. The next day, one Company E man was wounded. On August 12, deadly Confederate sniper fire killed Company E's first sergeant along with privates from

Companies F and G. The following day, the first sergeant of Company D was killed. An additional three men from Company I died from wounds received in action around Atlanta. Part of the annoyance came from Confederates in rifle pits about eighty yards from the First Brigade. About an hour before daylight on August 17, Captain John Murphy, Company G, with a detail of forty men from the 90th and 26th Illinois, captured three of the Confederate skirmish pits. Captain O'Connor reported that they "succeeded in capturing 8 of the enemy from one pit and driving him out of two others, killing and wounding several," with a loss of one man killed. However, according to Adjutant Davis, "A heavy fire from the enemy's reserve line prevented the captain from holding the works taken." The 90th Illinois "remained on this line—occasionally making demonstrations to draw the enemy out." One such demonstration by the brigade on August 18 discovered no reduction of Confederate troops in its front.[39]

First Lieutenant Patrick Campion, another of the regiment's "bad boys," was in the doghouse again for being a little too relaxed at his post. A thoroughly aroused Captain Samuel Brough, who commanded the brigade's pickets, filed charges of drunkenness and neglect of duty against Campion for going to sleep while commanding the outposts on August 5. The charges worked their way through channels to the Fourth Division's headquarters, but somehow or other Campion remained a first lieutenant. The regiment had only nine officers present for duty, and any lieutenant, drunk or sober, could ill be spared.[40]

From July 28 to August 26, Hood continued to hold Sherman's army in check as the XV Corps line moved forward less than a mile and a half in a general swing toward the southeast. The siege wore on everyone's nerves. According to Patrick Sloan, the Legion occupied a line so close to the Confederates that they could carry on a conversation when both sides felt so disposed. Sugar and coffee could be exchanged for Confederate tobacco, but "generally neither party dare show enough of their head to be a mark or they would soon get a bullet through it." Considering that Union troops wore wool uniforms year round and that August in Georgia meant high humidity, mosquitoes and chiggers galore, and intense heat with no shade unless a man contrived his own, it was a trying time for the Legion. Confederate general Manigault's graphic description of the effect of four weeks of trench warfare on Confederate soldiers would apply equally well to the 90th Illinois. He found it to be "the most anxious, exhausting, and perilous . . . of my experience as a soldier."[41]

The siege of Atlanta dragged on through August, with Sherman stymied in his attempt to capture the city and Grant likewise stuck before Petersburg, Virginia. Even worse, Grant's army had suffered horrendous numbers of casualties. By late summer, President Lincoln became convinced that he would be defeated in the upcoming presidential election. The Democratic Party platform drafted at the party's Chicago convention proclaimed the war a failure, justifying Lincoln's concern for the Union if the Democrats won the election. As Sherman explained, military success was "a political necessity; and it was all-important that something startling in our interest should occur before the election in November." The required "success," the capture of Atlanta, had to occur well before the elections.[42]

To evict General Hood from Atlanta and decide the campaign one way or the other, General Sherman relied once again on a flanking movement. By this time. Atlanta's defense line extended past East Point and bent to the southeast, protecting five miles of the Macon and Western Railroad. Leaving the XX Corps to hold a bridgehead at the Chattahoochee River railroad bridge, Sherman's three armies pulled out of the trenches and made a general left-wheel, pivoting on Major General John M. Schofield's Army of the Ohio near East Point, with Howard's Army of the Tennessee making a wide swing to the west, south, and then east toward Jonesborough (now Jonesboro; see Map 10). Thomas's Army of the Cumberland, minus the XX Corps, occupied the part of the arc between Schofield and Howard.[43]

During the night of July 26, the soldiers of the Army of the Tennessee pulled out of their lines and marched in the rain over difficult roads toward Sandtown before turning south and crossing Camp Creek. At 10 P.M., the 90th Illinois troops received orders to quietly evacuate their position and join their brigade. They marched all night toward the west and continued marching until 1 P.M. the next day, when they bivouacked near Wolf Creek about five miles from the West Point railroad, having marched fifteen miles. Company K reported it "formed line of battle at 3 P.M. and fortified," remaining in its "works all night." The Legion followed standard army policy, for from the start of the Atlanta campaign until the end of the war, Sherman's soldiers entrenched their position every night whenever "the proximity of the enemy rendered it prudent," according to Captain Poe of Sherman's staff. The 90th Illinois and other troops benefited from the careful planning and preparation for the march. During the night, small fires lighted the roads newly cut through the forest. While half of Oliver's First Brigade worked at thoroughly destroying the railroad, the 90th Illinois went back to guarding trains. The Irish troops left at 5 P.M. on July 28 and escorted the XV Corps wagon train eight miles, which about equaled the length of the corps wagons drawn up in marching order on the road. Sometime during the march on that day, Confederates, probably cavalry, captured Commissary Sergeant Lawrence W. Bracken and Private John Campbell of Company A. The next day, the 90th Illinois rested near Shadna Church, about two miles north of Fairburn on the West Point and Atlantic Railroad. The Legion remained with the wagon trains until the morning of August 30, when it rejoined the First Brigade. Meanwhile, Sherman's three armies thoroughly destroyed twelve and a half miles of the West Point railroad.[44]

On July 30, Sherman's three armies moved eastward toward the Macon railroad, Hood's last remaining supply line. The Army of the Tennessee had the greatest distance to travel, since it moved on an outer circle and the railroad bent to the east from East Point to Jonesborough, generally following a ridge east of the Flint River. After the 90th Illinois rejoined the First Brigade on the morning of July 30, they crossed the West Point railroad and marched some twelve miles to the vicinity of Jonesborough, arriving there about 8 P.M. When 90th Illinois troops deployed as pickets in front of their brigade, they "found the enemy in strong force about 300 yards in our front," according to Captain O'Connor. During the night, the men of the First Brigade fortified their position.[45]

By the morning of July 31, the XV Corps had strongly fortified its position on the highest ground between the Flint River and the railroad half a mile away at Jonesborough. Brigadier General William Hazen's Second Division lay to the left of the Jonesborough road, with his line bent back to the left. He received two regiments from Major General Peter Osterhaus's First Division. Harrow's Fourth Division, which included the 90th Illinois, connected with the right of Hazen and bent its line back to the right. To protect the southern flank, Logan moved the Second and Third Brigades of Osterhaus's First Division to extend the line on Harrow's right and connect with a brigade of the XVI Corps, whose flank rested on the Flint River. Logan knew that Confederate reinforcements had arrived during the night and expected to be attacked. For added strength, the remainder of the XVI Corps and the bulk of the XVII Corps were positioned just to the west of the Flint River.[46]

On August 31, the 90th Illinois remained deployed as skirmishers in front of the First Brigade, engaged in what Colonel Oliver termed "severe skirmishing until 2:30 P.M., when the enemy was seen forming columns for assault." The Battle of Jonesborough was about to begin. Captain O'Connor reported that the Confederates attacked in strong force at 2:30 P.M., driving in the Union skirmishers as they advanced. When the skirmishers on his left and right were driven back, he ordered the 90th Illinois "to fall back behind our main line." By that time, a heavy fire had opened both on his right and left. After firing from the main line ceased, the 90th Illinois advanced and reoccupied the skirmish line. He reported "gaining and holding . . . most of the pits, taking twenty-eight prisoners" in the process. The Legion lost three killed, thirteen wounded, and one missing. The Irishmen held the position until dark, when they were relieved. On September 1, they "built a line of works" behind the 70th Ohio, where they "remained until the morning of the 2nd when it was ascertained the enemy had retreated from Jonesborough."[47]

In August, the 90th Illinois reported twelve men killed or died of wounds received in action, one died of disease, and two discharged for wounds or disability. The aggregate present and absent declined another nineteen to 365 officers and men, with only 177 enlisted men present for duty, a decrease of six from July. The Legion had fifteen fewer absent sick, which helped make up for some of the losses.[48]

Following the repulse of the Confederate attack at Jonesborough, General Hood abandoned Atlanta. About 2 A.M. on September 2, the ground shook and the Legion heard heavy explosions from the direction of Atlanta, some twenty miles away. The honor of accepting the surrender of the city fell to the XX Corps, but Sherman could claim in his September 3 message to Washington: "So Atlanta is ours, and fairly won."[49]

There was still a war to fight and General Hardee's Corps to pursue, so later on September 2 the Army of the Tennessee marched south from Jonesborough in three columns paralleling the railroad (see Map 10). Some five miles south of Jonesborough, General Hardee's troops were found in a strong position north of Lovejoy's Station, prepared to resist an attack. The men of the 90th Illinois supported the skirmish line from their fortified positioned on a high ridge some nine hundred yards from the Confederate line. The assistant adjutant, blue-eyed and black-haired Lieutenant John McAssey, reported "skirmishing every day with the Enemy—until the night of the 5th when it was evacuated and we fell back to the line of works held on the 31st of August." Sherman considered the capture of Atlanta as sufficient accomplishment and abandoned the pursuit of Hood's army. Starting at 8 P.M. on September 5, the XV Corps withdrew by easy stages from the lines at Lovejoy's Station, reaching East Point about 11 A.M. three days later where the Legion went into camp. Captain O'Connor proudly reported that on September 7, the 90th Illinois was the rear guard for the XV Corps on the seven-mile march from Jonesborough to Grime's (Morrow's) Mill.[50]

The Chicago Board of Trade celebrated Atlanta's capture by quickly appropriating two hundred dollars to fire a salute, enlivening local celebrations of the event. Congress passed a joint resolution tendering the thanks of the people and of Congress to Sherman, who was soon promoted to major general in the regular army. President Lincoln ordered a salute of a hundred guns at the arsenal at Washington and at seven other cities. The capture of Atlanta revitalized support for the war and, along with Major General Philip Sheridan's victories in the Shenandoah Valley, secured the November election for the Lincoln administration. Sherman summed it up: "Success at Atlanta . . . made the election of Mr. Lincoln certain."[51]

{ 10 }

HAZEN'S SUMMER CAMP AND A STERN CHASE

With the end of the Atlanta campaign, the 90th Illinois went into summer quarters with the rest of the Army of the Tennessee at East Point, Georgia, remaining there until October 4, 1864 (see Map 10, in chapter 9). Both Union and Confederate armies needed time to rest and refit. The Irish Legion had earned a respite, having marched over 380 miles during the Atlanta campaign, most of it over muddy roads guarding trains. During the campaign, the Legion had lost 117 officers and men killed, wounded, and missing; however, of that total, 30 of the wounded had returned to duty by the end of September, increasing the number of enlisted men present for duty to 195. On September 9, Charles A. Thompson mustered in at East Point as the Irish Legion's surgeon, replacing Henry Strong, who had resigned some two months earlier. During September, six members of the 90th Illinois, paroled at Rough and Ready, about five miles south of East Point, and officially exchanged, returned to active duty. Five had been captured on July 22, and some had been confined at Andersonville.[1]

Several companies had new commanders. Captain John C. Harrington of Company C received a discharge for disability on September 8, and James Dunne, called "Old Shakehead" from his habit of expressing himself without words, replaced him. First Lieutenant Thomas Murray, who had commanded Company I since August 11, 1863, except for three months' recruiting duty during the spring of 1864, officially became its captain on September 13, 1864. First Lieutenant Lawrence McCarthy, who commanded Company H, remained detailed to the brigade. Colonel John Oliver appreciated having an Irish tenor at his headquarters, as had his predecessor, Colonel Reuben Williams. However, McCarthy obtained a poorly timed twenty-day leave dated September 23 and would not rejoin the Legion until

April 25, 1865. First Lieutenant John McAssey assumed command of Company K when Captain Patrick Real went on sick leave to Chicago at the end of September and resigned from the service on November 16, 1864, due to continued poor health. When Lieutenant William White, now recovered from his wound suffered in the fighting at Ezra Church, returned to the regiment on September 18, he immediately assumed command of Company F, replacing Captain Patrick Feeney, who remained in Chicago recuperating from wounds also received in the same battle. The discontinuation of the Fourth Division on September 15, 1864, directly affected the Irishmen of the 90th Illinois. Its First Brigade, now reduced to the 48th and 90th Illinois, 99th Indiana, 15th Michigan, and 70th Ohio, became the Third Brigade of Brigadier General William B. Hazen's Second Division of the XV Army Corps, where it would remain for the rest of the war. Colonel Oliver continued to command the brigade. On September 23, Brigadier General John M. Corse's former Second Division of the XVI Corps became the replacement Fourth Division of the XV Corps. The commander of the XV Corps, Major General John A. Logan, a congressman from southern Illinois before the war, returned to his home area to help the Republican Party carry Illinois in the coming election, and Major General Peter Osterhaus replaced him.[2]

The 90th Illinois now had a thirty-three-year-old West Point graduate with extensive combat experience for a division commander. A no-nonsense professional soldier, Hazen had not been pleased with the level of discipline, instruction, and administration he found in his new command or with the free and easy ways of his western troops. Hazen described the condition of the division upon his assuming command on August 15 as "wretched" and "deplorable" with many men "absent or non-combatant." He quickly issued a series of orders to correct the situation. The effect was magical; within a week, the numbers of men with muskets increased from 1,700 to 2,200. After joining Hazen's division in mid-September, the number of enlisted men of the 90th Illinois on detached or daily duty decreased to twenty-seven, fifteen fewer than reported in August.[3]

On September 29, Principal Musician Patrick Sloan, writing to his wife from the hospital at East Point, probably spoke for most of the 90th Illinois when he described his new division's commander as a "great disciplinarian" who "has the Division out nearly all the time drilling or exercising in some way." From September 19 to October 4, the troops of the Irish Legion would have, but probably did not welcome, the opportunity to improve their performance on the drill field. Exercises included daily company drills for an hour and a half in the morning and either battalion drills or "evolutions of the line" in the afternoon for an hour and a half, five days a week.[4]

Hazen was determined to make his troops look and act like soldiers. The Irish Legion received instructions on such basic military practices as writing reports and saluting. The men could look back and give thanks that Colonel Timothy O'Meara had trained them to perform such matters. Hazen also instructed his troops on proper methods of constructing breastworks, and to put theory into practice, he ordered one wagon with one hundred axes, one hundred spades and shovels, and fifty pickaxes attached to each brigade. If needed, the 90th Illinois would literally be prepared to dig in. He also ordered that when in the field, the men "will be ready to march at any time in ten minutes after the 'general' is sounded."[5]

Faced with the problem of expelling Major General William T. Sherman's army from Georgia, General John Bell Hood sought a rematch with Sherman at a place and time of Hood's own choosing near the Tennessee border. By the night of October 1, Hood's army had crossed the Chattahoochee River, prepared to move north and wreak havoc on Sherman's railroad supply line. This got Sherman's full attention, and the stern chase began on October 3. Hood's attack on Sherman's supply line and Sherman's attempt to herd Hood's army elsewhere involved little fighting other than daily skirmishes and much maneuvering by both armies, more closely resembling a high-stakes chess match than the series of bloody battles waged in July and August around Atlanta. Hazen, ever the hard-bitten professional, considered his division's pursuit of Hood "most uneventful." From October 4, when they left East Point and crossed the Chattahoochee River, until they returned to the old Smyrna Campground some 290 miles later, the men of the 90th Illinois commonly marched fifteen to twenty-two miles per day, but they never quite managed to catch Hood's army (Map 11).[6]

Their chase can be summarized as a lot of walking and one short train ride on October 11, when the Legion and the rest of the Third Brigade boarded freight cars at Allatoona and rode west to Rome. They accompanied Corse's Fourth Division on a brief reconnaissance south of the Etowah River, skirmished briefly with Confederate cavalry, and returned to Rome.[7]

Hood's army crossed the Coosa River and destroyed the Western and Atlantic Railroad from Resaca to near Tunnel Hill before passing through the mountain gaps in the general direction of Gadsden, Alabama, arriving there on October 20. Hood abandoned his plans to attack Sherman's army, deciding instead on an invasion of Tennessee, and left Georgia to its fate. He also left Major General Joseph Wheeler's cavalrymen to deal as best they could with Sherman.[8]

Meanwhile, the 90th Illinois rejoined its division at Ship's Gap on Taylor's Ridge and followed in the wake of Hood's army into Alabama, where they watched other troops skirmish with Wheeler's Confederate cavalry at Turkeytown. With Hood now near Decatur, Alabama, some fifty-five miles to the northwest, Sherman gave up the chase.[9]

After observing the Turkeytown skirmish, Captain Daniel O'Connor wrote Illinois adjutant general Allan Fuller requesting a Catholic chaplain to replace Father Thomas Kelly. Given the uncertainties of the mail, it would be some two

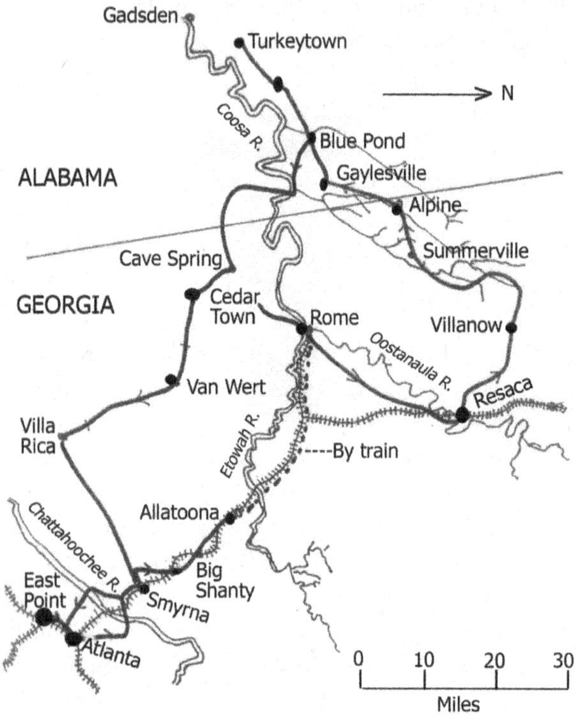

Map 11. Route of the 90th Illinois during pursuit of General John Bell Hood and return to Atlanta

months before he received an answer. On October 29, the men of the 90th Illinois began the march back to Atlanta, and by November 5, they, along with the rest of the Second Division, arrived back at the old Smyrna Campground. The Legion now had only 224 officers and enlisted men present—and of these, only 185 were present for duty—as the number of absent sick officers and men had increased by thirty-five. During the pursuit of Hood, the Irish Legion troops marched some 290 miles, retraced the territory of their spring campaign, and enjoyed beautiful autumn scenery in northern Georgia and Alabama, all at government expense.[10]

In his memoirs, Hazen posed the question: "What to do next?" He added: "There was scarcely a soldier in the command who did not think of it by day and dream of it by night." By implication, the troops of the Legion would have shared the same concern about military strategy. It really made no sense to go back to Chattanooga and start all over from there, but permanently holding Atlanta would be difficult, if not impossible. First, a large number of troops would be required to garrison Atlanta and protect the extended Louisville-Nashville-Chattanooga-Atlanta railroad supply line. Second, the vulnerability of this lifeline to Confederate raiders was a major concern. Certainly Sherman thought so when he wired Lieutenant General Ulysses S. Grant, "It will be a physical impossibility to protect the roads, now that Hood, Forrest, Wheeler, and the whole batch of devils, are turned loose without home or habitation." Sherman had a solution: "I propose we break up the railroad from Chattanooga forward, and that we strike out with wagons for Milledgeville, Millen and Savannah." Sherman pointed out that it was useless to occupy Georgia, adding rather ominously: "I can make this march, and make Georgia howl."[11]

It took time for Sherman to convince Grant and the army's chief of staff, Major General Henry Halleck, of the wisdom of his proposal. Finally, on November 2, Sherman received permission from Grant to make his march to the sea. How much the soldiers of the 90th Illinois knew about these future plans is not recorded, but Hazen wrote that "thousands of men, and of all grades, had solved the problem in their own minds precisely as did our commander . . . to move forward." One can expect that some very interesting rumors circulated in the Legion about the nature and ultimate destination of their next march.[12]

Some 219 officers and enlisted men of the Irish Legion judged able to stand the rigors of the planned march survived Sherman's culling. Those vigorous Irishmen who would make the march included Lieutenant Colonel Owen Stuart, now restored to command of the regiment. With proper care and timely extensions obtained by forceful argument, his twenty-day medical leave lasted a little less than sixty days before he returned to the field. His journey involved one day in Louisville, Kentucky, followed by five days in both Nashville and Chattanooga. At Chattanooga, he received orders placing him in command of the 2nd Battalion, 3rd Provisional Brigade, at the Camp of Detachments. Three days later, he received further orders directing him to move his battalion to the depot before taking the train to Tilton, Georgia, located between Dalton and Resaca, and to report to the headquarters at Chattanooga for final orders. This was serious business; commanding a battalion of strangers held little appeal to Stuart, who wrote, "But the majority of my men being drafted I was afraid of them in a fight. So I resolved to get relieved." Unimpressed by differences in rank, Stuart told Major General James B. Steedman that he "belonged to the department of the Tenn. and would not Serve out side of it." To his credit, Steedman released Stuart, and the final orders, also dated October 27, instructed Stuart upon arriving at Tilton to turn over command to the major of the battalion "and proceed to your proper command in the field." The Union army could devise an interesting way to get a wounded officer to return voluntarily to his command. Hoping to rejoin the Legion, Stuart started for Rome on a slow train that advanced only thirty miles in three days, so that when he arrived at Rome, the 90th Illinois had moved on. General Corse ordered him to Marietta to meet his regiment, which arrived nearby at Smyrna on November 5.

On November 8, Stuart, obviously glad to be back with his fellow Irishmen, wrote he had rejoined "the good old 90th. They are all well and glad to See me."[13]

By November 4, 1864, while at Marietta, Lieutenant Colonel Stuart already knew he would be on a march to the sea. A letter to his wife, Margaret, indicates some ambivalence: "Now about the future, the 14, 15, 17, and 20th [Corps] are going some where no body can tell, but Sherman told me at Rome to burn my Baggage and he would give us a Salt water Bath. I personally am stuck for this campaign but am going to see General Howard as soon as he arrives." On November 8, while camped near Vining's Bridge on the Chattahoochee River, Stuart added a few more details of their forthcoming march in another letter to his wife: "This army will move in a few days, and it is the opinion of all officers that we are going to Savannah or Mobile." His only problem was that he was "in a very bad way for horses. My Grey is hardly able to walk. I am trying to get another from the Govt." He added that after they left Atlanta, there would be no communication for some time, and no mail was currently "going North except we may find Somebody going up."[14]

On November 8, the men of the Legion received part of their back pay for duty from December 31, 1863, to August 31, 1864. Eight months' pay of over a hundred dollars formed too big a wad of cash for each private to carry around, so the next day General Osterhaus ordered Captain David Duffy, Company E, to go to Chicago, taking the troops' money to their families, and return as soon as practicable. These orders kept Duffy from making the march to the sea, depriving the 90th Illinois of another experienced company commander. His replacement, Lieutenant McAssey, commanded both Company K and Company E until February 21, 1865. For various reasons, Captains Feeney, Company F, and John Murphy, Company G, would also miss the march to Savannah.[15]

On November 10, the 90th Illinois marched to Turner's Ferry, about four miles downstream from the railroad bridge, to guard the crossing and allow the pontoon bridge over the Chattahoochee River to be put down. The Legion remained at Turner's Ferry until relieved by the Fourth Division on November 14 and then marched back to Atlanta.[16]

The 90th Illinois could readily observe that time was getting short as preparation for the march to the sea neared completion. Sick and wounded men and surplus stores at Atlanta had been sent to Chattanooga by rail. Wagon trains sat loaded and ready to move on short notice. Railroad and telegraph communication with Chattanooga had been severed on November 12. Captain Orlando Poe, Sherman's chief engineer, supervised the destruction so that "for military purposes the city of Atlanta has ceased to exist." By November 14, Sherman's army—62,000 strong, located in and around Atlanta—included 5,063 cavalry commanded by Brigadier General Hugh Judson "Kil-Cavalry" Kilpatrick. Sherman divided his army into right and left wings commanded by Major Generals Oliver O. Howard and Henry W. Slocum, respectively. The right wing included the XV Corps and XVII Corps, commanded by General Osterhaus and Major General Frank P. Blair, respectively. The XV Corps had four divisions, including Hazen's Second Division. The 90th Illinois belonged to Colonel John Oliver's Third Brigade of Hazen's Second Division. The XIV and XX Corps formed the left wing.[17]

If those in the 90th Illinois wondered how the march would be conducted, Sherman's field orders provided the details but left them guessing as to their final destination. Wagons would carry only provisions and ammunition. To limit congestion, the four corps would march on four nearly parallel roads. The columns would start at 7 A.M. and march about fifteen miles per day. The most quoted order explained how the troops would be fed: "The army will forage liberally on the country." Each brigade had an organized foraging party "under the command of one or more discreet officers . . . aiming at all times to keep in the wagons at least ten days' provisions for the command and three days' forage." Sherman expected his troops to live as much as possible off the country. Sherman forbade his soldiers from entering dwellings or committing trespass. Corps commanders alone had "the power to destroy mills, houses, cotton-gins, etc." Destruction of property was limited to cases where the march met local resistance. The troops were "to assist wagons at steep hills or bad crossings of streams." The 90th Illinois knew well what that meant.[18]

Rivers would be the major physical obstacles faced on the march, and both wings' pontoon-trains would allow them to bridge a river where they pleased. The pontoon-train of the right wing could build a bridge 580 feet long. To aid in overcoming the obstacles of poor roads with swamps, bogs, and other impediments to movement of wagons, ambulances, and artillery, the seven divisions of the right wing each had a pioneer corps of the "average strength of 100 whites and 70 negroes," giving the wing approximately 1,200 men as pioneers, according to Captain Poe.[19]

The army's 2,500 or so wagons, each pulled by a six-mule team, and six hundred ambulances, each with two horses, meant each corps had to protect some eight hundred vehicles occupying a distance of five miles or more on the march. The wagon trains and artillery would travel on the road while, except for rear guard troops and at bridge crossings, men would march on whatever paths they could improvise alongside the wagons. The trains would carry both ammunition and supplies, including bread for twenty days, sugar, coffee, and a double allowance of salt for forty days for the men but only three days' grain for the horses and mules. A herd of 5,000 head of beef, some forty-day supply, would accompany Sherman's army as it left Atlanta. Ammunition supplies included the forty rounds each soldier carried and another two hundred rounds per man carried in the wagons. In addition, there were two hundred rounds of ammunition for each field gun. The soldiers of the Irish Legion would not starve, but in order to live off the land as Sherman intended, they had to keep moving. If the army remained stationary, it would soon exhaust the food supply available from the surrounding country. There could be no extended sieges.[20]

Sherman summed up the situation: "It surely was a strange event—two hostile armies marching in opposite directions, each in the full belief that it was achieving a final and conclusive result in a great war."[21]

{ 11 }

AN ARMED PICNIC

On November 15, the Irish Legion began the great march to the sea. They and the rest of the right wing, accompanied by Brigadier General Hugh Judson Kilpatrick's cavalry, followed the railroad toward Jonesborough and then McDonough, Georgia. They had orders to make a feint on Macon, cross the Ocmulgee River at Planters' Factory, and rendezvous near Gordon in seven days (Map 12). Major General William T. Sherman planned to march his army between Macon and Augusta, forcing his Confederate opponent "to divide his forces to defend not only these points, but Millen, Savannah, and Charleston." The only organized resistance Sherman's army would face until his troops reached Savannah would come from General Joseph Wheeler's cavalry and small bodies of troops, many of them militia. According to Confederate major general Gustavus W. Smith, the Confederate cavalry "could not materially, if at all, affect the regular daily progress of Sherman's main forces, mainly serving to restrict the operations of the Union cavalry."[1]

The Atlanta campaign had instilled in the men of Sherman's army an air of confidence, self-reliance, and trust in their leader and the belief that their next campaign would bring an end to the war. As a result, the officers and men of the 90th Illinois most probably viewed the coming march with much the same attitude as that expressed by Brigadier General William Carlin, who described the soldiers' mood as "free and exuberant. We didn't know where we were going, but we felt certain that [we] were doing a work that would prove decisive." Carlin added, "Besides, there was a delightful relief in the minds of all, that for some weeks at least we would have some exemption from the carnage of battle."[2]

In addition to light hearts, the soldiers also lightened their loads on the march, according to the XV Corps scout from the 100th Indiana, Theodore Upson. In

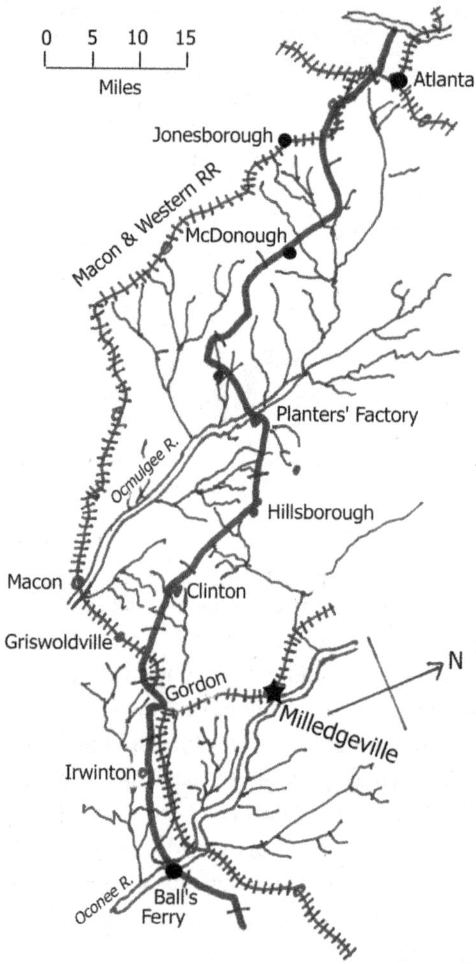

Map 12. March to the sea: route of the 90th Illinois through Georgia's Piedmont, November 15–27, 1864

addition to their "haversacks, canteens, guns, and cartridge boxes containing forty rounds of ammunition," all that many soldiers carried was a "blanket made into a roll" with a "rubber 'poncho' . . . doubled around and tied at the ends and hung over the left shoulder."[3]

Five rivers—the Ocmulgee, Oconee, Ohoopee, Canoochee (Cannouchee on some maps), and Ogeechee—formed the few natural barriers at which small forces of Confederate troops could dispute crossing points and temporarily delay Union forces. River crossings formed choke points that presented real difficulties for Union wagon trains and artillery if flooded. November weather in Georgia wasn't exactly summer, either, as November 23 produced ice some inch and a half thick.[4]

Although the march to the sea is the best-known event in which the Irish Legion took part, it is also the least well described and documented by its own members, with the fortunate exception of letters from Lieutenant Colonel Owen Stuart and Quartermaster Redmond Sheridan. By this time, brigade and regiment level reports had become routine, providing few descriptive details beyond the direction of march, cities and towns passed, miles covered, travel conditions, and actions related to encounters with the enemy, which for the 90th Illinois were few until the regiment reached the Ogeechee River some twenty miles from Savannah. The Irish Legion made relatively steady daily progress except for delays in crossing the Ocmulgee, Oconee, and Ogeechee Rivers (see Map 12; Map 13).

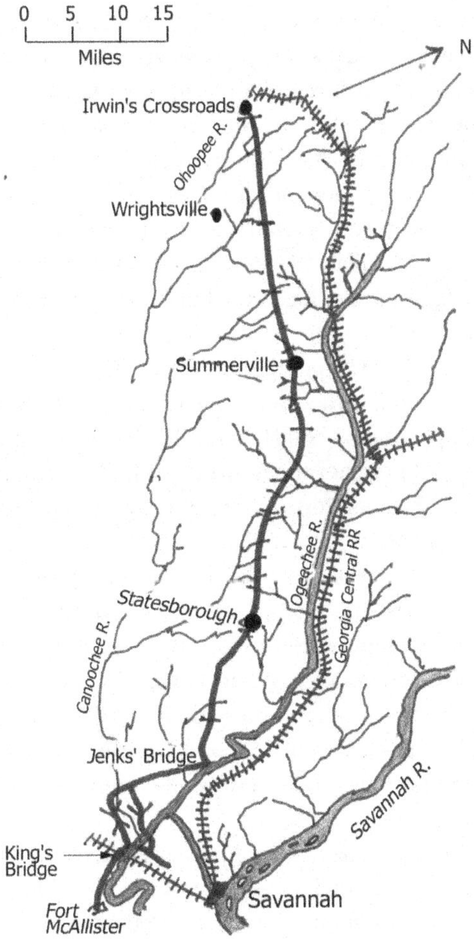

Map 13. March to the sea: route of the 90th Illinois through Georgia's Coastal Plain to Savannah

Despite General Carlin's description of the march as "an armed picnic," food availability and travel conditions varied considerably between units and changed as the march progressed due to regional differences in terrain and type and intensity of agriculture. The right wing, and thus the 90th Illinois, found food to be less plentiful than reported by members of the left wing. But for most of the first two weeks, the men of the Legion marched through the Piedmont, where that region's well-developed agriculture provided a sufficiency and in many cases an overabundance of hogs, various kinds of fowl, and potatoes, which, by Sherman's orders, could be theirs for the taking.[5]

In a letter to his brother, Quartermaster Sheridan described the food supply for the 90th Illinois during the march: "[We] received orders that another long, arduous, and dangerous campaign must immediately be proceeded on. So on we went with 15 days full rations of bread, sugar, coffee and salt and some beef on hoof, but this was unnecessary where there was plenty of hogs and chickens. They were easier dressed and I assure you no army ever lived better. No restrictions were placed on the men in obtaining food but were forbidden to pillage houses." The result, as Sheridan rather ruefully observed, "was feathers enough along the route daily to stuff feather beds for all Jersey and if the Hog Heads could have been collected into one great reservoir the Northern Millions could have feasted at least for one meal." Sheridan felt "sure the greatest lover of hog flesh must feel abashed to look a pig in the face hereafter, but these Yankees have no limit to their bashfulness."[6]

However, according to Corporal Simon Swan, Company G, meals resembled a feast or famine situation, with dinner sometimes consisting of meat from an old dead mule. The supply of food collected locally depended upon the ability of the foragers. Some, apparently less adept or more kindhearted, returned with little or nothing to show for their efforts; other more aggressive types always returned fully laden with their spoils.

Lieutenant Colonel Stuart wrote that the Legion traveled "over a great many miles and on all Sorts of roads, Swamps & Deserts." To allow the wagons to traverse wet or boggy stretches, pioneers corduroyed the road and could cover a quarter of a mile in as little as fifteen minutes. Where longer stretches required corduroying, officers assigned lengths of road to individual regiments to speed up the work. Brigadier General William Hazen's Second Division, which included the 90th Illinois, constructed 1,850 feet of bridging and corduroyed over six miles of road during the march to the sea.[7]

Partly to allay his wife's concern about his physical condition, Stuart wrote that during the march he spent "28 days and nights in the Saddle, but I Stood it much better than I expected. The whole Army lived on the Country, and you may judge we lived well, on Potatoes, Beef, Mutton, Chicken & Eggs, and the whole Army is much better, now than when we Started. Our Army moved from Atlanta in four

Columns," with the "15th [Corps] on the extreme right"; consequently, "we had all the fi[gh]ting to do, as Wheeler was on our right and rear after we left Macon." Stuart wrote that "no more than one Division marched on the Same road," so that "the whole army covered a front of Sixty miles cleaning everything before us." The order of march rotated within the brigade so that the lead regiment (advanced guard) for one day moved to the rear of the brigade the next day, becoming the rear guard. Brigades followed the same rotation within the division and divisions likewise within the corps.[8]

Quartermaster Sheridan commented on the lack of major battles during the campaign: "The principal warfare of our entire army" consisted of "a few skirmishes with Wheeler when crossing the Oconee, the Ogeechee and the Canoochee Rivers excepted till we reached the neighborhood of Savannah."[9]

The distance by highway from Atlanta to Savannah is 249 miles. The 90th Illinois took twenty-five days traveling 289 miles from Atlanta to King's Bridge outside Savannah, an average of eleven and a half miles a day. The march from Atlanta to Savannah followed a fairly direct route, with the line of march of the Second Division, and thus the 90th Illinois, from McDonough to Savannah deviating no more than fifteen miles from a straight line (see Maps 12 and 13). From Gordon to Savannah, the route of march lay from two to ten miles south of the Georgia Central Railroad.

From November 15 to November 27, the Legion marched some 143 miles through the Piedmont region east of Atlanta. River crossings formed potential bottlenecks, as shown by the full day and a half required for the 16,000 men, supply trains, artillery, and livestock of the XV Corps to cross the Ocmulgee River at Planters' Factory. The daily distance covered, excluding days involving river crossings, varied between a high of seventeen miles to a low of five miles when directional problems and a need by the Third Brigade and thus by the Legion to fortify their campsite slowed the march on November 23. Two days earlier, the 15th Michigan of Colonel John Oliver's Third Brigade had to fight off Confederate cavalry near Macon while guarding trains. One day earlier, Brigadier General Charles Walcutt's brigade of the First Division of the XV Corps had been attacked by Confederate infantry at Griswoldville, some ten miles east of Macon on the Georgia Central Railroad. Hazen responded to the Confederate attacks by ordering his brigade commanders to organize their mounted foragers into a force of mounted infantry to be used when necessary. Hazen's mounted force never exceeded more than 5 percent of his troops, so only a few of the Legion officially got to ride instead of walk on the march to the sea. The 90th Illinois passed through Gordon on November 23, where Company A reported burning the depot.[10]

On November 25, the 90th Illinois reached Ball's Ferry on the Oconee River, but Confederate troops on the opposite (eastern) shore prevented Union troops from crossing the river. The men of the Legion had a short time to admire the magnificent live oak trees draped with Spanish moss that lined the river at the ferry before Colonel Oliver deployed them along with the 99th Indiana as skirmishers to picket the river. The next morning, the Confederates had departed, and that night, November 26, the Legion crossed the river in small boats. Such action often occurred at river crossings, and Company F of the 90th Illinois reported skirmishes while crossing the Ocmulgee, Oconee, Ogeechee, and Canoochee Rivers.[11]

On the next day, the Third Brigade, including the 90th Illinois, marched eight miles to Irwin's Crossroads, where the troops camped at noon (see Maps 12 and 13). They now entered the transition from the Piedmont to the Coastal Plain, and many of the farmers in the Legion would have noticed the changes in vegetation and soil as the reddish clays of the Piedmont gave way to the light-colored sandy soils of the Coastal Plain.

Back in the North, Sherman's march generated headlines fueled by a mixture of fact, wild speculation, and silence. The authorities in Washington had no better information on Sherman's whereabouts. When questioned about Sherman's destination, President Lincoln reportedly responded: "I know the hole he went in at, but I can't tell you what hole he will come out of."[12]

The 90th Illinois marched some 119 miles in the Coastal Plain from Irwin's Crossroads to Jenks' Bridge on the Ogeechee River, an average of thirteen miles per day. Major General Peter Osterhaus, who commanded the XV Corps on the march to the sea, described the area as "almost a perfect wilderness—long-leaved pines cover the poor sandy soil but sparely, and exclude all other vegetation except where an occasional creek or marsh, lined with narrow skirts of shrub-like undergrowth, breaks this monotony." He added that "what makes the soil almost worthless for agricultural purposes rendered it favorable to our operations. An energetic corps of axmen to corduroy roads across the creeks and marshes opens in a short time enough space for any number of columns." The men of the 90th Illinois should have found much on the march through the Costal Plain to their liking. The area had good water, while the ground had a thick cover of soft "pine straw" and "wire grass." Camping among the dark pine trees under the clear starlight with the hazy smoke of campfires drifting among the tents held its own particular charm. Much of the area was sparsely inhabited with few farms along the main roads except for small cultivated patches, making food harder to find and requiring greater effort by the Legion's foragers.[13]

After passing Irwin's Crossroads on November 27, the 90th Illinois entered a continuous pine forest, crossing several swampy branches of the Ohoopee River before reaching Summerville on November 30 (see Map 13). As the Irishmen marched on the Old Savannah Road paralleling the right bank of the Ogeechee River, they crossed a series of low, broad marshes that required corduroying.

Contacts with Confederate forces, especially cavalry, became more numerous, and Colonel Oliver reported that near Statesborough (now Statesboro), about six hundred Confederate cavalry had attacked some of the division's mounted foragers, driving them back on the 70th Ohio, which fired a single volley, causing the Confederate cavalry to skedaddle.[14]

The Legion's amphibious assault across the hundred-yard-wide Ogeechee River at Jenks' Bridge, twenty-one miles from Savannah, earned the Irishmen another name to place on their flag. On November 6, Colonel Oliver's Third Brigade, including the 90th Illinois, attempted to capture intact Jenks' Bridge, located where the Savannah road crossed the Ogeechee River, near Eden Station on the Georgia Central Railroad (see Map 13). Oliver's troops moved out smartly from camp between 6 and 7 A.M. and, despite some skirmishing, covered the fifteen miles to the bridge in less than four hours' marching time. However, a wait of one and a half hours for the artillery partway on the march delayed their arrival at the bridge until noon. Apparently, somebody forgot to tell the artillery about the expedition.[15]

When Lieutenant Colonel Stuart arrived at Jenks' Bridge, he found the bridge burned and Confederates strongly fortified on the opposite or eastern bank of the Ogeechee River. According to Stuart, that night Oliver's Third Brigade, without the 90th Illinois, "started down the river to another bridge about 21 miles [away]," leaving "my Regt at Jenks' Bridge to watch the Enemy and Keep them in check until Genl. [Oliver] Howard arrived about 8 A.M. [on December 7]. The Genl. and his Staff came up, [and] sent for me. I told him the Enemy force was Small. He then ordered me to cross the river in a Pontoon boat with two or three companies and dislodge the enemy. I done it Successfully, but when we Started every one thought we were going to our grave." Stuart wrote that he kept General Howard's "order and will preserve it." Adjutant Edwin Davis made it sound more exciting, reporting the 90th Illinois "crossed the [Ogeechee] River next day in pontoon boats under fire from the enemy, but drove him [from his position] without any loss on our side."[16]

General Howard's account fills in some of the details. He reported that Brigadier General John M. Corse found "Colonel Owen Stuart behind a line of rifle pits exchanging shot with [a] considerable force on the other bank. Corse sent up a battery and located it so as to clear away all riflemen that would bother his boats. Then he sent Stuart's regiment across the river. As soon as the first troops got firm foothold east of the Ogeechee, the Confederates fell back to a prepared work, which formed a regular defensive connection from the river to the high ground." This allowed Union pontoniers to work unmolested as they laid a three-hundred-foot-long bridge across the Ogeechee River. The 90th Illinois got to observe as troops from Corse's division and Brigadier General Charles R. Woods's division, who had crossed farther upriver, encountered stiff resistance but drove the Confederate troops from their defensive positions, opening the road.[17]

While the 90th Illinois remained otherwise occupied at Jenks' Bridge on December 7, the Third Brigade made its way toward Bryant Courthouse near Eden just north of the Canoochee River (currently part of Fort Stewart Military Reservation) in an attempt to capture the nearby bridge over the Canoochee River (see Map 13). Following a skirmish at Black Creek, the brigade's sixty-man mounted force vigorously pursued the defending Confederate cavalry. Despite their efforts, the bridge at the crossing of the Canoochee River had been burned; however, they managed to save six-hundred-foot-long bridges across two lagoons. The brigade spent most of the next day skirmishing at the crossing with Confederate defenders. The rest of the Second Division soon joined them. The 90th Illinois remained at Jenks' Bridge until the morning of December 8, when the men crossed to the west bank of the Ogeechee River and marched twenty miles to rejoin their brigade. Content with having delayed the Union crossing of the Canoochee, the Confederate defenders fell back to Savannah during the night.[18]

On December 9, the Third Brigade, including the 90th Illinois, spent two hours crossing the Canoochee River in pontoon boats before rapidly covering the eight miles to King's Bridge but found most of it destroyed. The Third Brigade then destroyed fourteen trestles, ranging from 30 to 150 yards long, and the 500-yard-long "Gulf railroad bridge" across the Ogeechee as ordered. On the following day, the brigade recrossed the Canoochee River and marched to the Ogeechee River, crossed at Dillon's Ferry, and camped about ten miles from Savannah after marching eighteen miles. While the rest of the brigade rested in camp, on December 11 the 90th Illinois escorted the wagon train to obtain forage and marched back to King's Bridge the next day, rejoining the brigade. Big things were afoot as the Second Division had orders to cross the Ogeechee and "move down its right bank to Fort McAllister and capture it."[19]

{ 12 }

THE HANDSOMEST THING I HAVE SEEN IN THIS WAR

Major General William T. Sherman's troops ran low on supplies as they reached Savannah and began the siege of the city. In a letter to his wife, Margaret, Lieutenant Colonel Owen Stuart starkly summarized the situation the Union army faced upon reaching Savannah: "Our lines are now formed, and the Supplies all out." In Brigadier General William Hazen's Second Division, a First Brigade Regiment, the 55th Illinois, reported receiving "half rations of coffee, sugar, and hard-tack, the stores in the wagons being nearly exhausted" upon approaching Savannah.[1]

Starvation, at least in the short term, remained too dire a description of the army's situation. Rich oyster beds flourished nearby, and local plantations held piles of harvested rice. But before the rice could be eaten, it had to be hulled, which the troops accomplished in due fashion. Beef from large herds of cattle collected on the way supplemented the rice. According to Major Henry Hitchcock of Sherman's staff, ten days of rations remained for the troops, but they lacked fodder for the army's horses, mules, and cattle, and their supply of corn and oats would soon be exhausted. Another staff member, Major Thomas Ward Osborn, considered rice "poor food to feed an army on." The customary diet of the Irish Legion did not include brown rice, either, so they could be expected to have shared Osborn's opinion of such fare.[2]

With its large cannons covering the Ogeechee River, Fort McAllister effectively blocked river traffic, preventing resupply of Sherman's army by the Union fleet hovering offshore. This small, rather simple looking sand fort had withstood Union naval bombardment eight separate times from July 1862 through March 1863. During the attack on March 4, 1863, it survived bombardment by 345- to 350-pound shells from the fifteen-inch guns of the monitors *Passaic*, *Patapsco*, and *Nahant* from 8:30 A.M. to 4:30 P.M., with an hour and a half out for lunch. (Naval warfare still retained some degree of civility.) The fort remained defiant and largely intact with only one casualty, the garrison's pet cat, Tom. The shelling caused little damage, simply shifting the sand around, which the fort's defenders speedily moved back in place. Stuart bluntly stated the problem: "Ft. McAllister . . . was between the army and our Supplies, it must be taken or the army [will] starve."[3]

Sherman gave Major General Oliver Howard the job of opening up communications with the fleet. "Hazen's" was Howard's answer to Sherman's question as to which division to use to capture the fort. Sherman's agreement meant that the 90th Illinois would be part of the force attempting to take the fort by a frontal attack, which, based on past experience, would not be an easy thing to accomplish.[4]

Today, Fort McAllister, as restored by Henry Ford, who once owned the land on which the fort is located, may not look particularly impressive, but looks can be deceptive. As it existed in December 1864, it would have appeared formidable to the troops preparing for the attack. The fort's river frontage stretched only about 550 feet, but its circumference measured a little over 3,000 feet. A dry moat fronted three of its four land sides. The marshy terrain in front of the fourth land side made attack from that direction difficult (Map 14). Most of the fort's twenty-two guns fired over a protective wall or parapet. However, the five large cannon of eight- or ten-inch diameter mounted along the fourth land side faced downriver and thus provided little protection against a land attack from the other three sides. As Sherman's army neared Savannah, the land defenses of the fort had been strengthened and the fort resupplied to withstand a thirty-day siege. The Confederate defenders cut down trees and removed brush to provide clear fields of fire. To slow the approach of attacking Union troops, the Confederates placed abatis, trees cut down with sharpened branches facing outward, in front of the dry moat, a ditch some fifteen feet deep and six or seven feet across at the bottom. The fort side of the moat had an inclined slope or glacis that could be swept by fire from the defenders. To further delay enemy troops attempting to cross the moat, the fort's defenders had constructed a palisade, made by placing a row of stout, pointed poles set close together at an angle, on the bottom of the moat (Fig. 2). A single row of torpedoes, actually land mines made using seven- and eight-inch shells that exploded when stepped on, had been placed "just outside the abatis, and were about three feet from center to center," according to Captain Orlando Poe, Sherman's chief engineer. General Hazen noted that "the line of torpedoes . . . was continuous around the fort and about one hundred yards in front of the entanglements [abatis]. . . . The two flanks of the fort were the weak points,—the one on the Ogeechee side presenting a broad gravelly shore left by the receding tide." Abatis extended along only part of the fort's eastern and western faces, leaving the area near the river without entanglements. However, abatis protected the area in front of the long southern face of the fort, the area attacked by Colonel John Oliver's Third Brigade and the 90th Illinois. A Library of Congress map of Hazen's attack shows a similar placement for the abatis. A line of abatis and an earthen wall or "covered way" extended from the fort's southeast corner to an exterior mortar position that, while it complicated the movement of some, provided a measure of protection for other First Brigade troops attacking from the southeast. The fort's commander, Major George W. Anderson, had only 150 effectives (out of 230 total personnel) and no hope of reinforcement due to the isolated location of the fort. He realized that "holding the fort was simply a question of time" and determined "to defend the fort to the last extremity."[5]

On December 12, after Hazen received orders to cross the Ogeechee and take Fort McAllister, his Second Division marched five miles and camped near King's Bridge, in position to attack the fort the next day. Hazen's troops were supported by a section of Captain Francis De Gress's battery and the six guns of the 1st Missouri Light Artillery. The division crossed the newly rebuilt thousand-foot-long King's Bridge at 7 A.M. and marched thirteen miles along the right bank of the Ogeechee, reaching the fort between 11 A.M. and noon (see Map 13, in chapter 11). The men of the Irish Legion should have enjoyed the march through a nearly idyllic setting. According to Hazen's postwar account, "The day was bright, and the march, after leaving from rice farms, was along a lovely road of shells and white sand, under magnolias and wide branching live oaks draped in long, hanging moss." However the reality of war soon intruded about a mile from the fort when they captured a picket who revealed the location of a line of torpedoes (improvised land mines)

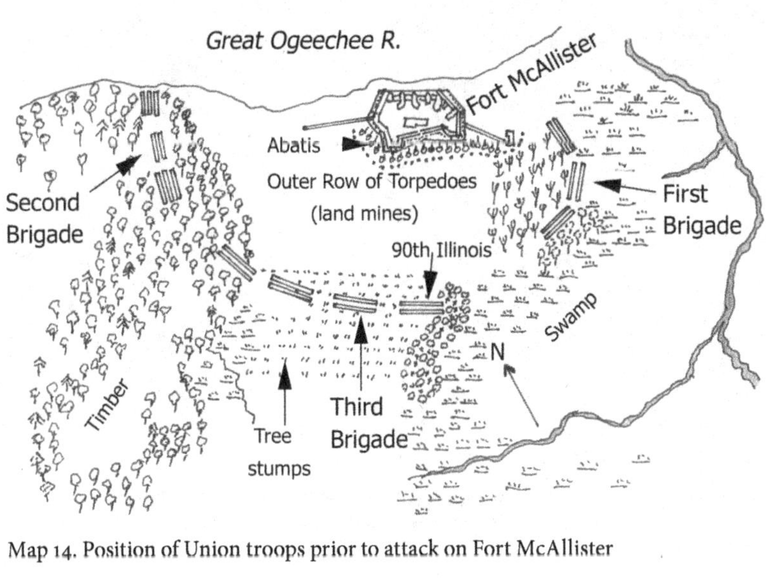

Map 14. Position of Union troops prior to attack on Fort McAllister

Fig. 2. Theodore Davis's sketch showing Brigadier General William Hazen's troops storming Fort McAllister at the moment their first regimental flags appeared atop the fort's parapet. The 90th Illinois is among the troops attacking on the right. (*Harper's Weekly*, January 14, 1865, 20)

across the road. It took some time to safely remove the mines. Hazen left eight regiments at that point and took his remaining nine regiments "forward to about 600 yards from the fort and deployed."[6]

Hazen sent three regiments from the Second Brigade to the left of the fort and three, including the 90th Illinois, from Colonel Oliver's Third Brigade to the center. A swamp delayed the three First Brigade regiments from reaching their position to the right of the fort (see Map 14). Oliver's Third Brigade deployed mostly in the open about seven hundred yards from the fort with the 90th Illinois on the right, 48th Illinois in the center, and 70th Ohio on the left. While the troops deployed for the attack, Hazen sent in skirmishers to suppress the fire from the fort. The skirmish line advanced at a run to within two hundred yards of the fort. Protected by high grass and tree trunks left by the defenders, the skirmishers kept "the gunners from working their guns with any effect," according to Hazen. Oliver credited Captain Stephen F. Grimes, Company A, of the 48th Illinois, who commanded the skirmish line, with silencing two ten-inch guns.[7]

As they waited in front of the fort for the signal to begin the action, the members of the 90th Illinois had time to speculate about what they would encounter during the coming attack. As they looked across open fields in their front, they could readily see some of Fort McAllister's defenses. Judging by photographs taken soon after the fort's capture, they would have seen its raised, sloping walls topped with field guns and could determine how effectively their skirmishers suppressed the fire from those same guns. They could also see one or more lines of abatis made of interlaced tree branches, knowing that they would have to cross these entanglements to reach the fort. Photographs show a line of abatis but also show clumps of tree branches scattered about, indicating the possible presence of more than one row of abatis at the time of the attack. The troops' location on somewhat lower ground than the fort made it difficult to detect the ditch in front of the fort and impossible to see the line of stakes, or palisades, at the ditch's bottom. However, being veterans, and thus intimately familiar with Confederate fortification techniques, they knew to expect such obstacles. They would not have known the number of defenders, but the apparent lack of Confederate skirmishers and rate of return rifle fire from the fort would have indicated the fort's limited troop strength. They would not have known the extent and placement of torpedoes around the fort; however, earlier that same day they had encountered such "infernal machines" buried in the road, as revealed by the captured picket, so the presence of torpedoes around the fort could not have been unexpected.[8]

Urged on by Sherman's signals, Hazen finally ordered his troops to attack. The marshy ground to the right of the fort had slowed deployment on that side, which was not completed until 4:45 P.M. when the bugle sounded forward. By 5 P.M., the Union soldiers had captured the fort. Hazen described the attack: "The troops were deployed in one line as thin as possible, the result being that no man in the assault was struck till they came to close quarters. Here the fighting became desperate and deadly." Hazen noted the placement of the torpedoes, which caused most of the casualties suffered during the attack. "Just outside the works a line of torpedoes had been placed, many of which were exploded by the tread of the troops, blowing many men to atoms, but the line moved on without checking, over, under, and through abatis, ditches, palisading, and parapet, fighting the garrison through the fort to their bomb-proofs, from which they still fought, and only succumbed as each man was individually overpowered." Theodore Davis's sketch (see Fig. 2) depicts Hazen's troops storming Fort McAllister at the moment their first regimental flags appeared atop the fort's parapet and shows the fort's defenses as described by Hazen, including exploding "torpedoes." The 90th Illinois scaled the fort's right face, shown in the sketch.[9]

Stuart described the attack in a letter to his wife: "Mind you the Rebs had 23 large guns in the fort, and 170 large Torpedoes buried out Side [the fort]. The attention was Sounded, advance—charge. When the men went with one tremendous yell and in 13 minutes from the time we charged we had possession of the Fort with all the Booty." Quartermaster Redmond Sheridan described the scene as the Legion moved to the attack: "At the sound of the charge they started on a run with fixed bayonet. In approaching the ditch the scene was horrible and grand and torpedoes bursting sending the object that pressed its cap disjointed and mutilated in air and eternity, guns of the Fort belching their ponderous solid shot, whilst along the ditch grape and canister swept like a whirlwind. Still down into the ditch they swept that escaped the fatal torpedoes." Sheridan described the scene as the Legion crossed the large ditch under fire and entered the fort: "As if to avoid them, to pull up the abattis was the work of a moment, and up the steep [slope] they rushed yelling—both defiance and agony when the latter was felt. The parapet was gained at the same instant by the color bearers of both the 90th Ill and 70th Ohio." According to Sheridan, the regiments raced to claim the honor of the first to enter the fort: "The bearer of the 70th was shot, and stumbled, ours also before he had time to plant the colors in the earth. An orderly of the 70th being on the spot like lightning stuck their color in the ground. The 90th was in ere his hand had accomplished the gallant task, yet an instant too late to claim preference. The fighting was terrific, meanwhile, the Rebs distaining surrender."[10]

Perched on the roof of a rice mill about three miles from the fort, General Sherman, ever impatient, waited for the attack to begin. Major Hitchcock gave an often-cited account of Sherman's reaction during the taking of the fort. The assembled "generals, officers and orderlies" observed the blue lines as they emerged from the woods surrounding the fort and watched to their dismay as the "head of the column seemed to sink down and disappear . . . the sign of a ruinous repulse if real." The blue lines soon reappeared, however, advancing through the enveloping smoke and swarmed onto the parapet. "The fort was ours!" Then all present atop the rice mill "joined in a yell of triumph."[11]

General Howard wrote that he and Sherman then proceeded "as fast as the oarsman could speed us down the Ogeechee to the vicinity of Fort McAllister." Unexploded torpedoes remained outside the fort, making it a dangerous place. Shortly after they landed, Howard "saw an ambulance, with the mules hauling it, run upon a hidden torpedo. Mules, ambulance, and men were blown into the air."[12]

An idea of the intensity of the combat and bravery of the Confederate defenders can be gained from the hand-to-hand fight between Union captain Stephen Grimes of the 48th Illinois and Confederate captain N. B. Clinch. This encounter received sufficient attention to be mentioned by Quartermaster Sheridan and in Colonel Oliver's brigade report as well as in Major Anderson's report. Captain Clinch put up a very good fight, giving Captain Grimes all he could handle and then some. Grimes required the assistance from other Union soldiers to subdue the Confederate captain, who received eleven wounds in the process of being overwhelmed. As Hazen leaped upon the parapet, he saw Captain Clinch "lying on his back, shot through the arm, with a bayonet-wound in his chest, and contused by the butt of a gun." Clinch recognized Hazen and spoke to him. According to Hazen, Clinch "was a brother-in-law of the Union General Robert Anderson, (defender of Fort Sumter in 1861) and I had known him before the war. Contrary to my expectation, he finally recovered." Clinch proved to be one tough cookie.[13]

As usual, the first regiment to plant its flag on the fort's parapet became the one honored with recognition in the battle reports. Colonel Oliver reported: "The flag of the Seventieth Ohio was the first on the fort, though the gallant veterans of the Forty-eight and Ninetieth Illinois were there with them almost at the same time." In his memoirs, Hazen spread the honors around, crediting the 34th, 47th, and 70th Ohio as being the first to plant their colors on the enemy's works, "followed in a moment by the colors of the entire command."[14]

As Civil War battles went, the Union suffered few casualties, with only 4 officers and 20 enlisted men killed and 7 officers and 103 enlisted men wounded for a total of 134. Over half the casualties were in Colonel Oliver's brigade, which lost 76 officers and men, and of these, the 90th Illinois lost 3 killed and 14 wounded severely. Torpedoes caused rather gruesome wounds as evidenced by a "primary excision" of three inches of the tibia for one 90th Illinois soldier and five inches for a second soldier. One of the wounded, Private Bernard Smith, Company E, had been reported dead after receiving a gunshot wound to the ear during the charge, the ball lodging in or near his brain. He unexpectedly recovered and convalesced in a hospital in New York City. In a letter to his wife, Stuart described Smith's reaction upon being wounded: "I thought of you, when he said to me about a second after he was shot when I wiped the blood off his face, and he came too a little, 'My Dear

Good Wife, Col. if I die will you write to her.' He was a good man and my dear if you go to Chicago do call and see the poor woman." Stuart had already written to Bernard Smith's wife giving her the details of her husband's wounding. The seventeen casualties suffered by the 90th Illinois at Fort McAllister, the Legion's only reported casualties on the march to the sea during the period November 15 to December 22, 1864, represented a significant loss as the December report showed 163 enlisted men present for duty, with 108 absent sick out of an aggregate total of 342 officers and enlisted men. Somewhat later Stuart wrote to Margaret, perhaps a bit ruefully, of their brigade commander's promotion: "Colonel Oliver, now Genl., we put a Star on his Shoulder in taking Ft. McAllister, and he made his appearance after all was over. But that is all right enough for it is the way all Genl. do these days. They never think of leading a charge, the cols. of Regts. has to do all that business now."[15]

With only twelve commissioned officers present for duty, Stuart felt the need for more help in running the regiment. On December 29, he appealed to higher authority, the XV Veteran Reserve Corps in Chicago, to order six of his officers on leave in Illinois for various reasons to return to the Legion without delay. Due to the location and rapidity of the movements of Sherman's army, none of the six would arrive until the war had essentially ended. However, it may have speeded the return of some to service, though not with the Irish Legion.[16]

Hazen listed the ordnance captured at the fort as "eleven siege-guns, one 10-inch mortar and twelve field-pieces," and sixty tons of ammunition. A more useful capture included "a large amount of commissary stores and liquors." In anticipation of a siege, the fort had been stocked just before Sherman's arrival with 2,200 pounds of hard bread, 1,000 pounds of bacon, and forty gallons of whiskey. Sherman reportedly liberated the fort commander's stash of fine Havana cigars and mischievously offered Major Anderson one of his own cigars following a meal they enjoyed that evening at Hazen's headquarters outside the fort. The division camped near the fort on Middleton's plantation, presumably relishing what Stuart termed their captured booty. Judicious appropriation of liberated booty may also explain Sherman's observation of soldiers at the fort sleeping very soundly "in the pale moonlight."[17]

After meeting with Hazen, Sherman and Howard secured what "Sherman called a yawl," and after rowing three miles down the river, they succeeded in reaching the dispatch boat *Dandelion*, opening communications with the fleet. The next day, General Hazen honored the 70th Ohio for its "conspicuous part" in the assault, appointing that regiment to garrison the fort. Along with the honor came the order to their colonel to "put the fort in order, cleansing it," including removal of the remaining land mines. Under the logic that "they put them there, they can take them away," the Southern prisoners, officers included, assisted in removing the naval mines (torpedoes) from the channel of the Ogeechee River and also in removing the remaining land mines from around the fort. Garrisoning a captured fort had its drawbacks.[18]

Praise for the conduct of the set-piece battle came from opposing quarters. Impressed by the performance of his old division, Sherman called the capture the "handsomest thing I have seen in this war." On the Confederate side, the December 14 issue of the *Charleston Mercury* reported the capture of Fort McAllister, paying a compliment to Hazen's troops: "We regret to announce the fall of Fort McAllister that post was carried early yesterday morning by assault, in which a heavy column of Sherman's best troops participated."[19]

On December 14, the day following the capture of Fort McAllister, General Hazen's Second Division camped near the fort at Middleton's plantation. The wounded remained in nearby hospitals until evacuated by hospital boat on December 24. Hazen also reported that he "made disposition of the captured property." The exact nature of the dispositions is not noted other than Sherman's appropriation of the fort commander's cigars and Hazen's requisition for his table of "wines taken at McAllister." Presumably the Legion, along with the rest of Hazen's troops, benefited proportionately from the spoils of the victory.[20]

Steamboats reached King's Bridge by December 16, and the naval supply line brought in much appreciated rations, letters from home, clothing, and forage, soon to be supplemented by siege guns and ammunition for use in subduing Savannah. The men of the 90th Illinois could relax a bit as the march to the sea had ended, as had their diet of rice. One of the letters that arrived contained Illinois adjutant general Allan Fuller's answer to Captain Daniel O'Connor's October 28 letter requesting a Catholic chaplain for the regiment. According to an 1861 act of Congress, the regimental commander could appoint chaplains, but to be commissioned they had to meet certain qualifications, which was impossible with the regiment now stationed in Savannah.[21]

Before General Sherman and his troops could party in Savannah, they first had to capture the city, and Sherman intended to do just that. It would not be an easy task, as the western approaches to the city were protected by a strong, fifteen-mile-long fortified line mounting some hundred cannon, with some of the largest guarding the approaches to the five narrow causeways leading into the city. Union forces prepared for an attack on Savannah with understandable reservations. Having already done their part, the Second Division got to sit this one out but kept busy by tearing up some twenty-two miles of the Gulf railroad. The men of the 90th Illinois along with their commander, Lieutenant Colonel Stuart, remained near Fort McAllister at the Second Division's Middleton's plantation camp until January 1, 1865, cleaning up the camp, unloading steamships at King's Bridge, and feasting on oysters. Obtaining oysters was not a problem, according to General Hazen, as "the coast, with its numerous bays, estuaries, and inlets was one continuous bed of oysters." By the time the 90th Illinois troops reached Savannah, their food preparation should have improved markedly, as Hazen ordered on December 26, 1864, that Black "authorized company cooks, and servants for officers entitled to them, will be permitted to remain with the division." They received "tickets" issued by the brigade adjutants that provided evidence of this permission.[22]

In a December 17 letter, Stuart, delighted to have a chance to write his wife, described the scene in camp: "You would think the camp was a large School every man with a piece of paper on his Knee writing to his friends while the Guns can be heard Pounding at Savannah, but we have got So use[d] to that Kind of Music that we can hardly Sleep if it is Still." He added: "I do wish you were here, it is a beautiful climate as warm as the 4th of July in Chicago. I am going to Send a party out tomorrow to fish Oysters." In another letter, he described going to the coast in a boat and finding "Oysters by the Millions." Stuart had finally found a source able to satisfy his voracious appetite for oysters.[23]

Beginning the evening of December 20, Lieutenant General William Hardee's Confederate forces successfully evacuated Savannah, escaping to Hardeeville, South Carolina, using improvised pontoon bridges and causeways that Sherman had failed to block. The next morning, the Union troops discovered that the Confederates had gone. This came as a relief to many of the soldiers on both sides, as the assault promised to be bloody. Certainly Major George Nichols, an aide to Sherman, saw the positive side: "We are in Savannah, in the full enjoyment of superb quarters, fish, oysters, and other good things, and our army relishes the condition of affairs." Stuart could agree completely.[24]

On December 22, 1864, General Sherman sent his often-quoted letter:

> To His Excellency, President Lincoln, Washington, D.C.
>
> I beg to present to you as a Christmas gift the city of Savannah, with 150 heavy guns, and plenty of ammunition; also about 25,000 bales of cotton.
>
> W. T. Sherman
> Major General

Sherman seriously underestimated; Savannah actually held 38,000 bales of cotton.[25]

Now that he had a little time to catch up on paperwork, on December 22 Stuart recommended six from the 90th Illinois for promotion and started the recommendations on their journey upward through the proper channels. Five of the six would eventually be promoted, though some had to wait until April 7, 1865.

Quartermaster Redmond Sheridan's position and sense of duty prevented him from requesting a leave. Sheridan wrote to his brother that he had "hoped to have obtained a leave of absence, but continued service called" for his presence with the Legion. By way of explanation, he added: "You know what the chances of a Q. M.

are to obtain leave, therefore need not explain. If our old commander was living, I should have visited home ere this, though I have nothing to say in complaint of our present." He then described his relationship with Owen Stuart: "We are old acquaintances in civil life retaining our old familiarity; of course I know enough to take no advantage by neglecting or showing a disregard for orders. Thus our relations may remain reciprocally courteous until we resume our respective social positions in society at the end of our term of service." Father Dunne had chosen wisely in selecting Sheridan for quartermaster of the Irish Legion. Sheridan also described the year's activities, ending with the conclusion: "Since May last the duties of this Western Army has been severe in the extreme." Many others in the regiment and in that army might well have agreed. The 90th Illinois regimental report for December 1864 showed only 163 enlisted men present for duty. Company B, the largest, had an aggregate present and absent of fifty-three EM and officers and the most EM present for duty, twenty-five. Company I, the smallest, had an aggregate present and absent of twenty EM and officers and only eight EM present for duty.[26]

On December 23, the 90th Illinois received word of the success of Major General George Thomas's first day's attack on General John Bell Hood's Army of Tennessee in front of Nashville and of Thomas's expectation of destroying Hood's entire army the next day. Less welcome news arrived on December 29: no leaves would be granted from the regiment. According to General Howard's order, the army needed all to be present "for another short and decisive Campaign." Howard also attempted to interfere with his soldiers' traditional pastimes, denouncing gambling as "criminal and detrimental to the interests of the service." He warned it must be stopped and threatened arrest and even worse: "offender's winnings will be taken."[27]

On New Year's Day, January 1, 1865, the 90th Illinois, along with the rest of the Second Division, marched about twenty-two miles toward Savannah by way of King's Bridge. The next day, they continued toward Savannah, marching four miles and camping on the west side of the city. The 90th Illinois remained there until January 14 and completed resting and refitting. Most of the time the men built fortifications, but they took time from their labors on January 7 to join in a parade through downtown Savannah. Stuart's description of the event to his wife reveals something of the condition of the troops, including the 90th Illinois: "Yesterday was a great day for the 15th Corps. General Sherman Reviewed his old Ragged Corps and marched them through all the principal Streets in the city. This makes the Second time they had to march through Savannah. The first day was bad and the Second was worse. The Genl. remarked that he had seen them form a better line of Battle in front of the Enemy." Sherman still managed to keep his sense of humor, according to Stuart: "Still Old Billy would laugh and Point to parts of the flags in the different Regts. Genl. Logan arrived here in the morning in time to see his favorite Corps out on Review." As to the future, Stuart looked for "another short and decisive campaign, no body can tell where. I can mention one of four places, Augusta, Charleston, Wilmington or Richmond and the move will be made as soon as we can get supplies here." In common with Confederate leaders, Stuart guessed wrong on all four.[28]

While stationed near Savannah, Stuart had another worry: the regiment needed a new green flag. His letters never did explain why the 90th needed a replacement for the old green flag, but it probably related to the capture of the Legion's color sergeant and flag at the Battle of Atlanta on July 22, 1864. Silk regimental flags deteriorated through wear and tear, and both the flags and their bearers, obvious targets in battle, suffered accordingly. Apparently reflecting his regiment's earnest desires, Stuart definitely wanted that new regimental green flag, as shown by his emphatic instructions to his wife in his December 17 letter: "My Dear there is one thing I want you to do and that is to Buy that Flag." Regimental politics involving the absent Major Patrick Flynn played some part, because Stuart wrote, "Flynn is writing to the officers Saying that the Regt. is disgraced that I ordered the Flag and then refused to Pay for it." Flynn had written to an officer of the Legion "that if they Send him fifty Dollars he will raise the Balance and give it [as] a present to the Regt." Stuart further encouraged Margaret to act: "By you getting the Flag and Sending it to the Regt. you gratify me very much and I think will not loose anything by it." Margaret responded in a January 8 letter that began, "Now dear about the Flag." Due to her mother's illness, she had been unable to go into the city to see about the flag, which had wound up in Smith McCleavy's hands with forty dollars due. Not deterred in the least, Margaret obtained the flag by threatening a Dr. Bois "that I would hold him responsible for it." She added: "I paid for it 81.25 dollars [and] it will leave Thursday night for the regiment." She then commented on Flynn's actions: "This is all Flynn's doing. He is the biggest rascal ever lived. I am glad he will not trouble you anymore as he is mustered out of the Service since he went to Washington with recommendation to the president to appoint him Pay Master but did not succeed in being appointed. He made speeches in Rockford for Lincoln and indeed in every little town. McCleavy said he [Flynn] was glad that I got the flag, but I don't believe it." Margaret also had news about other officers of the regiment: "Capt. John Murphy [Company G] and [1st Lieutenant Lawrence] McCarthy [Company H] are here in plain clothes. They are waiting to be dismissed. They say they will never go back, but I hear there is an order for all absent without leave to go to their regiment to be tried by court martial." Margaret's January 13 letter instructed her husband that Captain David Duffy, Company E, would leave for the regiment the next day and would take the flag with him. The Legion's current location and subsequent movements through the Carolinas considerably delayed Duffy's, and thus the flag's, arrival, so that Stuart had seen neither when he wrote his wife on April 21. He took a philosophical view of the situation: "Still it can't be helped and I am not going to fret about it. Particularly when I am so near to going home." Captain Duffy finally returned to the 90th Illinois sometime between April 21 and April 29, when the regiment began the march to Washington, D.C., guaranteeing that the men of the Irish Legion received their new flag in time for the Grand Review.[29]

The march to the sea was over, and a new march would soon begin. Sherman felt a great deal of satisfaction with the results of his march through Georgia and planned for his army's next march to bring an end to the war.[30]

{ 13 }

ROCKING THE CRADLE OF SECESSION

In his letter congratulating Major General William T. Sherman on his successful march to the sea and his thoughtful Christmas gift, President Lincoln, ever the realist, asked the pertinent question, "But what next?" While the 90th Illinois approached Savannah and participated in capturing Fort McAllister, General Sherman and Lieutenant General Ulysses S. Grant grappled with the "what next" of how to unite their two armies near Richmond, where they could jointly operate against Confederate general Robert E. Lee's Army of Northern Virginia and end the war. Grant, writing on December 6 from City Point outside Petersburg, Virginia, suggested that Sherman "with the balance of your command come here by water with all dispatch." Grant soon changed his mind, due to the lengthy delay required to collect the shipping for such a major transfer of troops, and agreed to Sherman's suggestion to march his troops north through the Carolinas. Grant summarized the obstacles faced in such a march: "The season was bad, the roads impassable for anything except such an army as he [Sherman] had, and I should not have thought of ordering such a move." Sherman thought the march could be done, and Grant willingly let him try. Moreover, after the march to the sea, Sherman's troops felt ready to go wherever he might lead them.[1]

For the Irish Legion, the new campaign began on January 14 when the troops marched to Fort Thunderbolt on the Wilmington River. The next day, they boarded the gunboat *Wenonah* and sailed for Beaufort, South Carolina, arriving there on January 16 (Map 15). Bad, rainy weather made the trip "a rough and in every way uncomfortable passage," according to Brigadier General William Hazen. Lieutenant Colonel Owen Stuart described the trip, remarking on "the rolling of the Ship on Salt water." He expressed amazement at their destination in a letter to his wife: "I had no idea that my next [letter] would be from this Rebel state. . . . No body knows where we are going. Pap Sherman has not arrived yet, He keeps his own Secrets." After landing at Beaufort, the Legion marched four miles and camped. Stuart was not impressed with his location "where I am now writing this letter, in a dismal Swamp without any fire or W[his]ky, but will have some tonight when my baggage comes, as my good old friend Col. Condit Smith [chief quartermaster, XV Army Corps] sent me a gallon of good old B[ourbo]n and a box of Segars. It will be a treat to smoke a good Spanish." Very cold weather, combined with a severe wind blowing sand and dust everywhere, made their stay somewhat uncomfortable. Stuart benefited from having such a helpful friend as Condit Smith, but most

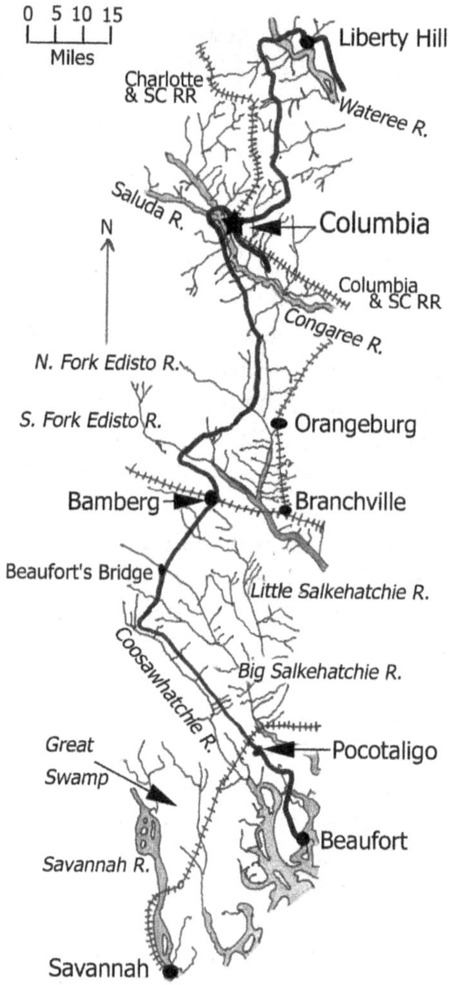

Map 15. March through the Carolinas: route of the 90th Illinois from Beaufort to Liberty Hill, South Carolina

of the Irish Legion would not be so fortunate. Major General Oliver O. Howard, commander of the Army of the Tennessee, ever the spoilsport, restricted the availability of whiskey to the troops in his Special Field Orders No. 15. He attempted to stop the "nefarious practice" of officers "purchasing whiskey from the commissary on their own certificates, for the purpose of distributing it to their men." Howard had definitely "quit preaching and started meddling."[2]

During their stay until January 30 on Port Royal Island, the men of the Legion presumably enjoyed the natural beauty of the region, and those who desired could feast on oysters available from the numerous beds in the area. However, it would not be a time of rest for the "boys" as from January 19 to January 24 General Hazen again shaped up his troops, ordering daily battalion drills and "evolutions of the line." The Second Division must have been an interesting looking bunch of individuals, for on January 21 the Irish Legion received the following order from Hazen: "The practice in many commands of allowing soldiers to wear officers' badges, and those of other arms of the service, is not only prohibited by all the rules of the service, but by this order." Another part warned that previous orders requiring that hair "be kept short having been in many cases disregarded, hereafter any enlisted man of the command seen with long slovenly locks will be arrested and put at hard labor. Officers . . . have been no less derelict with regard to themselves than with their men." On January 20, Stuart felt a bit ill and stayed in his tent, writing that "the Regt. is out on review and inspection. The Capt. [Daniel] O'C[onnor] has command, I thought I would lie off as pay is about the Same, and I believe the less a man does in the army, the more credit he gets and I believe I will try the game, and see how it will work." Stuart's ironical statement about pay served to remind his wife that the regiment had not been paid since the previous August.[3]

While at Beaufort, Stuart received news that several absent officers, Major Patrick Flynn and Captains John Murphy of Company G and David Duffy of Company E, planned to return to the regiment. The next news of Flynn came from Sergeant Charles Stuart of Company A, one of a group of returned prisoners taken at Missionary Ridge and the July 22 and 28, 1864, battles around Atlanta. Stuart wrote that the sergeant "says Flynn the Toothless Red Headed Maj. is on his way back. I tell you I am glad, as [I] want to have him under me for the balance of my time in the army. I intend to treat him well, but he has got to do a good deal of duty Such as he has never done before." On the brighter side, Stuart's stay at Beaufort gave him the opportunity to indulge his love of oysters. He wrote Margaret that he wished she were there, "although it would not be a very pleasant place for you, but on account of the fine Oysters, knowing that you like them so well. Still they are fine, I roasted one this morning it is what they call a bunch, and well it might be called one for it had fifteen of fine fat oysters as you ever saw. I thought while at home that a dozen was a big thing, but know I can eat over one half Bushel, Raw and Roasted, gives me an appetite before breakfast." That morning Stuart and Adjutant Edwin Davis ate nearly a bushel. Stuart wrote that Davis's "hands are all cut opening them. I play off on him there. He has tried to learn me but I don't want too." Stuart had acquired a new horse, which he proudly described to his wife: "I believe I never told you about my fine mare. She is pronounced to be the best animal in the army, and I had [a] deal of trouble to keep her as she has a sister in the Division and the Genl. wanted both of them." More ominously, he wrote: "This Campaign is going to test the Quality of men and officers as a Genl. Order deprives them of tents except the Dog ones, I am going to take a Fly and perhaps a wall tent and my little Stove." Stuart's stove came in handy because "we had Frost here last night and was quite cool all day for the wind is Blowing keenly, a North Eastern." Stuart observed the effect of the weather on the troops: "The 3rd Div. 15th A.C. are now passing and one would imagine that he was in Ill[inois] to look at them Belt their arms around their Body to warm their Fingers, but I am comfortable enough, at this time a good Fire in my ten-inch Stove and nothing on my mind while writing but your Self and hoping that there may be a letter in the Ship that arrived last night from you my Dear."[4]

It had been rainy for several days, leading First Lieutenant William White on January 22 to write to his wife that "nothing can be done, and we have nothing to do. Beaufort is a dull place to loaf, and the result is we lay a round the tent in each others way." Brigadier General John Oliver did his part to break up the boredom, holding a brigade drill that afternoon, which of course included the 90th Illinois. By the next day, the weather improved, the sun came out, and Hazen had the division out drilling that afternoon. White took his turn as regimental officer of the day, which kept him in camp. This brief period of relative inactivity ended on January 24 when three regiments from each brigade began repairing the shell road to Port Royal Ferry, a task requiring corduroying 3,670 yards of road. White wrote that satisfactorily shorn or not, the men of the 90th Illinois left their camp unexpectedly the morning of January 24 "and marched out here about 5 miles Scattered along a Regt in a place, and working on the road." White approved of their new location: "Our Regt. is camped in a nice place and we are no longer at a loss for something to do. Half the Regt. works in the forenoon and the other half afternoons, we are corduroying the road out from Beaufort on which the trains will have to move on the prospective campaign."[5]

While at Port Royal Island, Company C of the 90th Illinois gained four by enlistment; in addition, a first sergeant and two privates returned from missing in action. The regiment also received a hospital wagon to be shared with the 48th Illinois. Stuart took the opportunity to send a final letter to his wife before departing on the march, writing that "W. T. or 'Old Billy' in his order to his command says that the campaign will be Short and decisive and the Shorter the better for I will try and get home on a thirty day leave after having the honor of marching into the City of Charleston. My Dear this is the last letter from Beaufort as we are ordered to march tomorrow morning." He expected that "we will meet with very little resistance from the Enemy as they are nearly plaid out except Lee's army."[6]

Their road-building completed, on January 30 the men of the 90th Illinois crossed Port Royal River on a pontoon bridge at the ferry landing and marched seventeen miles to Pocotaligo, South Carolina. Sherman selected Pocotaligo as the concentration point for Howard's right wing, partly because of its nearness to "the sandy pine-land which connected with the firm ground extending inland." Afterward, the soldiers could justifiably question just how much firm ground they actually found on their march through South Carolina.[7]

Prior to leaving Pocotaligo, Hazen restated orders to his division strictly regulating the foraging required to obtain some seven thousand pounds of food each day. He authorized foragers to discharge firearms only "at the enemy" and forbade them from "pillage" of houses, but they "may take from them salt, flour, meal, and meat, if by so doing they do not leave the occupants destitute." Hazen also specified the organization of pioneer (construction) troops by brigade commanders, who were "also directed to gather up able-bodied negroes for this service." These pioneers would play an essential part in the passage of the army through South Carolina, as they had through Georgia on the march to the sea. Writing some twenty years after the war, Hazen continued to be impressed by his troops' efforts on the march through the Carolinas: "Long stretches of marsh and quicksand required corduroying, and my command became very expert at it. The amount of work of which a large body of troops is capable is almost incredible. When the will is right, the question is one merely of organization. . . . The men had only to be shown what was wanted, and it was soon done. The rapidity of the road-making was remarkable, and our march was scarcely impeded by obstacles thought by the enemy to be insurmountable."[8]

For the march through the Carolinas, Sherman again divided his troops into two wings. The XIV and XX Corps again formed the left wing under the command of Major General Henry Slocum, and the right wing again consisted of the XV and XVII Corps under the command of General Howard. To minimize congestion, each of the four corps again marched by a different road. To aid in keeping the troops together on the march, the route of the XV Corp would be marked (blazed) with "+," and the route of the Second Division was marked by "±," an addition the men of the 90th Illinois no doubt found useful whether or not they appreciated its mathematical significance. The two wings traveled on more or less parallel courses often ten to thirty or more miles apart, reducing congestion and allowing them to more effectively forage off the land. Sherman's feints toward Augusta and Charleston as his army moved toward Columbia forced Confederate general P. G. T. Beauregard to divide his forces to protect both threatened cities, proving the maxim of Fredrick the Great that "he who defends everything, defends nothing."[9]

Exchanges between the army's chief of staff, Major General Henry W. Halleck, and Sherman clearly indicated that the march would be hard on South Carolina. In a letter dated December 18, 1864, Halleck, deskbound in Washington, D.C., expressed frustration with the "cradle of secession": "Should you capture Charleston, I hope that by some accident the place may be destroyed; and if a little salt should be sown upon its site, it may prevent the growth of future crops of nullification and secession." Sherman replied in the same spirit: "The whole army is burning with an insatiable desire to wreak vengeance upon South Carolina. I almost tremble at her fate, but feel that she deserves all that seems in store for her."[10]

Fortunately, Lieutenant White, who commanded the Irish Legion's Company F on the march, proved to be a keen observer and gifted writer and, in a long letter to his wife, described in considerable detail the march and actions of 90th Illinois soldiers during the march through the Carolinas.

The march definitely started on the wet side. Sherman's medical director, Surgeon John Moore, described the difficulties faced by soldiers during the march through South Carolina, which of course included the 90th Illinois: "By far the most serious obstacle encountered during the first ten days was the bad condition of the roads. . . . Several days' heavy rain so swelled the streams as to cover the whole face of the country with water, so that the marching columns were almost constantly in water, often knee deep." Writing at the start of the march, Major Thomas Ward Osborn of Sherman's staff described the road conditions encountered by the army, praising the work of the pioneers. The few available roads "cut through" after as little as "two hours use" and had to "be corduroyed" with "rails and timber" before the trains could move over them. He considered Sherman's army's "superior pioneer organization . . . composed mostly of negroes" to be "of great value" and "probably superior to that of any other Army."[11]

The route of the 90th Illinois from Pocotaligo passed to the southwest or left of McPhersonville, located only two miles from Pocotaligo, and hugged the northern bank of the Coosawhatchie River for some thirty-five miles to the vicinity of Loper's Crossroads (see Map 15). From there, the direction of march became north-northeasterly toward Bamberg. Wherever one found water in South Carolina, there seemed to be those magnificent live oaks, literally dripping Spanish moss, although by this time such sights no longer provided enough novelty to warrant comment in letters home. Lieutenant White described the first day's thirteen-mile march, which began at 7 A.M., indicating the mood and conduct of the Legion's troops: "We left on the 1st of February, and a beautiful day it was, an omen perhaps, of the success that was to attend us. The trains were loaded to their capacity with ammunition and supplies. Everybody was in good humor and confident in the skill of our chief, with cheerful hearts bid adieu to line and base and land on the ocean of the Confederacy." White wrote that the first day's march "was in a northwesterly direction, the road pretty good save where it crossed a marsh or slue, and invariably at such places it had been obstructed by fallen timber, but the pioneer corps without assistance from the troops were able to remove such paltry 'obstacles' in advance of the column." White described the destruction visible along their line of march: "The houses . . . were nearly all vacated, and such as were so we left in ashes. The fences, woods, and everything combustible, was on fire." The village of McPhersonville on their right "shared the fate which the conduct of our men today seemed to threaten all South Carolina." That evening the regiment halted "at a plantation, the outhouses of which were all on fire." A high wind "wafted the flames to the dwelling which burned so furiously, the family saved nothing but themselves." White denied "that this desolation was the work of our regiment. There was thousands in advance of us, and to them belongs the credit or disgrace which ever it may be. I never knew a man of our regiment to fire a building without orders, though I do not say some of them have not done things as bad."[12]

Sherman had been rather loose with respect to the level of discipline imposed on the army during the march from Atlanta to the sea, and stricter constraints on his army's behavior proved difficult to impose during the march through South Carolina. General Hazen's comments illustrate the difficulty encountered in trying to stop looting and burning, some by stragglers: "No sooner had we passed Pocotaligo than the demon of destruction seized possession of everybody. South Carolina had fired the first gun, and even the smallest drummer-boy seemed determined to get even. . . . We were not out of sight of Port Royal Ferry when the black columns of smoke began to ascend. . . . Here began a carnival of destruction that ended with the burning of Columbia, in which the frenzy seemed to exhaust itself. There was scarcely a building far or near on the line of that march that was not burned." Hazen summed it up: "Thus we soldiered in South Carolina. An order prohibiting the destruction of property in any particular case was of no effect beyond one's immediate presence and power to enforce it."[13]

White continued his description of the march: "Next morning [February 2] at an early hour found us again on the road. Fallen timber was occasionally met until we came to a place where there was a number of trees half cut, as though they had not time to finish their design, and from here we found no more obstructions of this sort."[14]

According to Hazen, the road conditions on February 2 included many swamps, which made the march "very severe, the infantry . . . crossing all the swamps on felled trees." Lieutenant White wrote that a skirmish occurred toward evening with the result that "the Rebs. retired across a small stream at 'Windham's Mill' and declined to yield further. Our Division moved up and encamped so close that the Rebs favored us with an occasional shot during the night."[15]

The next morning, the Third Brigade, including the 90th Illinois, skirmished with Confederate troops at Duck Creek and drove them three miles beyond the creek. White commented on the weather conditions: "It was raining which is always a disagreeable circumstance when there is a fight in prospect. It happened also to be the 3rd Brigade's turn in advance and of course that made it our duty to dislodge the enemy and accordingly everything not needed for the fight was left in camp." White described the Third Brigade's tactics, which were used repeatedly by Union troops to overcome Confederate resistance at other stream and river crossings: "The 48th Illinois went down the creek some distance, waded across and [in] due time made its appearance on the Rebel flank when they took alarm and left in a hurry much to the delight of us who did not expect to get out of it so easy." The 90th Illinois "returned to camp and remained until noon the next day."[16]

Bad road conditions on February 4 required corduroying long stretches, and Confederate troops continued harassing the division. In spite of these difficulties, the division still marched eight miles, camping seven miles from the Big (Great) Salkehatchie River. White wrote that the Legion "turned to the right, the 17th Corps was on that side of us, and artillery was heard in that direction in the morning." Although the weather had cleared by noon, "the road after the rain was in a bad condition." The Legion was one of three regiments sent ahead of the column to corduroy the road, "for which purpose the fences within reach were appropriated." White added, "Orders had been issued against firing buildings, but still there is some of it done."[17]

The division crossed the Great Salkehatchie River at Beaufort's Bridge on February 5 and camped one mile past the bridge after marching a total of eight miles. White added: "This crossing had been fortified and from the front was impregnable," but after "quite a severe skirmish" the XVII Corps "with Shermanic tactics had flanked them" by crossing at River's Bridge some six miles downriver from Beaufort's Bridge. This caused the Confederates to abandon their prepared defense at Beaufort's Bridge. The XVII Corps attack had been the source of the firing heard the previous morning. White described the country the Legion traversed between Beaufort and the Salkehatchie River as "a level plain, divided between plantations, pine woods, and swamps," but after they crossed the Salkehatchie, "the land became more rolling and in places too rugged for cultivation."[18]

On February 6, the division marched on the Orangeburg road, crossed the Little Salkehatchie River at dark, and camped a mile past the river. According to White, the regiment got into camp early on the evening of February 5 and expected to remain there for a day or two. However, the next morning, February 6, the Legion yet again endured the frustrating experience of "hurry up and wait." As White described it, "while some were drawing rations and others enjoying the supposed rest by a prolonged sleep, the brigade bugler very unexpectedly 'sounded the general' which means whatever you are doing stop and pack up ready to move in two minutes." This caused "a pretty mess" as the Legion "bundled out . . . in great haste and confusion . . . only to cross the road and wait three whole hours." The reason for "such a hurry" remained unexplained. The Legion "was in advance for pioneer duty. A regiment from each brigade has to do this each day in its turn, and by this means unless the road is very bad the trains will not be delayed at all." The regiment "soon caught up with the 1st and 3rd Divisions which had been skirmishing with some Rebel cavalry across a swamp," where the Irishmen "had to wait over an hour till the road was clear." To speed things up, the trains marched "in double column, one across the bridge and the other through the water up to the wagon beds." The Legion "camped about dark," but White and his messmates waited in the rain for two hours until the wagon arrived with their tent. White wrote that meanwhile, "we had improved our time by collecting boards and drying them by the fire to lay on, and when the tent was up we slept quite comfortable."[19]

According to Lieutenant White, it was still raining on February 7, "and we expected a skirmish at the railroad, but no, the Johnnies had gone." They "met a Cavalry man with a box of tobacco. The 90th made a raid on him and captured it, telling him as he was mounted he could go look for more." The 90th Illinois reached the Charleston and Augusta Railroad at "Bamberg Station" about 11 A.M. The regiment spent the rest of that day and the next destroying the railroad toward Midway "by piling up the ties, then laying on the iron, set fire to it and when it is hot, twist and bend it." He added, "It will require the action of a rolling mill to render it again fit for use."[20]

The 90th Illinois left Bamberg at daylight on February 8 and marched to Holman's Bridge on the South Fork of the Edisto (see Map 15). White noted that "the day was pleasant and the country good, which is always a sure omen that the foragers would return laden." The foragers did not have to walk as they were "permitted to mount themselves and required to bring in horses, mules, cattle and all kinds of food for men and animals," according to General Howard. White wrote that they "got into camp early and threw up a temporary work. The advance had reached the Edisto River and had been skirmishing."[21]

Company E of the 90th Illinois reported reaching and presumably camping at "O'Reilly's plantation on the Edisto River," where they found "the enemy was entrenched at the opposite side to prevent our crossing." To force a crossing of the South Fork of the Edisto River, the First Brigade sent a battalion three-quarters of a mile upstream from the bridge, where they crossed on fallen trees and advanced into the swamp beyond. Concerned about being flanked, the Confederate forces guarding the bridge withdrew during the night.[22]

The Second Division spent February 10 crossing the Edisto River, corduroying three-quarters of a mile of swamp land, and entrenching after marching only two and a half miles. The infantry had an easier time staying dry during the crossing than did the wagon train. According to White, pontoons easily bridged the river, but "beyond it was a swamp of near half a mile in length over which a temporary bridge of rails was built for the infantry to pass. The trains had to take it through the water." The Legion went only a short distance past the bridge before the troops camped and "threw up works" to guard against a surprise attack.[23]

The Second Division led the XV Corps advance on the relatively level Orangeburg road on February 11. The men reached Poplar Springs about 4 P.M. and entrenched, having marched fifteen miles. The 90th Illinois again had "pioneering" duty, according to White. As they worked at corduroying the road, some of the farmers within the Legion may have noticed the changing soil colors, which ranged from white to yellow-orange. An unexpected mail delivery came via the arrival from Savannah of Brigadier General John M. Corse's Fourth Division. White considered Poplar Springs "a village of a few houses, but has some notoriety as a fashionable resort in the summer season."[24]

The following day, the Second Division again led the advance and reached Shilling's Bridge on the North Fork of the Edisto River at about 9 A.M., where the troops found the bridge burned. The Second Brigade tried to cross the river but got into a sharp scrap with Confederate troops dug in on the opposite side. Hazen attempted to capture the Confederates at the bridge and secure the crossing by sending the First and Third Brigades across the river two miles below the bridge. Lieutenant White described how the 90th Illinois crossed the swamps of the Edisto: "We got over the river on a raft built of hewn timbers which fortunately lay on the bank." They then faced "a swamp of unknown width and deepness. The firing at the bridge a few moments before had been very brisk." General Hazen, anxious to push on, dismounted and took the lead on foot. White wrote that Hazen "plunged into the swamp and bade us follow, which we did." The water was ice cold, "most of the way waist deep and in places up to the arm pits," which produced "such hallowing as was then heard never before woke the echoes of that swamp." According to Hazen, the officers and men crossed the three-quarter-mile swamp "with cheerfulness and enthusiasm." White wrote that the swamp "was covered with timber and brush so you could not see the end and could not tell whether you were going up down or across. . . . One man took cramps and had to be carried and several fell down and lost their guns." He added that "an old citizen told us he had lived there for twenty years and never knew a man to cross that swamp before." While the 90th Illinois crossed the swamp, Hazen's Second Brigade had attacked and driven the Confederates from their entrenchments.[25]

White continued: "When we got through our clothes were a little damp, but we had the satisfaction to learn that the Johnnies had skedaddled, leaving fifty prisoners and about two hundred guns in our hands." The Legion then "marched about two miles and encamped as we supposed for the night and had collected rails, fodder, etc. to make ourselves comfortable and were drying ourselves by the fire when the 'general' sounded and we were again moving and marched about two miles to where the other troops were camped." The men of the Irish Legion had slim pickings at their new camp as earlier arrivals had taken most of the available firewood. White's wagon carrying their food, tent, and blankets did not arrive until midnight. White explained that their "pack mule had given out and we had to put them in the wagon, but from the time they came we slept comfortable until morning." There was some compensation for wading the swamp: "A ration of whisky was then issued to counteract the effects of the wetting. The wetting did not seem to hurt anybody in our regiment except Capt. [Daniel] Corcoran of Company A who has since been laid up with rheumatism." The Legion definitely had a wet and cold crossing of what the men referred to as "Chocktaw Swamp." Company E troops reported being up to their necks in water, while Company K maintained the water was only four feet deep.[26]

After the troops waded through the Edisto swamps near Orangeburg, their wet clothes froze, crackling and snapping as they moved about, making the whiskey ration all that more welcome. Frozen or not, wading the Edisto swamps left a lasting impression on some of the 90th Illinois. In his application to the Pension Office in 1886, Corporal Simon Swan, Company G, claimed disability by chronic rheumatism incurred "while wading swamps at South Edisto River on the march from Beaufort, South Carolina, in February 1865."[27]

February 13 became another day of crossing swamps. The troops first crossed Caw-Caw Swamp in rear of the Third Division and then crossed what Hazen called "Saddler's and Little Crotchpen swamps." They still marched thirteen miles on the gently rolling landscape before camping. White noted that "the 17th Corps was on the Railroad at Orangeburg to the right of us. We moved towards there as far as 'Andrew's Plantation' which is the largest and best appointed I saw in South Carolina until then. . . . From here we turned off towards Columbia and the 17th Corps followed the railroad strewing destruction in their path."[28]

The next day, the 90th Illinois marched seventeen miles, camping seven or eight miles from Columbia. According to Lieutenant White, the Legion spent an unpleasant night: "It rained all night, and occasionally you could hear a shot from the Johnnies and a return with interest from our fellows. The 1st Div. being in advance of us, of course we were out of range." Also on the same day, Major General John A. Logan issued an order that the XV Corps badge, a miniature cartridge box with the motto "Forty Rounds," was to be worn on the hat or cap by every officer and soldier in the corps. Writing eleven years after the war, George Woodruff named Sergeant William McGuffy, Company G, as the person responsible for the motto, as described in chapter 7.[29]

White recorded that on February 15, "Our regiment on account of being small was detailed to guard the train, and the 1st and 2nd Div. unencumbered moved on. The 1st had some pretty sharp skirmishing, and artillery was used quite freely, but nothing like a battle took place." The road was bad and the "whole corps train of fourteen or fifteen hundred wagons" moved slowly, advancing only three miles. White wrote that the train was heavily guarded with "a guard like ourselves with each division train besides a rear guard. The 99th Ind. of our brigade had been rear guard of our division that day, and had camped with the train, but about 9 o'clock [P.M.] were ordered to the front, and had to tramp out in the mud and dark with a brisk artillery fire from the enemy to steady their nerves. We wished them no harm, but thanked our stars that it was not us." It was not a restful night as, according to White, "the Rebs continued to ply their artillery all night, and we could hear locomotives continually whistling. No doubt they wished us to believe reinforcements were arriving, but the same bustle has always been as far as my experience goes, rather indicative of an evacuation."[30]

With Sherman's army of nearly 60,000 men virtually at its gates, General Beauregard's February 16 letter to General Robert E. Lee described the hopelessness of the Confederate position at Columbia: "Our forces, about 20,000 effective infantry and artillery, more or less demoralized, occupy a circumference of about 240 miles from Charleston to Augusta. The enemy, well organized and disciplined, and flushed with success, numbering nearly double our force is concentrated upon one point (Columbia) of that circumference. Unless I can concentrate rapidly here, or in my rear, all available troops, the result cannot be long in doubt." Newly promoted Lieutenant General Wade Hampton, suddenly placed in charge of the defense of Columbia, felt otherwise and prepared to fight to defend Columbia, his home.[31]

The men of the 90th Illinois had no way of knowing that one of their own, First Lieutenant Andrew Phinney, Company A, had been imprisoned just outside Columbia in Confederate prison camps since his capture at the Battle of Atlanta on July 22, 1864. However, when the 90th Illinois arrived at Columbia, he no longer remained there. Confederate authorities had moved the 1,200 prisoners at Camp Asylum on February 14 or 15, 1865, to Charlotte, North Carolina, to prevent their release by Sherman's troops. Fortunately, Phinney did not have long to wait as he received a parole on March 1, 1865.[32]

On February 16, the 90th Illinois neared Columbia under clear weather. Lieutenant White described their approach: "The enemy had been driven across the Congaree River and the train ordered up." The Legion "found it difficult to get along in daylight" and "had reason to commiserate [with] the 99th on their night march." To avoid crossing the broad Congaree River "in the face of the enemy," Sherman's army moved two miles above Columbia and crossed the Saluda and Broad rivers above their junction forming the Congaree (see Map 15). White described the action when wagons of the XV and XVII Corps trains "passed within shelling distance" of Columbia: "The Rebels did not neglect the opportunity to give them a few." An experienced infantryman, White enjoyed the response of the teamsters, writing, "It was amusing to see them hurry past. One teamster had a mule killed but he could not stop for such trifles while himself was in danger, but dragged the dead animal till he thought it safe to wait and unhitch him."

On their way to the river crossings, the Legion passed by Camp Sorghum where Union prisoners had been held. White described it as "a miserable abode . . . on the edge of a swamp." When the Confederates evacuated their Union prisoners, many "escaped and made their way to our lines."[33]

It took all night for the wagon train to cross the Saluda River. White noted that due to the resulting traffic jam, "We were kept on our feet moving a few yards at a time until near daylight. Always in crossing a river there is a jam and especially with so large a train, and it is a great deal more tiresome loitering along than to go ahead and be done with it." When they finally crossed the river, they found "the ground was high and dry. We were again out of the mud. Trains were all corralled and we lay down to have a nap before breakfast." The Confederates still held the city. White wrote: "The advance was still skirmishing for a passage over the Broad River. De Gress' Battery was in position to send his compliments since the day before and was occasionally doing so. [Large bronze stars currently mark the location where shells fired by Captain Francis De Gress's battery struck the unfinished Capitol building.] The day [February 17] was pleasant and we lay around on the grass in supreme comfort waiting the fall of Columbia."[34]

{ 14 }

HAIL COLUMBIA, HAPPY LAND

When Union troops arrived on February 17, 1865, the capital city of Columbia served as South Carolina's educational center, a major railroad center, and an important center for manufacture and storage of war matériel for the Confederacy. It was also a tinderbox. Most structures in the city had been constructed with wood. In their hurried retreat, Confederate troops left behind artillery shells stored on the grounds of the old Statehouse and elsewhere in the city. More than four hundred bales of cotton lay grouped in four or five piles in Richardson Street, the city's main street, placed there by Confederate troops to be burned. Large amounts of cotton had been placed in four other streets. During the day, a high wind blew from the northwest, widely scattering the loose cotton. Retiring Confederate forces set fire to the Charlotte railroad terminal, and arriving Union troops found piles of cotton smoldering and some burning. The troops joined the city's firemen in fighting a blaze involving a hundred or more cotton bales near the town hall on Richardson Street. By one o'clock, the firemen, aided by Union troops, had the cotton fire nearly extinguished. During the day, other fires broke out and some cotton fires rekindled, requiring efforts to control them.

Citizens had stored large amounts of liquor in the city, making liquor easily obtainable by the troops, which reduced the effectiveness of the brigade charged with maintaining order. Numbers of straggling troops, some of them drunk, thronged the city. Some sixty or more Union soldiers held near Columbia as prisoners of war had escaped during their removal. Highly resentful of their treatment and under no one's control, their presence further added to the confusion. By dark, the wind speed had increased. The necessary conditions for a major conflagration existed, which is precisely what occurred.[1]

The entry before noon of the XV Corps into Columbia foreshadowed trouble. General John A. Logan's biographer, James Pickett Jones, reported that "as the men marched they sang: 'Hail Columbia, happy land. If I don't burn you, I'll be damned.'"[2]

The Second Division marched through Columbia about 5:30 P.M. and camped a mile beyond near the Columbia and South Carolina Railroad. Irish-born First Lieutenant William White's comments on Columbia indicate something of the attitude of the troops of the XV Corps and the Legion toward the city: "And if we review the history of the city, we shall find little in it to conciliate the favor of a Yankee army. Here it was the first ordinance of secession was adopted. Here was the germ of all the evils that for four years have beset the nation, and this the capital of the state, which by a bullying spirit and violent fanaticism frightened other states into following her example. Here it was they shaved men's heads, tarred and feathered them and rode them on a rail, for no other offence than loyalty to the old flag." White described the case "of an Irish stone cutter who worked on the new state house. Powers by name, and those who knew him say as fine a young man as there was in the city, had been served in this manner by the vigilance committee, shipped to Charleston and warned, by the first steamer to quit the Confederacy. When I think of this, as I heard many of those deeply interested say, 'if only the guilty suffered it would be well.'"[3]

The morning of February 17 started out uneventfully for the soldiers of the 90th Illinois. According to Lieutenant White, the troops had a bit of fun as they relaxed near the present location of the city's zoo and waited to enter Columbia: "The boys had caught a fox and were having lots of sport chasing him, until about ten o'clock when the voice of the artillery was hushed, the river was passed, and finally the firing died away in the distance and Columbia was ours! It had been formally surrendered to a brigade commander of the 1st Division by the Mayor." At 3 P.M., the 90th Illinois troops joined their brigade and crossed the pontoon bridge over the Broad River. White saw a number of rather ominous sights upon entering the capital: "Towards town we passed any number of stragglers coming out with boxes of tobacco, sugar, whiskey, wine and all manner of plunder, and nearly all half-tight, some wholly so." But White liked what he saw of the city itself, finding "the place much nicer than I expected. In fact considering locality and everything else I think it the most desirable city to live in I have seen [in the] South." White observed that "it had the appearance produced by a snow shower or cotton shower for such it was. Cotton was everywhere in the trees, streets, and all around for all the world as if it snowed there. In places there was bales of it and I noticed some of them were on fire." The accumulation of loose cotton in the shade trees reminded General Oliver O. Howard of "a grove in Maine after a snow storm."[4]

Upon entering the city, Brigadier General William Hazen noted large number of troops "straggling about the city" and citizens treating the troops "very unwisely, to wines and liquors . . . passed along the line in buckets and tin pans, and in one case a large tin boiler." White saw few white but many black citizens on the streets and observed "soldiers everywhere, many half drunk, and even some of the guard stationed to keep order were far from being sober. Even some of the 90th were getting funny while yet marching along the streets." There were "quite a number of small union flags displayed and a lot of little boys hurrahed for the union. But the soldiers regardless of this went about taking whatever they fancied." White "saw trouble ahead, and remarked to Capt. [Michael] Murphy near me, who is like myself a kind of sober-sides, who preserve our equilibrium under all circumstances."[5]

White described what happened next: "We marched through town and camped on the southeast side. Soon as the men got their suppers, and some before it, they began to put for town and ere long the camp was almost deserted, even some out on picket left their posts and went. It may appear strange that such looseness was permitted, but the truth is the demoralization extended to officers as well as men." Captain Murphy, Company B, and White remained in camp and tried unsuccessfully to sleep. There was just too much disturbance: "The hollowing, shooting, and all sorts of noise downtown was continually ringing in our ears."[6]

White detailed the resulting chaos:

> Fires broke out, the wind arose and the commotion became dreadful. The fire spread with resistless fury, and soon the body of the town was in flames. Men [were] returning to camp with jugs and buckets of whiskey, kicking us up to drink, and telling wonderful tales of doings downtown. Murphy and myself could stand it no longer but got up to go behold a scene, which we deemed would become historic. We did not however go far into the city, but stood for a while contemplating the scene in the distance which was indeed terribly grand. Citizens in groups were standing here and there as if consulting what was best to be done. Many who were not in the least danger, had left their houses and saved what they could. We endeavored to console them and offered advice, but they were suspicious of our council and showed a willingness to be left alone. They thought the city had been fired by order and that none would be spared. Others were more confident and would pray any soldier who seemed well disposed to remain with them as a sort of safe guard. A great many had displayed white flags, but their present enemy (fire) would accept no truce.[7]

Then things really got out of hand. White described the streets as full of drunken men, soldiers, white and black citizens, and even some women. He continued: "I never saw whiskey so profuse, nor so many under its influence. Totally convinced of the depravity of human nature, I and my friend returned to camp."[8]

White's account of what he observed is supported by others present at the scene. The large quantities of liquor supplied to Union troops by citizens of the city resulted in a general loss of control by the provost guard and their replacement by the First Division's First Brigade. The brigade faced the dilemma of either restoring order or fighting the fire, now expanded into an inferno by the high wind. About 8 P.M., XV Corps scout Theodore Upson of the 100th Indiana of the First Brigade received orders to go to the city. He found that "the row of cotton bales was burning fiercely," along with "some of the buildings along the street." But before the men of the First Brigade could fight the fire, they first had to round up the drunken soldiers and get them out of harm's way. Upson described how the fire spread: "The wind blew terribly. It would pick up flakes of the burning cotton and carry it a long ways. If it fell on a roof it set fire to that building. Burning shingles and pieces of boards flew before the wind. We soon began to help the women and children." To add to the confusion, large quantities of artillery shells, some very large, that were stored throughout the city exploded when fire reached them.[9]

Major Thomas Ward Osborn, chief of artillery of the Army of the Tennessee, described a hellish scene at midnight. The fire occupied a square mile where "flames rolled and heaved like the waves of the ocean." The high wind filled the air with "burning cinders," making the road a virtual "cataract" of fire. He observed an appalling "scene of pillaging" combined with "suffering and terror"-stricken citizens, "the arresting of and shooting negroes," and "frantic and drunken soldiers."[10]

Undeniably, a riot occurred. General Howard blamed a combination of "escaped prisoners, convicts from the penitentiary just broken open, army followers, and drunken soldiers" for what happened. The riot interfered with fighting the fire. Force had to be used to restore order. Hazen wrote that he directed several isolated firefighting efforts before sending Brigadier General Oliver's Third Brigade at 2 or 3 A.M. to "patrol the city, and arrest all soldiers and disorderly persons. . . . They marched to the north end of the city, and deploying, moved through the town like a drag-net. The haul was by no means a light one. About twenty-five hundred citizens and soldiers, including officers of nearly every grade, were turned over to the provost-marshal." Oliver accomplished his mission by 5 A.M. and returned to camp to report to Hazen.[11]

Reports differ as to time and number apprehended. According to Oliver, at 4 A.M. his Third Brigade, including the 90th Illinois, had been called out to suppress a riot. He reported: "Did so, killing 2 men, wounding 30, and arresting 370." Adjutant Edwin Davis reported rising at 2 A.M. and proceeding under orders "to restore order in the city and arrest all straggling and disorderly soldiers. The greater part of the city was then in ruins." The Irish Legion remained on duty until 10 A.M. the next day, by which time order had been restored.[12]

William White, in command of Company F, reported the regiment's less-than-stellar condition and encounters as the men proceeded to clear the streets of Columbia: "About three o'clock in the morning our brigade was out with peremptory orders to clear the town of stragglers, and for this purpose my company was able to muster four men, and one of them was so drunk, he thought we were going out to attack the enemy. Other companies were as bad, so you may judge how efficient for the work before it was our brigade." White wrote the Legion moved out, "a company or two to each street[, and] cleared everyone before them. Passing the state house Tim [probably First Sergeant Timothy Mahoney] and myself had a very narrow escape. There was a pile of heavy ammunition in the yard and shells had been exploding from time to time all night. Everything around was burned so there were hundreds of them lying in a heap of live coals. An unfortunate soldier wandering among the rubbish struck one and sent him to eternity in an instant." White wrote that he was so close "when it exploded" that "the ashes was thrown over me and I held my breath in expectation of a piece to strike. But they did not and soon as I recovered from the shock I fervently thanked God for my escape."[13]

White took note of what he saw as the regiment moved through the city:

> Further on the scene presented was indeed deplorable. It would be vain for me to attempt a description. The streets were filled with furniture, the finest and meanest, broken and burned scattered promiscuously. Families of wealth and refinement crouching beside a few tattered remains of their once splendid establishments, for to save anything it was not only necessary to get it out of the house but out of the neighborhood. The Park was filled with such as lived near enough to avail themselves of its sheltering space. I went to the convent purposely to ascertain its fate, and was sorry to find only its blackened walls and burning casement. It was situated in the heart of the city. Gen. Sherman had sent it a special guard, but against fire they could not protect it. The Sisters and their charge took refuge in the church which fortunately escaped. I saw them all standing in the church yard, and had quite a talk with the priest. He was very unreasonable and blamed Sherman severely. I explained to him that this was the work of lawlessness and no man would regret it more than Sherman. I was afterwards glad to hear that the General called on them next morning, and did what he could to alleviate their condition. They had purchased a place in the country and he sent ambulances to take them out there, and sent them provision. About eleven o'clock order was so far restored that what stragglers we had collected were turned over at corps headquarters and the brigade returned to camp. The new state house remained intact, but the old one was destroyed. . . . In the yard was erected a handsome palmetto tree of cast iron, in honor of the Palmetto Regiment which went from South Carolina to the Mexican War. It was painted green and some mistook it for a living tree. It remained uninjured.[14]

By afternoon of February 18, it was business as usual for the 90th Illinois. Adjutant Davis reported that the regiment "moved seven miles out on the Wilmington R.R. with the Division, and destroyed it." White described the activities of those soldiers of the Legion sufficiently recovered to walk: "Afternoon we were ordered out to assist in tearing up railroad, and collecting all that were sober enough to go we marched out about seven miles and commenced work." The next day, as the men of the Legion returned to Columbia, they "passed the extensive plantation of [General] Wade Hampton, when on leaving he had destroyed two thousand bales of cotton and several cribs of corn. When we got back we found our stragglers all sober and ready for duty. The Columbia spree was over."[15]

Lieutenant White commented on the aftereffect of their occupation of Columbia: "On the morning of Feb. 20th, we bade Columbia farewell, and no doubt those who remained saw us depart without regret, and who would blame them, for instead of a fair and lovely city we left them a forest of blackened chimneys and a heap of rubbish." General Hazen summed it up this way: "Thus the city where secession was first proclaimed was turned to ashes." He "never doubted that Columbia was deliberately set on fire in more than a hundred places. No one ordered it, and no one could stop it."[16]

In White's opinion, "the burning of Columbia was a disgraceful affair" whose responsibility could be shared rather widely: "The rebels say Gen. Sherman, but of course they could not think of blaming themselves. When it became known to Gen. [P. G. T.] Beauregard that Sherman intended going there, he advised the evacuation of the place by the military, and for a deputation to meet Sherman at Orangeburg and surrender the place, and this the Mayor and citizens were anxious to do. Had they done so there is no doubt they would have been treated as such conduct deserved." But that was not to be the case as "their brave Governor would defend the place to the last man, and the chivalric Wade Hampton would fight us from house to house." White concluded: "Thus they were throwing dust in each others eyes until Sherman was at the gate, and then our gallant Governor, as all their leaders will do some day, took to his heels leaving the Mayor to surrender the town when it was ours, in spite of him. And when the troops entered they commenced, by giving them whiskey, the work of their own destruction." After the war, intense debates raged over the question of who burned Columbia, and even today it remains a matter of considerable controversy.[17]

{ 15 }

LEAVING THE CRADLE

The speed with which Major General William T. Sherman's army traversed South Carolina's flooded rivers, numerous swamps, and nearly impassable unpaved roads in winter lent an aura of invincibility to his troops' northward march. They treated wading through hip- to arm-pit-deep icy water in order to dislodge Confederate defenders from entrenched positions at river crossings as standard procedure, with little complaining. Confederate military authorities viewed Sherman's march through the Carolinas in amazement. Confederate general Joseph E. Johnston's engineering officers all considered such a march in winter as a complete impossibility, leading Johnston later to comment that "there had been no such army since the days of Julius Caesar."[1]

On February 20, the men of the 90th Illinois began the next leg of their march, bound for Goldsboro, North Carolina, by way of Camden and Cheraw, South Carolina, and Fayetteville, North Carolina (see Map 15, in chapter 13; Map 16). They left Columbia at 8 A.M., marching east to Travelers Rest and north toward Liberty Hill, and before camping at 5 P.M., they had covered twenty miles. The fifty or so miles of country they crossed between Columbia and the Wateree River lay over a higher, more productive area with rolling topography. The general direction of the march, which had been northerly until Columbia, became northeasterly from Camden, as far as Goldsboro, roughly paralleling the coastline, but displaced some 70 to 110 miles inland.[2]

A "multitude of fugitives, both black and white," accompanied the Second Division's march, according to Brigadier General William Hazen, who formed them into a column directed by recently freed Union officers. First Lieutenant William White described "the scene on the road. Refugees, white and black and

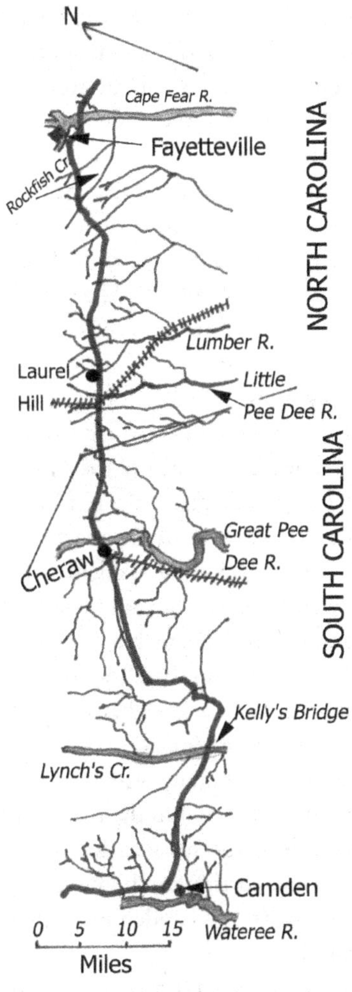

Map 16. March through the Carolinas: route of the 90th Illinois from Camden, South Carolina, to Fayetteville, North Carolina

some between those colors filed in vehicles of every description from an army wagon to a one-horse cart thronged the way, all following the Moses of their day to the land of promise."[3]

It proved hard going on February 21 as hills, mud, and quicksand slowed the march, but the Third Brigade still covered twenty-two miles. The 90th Illinois had been detached from the Third Brigade for part of the day. Lieutenant White described their adventures: "Our brigade was in advance, and about nine o'clock our regiment was sent a mile to the left to hold a bridge on Wateree Creek until relieved. There was some Johnnies out across, and foragers coming in from there reported they had captured and murdered two of our foragers. Those who brought this intelligence also brought in with them about twenty-five splendid mules which they found in a swamp. We remained there about four hours and were then relieved by the 52nd Ill. of the [Fourth] Div."[4]

The following day, they passed through Poplar Springs and had to wait to cross the Wateree River at Peay's Ferry, just above Taylor's Creek, until the completion of the pontoon bridge. They then camped two miles from the river after marching only eight miles. Lieutenant White wrote that the 90th Illinois rejoined the Third Brigade "on the top of a hill across the Wateree River." Peay's Ferry operated some four miles to the west of Liberty Hill.[5]

On February 23, the Legion marched about eighteen miles in the direction of Camden. According to Lieutenant White, the troops "passed through the village of 'Liberty Hill' which was a scene of a battle of the American Revolution [see Map 15, in chapter 13]. It was a neat little place. Do not know whether it was burned after we passed or not. It rained nearly all the afternoon and we camped early at a place called Flat Rock." Two days later, a resident of Liberty Hill wrote that the area had suffered severely with "twelve burning residences" lighting the route of march. The weather did not cooperate, as Lieutenant White found it still raining the next morning, February 24, so that "the roads were in awful condition." However, by that "afternoon they were some better but the rain did not cease, and through it we made a march of twenty miles but did not get to camp until after ten o'clock. Our regimental wagon and many others was capsized back on the road. Everything all wet and mud, and to add to the rest it was my turn for picket, but fortunately we go[t] in so close to another division that no picket was needed. Tis such nights as this makes a soldier think of home and sigh for its comforts." The Irish Legion camped one mile from Camden near the site of the Revolutionary War battle of the same name.[6]

The route the 90th Illinois followed from Columbia to Camden resembled a Z, which lengthened the distance traveled to some eighty-five miles, greatly exceeding the most direct route of about thirty-six miles (see Map 15, in chapter 13; Map 16). Lieutenant White attributed the army's movements as an attempt to mislead the Confederates "by marching towards Charlotte, from Columbia, and when near there suddenly changing his direction to where his was least expected. Thus in getting from Columbia to Camden we marched twice as far as one place is from the other in a direct line, and for this, I have heard many a 'mick' say Sherman was 'a fool and didn't know where he was going' forgetting the old adage that 'the longest way round was the safest way home.'"[7]

The Confederacy was clearly running out of troops. At Camden, General Hazen recounted meeting "a mounted home-guard on duty for some inscrutable purpose." One of the captives, a sociable clergyman "of Jacksonian type" was released after a couple of days along with his horse and shotgun. One of Hazen's columns captured "a platoon of venerable home-guards, with their arms and ammunition carefully packed away in a wagon." Hazen quartered them in tents near his headquarters and wrote that "in the evening they all came over to my camp-fire, and entertained me with an account of their novel war experiences. Each man had some peculiar and personal malady, an account of which figured largely in the conversation. In the morning I had a handsome walking-stick cut for each, gave them a good breakfast, and let them go. They thanked me pleasantly for their entertainment, liked the walking-sticks, and did not see the joke." Hazen also captured several Confederate staff officers but let most go, considering them to be noncombatants. At this stage of the conflict, Hazen apparently viewed Confederate staff officers as relatively harmless. The end of the war approached, but it wasn't over quite yet.[8]

On February 25, the 90th Illinois marched only eight miles on the Society Hill road. Lieutenant White described the road as good and the day as fine, adding, "We jogged along quite leisurely and camped early." However, the next day's travel proved more challenging. After marching some ten miles, the Legion managed to cross the rapidly rising waters of Lynch's Creek at Kelly's Bridge, but the trains could not follow (see Map 16). White noted their difficulties. On the previous day, Lynch's Creek had flowed "placidly within its banks but was now so swollen as to be waist deep two hundred yards each side of the bridge. We had to wade across and the sooner we did so the better, as the water was still rising. We got over without difficulty. The crossing of this bore no comparison to our experience at North Edisto." It was Lieutenant White's turn to go on picket, but he "had a good post and got along very well. The trains did not get over that night, and by morning the water was so high it took away part of the bridge so they had to go to work and bridge the whole space covered by water. It took three days to do it, during the most of which time it was raining." Hazen described Lynch's Creek as "a seething torrent half a mile wide," much of it four feet deep. To get the wagons over, the creek required building a bridge, which commenced on the last day of February with the creek still slowly rising. Hazen proudly stated: "In just twenty hours, with only the men and tools of my command, actually built a bridge nineteen hundred feet long on ninety trestles, over which an army corps passed in safety."[9]

Major General Oliver O. Howard had good reason to doubt Hazen's claim of safe passage, because on March 1 the bridge collapsed under the weight of the general's heavily loaded mess wagon. The wagon ended up "top down and wheels up," considerably reducing the general's mess, as related by Major Thomas Ward Osborn. However, Howard bore no grudge over the incident, as Hazen soon received a promotion to major general.[10]

The men of the 90th Illinois probably missed that little bit of fun, as they left Kelly's Bridge on March 1 bound for Cheraw, South Carolina. However, they camped close by at Kelly Town, which White described as "no town at all but a group of planters of that name living near each other, all immensely rich and inveterate rebels. None of them were at home. From here until our arrival at Cheraw, nothing of note transpired. The weather was showery and the road very bad but it had been fixed by other troops ahead of us." On March 2 and 3, the Irish Legion troops marched in a northerly direction until they neared Juniper Creek. There, the direction of march changed to northeast, directly toward Cheraw, paralleling Juniper Creek (see Map 16). They marched through a rolling sand hill area (now the Sand Hills State Forest), reaching Cheraw on March 4, and camped on a ridge north of the town.[11]

At Cheraw, Hazen established his quarters in the house of a judge who possessed a fine library with a collection of Sir Walter Scott's novels. While visiting Hazen, Sherman appropriated several of the novels, claiming "that reading-matter was necessary food, and that we had a right to forage for it." No wonder South Carolinians considered Sherman a barbarian, although a well-read one.[12]

Cheraw had already been captured by the XVII Corps the day before the 90th Illinois arrived. According to Lieutenant White, "It cost them but a slight skirmish. The place [in and] of itself was of little value but large quantities of every kind had been shipped there for safety as they did not think we were going there. And when they found their mistake it was too late to correct it." According to White, the 90th Illinois found Cheraw under firm control: "Guards were stationed everywhere and good order prevailed." Sherman clearly wanted no repeat of the riot at Columbia. According to White, the members of the Legion took advantage of the time to rest and used the brilliant sun "to air our blankets and clothes which from successive rains had grown damp and moldy." White described the destruction of everything of military value: "There was a large quantity of cotton, military stores, and an extensive turpentine mill, all of which were destroyed. I believe there was more ammunition destroyed here than at Columbia, and about twenty pieces of artillery fell into our hands which were consigned to the great Pedee (river) and the carriages burned. In hospital there was some three or four hundred rebel sick and wounded, which I suppose were paroled."[13]

A local resident described the destruction around Cheraw: "The entire neighborhood was on fire; the stables still smoking in the barnyard, the railroad burning in the distance both north and south for miles, the Ridgeway depot, three miles off, burning brightly. Nothing but flames, smoke and destruction were to be seen in every direction."[14]

Lieutenant White commented on Cheraw's historical significance: "This place was connected with the history of the Revolution. There is still standing in good repair the Church [Old St. David's Episcopal Church] that General Green [Nathaniel Greene] used for a hospital after the battle of 'Eutaw Springs.'" White wandered about in the church's graveyard, examining the headstones. He came upon one, a descendent of "a member of the Constitutional Convention, in the days when American patriotism was pure." On the back of the monument he found "the following reflection of a Yankee bard." It concluded with:

> Rise! Slumbering patriots, view the ruin made,
> And bid the traitor crew in shame disperse,
> Bid them restore the union they've betrayed,
> Or doubly damn them with a father's curse.
> (Signed) H. B. Fitzpatrick Co. "D," 6th MO.

"The above was copied by a great many. I think it pretty good."[15]

Lieutenant White described the Legion's march to the North Carolina state line, after leaving Cheraw and crossing the Great Pee Dee River the night of March 5: "A moonlight march of three miles brought us to Col. John Harington's plantation, where we encamped. There had been a [Confederate] commissary here but unable to get the stores away, they destroyed them. Next day our division did not move, but the regiment with a detail of wagons went out a few miles for corn." The following day, March 7, the Legion "had a pleasant march of about seven miles" toward Fayetteville.[16]

Lieutenant White commented on the number of "Jonnies . . . picked up by our foragers" as well as on the dangers facing Union foragers. "The foragers were out every day and once in a while there was a few of them captured. [General] Wade Hampton's cavalry was around and most of them had uniforms very near like ours, so they could not always tell them from our men. They also had murdered some of our men after taking them, and labeling their bodies 'Death to Foragers' left them in a conspicuous place to be found by us." White added that such murders did not stop foraging but that "a like number of their men in our hands were disposed of and labeled 'Retaliation.' A correspondence [dated February 24] between Hampton and Gen. Sherman was held on this subject." Such news traveled rapidly within the army, and Union foragers were well aware of the hazards they faced. On March 6, the soldiers of the Legion received word of another sort of hazard in the form of one of General Howard's numerous field orders, which in this case called their attention "to the gross and criminal practice of profane swearing which prevails and is increasing in amounts amongst us, so much so, that every sense of principle and good taste is outraged."[17]

{ 16 }

TOURING TARHEEL COUNTRY

Brigadier General William Hazen did his best to curtail unauthorized foraging in North Carolina by issuing orders regulating foraging and forbidding the possession of unauthorized property such as horses or any other visible means of locomotion. Thus chastened, on March 8 under a misting rain, the men of the 90th Illinois marched on the Telegraph road to Fayetteville (currently South Carolina SSR 165), crossing into the state of North Carolina one mile after leaving camp (see Map 16, in chapter 15). They crossed the railroad connecting Wilmington and Charlotte some five miles farther before camping near Laurel Hill. Lieutenant William White commented that "the appearance of the country improved" when the Legion entered the Old North State; however, the weather did not, as "it rained all that afternoon and night." According to White, the Legion heeded Hazen's orders restricting foraging. "What we had seen of the old north state so far prepossessed us in its favor, and the conduct of the troops towards the inhabitants underwent a marked change." So far, the march from Cheraw had been relatively easy, but that would soon change.[1]

The Legion started early the next day, March 9, and marched on the Fayetteville road. The men crossed the Lumber River on a pontoon bridge at Gilchrist's Bridge and continued on to near Bethel Church. Supper would be delayed as rain made the road impassible, stranding their wagon train. In an attempt to bring the trains to Bethel Church, the 90th Illinois spent the next day helping to corduroy nearly four miles of roads. Lieutenant White described the difficult road conditions the regiment faced after crossing the Lumber River: "We got in camp about dark, but before fixing up were ordered out to assist the train up, which was stuck in the mud, a few wagons in a place, four miles back along the road. We went, but after two or three hours of fruitless toil, in the dark, rain, and mud, we gave it up for a bad job and returned to camp." White added that everyone suffered, including Major General William T. Sherman, whose "headquarters train was in the mud among the rest and in its absence he put up at Bethel Church, which on such a night was certainly preferable to a tent. The rain was so heavy that some places water was knee deep coming back, that were dry going out, and it raised in the floor of some of our tents so they had to be moved. Everything considered it was a miserable night, and we began to think the Rebel hope of our sticking in the mud of the old Tar State was about to be realized." However, the next morning, March 10, "heavy details were out pioneering and trains worked along." Off to his right, White "heard a brisk artillery fire, which we afterwards learned was a sudden attack on Brigadier General Hugh Judson Kilpatrick's cavalry by General Wade Hampton's. Both claimed victory." Disbelief in Kilpatrick's veracity probably prevailed in the army, or perhaps this comment simply represented the natural antipathy of infantrymen for their brethren in the cavalry who got to ride while they slogged through the mud. White continued: "Towards evening we moved on again fixing the road as we went. Our regiment camped in a pleasant place by itself, and corduroyed a piece of road by moonlight after supper."[2]

On March 11, White, as part of a work detail, accompanied the regimental wagons "to help them along if they needed it." He added: "We got along very well. March about eighteen miles and reached camp on Rock[fish] Creek about 8 o'clock." They were about seven miles from Fayetteville and received "information that the 17 and 20th Corps had entered there early in the day." White wrote that the Legion "expected to remain a day or two and were very glad to hear that boats had come up the Cape Fear River and there would be a chance to mail a letter." Given the opportunity, White visited Fayetteville "more on account of its Revolutionary fame than anything else." Accustomed to rapidly expanding western cities, he found it "a very ancient looking place, not a house in it under twenty years old." As usual, items of military value were destroyed. Sherman's chief engineer, Brigadier General Orlando Poe, oversaw the thorough destruction of the large U.S. Arsenal at Fayetteville that produced arms for the Confederacy. Contact with the outside world was temporarily reestablished by the arrival of transports on the Cape Fear River laden not with shoes and socks but with oats, which then departed carrying the sick and wounded. Some clothing arrived later by boat, but there is no mention as to whether the 90th Illinois received any. White noted the departure of the refugees "for Wilmington, some on boats and others in wagons." The boats brought some items of interest to the soldiers. White reported: "We were all anxious for the latest news from the United States and to get it paid fifty cents for a *New York Herald* of March 6th. All the news we had lately came from rebel papers and if they were true the end of Yankeedom was near at hand. The news in the *Herald* was quite refreshing."[3]

On March 14, the Irish Legion crossed the Cape Fear River on a pontoon bridge and camped on the Warsaw road a few miles from the river (Map 17). The next day, the Legion reported to Brevet Brigadier General William B. Woods, who commanded the XV Corps train guard. The corps train of 550 wagons extending some four and a half miles on the road would have been an impressive sight to local inhabitants and a tempting target for Confederate raiders. Woods's brigade plus three regiments served as train guards. The Pioneer Corps and half a mounted infantry regiment marched ahead of the train. The 90th Illinois marched along the left flank guarding one hundred wagons, helping move the wagons along the muddy roads when required. As the Second Division marched ahead toward Goldsboro, the 90th Illinois followed somewhere in the rear of the corps with the trains from 6 A.M. on March 16 until relieved from duty as train guards on March 20. It was a strenuous trip over bad roads that required crossing the South River and Little and Big Coharie rivers, all of which had to be bridged. The night of March 20, the Legion camped twelve miles southwest of Goldsboro.[4]

Lieutenant White explained that since a Confederate attack on the army's left wing was expected, "a guard was detailed to take charge of the trains, so the troops might move unencumbered, and if they met the enemy be in a condition to receive them. Our regiment was among those so detailed."[5]

White's description of the regiment's sobering experience of escorting trains on St. Patrick's Day also illustrates the major impact of weather on the movement of wagon trains: "During the afternoon [March 15] it rained heavily but through the driving storm the boom of the cannon in the distance was distinctly heard. Next morning the train was moving. The roads for awhile were pretty good but grew worse and rain again began to fall, which did not improve them. About dark we blocked up at a broken bridge, and were kept two or three hours in suspense not knowing whether to camp or not, but finally settled down for the night. The train was all night closing up." White wrote that the next morning ushered in "a fine day, and unusual thing you know for St. Patrick's, but all the more acceptable on that account. And for once on a remarkable day [St. Patrick's] the 90th were all sober. The only wet to be had was what they got crossing the broken bridge." However, they did not go far, as "a short distance from the creek we halted and remained all day while the train was getting over. About dark we moved on a mile or two further, camped and after supper worked on the road until 12 o'clock. Thus we spent last St. Patrick's." The next day, March 18, the Legion served as the rear guard. For a while, the road "was miserable but grew better as we advanced. Towards evening the train blocked up again at a creek, and we did not get over until after dark, and then we had a sort of Blondin [tightrope-walking] performance on a single log across the stream. All got over without accident and continued our way over a miserable road until 3 o'clock in the morning [March 19], and were then permitted but a few hours rest."[6]

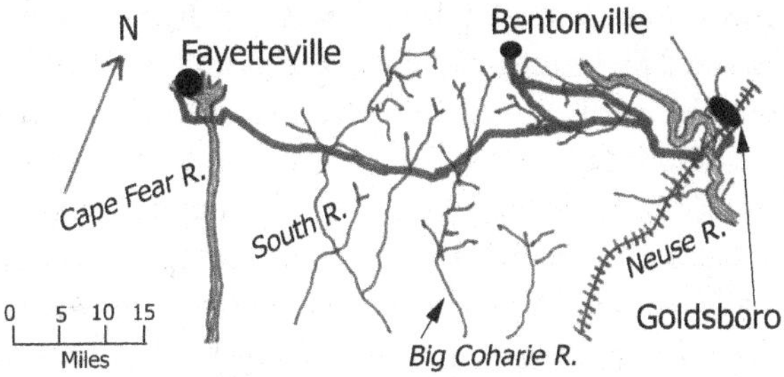

Map 17. March through the Carolinas: route of the 90th Illinois from Fayetteville to Goldsboro, North Carolina

On March 19, the Irishmen "were in the rear again and again towards evening the train blocked up at a swamp, and the troops halted for supper. . . . About 8 o'clock we crossed the swamp and camped near Sashen Church."[7]

Previously, on February 23, General Sherman's old foe, General Joseph E. Johnston, had received orders appointing him to the command of what remaining Confederate forces could be scraped together in the Carolinas, some 16,000 or so, with instructions to "concentrate all available forces and drive back Sherman." Johnston had no illusions, believing that "we could have no other object, in continuing the war, than to obtain fair terms of peace; for the Southern cause must have appeared hopeless then, to all intelligent and dispassionate Southern men." Johnston's first chance to stop Sherman occurred at Averasborough (Averysboro to Sherman), North Carolina, where Confederate lieutenant general William Hardee fought a successful delaying action on March 16 against Sherman's left wing. By March 18, both wings of the Union forces had passed Fayetteville, marching toward Goldsboro on roads ten to twelve miles apart. Confederate reports indicated nearly a day's march separated the heads of Sherman's two wings, presenting Johnston a chance to strike Sherman's isolated left wing. Reinforced by some 8,700 troops under General Braxton Bragg, Johnston's Confederate forces vigorously attacked and forced back the forward units of the XIV Corps at Bentonville on March 19. The Union troops eventually rallied and with the assistance of the XX Corps repulsed further Confederate attacks.[8]

Reuniting the two wings of the Union army at Bentonville required the XV Corps to reverse direction and rapidly move to the sound of the guns. By about 1 A.M. on March 20, Hazen had his division underway and after backtracking some fourteen miles reported to Major General Henry W. Slocum at 6:30 A.M., where they reinforced the XIV Corps. On March 21, Hazen's Second and Third Brigades corduroyed a road to the rear of the First Brigade line on the right of the XIV Corps before throwing up works on the same line.[9]

The 90th Illinois almost missed this last battle of the campaign, arriving near the end. As described by Lieutenant White, the part played by the Legion in the Battle of Bentonville mainly involved getting there: "Next morning (20th) about sunrise a brisk cannonade was heard to the front and lasted about an hour. We had heard firing occasionally for several days past but not so heavy as this, and we judged they had found the battleground and would soon be sending for us, which proved to be the case." White wrote that "about sundown" the Legion "got the order, left the train, and moved up to the 17th Corps train." For some unknown reason, the Irishmen "lay around loose" until nearly midnight before they "moved on, crossed a slue about knee deep in water, and marched until about half-past three o'clock in the morning, and then lay down for a short rest." White wrote: "At sunrise we were on the road again and did not halt until we had marched thirteen miles and joined the brigade, and even then we hardly had time to get dinner before they had us out corduroying with the rest of the brigade." White then learned that "there had been considerable fighting. The 14th Corps had done the most of it and at one time were in a critical situation but got out bravely. Our Division was sent to their support but did not become engaged. The fighting in front of the other corps might all be called skirmishes, although some of them were pretty severe. It rained all the afternoon, and just before dark our own brigade went into line in the left of the corps." White described the Legion's part in the battle: "The Rebel skirmishers were pretty active, but we got up a breastwork of logs without accident. . . . It was about 11 o'clock when we got the works completed, and putting out a strong skirmish line, we lay down to rest." It couldn't have been a very sound sleep, as according to White, "The skirmishers kept banging away, and a battery on our right at regular intervals put in its say. It was said that in the morning we were to charge the Rebel works, but when morning came they were gone. And from the number of traps [wagons] left I should say they left in a hurry, for which we were much obliged to them. Gen. Sherman announced the close of the campaign, and we moved towards Goldsboro."[10]

Major General Alfred H. Terry's army made contact with Sherman's army at Cox's Bridge on the Neuse River, some eight miles outside Goldsboro. Terry's soldiers looked forward to meeting Sherman's veterans, and one from the 47th New York gave the following colorful description of that meeting: "A corps of infantry came by, preserving little or no order of march. One-half of a regiment would be mounted, and the other half on foot. Their dress was of every conceivable variety, and, like their manners, free and easy." To his utter amazement, "one would ride by, sitting on a side-saddle, and behind him would come a carriage and pair, the occupants being two high privates, fully accoutered, but wearing stove pipe hats and smoking cigars. High-bred and well-conditioned horses, broken-down jades, mules, donkeys, and oxen, harnessed in every kind of style, and driven according to the caprice of the possessor, moved along in mass." If nothing else, this description demonstrates the utter futility of Sherman's attempts to dismount his infantry. Terry's soldier observed that "in the rear of the column came all manner of vehicles, laden with pigs, sheep, goats, forage, and negro women and children. The spectacle was strange, picturesque, and brimful of the comic element. There was nothing strictly 'military' about it, but these men had, just a little while previous, been engaged in deadly conflict, where they had displayed the highest qualities of the soldier."[11]

Adjutant Edwin Davis reported that the 90th Illinois "crossed falling creek on the 23rd and Neuse River on the 24th. On the same day the campaign being ended we marched through Goldsboro and went into camp two miles east of the town." The Irish regiment marched some 172 miles during the month of March. At Goldsboro, the First and Third Brigades entrenched in their division's front line, which helped keep the 90th Illinois occupied.[12]

After what had been a long, grueling march through the Carolinas, Lieutenant White could finally relax: "Our march to Goldsboro was easy and pleasant, our first bivouack was in company with a part of Gen. Terry's command. The first of the cooperating column we had seen, and that night for the first time since leaving the coast, I slept out of my pants. Next day we crossed the Neuse River, marched in Review through Goldsboro and thence to our present camp. So ended the campaign."[13]

As White indicated, Sherman's army united at Goldsboro with those of Major Generals John M. Schofield and Alfred H. Terry for a combined total of nearly 89,000 Union troops, including 81,000 infantry, significantly increasing their dominance over General Johnston's Confederate forces before they headed for Raleigh, North Carolina.[14]

The 90th Illinois marched some 590 miles from Beaufort, South Carolina, to Raleigh, North Carolina, when railroad destruction, forage, and other expeditions are included. This considerably exceeds the most direct route of about 400 miles between cities visited on the march. The flooded nature of portions of the area traversed, the need to use separate routes for each of the four corps, the roundabout path followed between Columbia and Camden, South Carolina, and the extra miles added by the march to and from the Bentonville battlefield all increased the distance marched. During the fifty-two days from their leaving Pocotaligo to their arrival at Goldsboro, the men of the regiment marched a total of some 460 all-purpose miles, an average of 8.8 miles per day. Considering weather and road conditions faced, this rate of march compares favorably with their figure of 11.5 miles per day on the march to the sea. Confederate general Johnston's engineers clearly had a right to be amazed at the progress of Sherman's army across the Carolinas.[15]

During the march though the Carolinas, the 90th Illinois had two enlisted men wounded and seven missing. The Irish troops had been kept busy as four regiments of Brigadier General John Oliver's brigade (15th Michigan, 70th Ohio, 48th Illinois, and 90th Illinois) each corduroyed three miles of road and the 99th Indiana did four miles. The road conditions during that march had been much worse (four hundred miles corduroyed) than during the campaign for Atlanta (one hundred miles) or the march from Atlanta to Savannah (sixty miles). Interestingly, the troops had less sickness during the campaign in the Carolinas than would have been expected of garrison troops.[16]

On March 25, some 350 recruits and convalescents rejoined the Second Division, and reinforcements continued to arrive through the end of the month. The 90th Illinois apparently received a small number of reinforcements while at Goldsboro, as the number of enlisted men present for duty in March increased to 165, sixteen more than in February, while the absent sick decreased to ninety-eight, eleven less than in February. One of those returning was Captain Patrick Feeney, who resumed command of Company F, replacing First Lieutenant William White. Lieutenant Colonel Owen Stuart appointed White as acting regimental quartermaster on April 1, replacing Quartermaster Redmond Sheridan, who went on thirty days' leave beginning April 3, 1865. While recuperating in Chicago from his wound received at the Battle of Ezra Church, Captain Feeney had been detailed for three months' duty at Camp Douglas. Upon attempting to return to his regiment, he arrived at Nashville, Tennessee, while it was under siege by the army of Confederate general John Bell Hood. Feeney commanded a battalion of the Provisional Division during the Battle of Nashville. Other duties prevented his rejoining the 90th Illinois until near the conclusion of the march through the Carolinas in the spring of 1865.[17]

Once the 90th Illinois started on the march through the Carolinas, it became almost impossible for soldiers left behind to return to the regiment until the Legion reached Goldsboro. Upon returning from leave, Captain John Murphy, Company G, had been assigned to duty at Blair's Landing, South Carolina, on February 9, 1865, in command of detachments of the XV Corps. He rejoined the 90th Illinois on April 25, after being wounded in the left wrist at Snyder's Cross Roads, North Carolina, sometime during the previous month. First Lieutenant Lawrence McCarthy overstayed his leave and also rejoined the 90th Illinois on April 25, 1865. He was not restored to command of Company H, as Michael M. Clark had been appointed to the command on April 7, 1865. After taking the troops' money to their families, Captain David Duffy, Company E, remained on special duty in Illinois from November 1864 through February 1865. Like the others, Duffy finally caught up with the regiment at Goldsboro. By September 1, 1864, Corporal Patrick Sloan's deteriorating health had finally forced him into a hospital at Marietta, Georgia. During mid-November, he had been at a convalescent camp near Chattanooga and then at Cleveland, Tennessee, where he served as a hospital steward. With his health somewhat recovered, he was ordered to Newbern, North Carolina, and by

February 15, 1865, was serving as chief hospital steward of the department hospital, which logically included supervising its construction. He described his work at Newbern as "superintending everything about the hospital. All orders must go from and though me." His work included "overseeing the wards" and "the receiving and discharging of patients." He remained at Newbern through mid-March before rejoining the Legion at Goldsboro.[18]

The 90th Illinois spent March 28 guarding the forage train as it traveled fifteen miles east of town to secure forage and returned to camp the same day. At Goldsboro, Stuart issued General Orders No. 1 on April 1, and it was no joke. The streets, parade grounds, tents, and quarters would be regularly swept, cleaned, and ditched. Knapsacks would be stacked neatly at the head of bunks. Company officers would be responsible for daily roll calls at reveille, retreat, and tattoo. There would be Sunday morning inspections, and drill parades would be held regularly. The Irishmen were back in the army.[19]

On April Fool's Day, the Second Division reported complying with the order suspending foraging and requiring that "all surplus vehicles and animals" be "turned over to the Quartermasters Department." Whether or not Stuart relinquished his private milk supply is not recorded. He had acquired a cow somewhere during the Legion's travels through South Carolina, which allowed him to enjoy the luxury of mush and milk for supper. Troops of the Second Division kept busy building fortifications, policing the camps, replacing worn-out clothing, and going on details to obtain forage for their animals. Hazen resumed drilling his troops with battalion drills on April 3. The next four days' activities included drills at various levels of command. Hazen personally conducted drills on April 7 and 8 and liked the results so much that he wrote: "When, on the 10th of April, the Army of the Tennessee set out for Raleigh, it was in better condition than I had ever seen it. It was, in fact, with certain exceptions, as nearly perfect, in instruction, equipment, and general efficiency, as volunteer troops can be made while in the field."[20]

While the 90th Illinois camped at Goldsboro, the troops celebrated Lieutenant General Ulysses S. Grant's capture of Richmond. In a letter to his wife, Stuart commented on "the Glorious News from Genl. Grant. Are now firing a Salute along our entire line in honor of it. I do hope he whipped Lee as bad as is reported, and if so the War is near at an end. What a Blessing that well be. . . . At least I hope the 90th has fired their last Shot." Stuart had new information regarding Major Patrick Flynn: "I managed to figure Flynn after all. you know he was discharged and re-instated again. . . . He reported at Beaufort, S.C. and there got Detailed. Wrote from there to the Department, or to his friend Genl. Logan, and then when he was ordered back to N.Y., and if permitted, to proceed to Washington, there to have his re-instatement revoked. I received a notice from Washington discharging him from the Service. He failing to report to the com. Officer of his Regt. So that ends little Red-Head. He is now paid for his Flag arrangement." Flynn had good reason to complain that life wasn't always fair. On the other hand, First Lieutenant John McAssey had reason to celebrate, being officially mustered as captain of Company K on April 8, 1865.[21]

Good news arrived thick and fast. By April 12, the 90th Illinois received word of the April 9 surrender of Lee's Army of Northern Virginia. The soldiers reacted strongly to the news. Brigadier General Charles Woods, commander of the First Division, jubilantly hosted a celebration that concluded with the general in a convivial mood leading a tour of the division's camps while pounding on a large bass drum. Scout Theodore Upson, Company C, 100th Indiana, explained the activities as a necessary outlet for pent-up emotion. Exactly how the 90th Illinois celebrated the news, while not recorded, can best be imagined.[22]

On April 10, the march toward Raleigh began. On April 14, the Legion crossed the Neuse River, entered Raleigh, the capital of North Carolina, and camped four miles northwest of the city. Sherman took the opportunity to review his troops while they marched through the city. That morning, Sherman received a request for a truce from Confederate general Johnston, which interrupted the army's march toward Charlotte, North Carolina. For Sherman's army, the war had effectively ended, but arranging the surrender of General Johnston's forces would have its unique complications.[23]

The XXIII Corps got the job of guarding the city of Raleigh while the XV Corps remained camped outside. During a visit to Raleigh, Stuart found it "beautiful but rather old Fashioned, there is a guard on every house and the most perfect order prevails." Sherman wanted no repeat of Columbia. Stuart expressed his satisfaction at having seen the war to its end and was clearly looking forward to what lay in the future and how the officers and men of the regiment would be viewed when he wrote his wife, "Home is all the talk." He added: "I know you are glad . . . that I have remained to see it finished. I know your are and every body must say that my Self and Regt. has done our part. Thank God I have got to Say, I have been in every Battle that Sherman fought since the fall of Vicksburg and that is enough for any one man, and in one year assisted in the capture of Milledgeville the Capital of Geo., Columbia, S.C., Raleigh the Capital of North C." The time to go home had finally arrived, or so they thought.[24]

As the men of the Irish Legion remained in their camp near Raleigh, two nearly simultaneous events markedly affected their attitude and that of their fellow soldiers. The 90th Illinois received the news of President Lincoln's assassination in Sherman's April 17 Special Field Orders No. 56. The order reflected Sherman's deep concern that the war could degenerate into drawn-out partisan warfare, which may partly explain the generous terms of surrender he offered to General Joseph E. Johnston. The news of the assassination produced strong responses in the troops, ranging from bitter talk to weeping to silence. Some had a more violent reaction.

A mob of two thousand started for Raleigh bent on destruction. Major General John A. Logan stopped them by threatening to turn nearby artillery on them. Black Jack proved he could stop a charge by his men as well as lead one.[25]

The second event, the treatment accorded General Sherman by the cabinet of President Andrew Johnson, had immediate and lasting effects on his army. On April 17 and 18, after General Robert E. Lee's surrender, Sherman and General Johnston developed lenient terms of surrender for all remaining Confederate armies that restored state governments in the Confederacy on conditions highly favorable to the seceded states. Approval from the authorities in Washington had to be obtained in order for the terms to go into effect. Johnston's and Sherman's armies stayed put as prescribed in the terms, resting on their status quo and waiting for Washington to respond.[26]

Lieutenant Colonel Owen Stuart described the scene of the two armies at peace camped outside Raleigh: "It is a beautiful Sight when the camp fires are light in the evening as the whole army are in one line, but in Groups by Corps, with the Reb's in our front both armys patrolling on their own ground protecting the citizens from plunder by either armys. They often meet at the same house, quite friendly. The majority of the Rebs say they will not fight any more. The officers are very bitter." Stuart wrote of his desire to go home and his concern for the Confederate soldiers: "My Dear after all I hope I will be home to enjoy the fruits of your garden labor, I can assure I can hardly rest thinking of it, and it coming so Sudden to us all, it will be a great Blessing to the both Sections of the country, Particularly the South, God help their poor Soldiers going home to an empty house without anything to eat or sleep on. I mean them that lives in the Section of country that this army passed through as they are Destroyed for years to come." The 90th didn't exactly relax while at Raleigh as their brigade commander, Brigadier General John Oliver, ordered drills to be held daily from 9 to 10 A.M. and 4 to 5 P.M. to keep his boys occupied and out of trouble.[27]

While the armies remained static, President Johnson and his cabinet unanimously and resoundingly rejected Sherman's seven-point memorandum for the surrender of Confederate forces. Secretary of War Edwin Stanton condemned Sherman's actions in no uncertain terms. Not content with handling the rejection internally, Stanton created a firestorm of indignation against Sherman in the press by having Sherman's dispatches, including the surrender terms, and his point-by-point rejection of them appear in the Sunday papers. Under the influence of Stanton's paranoia, Chief of Staff Major General Henry Halleck overreacted, ordering Generals George Mead, Philip Sheridan, and Horatio Wright into North Carolina with instructions to "pay no regard to any truce or orders of General Sherman respecting hostilities," and more specifically for Wright and Brigadier General James Wilson to "obey no orders from Sherman." All of this conveyed a not-so-subtle suggestion that Sherman had "gone over to the other side."[28]

The press picked up Stanton's attack on Sherman, and some of those papers reached his soldiers outside Raleigh. Theodore Upson of the 100th Indiana described the troops' reaction: "We don't propose to have our General called such names. 'Sherman a Traitor!' The idea!" Some soldiers took matters in their own hands by burning a cart of New York papers containing articles attacking Sherman.[29]

Sherman had clearly overstepped the bounds the administration was willing to grant to any general, even General Grant. Sherman never received Stanton's coded instructions to Grant forbidding him from dealing with political questions during General Lee's surrender, so he proceeded to draft his terms of peace based upon his understanding of Lincoln's intent. Unfortunately for all concerned, Lincoln was no longer in charge of events.[30]

General Grant visited Sherman in Raleigh and broke the news of President Johnson's rejection of his proposed terms of surrender. Ever the good friend, Grant sent Sherman to negotiate new terms of surrender based on those Grant gave to Lee. On April 26 near Durham Station, General Johnston surrendered the troops under his command. The Irish Legion's role in Civil War history may have ended, but Sherman's war with Stanton and Halleck had just begun. Some of Sherman's animosity may well have affected the attitude of his troops, giving them a very large chip on their collective shoulders when they next came in contact with their eastern counterparts.[31]

The 90th Illinois found time in April to update the regiment's returns for the enlisted men. Twenty-three prisoners of war appeared on the Legion's rolls. Six had been captured at Missionary Ridge, twelve during the Battle of Atlanta, and one each at Ezra Church and Jonesborough, while three were taken near Kingston, Georgia, on October 16, 1864. Seven other men had been discharged for disability, and two died of disease. One had deserted, and one returned from missing in action. Five recruits were added to the regiment. All these changes resulted in 193 enlisted men reported as present. Out of an aggregate total of 368 officers and men, ninety were absent sick and fifty-two were absent detached to other commands.[32]

{ 17 }

LIKE THE LORDS OF THE WORLD

On April 28, before the march home began, Major General William Hazen again warned his troops that foraging and the use of animals and vehicles were prohibited. The free and easy days of their march through Georgia and the Carolinas had ended, and the men of the 90th Illinois would have to march with no opportunity to acquire alternative means of transportation. On April 29, the Irish Legion began the long march to Washington, D.C., to be paraded and mustered out. The distance from Raleigh to Washington by road is about 254 miles, but the division covered some 280 miles or 290 miles in twenty-three days to reach Alexandria, Virginia, some six miles southeast of Washington, an average of about twelve miles per day. The march became a grueling experience for the troops. In the six days starting May 1, they marched 126 miles from the Neuse River to within six miles of Petersburg, Virginia, covering thirty miles on May 5. Theodore Upson, Company C, 100th Indiana, described the march as "fearfully hard." Warm weather and the unnecessarily fast pace, reportedly caused by competition between units, led to fatal sunstrokes in some regiments.[1]

Near Petersburg, the 90th Illinois passed through or nearby a series of battlefields, the scene of much hard fighting between the Army of the Potomac and General Robert E. Lee's Army of Northern Virginia. The soldiers could make their own professional assessment of the relative merits of the fortifications encountered. Major General Oliver O. Howard reviewed the Second Division, including the 90th Illinois, as the troops passed through Petersburg on May 9. Four days later, after crossing the James River on a pontoon bridge, the men of the Irish Legion had a firsthand view of Richmond while they paraded eight ranks abreast, as part of the Second Division, through what had been the Confederate capital city. They then crossed the Chickahominy River and camped.[2]

Major General William T. Sherman's resentment toward his former friend Major General Henry Halleck showed itself at Richmond in his refusal of Halleck's offer of hospitality. He also forbade the XIV Corps from being reviewed by Halleck. Whatever message Sherman's troops drew from his actions, it likely did not increase their willingness to submit tamely to any perceived insults during their remaining time in the army, or afterward, either, for some.[3]

From May 15 through May 19, the 90th Illinois marched ninety-six miles to within four miles of Alexandria, Virginia, an average of nineteen miles per day. This rapid pace in the heat overcame Captain David Duffy. Surgeon Charles A. Thompson of the 90th Illinois swore an affidavit that Duffy "was prostrated with heat, suffering a severe sun-stroke, falling by the road side, when I treated him till he sufficiently recovered to be taken with an ambulance. He was sick for several days before able to join his command in the line of march, and had not fully recovered from the affects of the sun-stroke when we were mustered out in June, 1865." The division, including the 90th Illinois, rested on May 20 but moved to Fairfax Seminary the following day. On May 22, the troops prepared for the Grand Review of General Sherman's army to be held on May 24, following the review of the Army of the Potomac on May 23. The men of the 90th Illinois, along with their Second Division comrades, had little opportunity to view their competition as they moved five miles to the south end of the Long Bridge, where they camped for the night, anticipating their moment in the limelight the following day.[4]

A feeling of competition with the eastern army motivated Sherman's troops to make a good impression during the review. Their pride was at stake, and newspaper articles critical of their discipline and military bearing only increased their determination. How could Sherman's army outshine the Army of the Potomac? Sherman met with some of his officers at his headquarters to prepare for the next day's review. They agreed that their troops could not match the appearance of the eastern troops attired in new uniforms, paper collars, and white gloves and moving with their regulation march step. Sherman and his officers decided not to try to excel in these areas but to pass in review just as they had marched through Georgia on the way to the sea and to include foragers in their columns. They intended to turn the rather uncouth appearance of Sherman's western troops into a major advantage over the spit and polish of the Army of the Potomac's troops. Lacking modern polling capabilities, crowd reaction and newspaper commentary would largely determine which army won this particular popularity contest.[5]

To improve their appearance, Brigadier General Hazen ordered his troops to crop their hair, trim their beards, and wash their haversacks and again forbade them from being out of uniform. As usual, many of Hazen's soldiers ignored his orders regarding hair.[6]

The 90th Illinois would have a new set of brigade, corps, and army commanders during the Grand Review. A few days earlier, General Howard had turned over command of the Army of the Tennessee to Major General John A. Logan. Thus, by May 24, General Hazen had replaced "Black Jack" Logan in command of the XV Corps and Brigadier General John Oliver had replaced Hazen in command of the Second Division. Out of a total present and absent of 357, the 90th Illinois had only 23 officers and a maximum of 223 enlisted men present to march down Pennsylvania Avenue. The absent included 35 officers and men detached and 12 men absent for other reasons but only 64 absent sick; apparently the prospect of being discharged had sped up many soldiers' recovery.[7]

Sherman's troops received some new uniforms, but need outpaced available supply, and some troops logically preferred to keep their clothing allowance rather than spend it for a somewhat useless new uniform. As a result, most paraded in well-worn uniforms and some in quite ragged clothing. The appearance of the 90th Illinois at the Grand Review matched that of their Second Division comrades: their uniforms showed the wear of their long service, and their hair failed to meet Hazen's strict standards of grooming.[8]

After a breakfast of coffee, hardtack, and whatever else they acquired to supplement the government's standard issue, the 90th Illinois, as part of the Second Division, crossed the Long Bridge with the rest of the XV Corps and formed by 8 A.M. on Maryland Avenue and adjoining streets north and east of the Capitol Building. Following the boom of the signal gun at 9 A.M., the corps moved forward onto Pennsylvania Avenue, led by Generals Sherman and Logan and their staffs.[9]

It was indeed a proud day for the men of the Irish Legion as they marched in route step with the long, swinging gait of veterans down Pennsylvania Avenue in a twenty-file front under their new emerald green flag emblazoned with the golden harp, the symbol of Ireland dating back to the seventeenth century. Richly decorated, the Legion's flag stood apart from standard government-issued regimental flags and left no doubt as to the troops' nativity. The elegance of their flag contrasted sharply with their worn uniforms and footwear, which showed the effects of hard service. Onlookers would have seen the names of many battles listed on their flag and would have recognized some, such as Mission Ridge and Vicksburg, but many would have been unfamiliar, especially to easterners. The experience of the review deeply impressed Corporal Patrick Sloan, now reunited with the 90th Illinois. Normally able to clearly and succinctly state his experiences and feelings in his letters, he struggled to describe the review to his wife: "My head is fuddled yet from all I seen and felt yesterday in Washington. Don't misunderstand that I was drunk. I tasted nothing Stronger than water but it was my feelings like many others I could not control them."[10]

Hazen considered the review to be "most satisfactory." He added, "The most gratifying acknowledgements were everywhere showered upon the officers and men of the command." Upson, from his place in the First Division, described with pride what he saw: "Our boys fell into the long swinging step, evry [every] man in perfect time, our guns at a Right Shoulder Shift . . . the men never had marched so well before. The sidewalks were packed with people, and my! How they cheered! It was a constant roar. . . . On the faces of the men was what one might call a *glory look*."[11]

Sherman also expressed pleasure with the performance of his boys. No longer the unkempt "Uncle Billy and his white sox" of the Carolinas and Georgia but now resplendent in a new uniform, he rode slowly down Pennsylvania Avenue. He recorded that on reaching the Treasury Building he looked back, and "the sight was simply magnificent. The column was compact, and the glittering muskets looked like a solid mass of steel, moving with the regularity of a pendulum." Sherman reached the reviewing stand and stood for six and a half hours watching 65,000 men of his army march past, division after division, all the while deliberately ignoring Secretary of War Edwin Stanton. Sherman liked what he saw: "It was, in my judgment, the most magnificent army in existence. . . . Many good people, up to that time, had looked upon our Western army as a sort of mob; but the world then saw, and recognized the fact, that it was an army in the proper sense, well organized, well commanded and disciplined."[12]

The review met with great success, proving Sherman's excellence as a showman. The addition of stalwart pioneers, the bizarre accoutrement of foragers and cooks, and the variety of vehicles mixed in with the marching units, portraying something of how the troops looked on their epic marches, greatly impressed the crowd, compensating for the lack of spit and polish of the troops. According to Major General Henry W. Slocum, "the attachments of foragers in rear of each brigade" most interested the spectators. "The men appeared 'in their native ugliness' as they appeared on the march through Georgia and the Carolinas. Their pack-mules and horses, with rope bridles or halters, laden with supplies such as they had carried on the march, formed part of the column."[13]

Sherman described scenes that drew "laughter and cheers" from the crowd. Six ambulances followed each division, representing its baggage train. In addition, some divisions added "goats, milch-cows, and pack-mules, whose loads consisted of game-cocks, poultry, or hams, etc.," while some divisions included the "families of freed slaves." A "corps of black pioneers" carrying picks and shovels led each division, adding "much to the interest of the occasion."[14]

Sherman's army received very favorable press coverage immediately following the review. The May 27, 1865, issue of the *New York Times* provided a description: "Bronzed, bearded, clear-eyed, lithe-framed, intelligent, independent, fearless young American men are these soldiers of Sherman. 'They march like the lords of the world' said the venerable Thomas Corwin, as the vast volumes swept up the great avenue of Washington. . . . They feel proud of their achievements, proud of the triumphant termination of this great war, proud of the country which they have saved, proud of the freedom and unity which their valor has secured to the republic. You see it in their port, you see it in their faces, and you hear it in the victorious notes that rise and swell in the evening heavens."[15]

Corporal Simon Swan's oldest son related a story that must have come from his father about the German ambassador's comments on Sherman's army during the Grand Review. Lloyd Lewis repeated the same story in his biography of Sherman. Obviously impressed as the first of the army corps passed, the ambassador commented, "An army like that could whip all Europe." As more corps passed, his exclamations increased until finally he exclaimed, "An army like that could whip the World!" Lewis's version adds a more elaborate ending. One suspects that this story made its rounds at various veterans' reunions, but however apocryphal, the story illustrates the pride felt by Sherman's soldiers, including the Irish Legion, in their achievements. It had been a great day for the soldiers of the 90th Illinois, one they would long remember.[16]

After passing by the reviewing stand, the Second Division's part of the review ended. The troops marched some four miles on Seventh and Fourteenth streets and camped between them near Fort Stevens. The men of the Irish Legion did not have their free run of the city, as General Hazen promptly issued orders allowing only a limited number of his troops to receive passes to visit "Washington City" each day and attempted to keep the rest in their camps, containing thousands of small white tents. Captain Michael Murphy happened to be one of the lucky ones who received a forty-eight-hour "leave of absence . . . to visit Washington City" by order of General Oliver. As they waited to be discharged, they bided their time as best they could. Thirty-eight enlisted men of the 90th Illinois whose term of service did not expire before September 30, 1865, were transferred to the 48th Illinois and waited until August 15 to be mustered out.[17]

Hazen probably wished the distance marched from the city had been a great deal longer in order to assure that his boys in the XV Corps behaved themselves. Unfortunately, that was not the case as on May 26 he issued orders instructing the division commanders to post "strong guards about their encampments" and establish guard posts on the roads to limit access to the city. This action was intended to strengthen and enforce his previous orders, indicating the problems he had in keeping his soldiers in their camps. The boys had a hard time controlling certain well-established habits developed during past marches. According to an article in the *Chicago Times*, many of the soldiers "seem to regard themselves as having some kind of right to appropriate articles for their own use," with or without payment. Their resulting appropriations and shenanigans sped their departure from the vicinity of Washington and also from the army. Hazen described the actions of his troops and the response of the Washington authorities: "While we were about Washington, it was difficult to keep down the spirit of reckless appropriation of other people's property. Many scenes more ludicrous than evil were constantly occurring, and the robbery of a hen-roost, or the use of a few panels of fence, was sure to be reported directly to the War Department, and an amount of investigation and police-court work was done daily which very soon made it necessary to send the Army of the Tennessee away; so that our expected long rest at Washington was reduced to a few days." You can imagine Hazen smiling as he wrote the following: "Among the disorderly acts of my men [XV Corps] was the 'capture,' as they facetiously called it, of the Fourteenth Street Railroad [horse-car line], which they reported to General Sherman as a good joke. The Corps was camped on the heights just beyond, and the men ran the road for their own convenience. They also appropriated the horse and buggy used by the captain of the Capitol police. These are only examples of their daily mischief. Finally General Sherman received an order to get his army away from Washington as quickly as possible." Although the extent of participation by the 90th Illinois in these capers remains unrecorded, one can presume it formed the basis of much reminiscence by members of the Legion at reunions and personal get-togethers of various kinds.[18]

The antics of Sherman's troublemakers resulted in most of the Army of the Tennessee, but not the 90th Illinois, being speedily removed from Washington, D.C., to a camp near Louisville, Kentucky, while the Army of Georgia was moved across the Potomac River. On May 28, some of the 90th Illinois had strayed, and Lieutenant Colonel Owen Stuart, "in compliance with instructions received last night," had "the honor to report" to the Third Brigade the absence of three officers, one first sergeant, and two privates.[19]

Reportedly, by June 2 the bulk of the XV Corps had left for Louisville, apparently much to everyone's relief. But however much the authorities wanted to speed the troops' departure, making out muster rolls took some time, so the men of the 90th Illinois waited until June 5 and 6, 1865, to officially muster by company for discharge. Although their last pay date had been August 31, 1864, they had to wait for their pay until after their return to Chicago. Then the boys had a wee bit extra to spend. Also on June 6, Lieutenant Colonel Stuart detailed First Lieutenant William White to take charge of all the regiment's books and papers and to report for instructions to the division's mustering officer.[20]

Wasting no time, on June 7 the men of the Irish Legion left for Chicago—not marching but by train—and in better order than when they had left Chicago back in 1862, only far fewer in numbers. The *Chicago Tribune* reported "only 221 men of this regiment have returned, and of those, 41 were crippled beyond carrying a musket." The 90th Illinois reached Chicago at midnight on June 9 via the Pittsburgh, Fort Wayne, and Chicago Railroad. The superintendent of that railroad's eastern division reported taking "up transportation for 90th Ill. Regt. from Pittsburg to Chicago, 248 men and 2 horses." Apparently, Lieutenant Colonel Stuart continued to watch out for his horses.[21]

The Irish Legion's homecoming proved a distinct disappointment. Chicago's attention centered on welcoming the pair of conquering heroes: Major General William T. Sherman, who had arrived in Chicago on June 7, and Lieutenant General Ulysses S. Grant, who would arrive three days later. In addition, the three-week-long Second Northwest Sanitary Fair had opened on May 30. The city of Chicago had not received prior notice of the arrival of the 90th Illinois, and the ten-acre facility at Camp Fry in Lakeview on the north side of Chicago, where the troops would be housed, left much to be desired. By June 12, eight regiments had arrived at Camp Fry, located at the intersections of Broadway, Clark Street, and Diversey Avenue. Dirty barracks and woefully inadequate supplies of food and fuel for the large number of troops present only added to their disillusionment. However, it is difficult to see how the men of the 90th Illinois or any other regiment who had marched to the sea and through the Carolinas would be long deterred from feeding or warming themselves at somebody else's expense. The 90th Illinois troops took the direct approach and obtained fuel to cook their rations from the most readily available source, as shown by Camp Fry's assistant quartermaster's report of the "damage done to barracks at Camp Fry by the 90th Ill. Vols." that included "200 ft. B.M. lumber" along with "16 window sash glazed" and "4 window glass" for a total cost of $52.80. However, no record exists that the government collected any of the $52.80 from the regiment.[22]

The Chicago newspapers eventually woke up to the presence of their returning regiments and fell all over themselves attempting to apologize for their initial lack of attention paid to the troops on their return. The *Chicago Tribune* listed the regimental and company officers and gave a brief "Sketch of Service" for each of the regiments. For the 90th Illinois, it began: "Of the many regiments in the great Northwestern army, none bears a fairer record than the Gallant 90th regiment Illinois volunteers." The 90th Illinois rated the usual nine inches of column, which was good considering that the same edition covered the arrival of General Grant and his wife and the reception and "Levee at the Tremont" held for them. Although the food and barracks at Camp Fry left much to be desired, the paper did its best to make amends to the men of the Legion by publicizing the route they would take on their way to the Sanitary Fair on June 13 and calling "for our citizens to turn out and give the boys the reception they deserve." The 90th Illinois "will be escorted through the streets of Chicago to the fair by Colonel J. L. M. Loomis and the boys of his old command, with a band of music."[23]

Chicago also gave a warm reception to the men of the 88th Illinois, the Second Board of Trade Regiment, and the 89th Illinois, the Railroad Regiment, who arrived at 9 P.M. on June 12 and were comfortably housed at Camp Douglas. Their June 13 visit to the Sanitary Fair, which included a welcoming speech by General Sherman, and subsequent reception at the Board of Trade, with a speech by Senator Richard Yates, was described in detail in three full-length columns by the *Tribune*. Sherman's speech included the admonition: "Boys, I want you to go to your homes and behave yourselves. Illinois is proud of you." He clearly wanted no repetition of the "excessive exuberance" displayed by his army while in Washington. The paper also devoted a short paragraph to the visit of the 90th Illinois to the Northwest

Sanitary Fair and described their exchange of "congratulations" with the 88th Illinois and 89th Illinois "as they passed each other, some of the remarks made being funny and quaint."[24]

The *Republican*, the successor to the *Chicago Post*, contained a more complete description of the visit to the fair by the Legion. "The gallant old 90th, one of the oldest regiments in the field, having entered Sherman's army at Vicksburg, came marching into the Washington street entrance of Union Hall, having come from Camp Fry." The article reported that the Legion made "a detour of the main hall . . . halted in front of the platform, and were greeted with three hearty cheers. Hon. T. B. Bryan then introduced Hon. Richard Yates, United States Senator from the central district who, in one of his happiest efforts, gave them a hearty welcome; referred with pride to their organization under the gubernatorial authority; praised their officers; paid a high tribute to the late heroic Colonel Mulligan, and mentioned with pride the valor, on so many fields of the gallant men before him." Unfortunately, Yates confused his Irish regiments, omitting Colonel Timothy O'Meara of the 90th Illinois and naming instead another Irishman, Colonel James Mulligan of the 23rd Illinois. As Yates closed "amid hearty applause, calls were made for Brigadier General J. M. Loomis, of Chicago, in whose brigade the 90th had fought so much and so nobly. His response was brief, but complimentary to the boys in the highest degree. The speeches ended, the regiment filed into Horticultural Hall, thence through Union Hall, taking their departure." While touring Horticultural Hall, the 90th Illinois repeated the experience of the 88th and 89th Illinois by "inspecting its beauties, drinking lemonade at Jacob's well [most of the beauties were there serving lemonade], and passing through the main departments of the fair, gazing upon its hundred thousand curiosities with joy and pride."[25]

The *Chicago Times* also described the visit by the 90th Illinois troops to Horticultural Hall. Their appearance still showed the effects of their arduous campaign through the Carolinas, including their "coarse and worn" clothing, "travel stained" shoes, "unkempt" hair, and "blue uniforms sadly the worse for service." They had obviously ignored Hazen's orders to cut their hair before the Grand Review. "There were old men among them, who seemed scarcely able to drag their limbs along the gravel path, and there were young boys there, seemingly not over sixteen years old. Weary travelers all. . . . The stock of lemonade must have suffered considerably before the whole company was supplied."[26]

Upon leaving the fair, the Legion's soldiers next "proceeded to the residence of the Rev. Dr. Dunne, adjoining St. Patrick's Church, on Des Plaines Street, and paid their respects in military style to their first colonel and to 'the father of the regiment.' The Reverend gentleman invited the regiment into the adjoining hall of the Young Men's Library rooms where the Rev. Mr. Brennan, addressing the regiment read to them" a series of "Resolutions by the Irish Catholics of Chicago on the Return of the Irish Legion." The resolutions began by expressing "a generous and heartfelt welcome to their peaceful homes, and the blessings of a free government which they have so nobly defended." The Reverend Dr. Dunne then addressed the regiment, beginning by expressing his feelings of pride in welcoming them back to Chicago. Father Dunne eulogized Colonel O'Meara for his bravery, honor, gallantry, and achievements and complimented Lieutenant Colonel Stuart for his bravery and efficiency. Following a brief review of their accomplishments and sacrifices, Father Dunne concluded his speech: "As for you, my friends who have escaped the perils of the battlefield and returned to resume your civic pursuits, I wish you every happiness. I hope your lives may be long, happy and prosperous, and that you may meet with a fair and large measure of worldly success. And as for me I will always feel proud, it will always be my boast that I too, in some measure, belonged to the Chicago Irish Legion—the brave, the gallant and chivalrous 90th Illinois."[27]

Lieutenant Colonel Stuart responded on behalf of the regiment by following General Grant's example and declining to make a speech. According to the *Republican*, Stuart's speech, or rather the lack of one, received an "enthusiastic response," probably because of the inviting smells that permeated the hall from the dinner waiting to be served. "The regiment was then invited to partake of a handsome collation which had been spread in the library rooms, and officers escorting Dr. Dunne to his residence, were entertained by him in his own hospitable style. After doing full justice to the good things before them, the regiment was again put into line, and after sainting Dr. Dunne and echoing cheer after cheer, they resumed their march and returned to Camp Fry. The reception was rendered more agreeable by choice music from the band of the Christian schools."[28]

All that remained for the regiment was to complete the discharge process and be paid. The return home for an individual company could be as impressive as their departure. When Company B, the Ryan Guards, arrived in Galena, Illinois, on June 15 on the 7:30 train from Chicago, they received a hero's welcome, according to the *Galena Gazette*. They were met outside town by "a delegation from the Committee of Arrangements and the Germania Band, who escorted them home. As they entered the city they were greeted by cheer after cheer, and the waving of handkerchiefs from the houses and bluffs lining the railroad track and on nearing the Depot the air was vocal with music, cheers, and the booming of cannon." After a parade, speeches, and a "magnificent supper . . . the Guards, accompanied by the Band, visited the home of the man whose name they bore, giving cheer after cheer for Wm. Ryan, after which they returned to the homes they had not seen for three years." Enough of the 90th Illinois remained in Chicago to form one of the regiments that paraded in the city's 1865 Fourth of July celebration.[29]

The men of the 90th Illinois saw their first action in late 1862 at Coldwater Station, four miles north of Holly Springs, Mississippi. After spending the spring of 1863 guarding the Memphis and Charleston Railroad, they went by boat to Vicksburg during the latter part of the siege, well after the severest fighting had occurred. After participating in the siege and recapture of Jackson, Mississippi, they marched across the length of the state of Tennessee, from Memphis to Chattanooga, before undergoing their first serious engagement, with Confederate major general Patrick Cleburne's forces at Missionary Ridge. There, the men of the 90th suffered their greatest losses in a single battle, 117 casualties in the bloody repulse suffered by Sherman's troops. The regiment participated in the Battle of Resaca, Georgia, and all three of the Army of the Tennessee's major battles around Atlanta: the Battle of Atlanta, the Battle of Ezra Church, and the Battle of Jonesborough. They fought on the defensive in each of these battles, which reduced casualties, yet their losses in the Atlanta campaign equaled those suffered at Missionary Ridge. With the exception of an amphibious crossing of the Ogeechee River at Jenks' Bridge and their participation in the capture of Fort McAllister at Savannah, it was march after march after march: the relief of Major General Ambrose E. Burnside at Knoxville, the pursuit of General John B. Hood through northern Georgia into Alabama, the march to the sea, the march through the Carolinas, and the march to Washington, D.C. The 90th Illinois covered nearly 2,600 miles on foot during campaigns and on the march to Washington after the war ended. The Irish Legion did not achieve the fame shared by regiments such as the 1st Minnesota or 20th Maine, nor did its brigade receive the acclaim accorded the Lightning, Iron, Irish, or Stonewall Brigades. Fate, including proximity to reporters, population centers, and access to the telegraph, ensured that greater attention was received by the eastern units of both Northern and Southern armies. Consequently, few units in the West, whether Union or Confederate, achieved such fame, however justly deserved.[30]

EPILOGUE

The Irish Legion had one last, sad official duty to perform. The Reverend Denis Dunne died of a heart condition on December 23, 1868, and was buried in Cavalry Cemetery, Evanston, Illinois. Under the direction of the chief marshal, Lieutenant Colonel Owen Stuart, members of the 90th and 23rd Illinois led the funeral procession from St. Patrick's Church to the Northwestern Railroad Depot.[1]

Local members of the Legion met from time to time, holding annual picnics in Chicago and attending as a body the funerals of deceased members. The timing of their annual picnic held in late September or in early October 1871 proved most unfortunate. Three and a half years later, on April 18, 1875, Lieutenant Colonel Stuart explained to the assembled survivors of the 90th Illinois that the "regiment borrowed the old flag of the command from the Adjutant General of the State at Springfield, to use at a picnic given by the survivors of the Ninetieth." After the war, Illinois had required all volunteer regiments to turn in their regimental colors. "Soon thereafter, and before its return, the flag was lost in the great fire of Oct. 9, 1871. The Adjutant-General now called upon them for a new flag to replace that lost in the fire." A second meeting on May 6, 1875, reported "the flag to replace that lost in the fire of 1871 had been ordered and would be ready in time to use during the days of the reunion." This time the men of the 90th got all their battles listed on the flag, and a beautiful flag it still remains with its golden Maid of Erin harp, the symbol of the United Irishmen in the 1798 rebellion. However, a tiny remnant of the original flag of the Irish Legion reportedly made an amazing reappearance in 1900 in the possession of Sergeant Major T. R. Lonergan. Survival of the remnant was possible because, following his capture at the Battle of Atlanta and subsequent imprisonment in Andersonville, Color Bearer Corporal Henry Porter of Company C had managed "by stratagems and concealment" to save the Legion's flag, as recorded in a June 1865 letter from a Springfield, Illinois, hospital, where he was recuperating following his release and exchange.[2]

In one sense, the Irish Legion was reborn in September 1890 when several veterans of the 90th Illinois met at John McAssey's home at 478 West Taylor in Chicago. That in turn led to a meeting of surviving members of the Legion at the Grand Pacific Hotel in mid-October and formation of a regimental association. The association accepted Mrs. Stuart's invitation to meet at her home on November 25, the anniversary of the Battle of Missionary Ridge, which established something of a tradition. The association also sponsored a lecture on Major General James B. McPherson and established a headquarters for the 90th Illinois in connection with a Union veterans' encampment in August 1900.[3]

After the war, the members of the Legion dispersed, literally scattering from Wilmington, North Carolina, on the East Coast to Riverside, California, on the West Coast and many locations in between. Members of the regiment would found several towns: Dunnington, Indiana, named for Captain James Dunn; Corley, Iowa, named for the wife of Sergeant Major Thomas McDonald; and Miles, Oregon, named for Private William Miles. Captain Patrick Real was instrumental in laying out and building Grafton, Nebraska.[4]

It is possible to follow the lives of some of the officers and enlisted men of or closely associated with the Irish Legion after their return to civilian life. First Lieutenant William White, whose letters contributed so much to this history of the regiment, returned to Springfield, Illinois, where he developed a highly successful construction business. He also owned White's Planing Mill, which, by hard work and excellent management, he developed into prominence. Seriously injured in August 1889 when a horse he was driving spooked and overturned the buggy, he died some three weeks later at the age of fifty-eight. His obituary described him as a "great reader" and "a man of good literary and scientific attainments." These statements are fully supported by his letters written during the war.[5]

The experience of the war and its aftermath altered some deeply held political and social views, and a number of the Legion would leave the Democratic Party to join the Republican Party. Before a local group in Springfield in 1868, White eloquently expressed such changes in a strong speech in favor of the Republican candidates, both national and in Illinois, and of equal treatment for all men before the law. "It is my belief that peace and prosperity in all sections of our diversified country can only be secured by the development and application of the principle that all men are created free and equal, admit this and you guarantee a man all his rights . . . deny it and you open the way for every form of tyranny that since the creation of the world has been his scourge."[6]

In 1870, Lieutenant Colonel Stuart farmed near Wheeling, Illinois, in Cook County but soon changed to the job of an assistant assessor, U.S. Internal Revenue.

His two daughters were born soon thereafter, Rose in 1870 and Margaret in 1872. By 1880 he lived at Jefferson, Illinois, and worked as a U.S. gauger at the Custom House, which involved serving as a revenue officer inspecting bulk goods subject to duty. Owen maintained his interest in military societies by attending the Soldiers and Sailors National Convention in Cleveland, Ohio, in September 1866. In 1877, he was elected as marshal of the Chicago Union Veterans' Club and vice president the following year. The club pledged to uphold the principles of the Republican Party, find jobs for unemployed Union veterans, and strengthen soldiers' social ties. His election brought with it an active role in organizing and equipping a force of the Union veterans sworn in as special policemen who helped preserve public order during the labor riots of July 1877. By 1900, he had moved to Park Rapids, Illinois. In October 1910, Owen, now eighty-two years old, and Margaret were living in Riverside, California, near their daughter Margaret Herrick.[7]

Stuart's friend and fellow printer Adjutant Edwin S. Davis returned to Chicago after the war where he worked as a printer at the *Chicago Evening Journal* from 1881 to 1891. He died in 1897.[8]

Quartermaster Redmond Sheridan formed part of the honor guard when President Lincoln's body lay in state in Chicago's courthouse. He was appointed justice of the peace and then clerk of the West Twelfth Street Police Court. He lived at 375 West Taylor Street all of his years in Chicago until his death in October 1885. Sheridan was buried in Calvary Cemetery, and in his obituary, the *Chicago Citizen* emphasized that he was known for his integrity.[9]

Corporal Patrick Sloan returned to Illinois and worked as a custom house officer in 1870 and bricklayer in 1880. In 1888, at age fifty-five and no longer able to perform manual labor, he applied for admission to the Illinois Soldiers' and Sailors' Home at Quincy, Illinois. He died in August 1906 and was buried in Arlington National Cemetery, site 17153.[10]

Major Patrick Flynn returned to Rockford and in spite of his war wound served as sheriff of Winnebago County from 1868 to 1872. He received a disability pension of twenty-five dollars per month, which he supplemented by selling insurance and doing various jobs not requiring physical labor. In 1901, he was reported to be deputy revenue collector.[11]

James Washington Sheahan, who had been involved in the founding of the Irish Legion and covered its actions in his newspaper throughout the war, had a long and distinguished career in journalism in Chicago. He sold his newspaper, the *Chicago Post*, in April 1865 and for a few months remained with its successor, the *Republican*, which was under the editorship of Charles A. Dana, who had been an assistant secretary of war under Edwin Stanton. In September 1865, he took an editorial position with the *Chicago Tribune*, where he remained for the rest of his career. Active in civic affairs, he served on the Chicago Public Library Board and the city's Board of Education and was president of the St. Patrick's Society.

His literary accomplishments included his comprehensive biography of Stephen A. Douglas and *The Great Conflagration*, the definitive account of the Chicago fire of 1871.[12]

Colonel John Mason Loomis, who led his First Brigade and thus the Legion, through their tests of fire at Jackson and Missionary Ridge, returned to Chicago and reestablished his fortune through his firm of John Mason Loomis and Company, lumber commission merchants. During the war, his wife, Mary, had accompanied him to the field and headed a company of Red Cross nurses. A prominent citizen in Chicago, Colonel Loomis remained active in Union Veterans' organizations, serving as chairman of the finance committee of the 1868 reunion of the officers of the Armies of the Tennessee, Cumberland, Ohio, and Georgia held in Chicago. Colonel Loomis and others of his family founded the Loomis Institute at Windsor, Connecticut, to which his wife left a $1.2 million endowment. The Loomis Institute is now the Loomis Chaffee School. Colonel Loomis died August 2, 1900. Major General Joseph Wheeler served as one of the honorary pallbearers at his funeral.[13]

The female soldier mentioned in chapter 1 and known variously as Eliza, Frank, or Francis Miller, or Francis Hook in subsequent accounts, appears in the Carded Medical Records in the National Archives for the 90th Illinois Volunteer Infantry in an entry for a Frank Miller: gunshot wound, left leg, "(female soldier), simple flesh wound left thigh." The list of hospital admissions included Hospital No. 1 at Chattanooga on February 18, 1864. She was then sent to Nashville on March 1, 1864, and admitted to Hospital No. 17 and was subsequently transferred to Hospital No. 1 on May 3, 1864. She was then "sent North June 10, 1864."[14]

Her presence with the 90th Illinois is explained in a newspaper account from the April 1, 1863, *Memphis Bulletin*. After being mustered out of the service with the 90th Illinois in Chicago, Francis or Frank Miller "married an excellent young man, a 'member of her mess,' and remained with the regiment ever since. She was with the regiment at Cold Water when the Van Dorn raid had taken place." She "shouldered a musket and took her place in the ranks by the side of her husband. . . . She fired two volleys into the rebel ranks with the coolness of a veteran. . . . The 90th is now quartered at Lafayette, Tennessee. 'Frank" is still living in union with her husband, is loved and respected by the entire regiment, and declares that 'she is for the Union of State, union of hearts, and the union of all loyal men and women to put down this rebellion."[15]

A *New York Times* correspondent interviewed a Francis Hook in an officers' hospital in Nashville and wrote that she had enlisted in August 1862 in "O'Meara's Regiment"—the 90th Illinois—under the name of Frank Miller. As a member of the regiment, she participated in the sieges of Vicksburg and Jackson, Mississippi, and was at Camp Sherman on the Big Black River. Later she had been captured at Florence, Alabama, while foraging and was seriously wounded while crossing the river with other prisoners. She had been taken to Atlanta, where her wound developed gangrene before her exchange in February 1864, which led to her hospitalization first in Chattanooga and then Nashville. A Davenport, Iowa, newspaper account, written long after the war, reported that Francis Hook had enlisted in the 90th Illinois and was taken prisoner in a battle near Chattanooga and wounded in the right calf while trying to escape.[16]

DeAnne Blanton and Lauren M. Cook describe Francis Hook's capture, wounding, and hospitalization in some detail. Their account agrees with that of the *New York Times* and also the Carded Medical Records of the Adjutant General's Office for Frank/Francis Miller but never identifies the regiment to which she belonged. However, no mention of such a person appears in the records of the 90th Illinois contained in the Illinois Adjutant General's Report or the material reviewed in the Illinois State Archives.[17]

Although the survivors of the 90th Illinois's campaigns were happy to return to civilian life, many counted their adventures in Sherman's army as the most exciting of their lives. Some, like Patrick Real, never tired of relating their amusing escapades.

Over the years, these Irishmen became integrated into their chosen communities, and many became leaders of them. All of these veterans remained proud of the role they had played in restoring the Union and helping to ensure, in Lincoln's words, "that this nation, under God, shall have a new birth of freedom; and that government of the people, by the people, for the people, shall not perish from the earth."

APPENDIXES

ABBREVIATIONS

NOTES

BIBLIOGRAPHY

INDEX

APPENDIX 1: MUSTER ROLL SUMMARY

	Present							Absent								
	Officers			Enlisted Men				Officers				Enlisted Men				
Year/ Month	For Duty	Sick	Total	For Duty	Extra Duty	Sick	Total	Detached	Sick	With Leave	Total	Detached	Sick	With Leave	Without Leave	Total
1863																
February	25	4	29	445	44	36	530	6	1	0	8	5	14	0	1	20
March	18	2	25	409	50	48	511	4	2	1	8	8	16	1	5	30
April	20	2	26	414	30	47	514	2	1	0	4	2	9	0	0	11
May	24	0	27	418	15	38	486	1	0	1	3	3	19	0	0	22
June	20	5	28	395	14	33	444	1	0	0	1	5	32	0	6	45
July	19	4	25	386	22	38	451	1	1	0	2	4	28	1	5	39
August	14	3	21	289	29	91	417	1	1	5	8	8	36	25	1	71
September	14	1	16	311	30	48	393	2	0	8	12	4	45	21	1	72
October	22	0	23	325	27	13	371	2	2	0	5	6	62	1	17	86
November	11	0	13	194	19	4	221	4	6	0	12	26	163	1	20	210
December	13	1	15	226	21	14	268	3	5	0	10	7	121	7	19	154

	Present							Absent								
	Officers			Enlisted Men				Officers				Enlisted Men				
Year/ Month	For Duty	Sick	Total	For Duty	Extra Duty	Sick	Total	Detached	Sick	With Leave	Total	Detached	Sick	With Leave	Without Leave	Total
1864																
January	16	0	16	225	28	16	279	2	5	0	9	27	106	3	10	146
February	13	0	14	250	25	13	295	3	5	0	10	24	79	13	7	123
March	12	0	14	262	39	11	321	2	5	2	10	12	72	2	4	90
April	13	5	20	285	35	7	328	2	1	0	4	8	64	0	3	76
May	13	0	16	241	20	4	271	1	6	0	7	27	94	0	6	127
June	17	2	20	254	37	7	303	0	2	0	2	5	76	0	7	91
July	9	0	11	183	37	4	238	1	7	0	8	4	110	0	10	127
August	12	1	13	177	42	16	236	1	6	0	7	3	96	0	7	109
September	11	1	14	195	27	28	256	1	3	3	7	7	73	6	2	84
October	10	0	12	175	29	3	212	1	5	3	9	11	106	0	3	124
November	13	0	15	182	14	3	204	3	2	0	6	20	97	0	6	127
December	12	0	14	163	20	4	192	3	2	0	7	14	108	0	2	129
1865																
January	13	0	15	150	15	6	184	2	0	0	4	25	108	4	2	144
February	11	1	14	149	16	7	178	3	0	0	5	25	109	3	7	150
March	12	1	15	165	12	11	194	2	0	0	4	19	98	1	10	134
April	17	0	20	168	23	2	193	2	2	0	4	50	88	5	5	151
May	21	0	23	197	18	8	223	3	0	0	3	32	64	4	5	108

Note: For December 1862, regimental total present and absent were 26 officers and 669 enlisted men. The following columns were omitted: Officers Present—on extra duty or in arrest; Officers Absent—without leave; Enlisted Men Present and Enlisted Men Absent—in arrest. The numbers in the Total columns include the data from the omitted columns.

Sources: Record Series 301.018, 90th Illinois Volunteer Infantry, Illinois State Archives, Springfield; Records of the Adjutant General's Office, Records of Volunteer Union Organizations, Record Group 94, 90th Illinois Volunteer Infantry, Muster Rolls and Returns, National Archives, Washington, D.C.

APPENDIX 2: REGIMENTAL ROSTER

The following roster lists the name and rank of officers and enlisted men of the 90th Illinois for each company and the field and staff. Names shown for company officers and field and staff are those of all who occupied those ranks. An asterisk following an officer's name indicates that the officer was not mustered in that rank. Rank shown for enlisted men is the rank at time of enlistment. An asterisk following a recruit's name indicates that the recruit was not enlisted or mustered. Additional information, including that recorded on muster and descriptive rolls regarding residence, nativity, and remarks concerning service, is available on the Internet at "The Illinois Civil War Muster and Descriptive Rolls Database," accessed through www.ilsos.gov/genealogy/.

FIELD AND STAFF

COLONELS

Timothy O'Meara
Owen Stuart*

LIEUTENANT COLONELS

Timothy O'Meara
Smith McCleavy
Owen Stuart

MAJORS

Owen Stuart
Patrick Flynn
Daniel O'Connor*

ADJUTANT

Edwin S. Davis

QUARTERMASTER

Redmond Sheridan

CHAPLAIN

Thomas F. Kelly/Kelley

SURGEONS

Henry Strong
Charles A. Thompson

FIRST ASST. SURGEONS

John B. Davidson
Darwin Hinckley*
John H. Scott

SECOND ASST. SURGEONS

Darwin Hinckley
Albert Honnold

NONCOMMISSIONED STAFF

SERGEANT MAJORS

Thomas R. Lonergan
Thomas McDonald

Q.M. SERGEANTS

Thomas McDonald
John F. Hoben

COMMISSARY SERGEANTS

John F. Hoben
Lawrence W. Bracken

HOSPITAL STEWARDS

Thomas Hendricks
Albert W. Potter

PRINCIPAL MUSICIANS

Charles Dunne
Patrick H. Sloan

COMPANY A

CAPTAINS

Patrick Flynn
James Conway*
Daniel Corcoran

FIRST LIEUTENANTS

James Conway
Daniel Corcoran*
Andrew Phinney

SECOND LIEUTENANTS

Daniel Corcoran
Andrew Phinney*

FIRST SERGEANT

Andrew Phinney

SERGEANTS

Michael Redmond
Charles Stuart
Michael Hayes
Owen Smith

CORPORALS

Maurice Kane
Henry Harris
Joseph Whalen
John Sullivan O'Brien
Robert Gubbins
Joseph P. Whalen
Henry Devine
Michael Lane

MUSICIANS

James Tully
Richard Listen
Henry Leonard

PRIVATES

Barrett, Patrick
Bracken, Lauren Henry
Broderick, David
Buckley, Cornelius
Burke, John
Burns, Michael Sr.
Burns, Michale Jr.
Butler, Thomas
Campbell, John
Carroll, John
Caton, William
Collinghan, James Joseph
Condon, James
Conley, John
Conley, Thomas
Conner, Eugene
Corcoran, Patrick
Cranney, Patrick
Crawley, John
Cronin, Patrick
Cullen, William
Devine, Henry
Devlin, Michael
Donahoe, Bernard
Dowd, Dennis
Doyle, Thomas
Dwin/Devine, Michael
Dwire, Martin
Fitzgerald, John
Fitzgerald, Richard
Fitzgerald, William
Fitzpatrick, William
Foley, James
Gaffenny, Patrick
Gavin, John
Harrity, Neal
Heffernan, Bartholomew
Harrington, Daniel
Kane, Hugh
Kane, Thomas
Kearns, Thomas
Kehoe, John
Kennelly, Edward
Kirby, Patrick
Lamb, Daniel
Lane, Michael Sr.
Laughnam, Thomas
Leahey, William
Lilas, Nicholas
Londregan, John
Malia, John
McCarthy, Edward
McCormick, Joshua
McGarry, Thomas
McGrath, John
McGrath, Owen
McKenna, John
McLaughlin, William
McMahon, Hugh
McMahon, John
Moore, James
Moran, John
Murphy, Dennis
Murphy, James
Murphy, William
O'Donnell, John
O'Neil, Francis
Ricely, Owen
Smith, James
Sullivan, Daniel
Sullivan, John
Tovey, John
Vaughan, Dennis
Wood, James
Young, George

RECRUITS

Cook, John
Dargan/Dorgan, John
Fanning, John
Gray, Robert
Listen, Richard 2nd
Ryan, Michael
Stewart, Charles M.
Thompson, Andrew

COMPANY B

CAPTAIN

Michael Murphy

FIRST LIEUTENANT

Thomas Gray

SECOND LIEUTENANTS

Charles Bellingale
Edward O'Neill

FIRST SERGEANT

Edward O'Neill

SERGEANTS

William H. Jones
James McCabe
John McDonald
Thomas Fitzpatrick

CORPORALS

F. E. Bale or Ball
Arthur Doyle
W. J. Burns
Thomas Long
Daniel Harnet
Jeremiah Quinan
James Wales
Hugh Callaghan

MUSICIANS

Edward Clark
John Shanan

WAGONER

Cornelius Lynch

PRIVATES

Baldridge, William
Beggan, John
Beggan, Patrick
Bell, Henry
Burn/Breen, Patrick
Burns, John 1st
Burns, John 2nd
Calaghan, Bernard
Calaghan, Daniel
Carroll, Mathew
Carry, Michael
Casper, Lorenzo
Clancy, Thomas
Connors, Patrick
Daily, Patrick
Donegan, Thomas
Donahoo, Michael
Doyle, Terrence
Everard, James
Fitzpatrick, John
Flynn, Daniel
Galagher, Neil
Gavin, John 1st
Gavin, John 2nd
Gavin, Joseph
Galvin, Daniel
Galvin, Philip I
Grace, John
Grady, Patrick
Griffith, Joseph
Hailey, John
Hynes, James
Hynes, John
Kinsella, John
Laffin, Martin
Longdale, Alexander
Mahan, Patrick
Mann/Mang, James
McCabe, Luther/James
McCardle, John
McCormack, David
McDonald, Alexander
McElroy, Thomas
McIntosh, Joseph
McKarney, Patrick
McKeene, Thomas
McKenna, James
McKernan, James
McKernan, Thomas
McNeary, James
Mehan, James
Monaghan, Malachy
Moore, John B.
O'Bryan, John
O'Byrne, William A.
O'Holonan, Edward
O'Rourke, William
Powers, John
Quinn, James
Roberts, Michael
Ryan, Thomas
Short, John
Snell, William
Sutter, Santy
Swift, James
Timmons, John
Todd, Henry
Welch, Charles
Welch, Edward
Williams, Thomas
Willson, John

RECRUITS

Donelly, Peter
Larkin, John
Norton, John

COMPANY C

CAPTAINS
Patrick O'Marah
John C. Harrington
James Dunne

FIRST LIEUTENANTS
John C. Harrington
James Dunne
James Casey

SECOND LIEUTENANT
Thomas Murray

FIRST SERGEANT
James Dunne

SERGEANTS
James E. Casey
Patrick Noonan
John J. Ryan
Dennis Sullivan

CORPORALS
Thomas McClelland
Henry Porter
Michael McDonald
Patrick Sloan
John Flaven
Patrick Ahern
John Blansfield
Trueman A. Robey

MUSICIANS
Michael Loughan/Loghan
James Stevens

PRIVATES
Bachand, Maglorie
Beach, William
Brady, Michael
Bryan, John W.
Byron, James
Carmichael, Dougald
Carr, William
Cary, Thomas
Cavenaugh, Joseph
Clark, James
Clayton, Thomas
Coomes, Cebert F.
Coomes, Robert
Crosby, John
Curley, James
Curran, Owen
Davenport, Thomas P.
Delaney, Richard
Donovan, Jeremiah
Doolan, James
Doris, Sylvester
Dougherty, Martin
Driscoll, John
Everett, Charles
Fleming, Thomas
Flynn, Timothy
Gannon, John
Gibbons, Edward
Gibbons, James
Grace, Patrick
Griffin, Edward
Griffin, John
Groundwell, John
Hamilton, Thomas S.
Hart, John
Hennebry, Thomas
Higgins, Peter
Hogan, Thomas
Hope, John
Jackson, Francis A.
Johnson, William W.
King, John
Klesner, Francis
Livers, Thomas R.
Lonergan, Thomas Ed.
Malloy, Patrick
McCafferty, John
McDonald, Thomas
McDonough, Bernard
McGrath, Patrick
Miles, William
Miles, William C.
Mortley, Edward
Murphy, Thomas
Newberry, Stephen
Newman, James
Nicholson, Patrick
Noonan, Thomas
O'Neil, Hugh
O'Reilly, John
Redmond, Edward
Reynolds, Thomas
Rice, James
Rowley, William
Ryan, John
Shay, John J.
Shannahan, David
Smith, William C.
Sweeney, Thomas
Swindells, George
Thompson, James S.
Wells, Joseph
Welsh, Edward
Wicker, Nelson S.

RECRUITS
Bell, James
Demuse/Demerce, David
Fitzgerald, James
Hair, Robert
Pursell, Henry
Thompson, Jason E.

COMPANY D

CAPTAIN

Daniel O'Connor

FIRST LIEUTENANT

John W. Kelley

SECOND LIEUTENANTS

Peter O'Brine/O'Brian
David A. Keys*
Peter McIntee/McIntire*

FIRST SERGEANT

David A. Keys

SERGEANTS

William H. Welch
Austin Needham
Martin Hicks
Peter McIntee/McIntire

CORPORALS

Michael Cunningham
Mathew Haley
Edward Cunningham
Michael Haley
John Casper
Peter Wilhelm
Thomas W. Smith
Thomas Burns

MUSICIANS

Charles Dunne
Philip Owens

PRIVATES

Bannon, Andrew
Bannon, Richard
Bloom, Frederick
Brown, Isaac
Bruce, Hugh
Bruce, William
Bugbee, James
Canna, John
Carney, James
Cassiday, Henry
Conchlin/Conklin, Simond
Cramer, James
Crow, Martin
Curran, William
Decker, Philip
Devlin, Patrick
Droydlin, Philip
Dudloff, David D.
Eckardt, Henry R.
Edwards, James
Garrity, Patrick
Glennon, John
Goodrich, James
Gossman, Conrad
Graham, William
Grant, John
Gray, James
Hendricks, Thomas
Hyers, James
Jones, George W.
Joyce, Austin
Judge, Bryan
Kane, John J.
Keffe, Richard
Kelly, James
Kelly, Robert
Keyser, Jacob
Lawhead, Peter D.
Leahey, Michael
Leonard, Henry
Lewis, John
Lively, David R.
Longhrea, James
Maher, John
Mahoney, Cornelius
Malone, James
Milgam, Matthew
Mock, Joseph
Moore, Joseph
Norton, Edward
Norton, Patrick
O'Boyle, Patrick
O'Brian, John
Oliver, John
Orker, John
Parker, John H.
Powers, William
Reele, John
Renne, Horace
Rowe, Anthony
Ryan, David
Sharkey, Edward
Shehey, George
Smith, Arnold
Smith, Frank
Smith, Martin
Smith, Richard F.
Smyth, Francis
Somers, Charles
Stalehey, Paul
Welch, William
Whalen, John
Wilch, William
Wiles, Michael
Wilkinson, David D.
Zolph, Simon

RECRUITS

Brondage, Alonzo P
Casey, John
Conway, Lawrence J.
Cutting, Henry P.
Denton, Thomas
Denton, William
Gannon, Peter
Smith, John W.

COMPANY E

CAPTAINS

Mathew Leonard
David Duffy

FIRST LIEUTENANTS

John McAssey
Timothy Mahoney
William Brice

SECOND LIEUTENANTS

Lawrence S. McCarthy

FIRST SERGEANT

Andrew E. Skelley

SERGEANTS

Joseph Gannon
John Marsh
Daniel J. Rock
Edward F. Scott

CORPORALS

Peter Trainor
Edward Wall
Michael Gallagher
John O'Connell
Edward Lynch
John Lyons
William Casey
James Coady

MUSICIANS

Michael Smith
Charles Docks/Cox

PRIVATES

Allen, Tipp
Ballard, Owen
Bergen, James
Blake, J. W.
Blessington, Philip
Brown, John
Buckley, Edward
Byrne, Peter J.
Cain, Robert
Call, Bernard
Cobert, William A.
Cody, Joseph
Corcoran, Robert
Costello, Joseph
Creammer, Henry
Daily, James
Daily, James
Daily, John
Daily, William
Dever, Edward
Dolan, Andrew
Dugdale, Thomas
Durkin, Peter
Flemming, Patrick
Flood, Patrick
French, Hugh
Galvin, Michael
Hasson, John
Haggerty, James
Haw, Robert
Heavy, John
Hoben, John F.
Houlahan, Andrew
Junker, Edward
Kelly, Patrick
Kennedy, John
Keogh, Edward
Lorden, Daniel
Loughan, Michael
Loutz, John
Malloy, John
Marshall, William
McCall, John
McCollough, David
McDonald, James
McDonald, John
McIntosh, David E.
Mongaven, John
Morrell, Bernard
Mulligan, Daniel
Murphy, Bernard
Murphy, John
O'Donnell, Michael
O'Kane, Francis
Ormsby, Henry
Prendergast, Jeremiah
Ryan, James
Ryan, John
Shaw, George
Smith, Bernard
Stone, John
Sweeny, Michael
Tieufel, Harmon
VanCleet, John
Walsh, John
Watt, James
Whitten, Robert

RECRUITS

Byron, Thomas
Fitzsimmons, Thomas
Furlong, William
Griffin, John
McAssey, John
Shery, Patrick

COMPANY F

CAPTAINS

Richard C. Kelly
Patrick Feeney

FIRST LIEUTENANTS

Patrick Feeney
William White

SECOND LIEUTENANTS

William White
Timothy Mahoney

FIRST SERGEANT

Timothy Mahoney

SERGEANTS

Francis A. Jackson
James Brady
Thomas White
James Healy

CORPORALS

Thomas Cox
James O'Donnell
Dennis Bartley
Michael Mahoney
Richard C. Stevens
John Ryan
John Kelly
David Fitzmorris

MUSICIANS

John Barry
William McIntyre

WAGONER

Christopher Staffen

PRIVATES

Allen, Tucker
Bailey, Thomas
Barry, Daniel
Barry, James
Burke, Edward
Callaghan, John
Carberry, Patrick
Carey, John
Casey, Edward
Clifford, Michael
Cunningham, Mark
Duhigg, Thomas
Durkin, Patrick
Dwyre, Michael
Ellis, Henry
Fahey, Patrick
Fallon, Patrick
Farrell, William
Faulkner, Patrick
Foster, William
Gillmore, James
Glennon, James
Gordon, James
Graham, John
Hanrahan, John
Hassan, John
Hessing, William
Hickey, William
Hickey, William 2nd
Hogan, Martin
Howard, Ulick
Hughes, James
Jordan, John
Keilley, Patrick
Kelly, Jeremiah
Kelly, William P.
King, John
Mahoney, Cain
Malone, Lawrence
Mathews, Alexander
McCann, Terrance
McCrea, Bernard
McMahon, Cornelius
McMahon, Michael
McVey, Samuel
Mooney, John
Moore, Alexander
Morrisey, James
Mullin, David
Murray, James
Naughton, Patrick
Oatis, Henry
O'Day, Simon
O'Neal, William P.
Parsons, John C.
Peters, Fenton
Purcell, Henry
Quirk, Jeremiah
Ray, John
Reevey, Hugh
Roach, Henry
Ryan, David
Scantlan, Patrick
Sherlock, P. F.
Slattery, John
Smith, Philip
Sullivan, John
Sullivan, John C.
Wynne, Simon

RECRUITS

Gilligan, Michael
Hartwell, Daniel
Rupert, John
Sullivan, Bryan

COMPANY G

CAPTAIN

John Murphy

FIRST LIEUTENANTS

David Duffy
Patrick Campion/Champion

SECOND LIEUTENANT

Patrick Campion/Champion

FIRST SERGEANT

Lawrence McNamara

SERGEANTS

John Cummings
Joseph Brennen
Dennis Meyers
William McGuffy

CORPORALS

William Jeffs
Luke Moore
George Donner
Edward Kelly
James Kayes
John Kelly
Edward Powers
James O'Conner

PRIVATES

Brenan, William
Brown, Frederick
Brown, John
Brusher, Justus
Burchill, Thomas
Connell, Edward
Connor, John
Cullen, Jeremiah
Cunningham, John
Currin/Curran, Patrick
Drennan, James
Duffy, David
Dunsmore, Phineas
Eaner, Charles
Foxton, John
Grady, John
Harcher, William
Harty, Thomas
Healy, John
Henry, John
Holahan, Michael
Holahan, Robert
Holahan, Thomas
Kane, Jerry
Keams, John
Keefe, John
Keefe, Patrick
Lawler, James
Leonard, Daniel
Maloy, John
Manning, William
Martin, James R.
McCarty, Dennis
McManus, John
Mead, Watson
Monroe, John
Moran, John
Morton, Samuel
Mullins, William
Murdock, Charles
Murphy, Michael
Nolan, Martin
O'Brian, John
O'Connor, Edward
O'Keefe, Patrick
O'Leary, Bartholomew
O'Neil, James
Potter, Albert
Redmond, Timothy
Reece, Jeremiah
Rierdon, Jeremiah
Rooney, Peter
Ryan, James
Ryan, John
Ryan, Timothy
Smith, Patrick
Swan, Simon
Treahey, Michael
Tully, John
Warner, Henry
Warren, Patrick
Welsh, Joseph
Whalen, Patrick
Wilkins, John
Williams, Frank

RECRUITS

Adams, James
Brown, James
Donahoe, Jeremiah
Dulanty, Michael
Etzenberger, John
Kaufman, Emel
Lewis, James
Lyon, John
Smith, John

COMPANY H

CAPTAINS

Peter Casey
Michael M. Clark

FIRST LIEUTENANTS

Andrew Liddle
Lawrence McCarthy

SECOND LIEUTENANTS

George W. McDonald
Michael M. Clark

FIRST SERGEANT

Michael M. Clark

SERGEANTS

John Dick
James S. Baxter
Thomas McLaughlin
Martin White

PRIVATES

Arlow, John
Augustine, John
Augustine, William H. H.
Bernard, Frederick W.
Borrigan, John
Bradley, Frank
Brandon, John
Brown, Charles
Brown, Oliver
Browne, Peter
Cahill, James
Clark, Firman B.
Cord, John L.
Corrall, Michael
Corson, John
Courtney, Thomas E.
Craig, William
Currie, George
Dacey, Timothy
Davis, David
Davis, Edwin S.
Devine, Patrick
Dodson, James S.
Egan, William
Fitzgibbons, John
Garrity, Daniel
Garrity, Edward
Gibbons, Patrick
Gibbons, Thomas
Gustus, Andrew
Haduk, Michael
Hansen, Christian
Hayes, Michael
Hill, Charles S.
Hollahan, John
Hopkins, Patrick
Jourdan, Michael
Kelly, Thomas
Kelly, Timothy
Lovett, William
MacIntire, James
Maguire, Charles
McCurdy, Michael
McDonald, Daniel C.
McGee, Michael
Mcguire, James
Meyers, Dennis
Monahan, Malachi
Morgan, David
Morris, Benjamin
Morrissey, Lawrence
Mulligan, James
O'Connor, James
O'Leary, Robert E.
O'Neil, Francis
O'Shaughnessy, Dennis
Padden, Owen
Price, Edward
Peura/Peuran, Joseph
Ready, Washington
Redmond, James
Roache, John
Robbinson, Edward
Scales, Thomas
Sellers, Henry
Shaw, Lorain
Shoop, Hiram H.
Skinner, John
Sloan, Michael
Smith, John
Smith, Patrick
Stein, Frederick
Stevenson, Charles A.
Sweeney, Thomas
Tatlow, Thomas
Thomas, Daniel
Thomas, Samuel
Thomes, John
Thompson, John/
George W.
Toomey, Michael
Woollett, Charles
Wright, Gilbert A.

RECRUITS

Hays, William
Mulligan, Patrick
Probst, Henry
Smith, Henry
Bryner, Michael*
Heart, James*
Hughes, Peter*
Hurley, John*

COMPANY I

CAPTAINS

William Cunningham
Thomas Murray

FIRST LIEUTENANTS

Joseph Teahon
James Geary*
Thomas Murray
Timothy Mahoney
William Brice

SECOND LIEUTENANTS

John J. O'Leary
Joseph Cavanaugh

FIRST SERGEANT

James Geary

SERGEANTS

Joseph Cavanaugh
John Doogan
William Brice
Neil O'Garry

CORPORALS

William Conwell
Thomas Julian
Lawrence Donovan
James Cribbins
Brennan Connor
Thomas B. Eagan
Tyler Polk/Tylor Pouk
Elisha N. Strong

PRIVATES

Brennan, Edward
Burns, Cornelius
Buckley, Timothy
Burns, Michael
Cane, James
Chichester, Merritt B.
Clark, John
Clyde, William
Colson, Charles
Coon, Henry C.
Cooney, Francis
Coughlin, John
Crawford, John
Curtis, William
Donovan, Daniel
Dougherty, James
Downs, James
Downs, Michael
Eich, John
Enright, James
Flannighan, Michael
Foley, William
Frazer, Robert
Frost, Hazen O.
Gallagher, George
Gallaher, Charles
Gallaher, Hugh
Griffith, Patrick
Hale, Francis
Hanrehan, James
Harris, William
Hart, James
Higgins, Andrew
Jordan, John
Kelly, Patrick
Kock, Jacob
Laferty, Michael
Laughran, James
Logan, Maurice
Londregan, John
Madden, Patrick
Malia, John
McAndrews, Michael
McIntire, Timothy
McLaughlin, Barnard
McNulty, Philip
McSweeney, Eugene
Meenahan, John
Milhorn, John
Mooney, Thomas
Moynahan, Anthony
Moynahan, John
Mulligan, James
Mulligan, James
O'Brien, Bernard
O'Connell, Daniel
O'Connell, Timothy
O'Connor, Charles
O'Connor, Thomas
Powers, John
Rosencrans, L. Willett
Ryan, John
Scanlan, Bernard
Scanlan, James
Sheppard, William
Shields, Francis
Sipple, Lewis
Smith, Henry
Smith, John
Stone, Charles
Sullivan, Patrick
Susan, Theodore
Thompson, John C.
Welch, James
Welch, Henry
Whalen, Michael
Wilkinson, James

RECRUITS

Gritzer, Francis
Hanley, John
Hawley, Michael
Lavell/Love, Daniel
Pearce, John
Redmond, John
Scanlan, Michael
Smith, Andrew B.
Zitwah, Lewis

COMPANY K

CAPTAINS

Thomas K. Barrett
Patrick S. Real
John McAssey

FIRST LIEUTENANTS

Patrick S. Real
Thomas Larkin
Jeremiah F. Riordan

SECOND LIEUTENANT

Thomas Larkin

FIRST SERGEANT

Jeremiah F. Riordan

PRIVATES

Allen, Charles
Armstrong, John
Barry, John
Bourke, Michael
Boyle, Patrick
Braning, Henry
Buckley, John
Buckley, Patrick
Byrd, John M.
Campbell, Martin
Campbell, Philip
Canty, Daniel
Clark, Henry
Closby, John
Coffey, Daniel
Coffey, John
Collins, John
Cox, Patrick
Curley, Thomas
Curtiss, William
Cusick, Michael
Darnes, Thomas W.
Daugherty, George
Daugherty, James
Deegan, James
Diggins, Thomas
Dillon, John
Dinan, John
Doolin, Michael
Doren, J. W.
Doyle, Thomas
Duffy, Edward
Duffy, John
Dunlop, John
Dwyre, Patrick O.
Gerenean, Nelson
Hall, Charles
Hanley, James
Hanrahan, James
Hart, Patrick
Hartnett, John
Hickey, John
Higgins, James
Highland, Robert
Homason, Thomas
Howard, James
Johnson, Peter
Jones, Jacob
Kalley, Timothy
Karnes, Stephen
Larkin, Thomas
Laycock, John
Leech, Theodore
Levanway, Joseph
Lynch, Patrick
Mathias, John
McAlear, William
McCormick, James
McFadden, Patrick/Philip
McGee, Philip
McInhill, James
McKey, A. B.
Meehan, Michael
Mohan, John W.
Naughton, Michael C.
Naughton, Patrick
Newman, James
Noonan, John
O'Leary, Jeremiah
O'Neill, William
O'Rourke, James
Osgood, H. J.
Pitzer, George H.
Porter, Samuel F.
Quinn, Michael
Real, Patrick S.
Reynolds, Barth G.
Reynolds, Patrick
Rierdan, Daniel
Riordan, Jeremiah F.
Riordan, Lawrence T.
Rock, Patrick
Roney, E. C.
Ryan, Hugh
Ryan, Patrick
Sanches, Francisco
Scales, Charles

COMPANY K

PRIVATES (CONTINUED)	RECRUITS	UNASSIGNED RECRUITS
Shaughnessy, John	Dorsey, John	Clark, John D.
Sherridan, Patrick	McGill, F.B.	Conly, John
Slaney, Edward	McFadden, Philip	Murphy, James
Stack, John	Middleman, Frederick E.	Powers, John
Stack, Patrick	Norton, Patrick	
Stephenson, Thomas	O'Rourke, James	
Sullivan, John C.,	Powers, Edward	
Tierney, Hugh	Riley, Timothy	
Trainor, John W.	Swartz, Nicholas	
Tye, Philip	Tyrrell, Thomas	
Welsh, Patrick		
Weston, John		
Williams, John W.		

Sources: Records of the Adjutant General's Office, Book Records of Volunteer Union Organizations, Record Group 94, 90th Illinois Volunteer Infantry, Vol. 1, Regimental Descriptive, Letter, and Order Book, National Archives, Washington, D.C.; *Report of the Adjutant General of the State of Illinois*, 5:289–308; Administrative Files on Civil War Companies and Regiments, Record Series 301.018; Muster and Descriptive Rolls, Record Series 301.020; Descriptive Roll for Field, Staff, and Line Officers, Record Series 301.023, 90th Illinois Volunteer Infantry, Illinois State Archives, Springfield.

ABBREVIATIONS

A.A.G.	Assistant Adjutant General
A.C.	Army Corps
AGR	*Report of the Adjutant General of the State of Illinois*, 9 vols. (Springfield, Ill.: Phillips Bros. State Printers, 1901)
ALPL	Abraham Lincoln Presidential Library, Springfield, Ill.
CCNMP	Chickamauga and Chattanooga National Military Park, Ga.
CHM	Research Center, Chicago History Museum (formerly Chicago Historical Society)
FO	Field Orders No.
GO	General Orders No.
ISA	Illinois State Archives, Margaret Cross Norton Building, Springfield, Ill.
NA	National Archives, Washington, D.C.
OR	*The War of the Rebellion: A Compilation of the Official Records of the Union and Confederate Armies*, 128 vols. (Washington, D.C.: Government Printing Office, 1880–1901)
RG94CMR	Records of the Adjutant General's Office, Record Group 94, 90th Illinois Volunteer Infantry, Carded Medical Records, Civil War, box 405, National Archives, Washington, D.C.
RG94MR	Records of the Adjutant General's Office, Book Records of Volunteer Union Organizations, Record Group 94, 90th Illinois Volunteer Infantry, Vol. 4, Morning Reports, Companies A, B, C, F, K, National Archives, Washington, D.C.
RG94MRR	Records of the Adjutant General's Office, Records of Volunteer Union Organizations, Record Group 94, 90th Illinois Volunteer Infantry, Muster Rolls and Returns, National Archives, Washington, D.C.
RG94RD	Records of the Adjutant General's Office, Book Records of Volunteer Union Organizations, Record Group 94, 90th Illinois Volunteer Infantry, Vol. 1, Regimental Descriptive, Letter, and Order Book, National Archives, Washington, D.C.
RS18	Administrative Files on Civil War Companies and Regiments, Record Series 301.018, 90th Illinois Volunteer Infantry, Illinois State Archives, Springfield, Ill.
RS20	Muster and Descriptive Rolls, Record Series 301.020, 90th Illinois Volunteer Infantry, Illinois State Archives, Springfield, Ill.
RS23	Descriptive Roll for Field, Staff, and Line Officers, Record Series 301.023, 90th Illinois Volunteer Infantry, Illinois State Archives, Springfield, Ill.

SFO	Special Field Orders No.
SO	Special Orders No.
SOR	Janet B. Hewett, ed., *Supplement to the Official Records of the Union and Confederate Armies*, pt. 2, vol. 13, serial no. 25 (Wilmington, N.C.: Broadfoot Publishing Company, 1995)

NOTES

Introduction

1. Woodruff, *Fifteen Years*, 361–62; RS20; Phisterer, *Statistical Record*, 18; *AGR*, 5:289–308.

2. Burton, *Melting Pot Soldiers*, 24; Laxton, *Famine Ships*, 2, 3, 18, 32, 43; Carman and Syrett, *History of the American People*, 451; Knight, "Catholic Encyclopedia: The Irish"; 1860 Federal Census.

3. Gould, *Investigations*, 16, 23, 24, 27, table 3; Burton, *Melting Pot Soldiers*, 113–16, 119, 120.

4. 1860 Federal Census; Gould, *Investigations*, table 3.

5. Ferrie, *Yankees Now*, 186; Chesterton, *Ballad of the White Horse*, book 2, "The Gathering of the Chiefs."

6. Burton, *Melting Pot Soldiers*, 134–38; Keneally, *Great Shame*, 317–18, 388, 501.

7. "Illinois and the War," *Chicago Evening Journal*, July 15, 1862; Scaife, *Campaign for Atlanta*, ii–iv.

8. McPherson, *Battle Cry of Freedom*, 322, 326; Wiley, *Life of Billy Yank*, 20, 26.

1. The Raising of the Irish Legion

1. Woodruff, *Fifteen Years*, 361–62; "Illinois and the War," "A New Irish Regiment," "City Matters," "For McClevey's Regiment," *Chicago Evening Journal*, July 15, 30, and August 1, 9, 1862; McCaffrey, "Preserving the Union," 62; "List of Recruiters," "A War Meeting: An Irish Regiment to be Raised Forthwith," "Novel and Interesting Ceremony," *Chicago Morning Post*, August 7, 9, and October 21, 1862 (hereafter *Chicago Post*); "More Men Wanted," "The Call for Troops," *Northwestern Gazette*, July 10, 21,1862; "The New Irish Regiments," "Progress of Recruiting," "Brownson on the Loyalty of the Roman Catholic Church," *Chicago Tribune*, August 7–8, 1862, July 22, 1863; Richard Yates to E. M. Stanton, August 7, 1862, *OR*, ser. 3, vol. 2, 123:315; "Adjutant General Fuller," *Illinois State Journal*, July 31, 1862; Burton, *Melting Pot Soldiers*, 139.

2. "City Matters; The Catholic Clergy and the War," "Another Irish Regiment," *Chicago Evening Journal*, August 5, 9, 1862; Karamanski, *Rally 'Round the Flag*, 114; Richard Yates to E. M. Stanton, August 7, 1862, *OR*, ser. 3, vol. 2, 123:315.

3. "Bryan Hall," "Hooley's Opera House," *Chicago Tribune*, October 30, December 14, 1870; "The War Meeting at Bryan Hall: Irish Element Aroused," *Chicago Post*, August 13, 1862; Karamanski, *Rally 'Round the Flag*, 127; "Illinois and the War," "Grand Rally at Bryan Hall Tonight," *Chicago Evening Journal*, July 15, August 12, 1862.

4. "Father Dunne's Legion, Capital Letter from Col. Mulligan," *Chicago Post*, August 19, 1862.

5. Karamanski, *Rally 'Round the Flag*, 77–78; Burton, *Melting Pot Soldiers*, 139; Eddy, *Patriotism of Illinois*, 567.

6. *Portrait and Biography Album*, 457; McPherson, *For Cause and Comrades*, 6.

7. Cunningham, *Three Years with the Adirondack Regiment*, 137–38, quoted in Botkin, "On Picket," 440–41.

8. Lonn, *Foreigners in the Union Army and Navy*, 70–75, 436–37; Burton, *Melting Pot Soldiers*, 112, 117, 120; Cavanagh, *Memoirs of Gen. Thomas Francis Meagher*, 369, 436–38; McCaffrey, "Preserving the Union," 54–56; McPherson, *Cause and Comrades*, 5–6.

9. "Local Military News: Presentation," *Chicago Post*, October 29, 1862; RS23.

10. *OR*, ser. 3, vol. 2, 123:206–7; Lonn, *Desertion during the Civil War*, 140; "Report of War Fund Committee," *Ottawa Free Trader*, September 20, 1862; "Board of Trade Subscribes $10,000," "Cook County Board of Supervisors Voted $200,000 for Bounties," *Chicago Evening Journal*, July 22, 24, 1862; Woodruff, *Fifteen Years*, 35, 43, 49, 367; "Volunteers Attention, Volunteers Wanted Immediately," *Northwestern Gazette*, August 4, 1862.

11. Stanton to Lincoln, December 1, 1862, *OR*, ser. 3, vol. 2, 123:903; "Scarcity of Laborers," *Chicago Post*, July 25, 1862; Hicken, *Illinois in the Civil War*, 124–25, 128–30; McPherson, *Battle Cry of Freedom*, 506; Lonn, *Foreigners in the Union Army and Navy*, 41–43; Nevins, *War for the Union*, 370; Karamanski, *Rally 'Round the Flag*, 113–14; Hallock, "Role of the Community," 124; *AGR*, 4:600, 651; 5:259, 287, 309, 358, 382, 434, 461, 568, 661, 686; 6:200, 512: 74, 75, 76, 88, 89, 90, 92, 93, 95, 96, 100, 104, 105, 113, 127 Illinois Vol. Inf. Regt. respectively; *OR*, ser. 3, vol. 5, 126:600, 677; vol. 2, 123:207.

12. "Enrollment of the Men of Illinois Preparatory to Drafting," "Honor for Illinois," *Northwestern Gazette*, August 2, 11, 1862; Karamanski, *Rally 'Round the Flag*, 114.

13. Skerrett, "Creating Sacred Space in an Early Chicago Neighborhood," in *At the Crossroads*, 27, 29; McCaffrey, "Preserving the Union," 62; Skerrett, "Irish in Chicago," 35–38; Andreas, *History of Chicago*, vol. 2, 400; "Novel and Interesting Ceremony," *Chicago Post*, October 21, 1862.

14. "City Matters," "Meeting at Bridgeport," *Chicago Evening Journal*, August 1, 12, 1862; "Military Matters," "Chicago," "The Irish Legion-Father Dunne's Regiment," "The War Meeting at Bryan Hall," "Death of Colonel Owen Stuart," *Chicago Post*, August 1, 6, 10, 13, 1862, and December 3, 1863; obituary, James W. Sheahan, *New York Times*, June 18, 1883; "Great Excitement on Dearborn Street," *Chicago Tribune*, October 12, 1861; U.S. Passport, April 28, 1862, Owen Stuart Letters, ALPL; Owen Stuart, Compiled Military Service File, NA.

15. Dunne to Yates, telegram, August 12, 1862, RS18; Mulkerins, *Holy Family Parish*, 471; Andreas, *History of Chicago*, vol. 2, 49; *Chicago City Directory*; Sheridan to Brother, February 12 and August 11, 1863, March 2 and December 29, 1864, private collection; Redmond Sheridan, Pension File, NA; Federal Census of 1880; W. H. Sheridan to P. B. Swan, July 27, 2004, personal communication; RS20; December 31, 1862, Report, RS23; "Dunne's Regiment," *Chicago Post*, August 14, 1862; "Catholic Item," *Chicago Tribune*, November 16, 1860; "Important to Volunteers: War Department Washington," *Northwestern Gazette*, August 26, 1862.

16. McIlvaine, *Reminiscences of Chicago*, xii; Gates, *Illinois Central Railroad*, railroad map of Illinois, 1857; "Illinois and the War," *Chicago Evening Journal*, July 15, 1862; *AGR*, 5:306–7; RS20.

17. Bruce, *Harp and the Eagle*, 104–12; Bilby, *Irish Brigade*, 50.

18. "Mulligan Guards," *Chicago Post*, August 21, 1862; Church, "Mulligan Guards," 94–95; *AGR*, 5:290–92; Melancthon Smith to Fuller, March 17, 1863, RS18; "The City," *Chicago Tribune*, September 9, 1862; RS23.

19. RS23; "Departure of the Ryan Guards," *Northwestern Gazette*, September 4, 1862; Michael W. Murphy, Pension File, NA.

20. Woodruff, *Fifteen Years*, 42, 49, 66, 367; Anon., "Major Daniel O'Connor," 316; *AGR*, 5:294, 295; RS23.

21. RS23 and RS20; *AGR*, 5:289–311; Karamanski, *Rally 'Round the Flag*, 106–7; "Postponed," "City Matters," *Chicago Evening Journal*, October 1, 2, 1862; "Negro Riot in Chicago," "Trial of Richard C. Kelly for Assault and Battery," "The Ridiculous Clark Street Imbroglio," "The Fraud upon the County," *Chicago Post*, July 15, 17, 18, and October 2, 1862; Civil War Soldiers and Sailors System Search, http://www.itd.nps.gov/, Detailed

Soldier Record, Richard C. Kelly; Peter Casey, "Note to History," June 9 [n.d.], and Casey to Wife, February 18, 1863, Peter Casey File, CHM; John Murphy, Pension File and Compiled Military Service File, NA; Dornbusch, *Military Bibliography*, 35; "The LaSalle County Regiment," "Last Notice," *Ottawa Free Trader*, August 16, 30, 1862.

22. RG94RD; RS20 and RS23; Gould, *Investigations*, 50, 95.

23. *AGR*, 5:309; Bross, "History of Camp Douglas," 160, 164–68; Karamanski, *Rally 'Round the Flag*, 141–44; Kelly, "History of Camp Douglas"; Faust, *Historical*, 558.

24. "Camp Douglas General and Special Order Book," CHM; *OR*, ser. 1, vol. 16, pt. 2, 23:661; *SOR*, 440, 446, 450.

25. "Camp Douglas," *Chicago Post*, October 4, 1862; *AGR*, 5:309; Karamanski, *Rally 'Round the Flag*, 142–43; "Camp Douglas," "More Outlawry at Camp Douglas," *Chicago Evening Journal*, October 2, 18, 1962; John C. Harrington, Pension File, NA.

26. Burton, *Melting Pot Soldiers*, 139; Andreas, *History of Chicago*, vol. 1, 244, 274.

27. Woodruff, *Fifteen Years*, 362; Lee to McClellan, June 19, 1862, Austin to Cravens, July 22, 1862, List of Officers Exchanged, September 21, 1862, *OR*, ser. 2, vol. 4, 117:41, 46, 578; Phisterer, *New York*, 2266; Farwell, *Ball's Bluff*, 109, 113; "Fourth of July in a Confederate Prison Pen," *New York Times*, August 8, 1862; *OR*, ser. 1, vol. 5, 5:320, 325; Goodwin to Wilder, June 6, 1862, *OR*, ser. 2, vol. 3, 116:892; Coyle, "Unknown Hero," 360; Timothy J. O'Meara, Microfilms, Regular Army Enlistments, T233, roll 25, p. 170, Third Cavalry, roll 29, NA; "Local Military," *Chicago Post*, November 25, 1862.

28. "The Irish Legion," *Chicago Post*, September 9, 1862.

29. Ely, "Memoir of Alfred Ely," 232; Coyle, "Unknown Hero," 362.

30. Bradwell to Fuller, August 15, 1862; O'Ryan to Yates, August 25, 1862; Knox to Fuller, September 6, 1862, RS18; Haines to Yates, August 11, 13, 1862, Yates Family Papers, ALPL; *OR*, ser. 3, vol. 2, 123:321–22.

31. Haines to Yates, August 29, 1862; Dunne to Yates, August 30, 1862; Officers of the 90th Regt. to Fuller, undated, RS18.

32. "The Irish Legion," *Chicago Post*, September 9, 1862; Dunne to Yates, September 10, 1862, RS18; Haines to Yates, September 17, 1862; O'Marah to Gooding, September 18, 1862, Yates Family Papers, ALPL; Sheridan to Brother, February 12, 1863, private collection. Punctuation added.

33. Snowhook to Hoffman, September 23, 1862, RS18; Burton, *Melting Pot Soldiers*, 139.

34. *AGR*, 5:289.

35. "The Irish Legion," *Chicago Post*, October 3, 1862.

36. "Presentation to Major Stuart: Sword Presentation," "Presentation of a Sword to Captain John Murphy," "Presentation at Camp Dunne: Presentation of a Sword to Capt. Casey," "Adjutant E. S. Davis Was Presented a Sword," "Excursion, Picnic, Sword and Banner Presentation," "Speeches: Local Military News," "Local Military," *Chicago Post*, October 3, 4, 5, 7, 24, 29, and November 26, 1862; "Sword Presentation," *Illinois State Journal*, September 29, 1862.

37. *AGR*, 4:600, 651; 5:259, 287, 309, 358, 382, 434, 461, 568, 661, 686; 6:200, 512: 74, 75, 76, 88, 89, 90, 92, 93, 95, 96, 100, 104, 105, 113, 127 Illinois Vol. Inf. Regt. respectively.

38. Number of enlisted men by company, October 19, 1862; Dunne to Fuller, November 13, 1862; Tucker to Fuller, November 23, 1862; RS18; RS23; Barrett to Fuller, October 20, 1862, RG94MRR, Cos. C–F, box 621; "W. B. Snowhook," "Local Military," *Chicago Post*, November 23, 25, 1862; "The LaSalle County Regiment," "Last Notice," "Report of War Fund Committee," *Ottawa Free Trader*, August 16, 30, and September 20, 1862; *AGR*, 5:289; "Irish Legion," *Chicago Evening Journal*, November 22, 1862.

39. "Irish Legion," *Chicago Post*, November 22, 1862; Sheridan to Brother, February 12, 1863, private collection; RG94RD; Burton, *Melting Pot Soldiers*, 140.

40. "A Female Soldier," *Chicago Post*, September 27, 1862; "City Matters, Daughter of the Regiment," *Chicago Evening Journal*, September 30, 1862.

41. RG94CMR; "A Female Heroine," *Memphis Bulletin*, April 1, 1863; "Story of Francis Hook," *New York Times*, April 21, 1864; "Francis Hook," *Davenport Daily Republican*, March 31, 1901; Blanton and Cook, *They Fought Like Demons*, 10, 44, 50, 75, 78, 96, 169, 183; RG94RD; RS20; *AGR*, 5:289–308.

42. John King to Fuller, November 27, 1862, RS18; "Town Election, South Chicago," *Chicago Tribune*, November 19, 1862.

43. Lonn, *Desertion during the Civil War*, 140–42; "Deserters Arrested in Illinois," *Northwest Gazette*, October 27, 1863; RG94RD.

44. *AGR*, 2:244–74; 5:289–308; 6:66–67; *OR*, ser. 3, vol. 5, 126:600, 677; *OR*, ser. 3, vol. 2, 123:207.

45. Sheridan to Brother, February 12, 1863, private collection; Woodruff, *Fifteen Years*, 368–69.

46. *AGR*, 5:289–308; "Local Military," *Chicago Post*, November 29, 1862.

47. *AGR*, 5:289–308; RG94RD; RS20 and RS23; Lonn, *Desertion during the Civil War*, 127–42.

48. *OR*, ser. 3, vol. 2, 122:207; Dunne to Fuller, November 13, 1862, RS18; RS20; Lonn, *Desertion during the Civil War*, 139; *AGR*, 5:302–6.

49. Barrett to Fuller, October 20, 1862, RG94MRR, Cos. C–F, box 621; Patrick Real, Pension File, NA; Prov. Mar. Gen. James B. Fry Rept. to Secretary of War Edwin Stanton, March 17, 1866, *OR*, ser. 3, vol. 5, 126:674, 678; 2nd Lieut. William White and thirty-seven men of Co. F to Gov. Yates, October 29, 1862; Unsigned to Gov. Yates, October 29, 1862, RS18.

50. J. Wallace, *Past and Present*; W. White, manuscript of speech presented March 18, 1861, in Cook's Hall, Springfield, IL, private collection.

51. "65 Years Ago Today, September 28, 1862," and "65 Years Ago Today, January 31, 1863," *Chicago Tribune*, September 28, 1927, and January 31, 1928; Faust, *Historical*, 242; Tap, "Race, Rhetoric, and Emancipation," 100–125; Rorabaugh, "Rising Democratic Spirits," 142; Commager, "XXV.7B.," 613–14.

52. *Treasury of Prayer*, private collection; "Local Military," *Chicago Post*, November 29, 1862; Woodruff, *Fifteen Years*, 369; December 1862 Report, RS23; Patrick Real, Pension File, NA.

53. "The 90th Regiment," *Chicago Evening Journal*, November 28, 1862; "Local Military," *Chicago Post*, November 29, 1862; Daniel O'Connor and John C. Harrington, Pension Files, NA.

54. *AGR*, 5:289–309.

55. 88th, 89th, 90th, 96th, 100th Illinois, RS23.

56. Dunne to Fuller, November 13, 1862, RS18.

2. Attention from Two Generals

1. "The Irish Legion," *Chicago Times*, December 8, 1862; December 1862 Report, RS23; Gibson and Gibson, *Army's Navy Series*, 116; *SOR*, 422.

2. Casey to Wife, November 30, 1862, Peter Casey File, CHM; December 1862 Report, RS23; George W. McDonald, Compiled Military Service File, NA.

3. D. Cameron to Dear Son and Daughter, December 12, 1862, Stuart Letters, ALPL; "From the Irish Legion," *Chicago Post*, December 5, 1862; December 1862 Report, RS23; Sayers, "La Grange, Tennessee."

4. "Army Correspondence: Convalescent Camp, La Grange, Tenn.," *Ottawa Free Trader*, December 27, 1862; Col. Norton to Maj. Gen. Grant, December 16, 1862, *OR*, ser. 1, vol. 17, pt. 2, 25:416–17; Bearss, *Vicksburg Is the Key*, 108–10, 233–34; *AGR*, 5:309.

5. *OR*, ser. 1, vol. 17, pt. 2, 25:380–81.

6. Ibid., 25:85, 285, 289; pt. 1, 24:58–60, 489.

7. Casey to Wife, December 6, 1862, Peter Casey File, CHM.

8. *SOR*, 423, 463; Woodruff, *Fifteen Years*, 369; *Lloyd's Map of the Southern States*; Northwestern Mississippi 1863 Map; McAlexander, *Southern Tapestry*, 35; *OR*, ser. 1, vol. 17, pt. 2, 25:28, 29, 32, 84, 286, 903; pt. 1, 24:439; "R. Sheridan, Letter from the 90th Illinois," *Boston Pilot*, October 17, 1863.

9. *SOR*, 423, 459, 463; RG94MR; Woodruff, *Fifteen Years*, 369; Davis, *Official Military Atlas*, plate 154.

10. Woodruff, *Fifteen Years*, 369–71.

11. U.S. Court of Claims, Congressional Jurisdiction, Case File 5762, Joseph H. Brooks, NA.

12. Sheridan to Brother, February 12, 1863, private collection.

13. *Mississippi 1860 Agricultural Census*; McAlexander, *Southern Tapestry*, 35, 56, 107, 160.

14. Military Pass, December 4, 1862; D. Cameron to O. and M. Stuart, December 12, 1862; Margaret to Family, December 17, 1862, Stuart Letters, ALPL; "Consolidation of the Irish and Scottish Regiments," *Chicago Evening Journal*, November 26, 1862; Hogan, *Williams's Memories*, 114.

15. Gray, *"Dear Darling Loulie,"* 50, 58–59.

16. Ibid., 59–60.

17. *SOR*, 463; Casey to Wife, December 14, 1862, Peter Casey File, CHM; Sheridan to Brother, February 12, 1863, private collection; McAlexander, *Southern Tapestry*, 107; John A. Griffin Diary, ALPL.

18. *SOR*, 463; Baumann, *Arming the Suckers*, 176; O'Meara to Fuller, December 5, 1862, RS18; O'Meara to Maj. Gen. John C. Sullivan, December 13, 1862, RG94RD; Woodruff, *Fifteen Years*, 371; *Story of the Fifty-Fifth Regiment*, 41; December 1862 Report, RS23.

19. Woodruff, *Fifteen Years*, 373–75.

20. Sheridan to Brother, February 12, 1863, private collection.

21. RG94RD.

22. Sheridan to Brother, February 12, 1863, private collection; Dupree, "Capture of Holly Springs," 55–58; Bearss, *Vicksburg Is the Key*, 275, 307–10; Faust, *Historical*, 365–66; *SOR*, 440, 450; Patrick Sloan to Wife, December 23, 1862, in Fulton, "Civil War Letters of Patrick H. Sloan" (hereafter Fulton/Sloan).

23. December 1862 Report, RS23.

24. Woodruff, *Fifteen Years*, 372; *SOR*, 446.

25. December 1862 Report, RS23; *OR*, ser. 1, vol. 17, pt. 1, 24:513.

26. Charles to Dear Sister, January 13, 1863, Wallace-Dickey Family Papers, ALPL.

27. Dupree, "Capture of Holly Springs," 59; *OR*, ser. 1, vol. 17, pt. 1, 24:503, 513; Bearss, *Vicksburg Is the Key*, 317.

28. Patrick Sloan to Wife, December 23, 1862, Fulton/Sloan; Patrick Sloan, Compiled Military Service File, NA.

29. Sheridan to Brother, February 12, 1863, private collection; Sheridan to Fuller, January 23, 1863, RS18.

30. Casey to Wife, January 7, 1863, Peter Casey File, CHM.

31. RG94MRR, box 622; Margaret to Sisters, December 1862, Stuart Letters, ALPL; "Letter from Capt. Barrett," *Ottawa Free Trader*, February 21, 1863.

32. *OR*, ser. 1, vol. 17, pt. 1, 24:525.

33. Woodruff, *Fifteen Years*, 373.

34. Ibid., 375–76.

35. Sheridan to Brother, February 12, 1863, private collection.

36. O'Meara to Loomis, January 3, 1863, RG94RD.

37. Sherman, *Memoirs*, 285–86; O'Meara to Loomis, January 4, 1863, RG94RD; Loomis to O'Meara, January 4, 1863; Rawlins to O'Meara, January 4, 1863, SO 4, RG94MRR, box 620; "The Cotton Speculating Generals," *Illinois State Journal*, February 16, 1863; Hurlbut to Rawlins, March 7, 1863, *OR*, ser. 1, vol. 24, pt. 3, 38:92.

38. McAlexander, *Southern Tapestry*, 16.

39. Main, "'A Sunday in the South.'"

40. "Forces in Northern Mississippi and West Tennessee," *Illinois State Journal*, December 30, 1862; "Cairo," "Capture and Plunder of Holly Springs," *Chicago Times*, December 25, 31, 1862.

41. RG94MR; December 1862 Report, RS23; RG94MRR, box 620; Long, *Civil War Day by Day*, 302–3, 306–7; Grant, *Personal Memoirs*, 225.

3. Life on "One Cracker a Day"

1. Grant, *Personal Memoirs*, 225.

2. Veritas to Editor, *Chicago Post*, April 28, 1863; McPherson to Grant, January 11, 1863, *OR*, ser. 1, vol. 17, pt. 2, 25:554; Grant to McPherson, January 8, 1863, *OR*, ser. 1, vol. 17, pt. 2, 25:545; M. Wallace, "Civil War Diary of Thomas K. Mitchell"; Microfilms, M594; *SOR*, 440; Thomas Larkin, Pension File, NA; Rawlins GO 6, January 20, 1863, *OR*, ser. 1, vol. 24, pt. 3, 38:3.

3. Woodruff, *Fifteen Years*, 376–78.

4. "A Day with the 'Irish Legion,'" *Chicago Post*, March 10, 1863.

5. RG94MRR, box 620; *SOR*, 446; "Woollett to Editor," *Chicago Post*, February 4, 1863; Baumann, *Arming the Suckers*, 176.

6. Patrick Sloan, Compiled Military Service File, NA; Patrick Sloan to Wife, February 4, 1863, Fulton/Sloan.

7. Patrick Sloan to Wife, April 6, 1863, Fulton/Sloan.

8. Casey to Wife, February 11 and 18, 1863, Peter Casey File, CHM; M. Wallace, "Civil War Diary of Thomas K Mitchell."

9. Hinckley to Sanitary Commission, Memphis, February 21, 1863, RG94RD; RG94MRR, box 620; Darwin Hinckley, Pension File, NA; *AGR*, 5:290–308; appendix 1.

10. O'Meara to Gen. Denver, 1st Div. XVI A.C., March 18, 1863, RG94RD.

11. Patrick Sloan to Wife, February 23, 1863, Fulton/Sloan.

12. *SOR*, 436; Woodruff, *Fifteen Years*, 378; Brig. Gen. Denver GO 16, March 6, 1863, RG94MRR, box 620; Stuart to Wife's Parents, April 12, 1863, Stuart Letters, ALPL.

13. Veritas, "The Chicago Irish Legion, 20 April 1863," *Chicago Post*, April 28, 1863; L. Wallace Duncan and Chas. F. Scott, *History of Allen and Woodson Counties*, 163–65; Henry Strong, Compiled Military Service File, NA; *AGR*, 5:289; Fuller to O'Meara, March 8, 1863, RG94MRR, box 620.

14. Patrick Sloan to Wife, March 12 and April 6, 1863, Fulton/Sloan.

15. RG94MR, Co. A; Edwin S. Davis, Pension File, NA; Loomis to A.A.G. XVI A.C., March 28, 1863, RG94MRR, box 620; Col. Timothy O'Meara, Pension File, NA; Loomis to A.A.G. 1st Div. XVI A.C., March 31, 1863, *OR*, ser. 1, vol. 24, pt. 3, 38:162; Veritas, "The Chicago Irish Legion," *Chicago Post*, April 28, 1863.

16. Tennyson, "Locksley Hall," 538; Lawrence McCarthy, Pension File, NA; M. Wallace, "Civil War Diary of Thomas K. Mitchell."

17. Dyer, *Compendium*, vol. 3, 1084; *OR*, ser. 1, vol. 24, pt. 2, 37:154, pt. 3, 38:949; RG94MRR, box 620; Stuart to Wife's Parents, April 12, 1863, Stuart Letters, ALPL; Baumann, *Arming the Suckers*, 176; *SOR*, 423.

18. Casey to Wife, April 13, 1863, Peter Casey File, CHM.

19. Ibid., April 23, 1863.

20. Stuart to Wife's Parents, April 12 and May 20, 1863; Margaret to Parents, April 11, 1863, Stuart Letters, ALPL.

21. HQ Dept. of the Tennessee GO 21, March 26, 1863, RG94MRR, box 620.

22. *AGR*, 5:290–308; Adj. Gen. Lorenzo Thomas SO 87, February 23, 1863, RG94MRR, box 621; Richard C. Kelly, Pension File, NA; RG94MRR, box 620; "65 Years Ago Today, January 31, 1863," *Chicago Tribune*, January 31, 1928; Woodruff, *Fifteen Years*, 363; Patrick Sloan to Wife, April 6, 1863, Fulton/Sloan; Peter O'Brien [or O'Brian], Compiled Military Service File, NA.

23. Hurlbut to Yates, May 15, 1863, RS18; RG94MR; Church, "Allen Curtis Fuller," 9–13; Welcher, *Union Army*, vol. 2, 145; Flynn to Fuller, May 13, 1863; O'Meara to Fuller, May 28, 1863, RS18.

24. Patrick Sloan to Wife, April 21, 1863, Fulton/Sloan; Casey to Wife, April 30, 1863, Peter Casey File, CHM; RG94MRR, box 621.

25. RG94MRR, box 620; appendix 1.

26. Casey to Wife, May 28, 1863, Peter Casey File, CHM; Williams, *Peoples History*, 39; Hernon, *Celts, Catholics and Copperheads*, 65–66; Meagher, *Columbia Guide*, 82–83.

27. Charles Woollett, "The Irish Legion of Chicago," Flynn quoted in "The Chicago Irish Legion," *Boston Pilot*, February 21, March 14, 1863; Charles Woollett, Compiled Military Service File, NA; Meagher, *Columbia Guide*, 84; Wright, *Oxford Dictionary of Civil War Quotations*, 156.

28. Williams, "Memories of War Times," *Warsaw Daily Times*, May 23, 1903; P. Flynn, "Letter from the Irish Legion," *Chicago Post*, February 27, 1863; Ezra J. Warner, *Generals in Blue*, 503; *OR*, ser. 3, vol. 3, 124:100; "The Following Speech Made to Troops at Helena, Ark, on April 6 by Adj. Gen. Thomas," *New York Times*, April 19, 1863.

29. Winther, *With Sherman to the Sea*, 55; Sherlock, *Memorabilia*, 275; *SOR*, 436.

30. "Lieut. Col. Owen Stuart," *Chicago Post*, July 3, 1863.

31. "Conversations with General Thomas," *New York Times*, July 20, 1863.

32. "Another Military Outrage," *Dawson's Daily Times and Union*, July 25, 1863; "Thomas' Published Account," *Defiance Democrat*, August 15, 1863; Styple, *Writing and Fighting the Civil War*, 204–5; *AGR*, 5:290–308.

33. "The Irish Legion, Futile Attempt to Abolitionize It," *Chicago Times*, May 25, 1863; Barrett to Fuller, July 21, 1863, RS18; Loomis to A.A. Gen. XVI A.C., May 29, 1863, and Adj. Gen. A. Thomas, SO 34, June 10, 1863, Thomas K. Barrett, Compiled Military Service File, NA.

34. "Irish-American Regiment," *Boston Pilot*, August 15, 1863.

35. Casey to Wife, May 28, 1863, Peter Casey File, CHM; *SOR*, 407, 423, 431; *AGR*, 5:290–308; RG94RD; R94MRR, box 620.

4. The Father of Waters Unvexed

1. Woodruff, *Fifteen Years*, 379; *SOR*, 407; Patrick Sloan to Wife, June 7, 1863, private collection.

2. Woodruff, *Fifteen Years*, 380–81; *SOR*, 428.

3. Casey to Wife, June 10, 1863, Peter Casey File, CHM.

4. Father Kelly to Mother Superior Mary Vincent McGirr, in Jolly, *Nuns of the Battlefield*, 262–63; *AGR*, 5:290–308; Hogan, *Williams's Memories*, 97; RG94MR.

5. Patrick Real, Compiled Military Service File, NA; Murphy, "Brief Sketch"; "Died," *Memphis Appeal*, April 15, 1862; MacManus, *Story of the Irish Race*, 473.

6. Jolly, *Nuns of the Battlefield*, 263; *SOR*, 407; Sheridan to Brother, August 11, 1863, private collection; "Resigned, Alderman Redmond Sheridan," *Chicago Tribune*, June 16, 1863; Woodruff, *Fifteen Years*, 381.

7. Bearss, *Unvexed to the Sea*, 748, 1080–81; Patrick Sloan to Wife, June 19 and September 23, 1863, Fulton/Sloan; *OR*, ser. 1, vol. 24, pt. 2, 37:154; Eddy, *Patriotism of Illinois*, 407–8; *OR*, ser. 1, vol. 10, pt. 1, 10:805.

8. Jolly, *Nuns of the Battlefield*, 263; "Bombardment of Vicksburg," *Chicago Tribune*, June 13, 1863.

9. Grabau, *Ninety-Eight Days*, 427; Urquahart, *Vicksburg*, 25, 37–38.

10. McLean to Mrs. Stuart, June 29, 1863, Stuart Letters, ALPL.

11. Adj. Gen. Office SO 260, June 12, 1863; King to Yates, June 28, 1863; O'Hara to Fuller, June 29, 1863, RS18; "Lieut. Col. Owen Stuart," *Chicago Post*, July 3, 1863.

12. Asst. Adj. Gen. to Yates, July 10, 1863; Judge Advocate to Stanton, July 10, 1863; Adj. Gen. Office to Yates, SO 331, July 25, 1863; Sheahan to Fuller, July 31, 1863, RS18.

13. Gen. Buford to Capt. Flange, July 12, 1863, Stuart Letters, ALPL.

14. Bearss, *Unvexed to the Sea*, 1089–92; *OR*, ser. 1, vol. 24, pt. 2, 37:533, 555, 628; pt. 3, 38:475; Grabau, *Ninety-Eight Days*, map 5.

15. R. Sheridan, "Letter from the 90th Illinois," *Boston Pilot*, October 17, 1863; *SOR*, 407, 436, 447; Davis, *Official Military Atlas*, plate 36, no. 1.

16. Patrick Sloan to Wife, June 23, 1863, Fulton/Sloan.

17. Ibid., August 10, 1863.

18. Casey to Wife, July 2, 1863, Peter Casey File, CHM; RG94MRR, box 622; R. Sheridan, "Letter from the 90th Illinois," *Boston Pilot*, October 17, 1863.

19. R. Sheridan, "Letter from the 90th Illinois," *Boston Pilot*, October 17, 1863.

20. Microfilms, M594.

21. Faust, *Historical*, 61; Grabau, *Ninety-Eight Days*, 22, map 68; *OR*, ser. 1, vol. 24, pt. 2, 37:628; Grant, *Personal Memoirs*, 253; Wills, *Army Life*, 188.

22. Patrick Sloan to Wife, June 30, 1863, private collection.

23. *OR*, ser. 1, vol. 24, pt. 3, 38:475; pt. 2, 37:555.

24. *SOR*, 411, 436, 441, 451; Sherlock, *Memorabilia*, 39, 41; *OR*, ser. 1, vol. 24, pt. 2, 37:628–30, 635, 639, 651; Woodruff, *Fifteen Years*, 382.

25. Sheridan to Brother, August 11, 1863, private collection.

26. R. Sheridan, "Letter from the 90th Illinois," *Boston Pilot*, October 17, 1863.

27. Casey to Wife, July 23, 1863, Peter Casey File, CHM.

28. Lawrence McCarthy and John McAssey, Compiled Military Service Files, NA.

29. Williams, "Memories of War Times," *Warsaw Daily Times*, June 20, 1903; James Conway, Pension File, NA.

30. *OR*, ser. 1, vol. 24, pt. 3, 38:481–82; pt. 2, 37:556, 580, 620; Bearss, *Siege of Jackson*, 66.

31. *OR*, ser. 1, vol. 24, pt. 2, 37:632.

32. Ibid., 37:556, 628–29; Grabau, *Ninety-Eight Days*, map 13; Davis, *Official Military Atlas*, plate 36, no. 1.

33. James Conway, Pension File, NA; Sherlock, *Memorabilia*, 40; Woodruff, *Fifteen Years*, 381; *OR*, ser. 1, vol. 24, pt. 1, 36:245; Bearss, *Siege of Jackson*, 67–68.

34. Sherman, *Memoirs*, 356; *OR*, ser. 1, vol. 24, pt. 2, 37:556, 629–30; *SOR*, 412, 424; Woodruff, *Fifteen Years*, 383–84.

35. *OR*, ser. 1, vol. 24, pt. 2, 37:632–33; Woodruff, *Fifteen Years*, 383–84; Hogan, *Williams's Memories*, 103.

36. Sherlock, *Memorabilia*, 41; *OR*, ser. 1, vol. 24, pt. 1, 36:245; pt. 2, 37:535; pt. 3, 38:502–3; Bearss, *Siege of Jackson*, 84.

37. James Conway and Darwin Hinckley, Pension Files, NA.

38. Casey to Wife, August 2, 1863, Peter Casey File, CHM; *New Encyclopedia Britannica*, 96; *OR*, ser. 1, vol. 24, pt. 2, 37:544; Col. Loomis to Capt. London, AAG First Div. XVI A.C., July 21, 1863, Loomis, Manuscript M107.

39. Johnston, *Narrative of Military Operations*, 208; O'Meara to Brother, August 5, 1863, Timothy O'Meara, Pension File, NA; O'Meara to Loomis, July 21, 1863, RG94MRR, box 620.

40. RS18.

41. R. Sheridan, "Letter from the 90th Illinois," *Boston Pilot*, October 17, 1863; Bearss, *Siege of Jackson*, 95.

42. *OR*, ser. 1, vol. 24, pt. 2, 37:529.

43. Casey to Wife, August 1, 1863, Peter Casey File, CHM.

44. Elder, "Diary of William Henry Elder," 47.

45. *OR*, ser. 1, vol. 24, pt. 3, 38:534, 537; Dyer, *Compendium*, vol. 3, 1084; Warner, *Generals in Blue*, 146; Howell, *Officers of the Army and Navy*, 327.

46. *SOR*, 412; Sherman, *Memoirs*, 370; RG94MR, Co. B; Winther, *With Sherman to the Sea*, 67.

47. R. Sheridan, "Letter from the 90th Illinois," *Boston Pilot*, October 17, 1863; Patrick Sloan to Wife, August 23, 1863, Fulton/Sloan.

48. Patrick Sloan to Wife, August 7, 1863, Fulton/Sloan; RG94MRR, box 620; RG94MR; appendix 1.

49. O'Meara to Brother, August 5, 1863, Timothy O'Meara, Pension File, NA; Woodruff, *Fifteen Years*, 365; Patrick Sloan to Wife, August 10, 1863, Fulton/Sloan.

50. "Camp Sherman, Mississippi," *Boston Pilot*, September 5, 1863; A. Cameron to Margaret, October 7, 1863, Stuart Letters, ALPL.

51. Casey to Wife, August 1, 1863; Casey to President Andrew Johnson, undated petition; O'Meara to R. M. Sawyer, November 20, 1863, Peter Casey File, CHM; Peter Casey and Lawrence McCarthy, Compiled Military Service Files, NA; Patrick Sloan to Wife, July 31, 1863, Fulton/Sloan.

52. "O'Marah's Candidacy for Board of Public Works," "Letter from William Sooy Smith," *Ohio Democrat*, October 9, 1879; Maj. Gen. U. S. Grant SO 268, September 30, 1863, RG94MRR, box 620; Thomas Murray, Compiled Military Service File, NA.

53. O'Meara to Services Rendered Claims Board, August 10, 1863, O'Meara to Fuller, August 12, 1863, RG94MRR, box 620; HQ 90th IL to Fuller, September 2, 1863, RS18.

54. Flynn to Fuller, January 28, April 6, May 13, November 18, December 22, 1863, and January 12, 1865; Lane to Fuller, December 28, 1864; Flynn to Gov. Oglesby, January 16, 1865; McAssey to Fuller, January 4 and October 22, 1864; 44 enlisted men of Co. E to Fuller, September 21, 1863; Daniel O'Connor to Fuller, January 23, 1865; Feeney to Fuller, February 16, 1863; McCarthy to Fuller, August 7, 1864; Casey to Fuller, March 7, 1864; Larkin to Fuller, July 23, 1864; Barrett to Fuller, July 21, 1863; unsigned letter from Freeport, IL, to Fuller, June 19, 1863; O'Marah to Fuller, July 22 and September 28, 1864; 27 enlisted men of Co. C to Fuller, September 18, 1864, RS18.

55. O'Meara to Brother, August 5, 1863, Timothy O'Meara, Pension File, NA.

56. Baumann, *Arming the Suckers*, 176; *AGR*, 5:289–308; RG94MRR, box 620.

57. *OR*, ser. 1, vol. 31, pt. 1, 55:630; Patrick Sloan to Wife, August 9, 1863, Fulton/Sloan; Sheridan to Brother, March 2, 1864, private collection; Sherlock, *Memorabilia*, 45; Margaret to Husband, September 26, 1863, Stuart Letters, ALPL; *AGR*, 5:289.

58. Sherlock, *Memorabilia*, 45; Patrick Sloan to Wife, September 23, 1863, Fulton/Sloan.

59. Sheridan to Brother, August 11, 1863, private collection.
60. Bearss, *Unvexed to the Sea*, 1313.

5. The March to Chattanooga

1. Long, *Civil War Day by Day*, 411–12; *OR*, ser. 1, vol. 31, pt. 2, 55:568–69, 630; Sherman, *Memoirs*, 373.

2. *OR*, ser. 1, vol. 30, pt. 4, 53:149; vol. 31, pt. 2, 55:569, 631; Woodruff, *Fifteen Years*, 385; *SOR*, 407, 424; RG94MR.

3. Margaret to Husband, October 3, 1863, Stuart Letters, ALPL.

4. *OR*, ser. 1, vol. 31, pt. 2, 55:569; Sherman, *Memoirs*, 376.

5. Woodruff, *Fifteen Years*, 385; Sherman, *Memoirs*, 376–78; *OR*, ser. 1, vol. 30, pt. 2, 51:757–60; Warner, *Generals in Gray*, 46.

6. Carmody, "Battle of Collierville," 466–70.

7. Sherlock, *Memorabilia*, 47; Woodruff, *Fifteen Years*, 385–86; RG94MR, Co. A; Sheridan to Brother, March 2, 1864, private collection.

8. Carmody, "Collierville," 469–70; Sheridan to Brother, March 2, 1864, private collection.

9. *OR*, ser. 1, vol. 30, pt. 2, 51:760–61; Sherman, *Memoirs*, 378.

10. Sherman Report, October 14, 1863, *OR*, ser. 1, vol. 30, pt. 2, 51:732–33; Sherman to Hurlbut, October 12 [13], 1863; Hurlbut to Carr, October 13, 1863; Sherman to Rawlins, October 14, 1863, *OR*, ser. 1, vol. 30, pt. 4, 53:304, 330, 355–56; Woodruff, *Fifteen Years*, 386.

11. Circulars, October 12, 1863, *OR*, ser. 1, vol. 30, pt. 4, 53:305–6; RG94MR, Co. A.

12. *OR*, ser. 1, vol. 31, pt. 2, 55:570–71, 630; Corse to Sherman, October 14, 1863; Corse's circular, October 14, 1863; Sherman's GO 80, November 16, 1863, *OR*, ser. 1, vol. 30, pt. 4, 53:359–60, 410; Faust, *Historical*, 332; Woodruff, *Fifteen Years*, 386–87; *SOR*, 408; RG94MR, Cos. A, B.

13. Sherman to Crook, November 6, 1863; Audenried to Grant, November 7, 1863; Sherman to Rawlins, November 8, 1863; Sherman to Hurlbut, November 9, 1863, *OR*, ser. 1, vol. 31, pt. 3, 56:69, 80, 90, 101; pt. 2, 55:569, 571; *SOR*, 408, 412, 432.

14. Sheridan to Brother, March 2, 1864, private collection.

15. Woodruff, *Fifteen Years*, 387; Sherman to Crook, November 6, 1863, *OR*, ser. 1, vol. 31, pt. 3, 56:69–70.

16. *SOR*, 412, 425; Woodruff, *Fifteen Years*, 387; QM Gen. Meigs to Grant, November 9, 1863, *OR*, ser. 1, vol. 31, pt. 3, 56:96; Hogan, *Williams's Memories*, 112; Cozzens, *Shipwreck of Their Hopes*, 109–10; *OR*, ser. 1, vol. 31, pt. 2, 55:571–73; G. Davis, *Official Military Atlas*, plate 117.

17. Wills, *Army Life*, 201, 231; Woodruff, *Fifteen Years*, 387; McDonough, *Chattanooga*, 47–48, 79–89.

18. Grant, *Personal Memoirs*, 312, 321, 331; Cozzens, *Shipwreck of Their Hopes*, 352, 386; Faust, *Historical*, 96–97.

19. *OR*, ser. 1, vol. 31, pt. 2, 55:572, 630–31; Sherman, *Memoirs*, 399; *SOR*, 413; Woodruff, *Fifteen Years*, 388; RG94MRR, box 620; Hogan, *Williams's Memories*, 115; RG94MR, Co. C.

20. *OR*, ser. 1, vol. 31, pt. 2, 55:588–89, 631; Woodruff, *Fifteen Years*, 388; RG94MRR, box 620; Sherlock, *Memorabilia*, 51.

21. RG94MRR, box 620; *OR*, ser. 1, vol. 31, pt. 2, 55:572, 577; G. Davis, *Official Military Atlas*, plate 49, no. 1, and plate 48, no. 1; Baumgartner and Strayer, *Echoes of Battle*, 191–92.

22. Col. Timothy O'Meara, Pension File, NA.

6. The Battle of Chattanooga

1. Sherman, *Memoirs*, 387; Grant, *Personal Memoirs*, 327; W. F. Smith, "Comments on General Grant's 'Chattanooga,'" in *Retreat from Gettysburg*, ed. Johnson and Buel, 715–17; Cozzens, *Shipwreck of Their Hopes*, 112, 144.

2. *OR*, ser. 1, vol. 31, pt. 2, 55:73–75, 572–73, 747; Wilson, *Under the Old Flag*, 294; *SOR*, 432, 437.

3. RG94MR, Co. C; Hogan, *Williams's Memories*, 119; *OR*, ser. 1, vol. 31, pt. 2, 55:573; Cozzens, *Shipwreck of Their Hopes*, 151.

4. Woodruff, *Fifteen Years*, 388; *OR*, ser. 1, vol. 31, pt. 2, 55:573–74; Sword, *Mountains Touched with Fire*, 199–200.

5. *OR*, ser. 1, vol. 31, pt. 2, 55:74–75, 633, 642; Wilson, *Under the Old Flag*, 295; Cozzens, *Shipwreck of Their Hopes*, 151–55; *SOR*, 437; Hogan, *Williams's Memories*, 120.

6. *OR*, ser. 1, vol. 31, pt. 2, 55:78; G. Davis, *Official Military Atlas*, plate 50, no. 1; W. Smith, "Comments on General Grant's 'Chattanooga,'" 716.

7. W. Smith, "Historical Sketch," 198, 208.

8. *OR*, ser. 1, vol. 31, pt. 2, 55:95, 349, 574–75; Cozzens, *Shipwreck of Their Hopes*, 213, 228.

9. Wilson, *Under the Old Flag*, 295.

10. *OR*, ser. 1, vol. 31, pt. 2, 55:747.

11. Ibid., 55:349, 574.

12. RG94MR, Co. C; Hogan, *Williams's Memories*, 120; Bloomfield to Carmen, November 21, 1907, 90th Illinois File, CCNMP; RG94MRR, box 620; *SOR*, 413; Henry Robinson, undated, 100th Indiana File, CCNMP.

13. Sherlock, *Memorabilia*, 54–55.

14. Bloomfield to Carmen, November 21, 1907, 90th Illinois File, CCNMP; Scott to Carmen, December 13, 1907, 12th Indiana File, CCNMP; Woodruff, *Fifteen Years*, 388, 389; Cozzens, *Shipwreck of Their Hopes*, 219–20; Map of Mission Ridge; Chickamauga and Chattanooga National Park Commission, *Map of the Battlefields of Chattanooga and Wauhatchie*.

15. *OR*, ser. 1, vol. 31, pt. 2, 55:633; Woodruff, *Fifteen Years*, 388; Williams, "Memories of War Times," *Warsaw Daily Times*, August 8, 1903.

16. "Two Stories of the Civil War: A Brave Commander," *Chicago Daily Tribune*, July 14, 1894; Mrs. Mary Hunt Loomis to Brother, December 6, 1863, John Mason Loomis, manuscript collection.

17. *OR*, ser. 1, vol. 31, pt. 2, 55:633.

18. Sherlock, *Memorabilia*, 54, 55; Henry Robinson statement, undated, 100th Indiana File, CCNMP; Chickamauga and Chattanooga National Park Commission, *Map of the Battlefields of Chattanooga and Wauhatchie*; G. Davis, *Official Military Atlas*, plate 45, no. 8; plate 49, no. 1.

19. Woodruff, *Fifteen Years*, 388–89.

20. *OR*, ser. 1, vol. 31, pt. 2, 55:633.

21. Duffy to Carmen, January 17, 1908, 90th Illinois File, CCNMP; Woodruff, *Fifteen Years*, 389; *OR*, ser. 1, vol. 31, pt. 2, 55:368, 652.

22. Woodruff, *Fifteen Years*, 389; *OR*, ser. 1, vol. 31, pt. 2, 55:87.

23. Alexander Moore, Pension Affidavit, Pension File, NA; *AGR*, 5:300.

24. R. Sheridan, "Letter from Quartermaster Sheridan," *Chicago Post*, December 8, 1863; John C. Harrington, Pension File, NA.

25. Woodruff, *Fifteen Years*, 390; RG94MRR, box 620.

26. Sherlock, *Memorabilia*, 69; Sherlock to Carmen, 1907 or 1908, 100th Indiana File, CCNMP.

27. *OR*, ser. 1, vol. 31, pt. 2, 55:735–36; Buck, *Cleburne and His Command*, 163.

28. *OR*, ser. 1, vol. 31, pt. 2, 55:749.

29. Ibid., 55:749; Sherlock to Carmen, February 10, 1908; Henry Robinson statement, undated, 100th Indiana File, CCNMP.

30. *OR*, ser. 1, vol. 31, pt. 2, 55:368, 633–34; Morrisey to Carmen, February 28, 1908; Bloomfield to Carmen, November 21, 1907, 90th Illinois File, CCNMP; Sherlock to Carmen, 1907 or 1908, 100th Indiana File, CCNMP.

31. Buck, *Cleburne and His Command*, 170; Hogan, *Williams's Memories*, 121; Henry Robinson statement, undated, 100th Indiana File, CCNMP.

32. "The Heroes of Chattanooga," *Rock Island Evening Argus*, January 5, 1864; *OR*, ser. 1, vol. 31, pt. 2, 55:634; Green B. Raum, "The Forgotten Fight on Tunnel Hill," in Cozzens, *Battles and Leaders of the Civil War*, vol. 5, 471–73; Sherlock to Carmen, 1907 or 1908; Bloomfield to Carmen, February 10, 1908, 100th Indiana File, CCNMP; Bloomfield to Carmen, November 21 and December 19, 1907; Duffy to Carmen, January 14, 1908, 90th Illinois File, CCNMP; Map of Tunnel Hill Area, CCNMP.

33. *OR*, ser. 1, vol. 31, pt. 2, 55:368, 370, 634; Duffy to Carmen, January 14, 1908, 90th Illinois File, CCNMP.

34. *OR*, ser. 1, vol. 31, pt. 2, 55:634, 643–44.

35. Ibid., 55:370, 652, 655.

36. Ibid., 55:82–88, 634, 655, 751–752.

37. Bloomfield to Carmen, November 21, 1907, 90th Illinois File, CCNMP; Hogan, *Williams's Memories*, 121.

38. W. Smith, "Comments on General Grant's 'Chattanooga,'" 210–12; Wilson, *Under the Old Flag*, 295–96.

39. *OR*, ser. 1, vol. 31, pt. 2, 55:96, 572, 576; Grant, *Personal Memoirs*, 358, 380; Warner, *Generals in Blue*, 185.

40. *OR*, ser. 1, vol. 31, pt. 2, 55:634; Woodruff, *Fifteen Years*, 390; "The Heroes of Chattanooga," *Rock Island Evening Argus*, January 5, 1864.

41. Winther, *With Sherman to the Sea*, 86–87; Bloomfield quoted in W. Davis, *Campfire Chats*, 80.

42. B. Davis, *Sherman's March*, 299; "Special Dispatch, Chattanooga, Nov. 25, 1863," *Chicago Tribune*, November 26, 1863; "Glorious Victory! General Grant's Great Success," *New York Times*, November 26, 1863; Winther, *With Sherman to the Sea*, 70, 86; *OR*, ser. 1, vol. 31, pt. 2, 55:632; vol. 32, pt. 3, 59:520; "The Battle of Tunnel Hill-Loomis Brigade," "The Late Colonel O'Meara," *Chicago Post*, December 31, 1863, and January 30, 1864.

43. Father Dunne to John O'Meara, December 7 and 31, 1863; Col. T. O'Meara, Pension File, NA; Penniman, *Tanner-Boy*, 249–50; "A Slander Refuted," *New York Times*, June 3, 1871.

44. Sheridan to John O'Meara, November 27, 1863; Col. T. O'Meara, Pension File, NA; R. Sheridan, "Letter from Quartermaster Sheridan," *Chicago Post*, December 8, 1863; Hugh O'Neil, Pension File, NA.

45. "The City Government, Preamble and Resolutions," "The Late Colonel O'Meara," *New York Times*, December 12 and 20, 1863; Coyle, "Unknown Hero," 365.

46. "Report Chattanooga," "The Irish Legion," "Death of Colonel Owen Stuart," *Chicago Post*, November 25, 28, and December 3, 1863; D. Cameron to Wife and Grandchildren, December 2, 1863, Stuart Letters, ALPL; *Oxford Dictionary of Quotations*, 554.

47. Mrs. Stuart to Mrs. Duffy, telegram, December 7, 1863; Stuart to Sherman, December 24, 1863; H.Q. Mil. Div. of the Miss. SO 39, December 19, 1863, Stuart Letters, ALPL; RG94CMR; *OR*, ser. 1, vol. 31, pt. 2, 55:86–88.

48. "The Heroes of Chattanooga," *Rock Island Evening Argus*, January 5, 1864; First Lieutenant James Conway, Pension File, NA; Andrew Phinney, Compiled Military Service File, NA.

49. *OR*, ser. 1, vol. 31, pt. 2, 55:86.

50. Strong to Fuller, March 4, 1864, RS18; *AGR*, 5:289–310; "The 90th Illinois Irish Legion," *Chicago Post*, January 1, 1864; *OR*, ser. 1, vol. 31, pt. 2, 55:86; RG94CMR; *SOR*, 452; Duncan and Scott, *History of Allen and Woodson Counties*, 163–65.

51. RG94CMR.

52. *OR*, ser. 1, vol. 31, pt, 2, 55:635; *AGR*, 5:289–308; RG94CMR; R. Sheridan, "Colonel Timothy O'Meara," *Boston Pilot*, December 26, 1863; Thomas E. Lonergan, Pension File, NA; RS23.

53. *AGR*, 5:289; RG94MRR, box 620; appendix 1.

54. Woodruff, *Fifteen Years*, 363; RG94CMR; Michael Murphy, Pension File, NA; *Medical and Surgical History*, 150, case 485.

55. *Medical and Surgical History*, 233, 254, 281, 405, 467, 480, 485, 498, 765, 771, 840, 941.

56. Patrick Sloan to Wife, April 12, 1864, private collection.

57. Henry Robinson statement, undated, 100th Indiana File, CCNMP; RG94MR, Co. C; *SOR*, 413, 452; Williams, "Memories of War Times," *Warsaw Daily Times*, August 15, 1903.

7. The Winter of Their Discontent

1. Woodruff, *Fifteen Years*, 391; Hogan, *Williams's Memories*, 123; Watkins, "*Co. Aytch*," 117, 120–21; *OR*, ser. 1, vol. 31, pt. 2, 55:87, 576, 635, 754–58.

2. Woodruff, *Fifteen Years*, 391; *OR*, ser. 1, vol. 31, pt. 2, 55:577, 635; pt. 1, 54:434; Sherman, *Memoirs*, 391; *SOR*, 413.

3. Grant, *Personal Memoirs*, 345–47; *OR*, ser. 1, vol. 31, pt. 2, 55:17, 577–79.

4. Woodruff, *Fifteen Years*, 391; *OR*, ser. 1, vol. 31, pt. 2, 55:577; Hogan, *Williams's Memories*, 125.

5. RG94MR, Co. C; *OR*, ser. 1, vol. 31, pt. 1, 54:431; pt. 2, 55:578; Woodruff, *Fifteen Years*, 391–92; *SOR*, 408, 413.

6. *SOR*, 413, 460; *OR*, ser. 1, vol. 31, pt. 2, 55:579; Sherman, *Memoirs*, 393.

7. Woodruff, *Fifteen Years*, 387, 392–93; *SOR*, 413, 433; *OR*, ser. 1, vol. 31, pt. 1, 54:435; pt. 2, 55:638, 640.

8. Sherlock, *Memorabilia*, 68; RG94MR, Co. C; Woodruff, *Fifteen Years*, 392; *SOR*, 413, 425.

9. *SOR*, 413, 433; Woodruff, *Fifteen Years*, 392; *SOR*, 408; *OR*, ser. 1, vol. 31, pt. 2, 55:580.

10. Lewis, *Sherman Fighting Prophet*, 317; W. Davis, *Camp-Fire Chats*, 299; Rossiter Johnson, "Minor Engagements of the First Year," 307; Sherman, *Memoirs*, 389; Woodruff, *Fifteen Years*, 393–94.

11. Woodruff, *Fifteen Years*, 394; *OR*, ser. 1, vol. 47, pt. 3, 100:142; vol. 31, pt. 3, 56:353; Faust, *Historical*, 443.

12. *OR*, ser. 1, vol. 31, pt. 3, 56:521; vol. 32, pt. 2, 58:23; Sherman, *Memoirs*, 413; Flanders and Swann, "Hippopotamus."

13. Davis to Stuart, January 6, 1864, Stuart Letters, ALPL; H. K Smith, "How Soldiers Build Shelters," *Chicago Post*, January 16, 1864.

14. Patrick Sloan to Wife, January 11, 1864, private collection; Patrick Sloan, Compiled Military Service File, NA; *SOR*, 413–14, 433, 438.

15. RG94RD.

16. Charges against Lt. Campion, January 3, 1864; Flynn to Harrow, January 1864, RG94MRR, box 621, Cos. C–F; Flynn to Campion, January 3, 1864, RG94RD; RG94MR, Co. A.

17. Davis to Stuart, January 6, 1864, Stuart Letters, ALPL.

18. Ibid.; Owen Stuart, Compiled Military Service File, NA; Stuart to Fuller, January 27, 1864; Flynn to Fuller, February 2 and 25, 1864, RS18; John McAssey and Thomas Murray, Compiled Military Service Files, NA.

19. Sheridan to Brother, March 2, 1864, private collection; Woodruff, *Fifteen Years*, 392; Patrick Sloan to Wife, January 31, February 14 and 27, April 3 and 12, 1864, private collection.

20. Flynn to Wilkinsen, A.A.G. Fourth Division, April 9, 1864, RG94MRR, box 620.

21. Patrick Sloan to Wife, January 31, 1864, private collection.

22. Patrick Sloan to Wife, January 31 and February 20, 1864, private collection; O'Meara to Services Rendered Claims Board, August 1, 1863, RG94MRR, box 620.

23. Patrick Sloan to Wife, February 17, 1864, private collection.

24. R.G. 123, Court of Claims, U.S. Congressional Jurisdiction, Case File No. 1694, J. P. Lewallen, NA.

25. Patrick Sloan to Wife, January 17, 1864, private collection.

26. McAssey to Loomis, January 5, 1864; McAssey to Fuller, January 4, 1864; War Dept. SO 57, February 5, 1864; Casey to Fuller, March 7, 1864, RS18; Darwin Hinckley, Pension File, NA; *AGR*, 5:289; RG94MRR, box 620.

27. Appendix 1; RG94MRR, box 620; Patrick Sloan to Wife, January 31, 1864, private collection; Maj. Gen. Logan SO 23; Timothy Mahoney, Compiled Military Service File, NA; Maj. Gen. Logan SO 33; Thomas Murray, Compiled Military Service File, NA.

28. *OR*, ser. 1, vol. 32, pt. 2, 58:23–24; Wills, *Army Life*, 220; Sherman, *Memoirs*, 463, 466–67.

29. *OR*, ser. 1, vol. 38, pt. 1, 72:117; pt. 3, 74:51; Hogan, *Williams's Memories*, 103–4; Risch, *Quartermaster Support*, 447–50; Patrick Sloan to Wife, March 6, 1864, private collection.

30. Winther, *With Sherman to the Sea*, 93; Eicher and Eicher, *Civil War High Commands*, 284; Warner, *Generals in Blue*, 211–12; Hubbell and Geary, *Biographical Dictionary*, 240; Hogan, *Williams's Memories*, 140; Wills, *Army Life*, 231–32.

31. Sheridan to Brother, March 2, 1864, private collection; Sherwin to Stuart, February 22, 1864; Murphy to Stuart, March 4, 1864, Stuart Letters, ALPL.

32. RS18; RG94MR, Co. A; Capt. Patrick O'Marah, Compiled Military Service File, NA; O'Marah to Fuller, July 22 and September 28, 1864, RS 18; War Dept. SO 57, February 5, 1864; Casey to Wife, March 17, 1864; Petition, Casey to President Johnson, undated; Flynn sworn statement, September 29, 1865, Peter Casey File, CHM; appendix 1.

33. "Political Movements—The Fenian Fair," *New York Times*, April 2, 1864.

34. Patrick Sloan to Wife, April 13, 1864, private collection; *OR*, ser 1, vol. 32, pt. 1, 57:630–35.

35. "A Voice from Father Dunne's Regiment," *Chicago Tribune*, March 24, 1864.

36. Wills, *Army Life*, 222, 225; Kennett, *Sherman*, 33, 36.

37. RG94MR, Co. A.

8. The Atlanta Campaign: Approach to Atlanta

1. J. Jones, *Black Jack*, 191–92; Grant, *Personal Memoirs*, 358; Sherman, *Memoirs*, 429; Johnston, *Narrative of Military Operations*, 261; appendix 1.

2. *OR*, ser. 1, vol. 38, pt. 3, 74:297; Williams, "Memories of War Times," *Warsaw Daily Times*, September 26, 1903.

3. Williams, "Memories of War Times," *Warsaw Daily Times*, October 10, 1903; *OR*, ser. 1, vol. 38, pt. 1, 72:103–6.

4. Castel, *Decision*, 68–69.

5. *OR*, ser. 1, vol. 38, pt. 1, 72:70; Castel, *Decision*, 123–24.

6. Sherman, *Memoirs*, 489–90; Castel, *Decision*, 68–69.

7. Sherman, *Memoirs*, 468–69, 495; *OR*, ser. 1, vol. 38, pt. 1, 72:115; Mruck, "Role of Railroads," 265–67; G. Davis, *Official Military Atlas*, plate 57, no. 1.

8. Castel, *Decision*, 121–23; *OR*, ser. 1, vol. 38, pt. 4, 75:126; Sherman, *Memoirs*, 496, 500, 504; Cox, *Atlanta*, 31.

9. *OR*, ser. 1, vol. 38, pt. 3, 74:90, 296–97; William White, Compiled Military Service File, NA; May 1864 Report, RS18; Hogan, *Williams's Memories*, 143.

10. *OR*, ser. 1, vol. 38, pt. 3, 74:296–97; pt. 4, 75:69, 90; *SOR*, 414; G. Davis, *Official Military Atlas*, plate 57, no. 2.

11. A.A.G. Townes SFO 3, May 8, 1864, *OR*, ser. 1, vol. 38, pt. 3, 74:31, 90–91; pt. 4, 75:87; Johnston, *Narrative of Military Operations*, 309.

12. Hogan, *Williams's Memories*, 147; *OR*, ser. 1, vol. 38, pt. 3, 74:90–91, 297.

13. Williams, "Memories of War Times," *Warsaw Daily Times*, October 10, 1903.

14. *OR*, ser. 1, vol. 38, pt. 3, 74:91, 297.

15. Ibid., pt. 4, 75:160; Hogan, *Williams's Memories*, 151; Flynn to Father Donelan, June 9, 1864, *Rockford Democrat*, July 6, 1864; Stuart to Wife, June 10, 1864, Stuart Letters, ALPL; *OR*, ser. 1, vol. 38, pt. 3, 74:91–92, 125, 278, 292, 297, 301, 308; G. Davis, *Official Military Atlas*, plate 58, no. 3; *SOR*, 414.

16. *OR*, ser. 1, vol. 38, pt. 3, 74:292, 302, 297, 308; May 1864 Report, RS18.

17. Castel, *Decision*, 162–63, 171, 173, 179; *OR*, ser. 1, vol. 38, pt. 4, 75:196–97; Secrist, *Battle of Resaca*, 41–43.

18. RG94CMR; Simon Swan, Pension File, NA; *OR*, ser. 1, vol. 38, pt. 3, 74:51.

19. *OR*, ser. 1, vol. 38, pt. 3, 74:278, 297–98; G. Davis, *Official Military Atlas*, plate 58, no. 2; Sherman to Halleck, May 21, 1864, *OR*, ser. 1, vol. 38, pt. 4, 75:274; William White, Compiled Military Service File, NA.

20. Sherman, *Memoirs*, 511; *OR*, ser. 1, vol. 38, pt. 4, 75:273.

21. Sherman, *Memoirs*, 511–15, 519–20; Sherman to Halleck, May 20 and 28, 1864, *OR*, ser. 1, vol. 38, pt. 4, 75:260, 331.

22. *SOR*, 415; *OR*, ser. 1, vol. 38, pt. 3, 74:297–98; Risch, *Quartermaster Support*, 420–21; Castel, *Decision*, 117; Sherman, *Memoirs*, 481; Gen. McPherson SFO 17, May 22, 1864; Hambright to Whipple, May 24, 1864, *OR*, ser. 1, vol. 38, pt. 4, 75:292, 306.

23. McPherson to Logan, May 25, 1864, *OR*, ser. 1, vol. 38, pt. 4, 75:313; Hogan, *Williams's Memories*, 155–58.

24. Sherlock, *Memorabilia*, 68; *OR*, ser. 1, vol. 38, pt. 3, 74:95, 278, 298; Flynn to Father Donelan, June 9, 1864, *Rockford Democrat*, July 6, 1864; Stuart to Wife, June 10, 1864, Stuart Letters, ALPL; *SOR*, 415, 453, 461; May 1864 Report, RS18.

25. Hogan, *Williams's Memories*, 158–59, 163.

26. *OR*, ser. 1, vol. 38, pt. 3, 74:298; pt. 4, 75:346; May 1864 Report, RS18.

27. Dawes, *Memoir*, 287–88.

28. *SOR*, 415; Sherman to Halleck, June 4, 1864, *OR*, ser. 1, vol. 38, pt. 4, 75:397, 285, 289, 400–401; G. Davis, *Official Military Atlas*, plate 59, no. 3; *OR*, ser. 1, vol. 38, pt. 3, 74:96, 97, 279, 298; June 1864 Report, RS18; Simon Swan, Pension File, NA.

29. Stuart to Wife, June 10, 1864, Stuart Letters, ALPL.

30. Stuart to Wife, June 13 and 26, 1864, Stuart Letters, ALPL; "Logan as the Hero of Atlanta," *Chicago Tribune*, July 21, 1897; Risch, *Quartermaster Support*, 451; *OR*, ser. 1, vol. 38, pt. 3, 74:298; pt. 4, 75:466.

31. Sherman, *Memoirs*, 520.

32. Stuart to Wife, June 13, 1864, Stuart Letters, ALPL; *OR*, ser. 1, vol. 38, pt. 1, 72:68.

33. Stuart to Wife, June 25, 1864, Stuart Letters, ALPL; John McAssey, Thomas Murray, and Patrick Real, Compiled Military Service Files, NA; RG94CMR.

34. May and June Reports, RS18; appendix 1; *SOR*, 434; Stuart to Wife, June 26, 1864, Stuart Letters, ALPL; *AGR*, 5:294; Henry Strong, Compiled Military Service File, NA.

35. *OR*, ser. 1, vol. 38, pt. 3, 74:287, 298; Sherman, *Memoirs*, 532; *SOR*, 415, 443, 461; John A. Logan to Condit Smith, July 11, 1864, RG94MRR, box 620; G. Davis, *Official Military Atlas*, plate 60, no. 1; Hogan, *Williams's Memories*, 173.

9. The Atlanta Campaign: Battles around Atlanta

1. G. Davis, *Official Military Atlas*, plate 88, no. 1; *OR*, ser. 1, vol. 38, pt. 1, 72:131–32; pt. 2, 73:907; Castel, *Decision*, 69, 347–48; Black, *Railroads*, 251–52; Sherman, *Memoirs*, 548.

2. *OR*, ser. 1, vol. 38, pt. 3, 74:53, 298.

3. Ibid., pt. 1, 72:156–57; pt. 3, 74:101, 287, 298; Johnston, *Narrative of Military Operations*, 349, 350.

4. *SOR*, 415–16; *OR*, ser. 1, vol. 38, pt. 3, 74:101, 298.

5. *OR*, ser. 1, vol. 38, pt. 1, 72:156–57; pt. 3, 74:101–2, 287, 298; Hood, *Advance and Retreat*, 165; July 1864 Report, RS18; *Story of the Fifty-Fifth Regiment*, 334.

6. *OR*, ser. 1, vol. 38, pt. 3, 74:39, 102; July 1864 Report, RS18.

7. *OR*, ser. 1, vol. 38, pt.1, 72:157; July 1864 Report, RS18; Sherman, *Memoirs*, 547; Castel, *Decision*, 391; Hood, *Advance and Retreat*, 173, 177; Hogan, *Williams's Memories*, 179.

8. Hogan, *Williams's Memories*, 179–80; *OR*, ser. 1, vol. 38, pt. 1, 72:72; pt. 3, 74:287, 631; G. Davis, *Official Military Atlas*, plate 56, no. 6; Sherman, *Memoirs*, 550–53; Castel, *Decision*, 392–93.

9. *OR*, ser. 1, vol. 38, pt. 1, 72:72–73; pt. 3, 74:285; Hogan, *Memories*, 180–81; Taylor, "My War," 26; July 1864 Report, RS18.

10. *OR*, ser. 1, vol. 38, pt. 3, 74:280–81, 294, 318–19, 342.

11. Ibid., 74:319, 342; Connelly, *History of the Seventieth Ohio*, 90–91; Hogan, *Williams's Memories*, 181.

12. *OR*, ser. 1, vol. 38, pt. 3, 74:287, 294, 319, 342; Hogan, *Memories*, 181.

13. *OR*, ser. 1, vol. 38, pt. 3, 74:246, 298–99; Hood, *Advance and Retreat*, 180–81; Castel, *Decision*, 405–6.

14. Hogan, *Williams's Memories*, 182–83; *OR*, ser. 1, vol. 38, pt. 3. 74:246, 287, 298–99; Castel, *Decision*, 405–6; Manigault, *Carolinian Goes to War*, 226–27.

15. *OR*, ser. 1, vol. 38, pt. 3, 74:298–99, 285, 287–88, 342, 779; Scaife, *Campaign for Atlanta*, 65–66; Hogan, *Williams's Memories*, 182–83; William Todd to Brig. Gen. John Cook, June 1, 1865, RG94MRR, box 620; Henry Porter, Compiled Military Service File, NA.

16. Manigault, *Carolinian Goes to War*, 228–29.

17. *OR*, ser. 1, vol. 38, pt. 3, 74:294, 319, 355–56; Saunier, *History of the Forty-Seventh Regiment*, 282–83; Connelly, *History of the Seventieth Ohio*, 96.

18. *Chicago Tribune*, July 21, 1897; Kurtz, *Atlanta Cyclorama*, 14–23; Jones, *Black Jack*, 216.

19. Hogan, *Williams's Memories*, 183–84; *OR*, ser. 1, vol. 38, pt. 1, 72:73–74; Castel, *Decision*, 409–10, 413.

20. Hogan, *Williams's Memories*, 184–85; July 1864 Report, RS18; Charles Woollett, Co. H, "Casualties in the 90th Illinois Infantry," *Chicago Post*, August 12, 1864; RG94MRR, box 620.

21. *OR*, ser. 1, vol. 38, pt. 3, 74:299; pt. 5, 76:232.

22. Ibid., pt. 1, 72:75–77.

23. Army of the Tennessee SFO 79, July 26, 1864; XV A.C. SFO 62, July 26, 1864, *OR*, ser. 1, vol. 38, pt. 5, 76:268–69; pt. 3, 74:288, 299; Hogan, *Williams's Memories*, 186.

24. *OR*, ser. 1, vol. 38, pt. 3, 74:40.

25. XV A.C. SFO 63, July 27, 1864, *OR*, ser. 1, vol. 38, pt. 5, 76:278; pt. 3, 74:281.

26. *OR*, ser. 1, vol. 38, pt. 3, 74:631–32.

27. July 1864 Report, RS18; Hogan, *Williams's Memories*, 186–87; *OR*, ser. 1, vol. 38, pt. 3, 74:288, 294, 305.

28. *OR*, ser. 1, vol. 38, pt. 3, 74:41, 104, 288, 294, 299; Hogan, *Williams's Memories*, 187.

29. *OR*, ser. 1, vol. 38, pt. 3, 74:41–42, 281, 294; Scaife, *Campaign for Atlanta*, plate 15.

30. *OR*, ser. 1, vol. 38, p. 3, 74:288, 299, 344.

31. Ibid., 74:288, 294; Hogan, *Williams's Memories*, 188.

32. *OR*, ser. 1, vol. 38, pt. 3, 74:41–42, 54, 105; *SOR*, 416, 454, 461; William White and Patrick Flynn, Pension Files, NA; RG94MRR, box 620; RG94CMR.

33. Charles Woollett, Co. H, "Casualties in the 90th Illinois Infantry," *Chicago Post*, August 12, 1864; RS18; Sergeant Charles Woollett, Compiled Military Service File, NA; appendix 1.

34. *OR*, ser. 1, vol. 38, pt. 3, 74:42; pt. 1, 72:75–79, 134; Sherman, *Memoirs*, 572–75; G. Davis, *Official Military Atlas*, plate 88, no. 2.

35. *OR*, ser. 1, vol. 38, pt. 3, 74:294–95, 299; August 1864 Report, RS18.

36. *OR*, ser. 1, vol. 38, pt. 1, 72:134; pt. 3, 74:282.

37. Stuart to Col. Clark, August 1864; Surgeon's Certificate, August 11, 1864; Maj. Gen. J. A. Logan SFO 79, August 17, 1864, Stuart Letters, ALPL; *OR*, ser. 1, vol. 38, pt. 3, 74:300.

38. *OR*, ser. 1, vol. 38, pt. 3, 74:282, 288–90, 299.

39. August 1864 Report, RS18; *OR*, ser. 1, vol. 38, pt. 3, 74:290, 299, 300; *SOR*, 443.

40. Capt. Samuel Brough, August 12, 1864, RG94MRR, box 620; RS18.

41. Patrick Sloan to Wife, August 12, 1864, private collection; G. Davis, *Official Military Atlas*, plate 59, no. 7, and plate 88, no. 1; Hogan, *Williams's Memories*, 192; RG94MR, Co. K; Manigault, *Carolinian Goes to War*, 238–39.

42. Sherman, *Memoirs*, 583; "The Opposing Forces at the Beginning of Grant's Campaign against Richmond," and "The Opposing Forces at Petersburg and Richmond," in Johnson and Buel, *The Way to Appomattox*, 182, 593; Phisterer, *Statistical Record*, 216–17; Donald, *Lincoln*, 527–30; Long, *Civil War Day by Day*, 559, 563.

43. Sherman, *Memoirs*, 578–80.

44. RG94MR, Co. K, NA; *OR*, ser. 1, vol. 38, pt. 1, 72:80, 136; pt. 3, 74:106–7, 290–91, 300; Scaife, *Campaign for Atlanta*, 108–9; G. Davis, *Official Military Atlas*, plate 60, no. 2, plate 57, no. 3; Osborn, *Fiery Trail*, 19; Hogan, *Williams's Memories*, 197; August 1864 Report, RS18.

45. *OR*, ser. 1, vol. 38, pt. 1, 72:80–81; pt. 3, 74:291, 300; RG94MR.

46. *OR*, ser. 1, vol. 38, pt. 1, 72:80–81; pt. 3, 74:43–45, 88, 108–9, 291; Castel, *Decision*, 501.

47. *OR*, ser. 1, vol. 38, pt. 3, 74:291, 300.

48. August 1864 Report, RS18; appendix 1.

49. Sherman to Halleck and Sherman's SFO 62, September 3, 1864, *OR*, ser. 1, vol. 38, pt. 5, 76:777, 789; pt. 1, 72:82; Hogan, *Williams's Memories*, 197.

50. September 1864 Report, RS18; *OR*, ser. 1, vol. 38, pt. 1, 72:82; pt. 3, 74:46, 110, 300, 633; G. Davis, *Official Military Atlas*, plate 60, no. 2.

51. Sherman, *Memoirs*, 582–83; *OR*, ser. 1, vol. 38, pt. 1, 72:87, 89; Goodspeed and Healy, *History of Illinois—Being a General Survey of Cook County History* (hereafter *Cook County History*), 489; Castel, *Decision*, 543–44.

10. Hazen's Summer Camp and a Stern Chase

1. *SOR*, 418; Sherman, *Memoirs*, 584, 604, 621; *OR*, ser. 1, vol. 38, pt. 3, 74:111, 115; RS18, RS20; RG94MRR, boxes 621, 620; Michael Clark, Compiled Military Service File, NA; appendix 1.

2. Thomas Murray, John McAssey, Patrick Real, Compiled Military Service Files, NA; Lawrence McCarthy, Pension File and Compiled Military Service File, NA; *AGR*, 5:294, 304; "James Dunn"; John C. Harrington, Pension File, NA; Daniel O'Connor to White, 90th Ill. Inf. SO 19, September 18, 1864, William White, Compiled Military Service File, NA; French, *Biographical History*, 272–77; September 1864 Report, RS18; Hazen, *Narrative*, vii–x, 71, 303; Sherman, *Memoirs*, 620–21; *OR*, ser. 1, vol. 44, 92:849.

3. Hazen, *Narrative*, 280–84; RS18; appendix 1.

4. Patrick Sloan to Wife, September 29, 1864, private collection; Hazen, *Narrative*, 303–4.

5. Hazen, *Narrative*, 303–5; Second Division GO 36, August 28, 1864; GO 31, September 4, 1864; GO 42, September 14, 1864; GO 48, September 24, 1864, RG94MRR, box 620.

6. Hazen, *Narrative*, 307–11; Hood, *Advance and Retreat*, 246, 259; John B. Hood, "The Invasion of Tennessee," in Johnson and Buel, *Way to Appomattox*, 425; Sherman, *Memoirs*, 615–16, 619, 621; Guernsey and Alden, *Harper's Pictorial History*, 670; Castel, *Decision*, 551; October 1864 Report, RS18; *SOR*, 418–19; *OR*, ser. 1, vol. 39, pt. 1, 77:576–77.

7. October 1864 Report, RS18; *OR*, ser. 1, vol. 39, pt. 1, 77:741, 745, 768–69.

8. Hood, "The Invasion of Tennessee," in Johnson and Buel, *Way to Appomattox*, 426–27.

9. October 1864 Report, RS18; *OR*, ser. 1, vol. 39, pt. 1, 77:743, 745, 807; Hazen, *Narrative*, 308–10; Hood, *Advance and Retreat*, 267–70.

10. *OR*, ser. 1, vol. 39, pt. 1, 77:745; O'Connor to Fuller, October 28, 1864, RG94MRR, box 620; Hazen, *Narrative*, 310–11; October 1864 Report, RS18; appendix 1.

11. Sherman to Grant, October 9, 1864, *OR*, ser. 1, vol. 39, pt. 3, 79:162; Hazen, *Narrative*, 312.

12. Hazen, *Narrative*, 312; Sherman, *Memoirs*, 639–41.

13. Surgeon Holden to Stuart, September 9, 1864; Moore to Stuart, October 24 and 27, 1864; Moe to Stuart, October 26, 1864; Earle to Stuart, October 27, 1864; Stuart to Wife, November 4 and 8, 1864, Stuart Letters, ALPL; Owen Stuart, Compiled Military Service File, NA; RS18; appendix 1.

14. Stuart to Wife, November 4 and 8, 1864, Stuart Letters, ALPL.

15. November 1864 Report, RS18; David Duffy, John McAssey, John Murphy, Lawrence McCarthy, Compiled Military Service Files, NA; French, *Biographical History*, 276.

16. November 1864 Report, RS18; *SOR*, 444.

17. *OR*, ser. 1, vol. 44, 92:56, 60, 849; Sherman, *Memoirs*, 642–43, 646, 649.

18. Sherman, *Memoirs*, 649, 651–53; *OR*, ser. 1, vol. 44, 92:8.

19. *OR*, ser. 1, vol. 44, 92:59.

20. Sherman, *Memoirs*, 653, 684; *OR*, ser. 1, vol. 44, 92:8.

21. Sherman, *Memoirs*, 644–45.

11. An Armed Picnic

1. *OR*, ser. 1, vol. 44, 92:7–8; Gustavus W. Smith, "The Georgia Militia During Sherman's March to the Sea," in Johnson and Buel, *Way to Appomattox*, 669.

2. William Carlin, "The March to the Sea, an Armed Picnic," in Cozzens, *Battles and Leaders of the Civil War*, 562; Sherlock, *Memorabilia*, 143.

3. Winther, *With Sherman to the Sea*, 134.

4. Hitchcock, *Marching with Sherman*, 120, 126; Wills, *Army Life*, 324.

5. Carlin, "The March to the Sea, an Armed Picnic," in Cozzens, *Battles and Leaders of the Civil War*, 562; O. O. Howard, "Sherman's Advance from Atlanta," in Johnson and Buel, *Way to Appomattox*, 664; Wills, *Army Life*, 320–21.

6. Sheridan to Brother, December 29, 1864, private collection.

7. Stuart to Wife, December 17, 1864, Stuart Letters, ALPL; *Story of the Fifty-Fifth Regiment*, 391; *OR*, ser. 1, vol. 44, 92:93.

8. Stuart to Wife, December 17, 1864, Stuart Letters, ALPL; *Story of the Fifty-Fifth Regiment*, 389.

9. Sheridan to Brother, December 29, 1864, private collection.

10. Hazen, *Narrative*, 314–17, 342; *OR*, ser. 1, vol. 44, 92:61, 84, 119–20; *SOR*, 419, 426.

11. *OR*, ser. 1, vol. 44, 92:120; November 1864 Report, RS18; *SOR*, 419, 444, 449.

12. Sandburg, *Abraham Lincoln*, 624; *OR*, ser. 1, vol. 44, 92:120; "Sherman's March," "Rebel Papers Are Preserving a Dismal Silence," "Richmond Paper Reports Sherman Heading for Beaufort," "Sherman's Army: The Seacoast Probably Reached Today," *New York Times*, November 18, 29, and December 1, 3, 1864.

13. *OR*, ser. 1, vol. 44, 92:84, 119–20; Wills, *Army Life*, 328, 330; Hitchcock, *Marching with Sherman*, 110–11, 116.

14. *OR*, ser. 1, vol. 44, 92:110, 120.

15. Ibid., 92:120.

16. Stuart to Wife, December 17, 1864, Stuart Letters, ALPL; *OR*, ser. 1, vol. 44, 92:61, 70, 120; December 1864 Report, RS18.

17. Howard, *Autobiography*, 82; *OR*, ser. 1, vol. 44, 92:70, 85, 86, 126.

18. *OR*, ser. 1, vol. 44, 92:110, 121; Hazen, *Narrative*, 321; December 1864 Report, RS18.

19. *OR*, ser. 1, vol. 44, 92:109, 121; December 1864 Report, RS18.

12. The Handsomest Thing I Have Seen in This War

1. Stuart to Wife, December 17, 1864, Stuart Letters, ALPL; B. Davis, *Sherman's March*, 96–97; *Story of the Fifty-Fifth Illinois*, 396.

2. Hitchcock, *Marching with Sherman*, 176; Osborn, *Fiery Trail*, 71; Cram, *Soldiering with Sherman*, 151–52.

3. Stuart to Wife, December 17, 1864, Stuart Letters, ALPL; Christman, *Undaunted*, 11–56; "The Bombardment of Fort McAllister," *Chicago Tribune*, March 17, 1863; D. Smith, *Civil War Savannah*, 93, 106–10.

4. Howard, *Autobiography*, 86–87.

5. *OR*, ser. 1, vol. 44, 92:61, 112; G. Davis, *Official Military Atlas*, plate 70, no. 2; Scaife, *March to the Sea*, 100; D. Smith, *Civil War Savannah*, 173–74; Hitchcock, *Marching with Sherman*, 189; Christman, *Undaunted*, 61; Faust, *Historical*, 1; Osborn, *Fiery Trail*, 47; Lawrence, *Present for Mr. Lincoln*, 185; Hazen, *Narrative*, 333; Ft. McAllister (map); Cooley, *Savannah, Georgia*; Sheridan to Brother, December 29, 1864, private collection.

6. Hazen, *Narrative*, 321, 331; RS18; O. O. Howard, "Sherman's Advance from Atlanta," in Johnson and Buel, *Way to Appomattox*, 666; *OR*, ser. 1, vol. 44, 92:72, 110.

7. *OR*, ser. 1, vol. 44, 92:61, 110, 121–22; Sherman, *Memoirs*, 675; Hazen, *Narrative*, 321–22.

8. Millhollen and Mugridge, *Savannah, Georgia (Vicinity)*; Cooley, *Savannah, Georgia (Vicinity: Fort McAllister)*; *OR*, ser. 1, vol. 44, 92:112, 121.

9. *OR*, ser. 1, vol. 44, 92:110; Scaife, *March to the Sea*, 97.

10. Stuart to Wife, December 17, 1864, Stuart Letters, ALPL; *SOR*, 420; Sheridan to Brother, December 29, 1864, private collection.

11. Hitchcock, *Marching with Sherman*, 179–80.

12. Howard, *Autobiography*, 91.

13. Hazen, *Narrative*, 333; *OR*, ser. 1, vol. 44, 92:122; D. Smith, *Civil War Savannah*, 178; Sheridan to Brother, December 29, 1864, private collection.

14. *OR*, ser. 1, vol. 44, 92:122; Hazen, *Narrative*, 322.

15. Stuart to Wife, December 17, 1864, and January 17, 1865, Stuart Letters, ALPL; *SOR*, 420; *Medical and Surgical History*, 450–51; *OR*, ser. 1, vol. 44, 92:95, 122–23; RG94CMR; RS18; appendix 1.

16. Stuart to Col. Strong, December 29, 1864, RG94MRR, box 620; appendix 1.

17. Hazen, *Narrative*, 322–23; Sherman, *Memoirs*, 675; Christman, *Undaunted*, 61; D. Smith, *Civil War Savannah*, 179; *Southern Historical Society Papers*, vol. 17, 66.

18. Howard, *Autobiography*, 91; Second Div. XV A.C. SO 194, December 14, 1864, *OR*, ser. 1, vol. 44, 92:711; D. Smith, *Civil War Savannah*, 179; *Story of the Fifty-Fifth Illinois*, 398.

19. Simpson and Berlin, *Sherman's Civil War*, 767; "News from Rebel Sources," *New York Times*, December 22, 1864.

20. Hazen, *Narrative*, 323–24, 334.

21. Sherman, *Memoirs*, 678–80; Fuller to O'Connor, December 6, 1864, RG94MRR, box 620.

22. Hazen, *Narrative*, 323–25, 334; Sherman, *Memoirs*, 686; D. Smith, *Civil War Savannah*, 165–66; Hitchcock, *Marching with Sherman*, 196; *OR*, ser. 1, vol. 44, 92:122, 731, 774; RG94MR.

23. Stuart to Wife, December 17 and 23, Stuart Letters, ALPL.

24. Nichols, *Story of the Great March*, 100; Alexander Robert Chisolm, "The Failure to Capture Hardee," in Johnson and Buel, *Way to Appomattox*, 680; D. Smith, *Civil War Savannah*, 189; Howard, *Autobiography*, 94; Winther, *With Sherman to the Sea*, 141–42.

25. Sherman quoted in Howard, *Autobiography*, 94; D. Smith, *Civil War Savannah*, 205.

26. Stuart to Geo. Nelson, December 22, 1864, Stuart Letters, ALPL; Sheridan to Brother, December 29, 1864, private collection; Stuart to Fuller, December 22, 1864; December 1864 Report, RS18.

27. O. O. Howard GFO 38 and 39, December 27, 1864, RG94MRR, box 620; *OR*, ser. 1, vol. 44, 92:795.

28. Stuart to Wife, January 7, 1865, Stuart Letters, ALPL; Hazen, *Narrative*, 325–26; January 1865 Report, RS18; Hirshson, *White Tecumseh*, 271.

29. Stuart to Wife, December 17, 1864, and April 21, 1865; Wife to Stuart, January 8 and 13, 1865, Stuart Letters, ALPL; Capt. David Duffy, Pension Files, NA.

30. Sherman, *Memoirs*, 697, 702.

13. Rocking the Cradle of Secession

1. Grant to Sherman, December 6, 1864; Lincoln to Sherman, December 26, 1864, *Report of Major General W. T. Sherman*, 279, 297; Grant, *Personal Memoirs*, 513.

2. Hazen, *Narrative*, 336, 339; January 1865 Report, RS18; Sherman, *Memoirs*, 734; Stuart to Wife, January 16, 1864, Stuart Letters, ALPL; Howard SFO 15, January 17, 1865, RG94MRR, box 620.

3. Hazen GO 4, January 20, 1865, RG94MRR, box 620; Hazen, *Narrative*, 339; Stuart to Wife, January 20, 1865, Stuart Letters, ALPL.

4. Stuart to Wife, January 17 and 20, 1865, Stuart Letters, ALPL.

5. "101-Year-Old Letter Reveals Thoughts of War Veteran," *Springfield Sun*, March 10, 1966; Hazen, *Narrative*, 339, 342.

6. Stuart to Wife, January 28, 1865, Stuart Letters, ALPL; RS18; Hazen GO 8, January 21, 1865, RG94MRR, box 620.

7. Sherman, *Memoirs*, 736; *OR*, ser. 1, vol. 47, pt. 1, 98:309–10.

8. Hazen, *Narrative*, 338, 340–42.

9. Fredrick the Great quoted in John Keegan, *Six Armies*, 23; *OR*, ser. 1, vol. 47, pt.1, 98:17–20; pt. 2, 99:1083; Sherman, *Memoirs*, 733, 749–50, 753; Osterhaus GO 3, January 6, 1865, RG94MRR, box 620; G. Davis, *Official Military Atlas*, plate 117.

10. Halleck to Sherman, December 18, 1864; Sherman to Halleck, December 24, 1864, *Report of Major General W. T. Sherman*, 286–87, 291.

11. *OR*, ser. 1, vol. 47, pt. 1, 98:187; Osborn, *Fiery Trail*, 92.

12. White to Wife, April 6, 1865, in Main, "Letter Home" (hereafter "Letter Home").

13. Hazen, *Narrative*, 336–38.

14. "Letter Home."

15. Hazen, *Narrative*, 343; "Letter Home."

16. *OR*, ser. 1, vol. 47, pt. 1, 98:310; "Letter Home"; Hazen, *Narrative*, 343.

17. "Letter Home"; Hazen, *Narrative*, 343.

18. "Letter Home"; Hazen, *Narrative*, 343; *OR*, ser. 1, vol. 47, pt. 1, 98:194.

19. "Letter Home"; Hazen, *Narrative*, 343–44.

20. "Letter Home"; Hazen, *Narrative*, 344.

21. "Letter Home"; *OR*, ser. 1, vol. 47, pt. 1, 98:194–95.

22. *SOR*, 445; Hazen, *Narrative*, 344.

23. "Letter Home"; Hazen, *Narrative*, 344.

24. "Letter Home"; Hazen, *Narrative*, 344.

25. "Letter Home"; Hazen, *Narrative*, 344–45.

26. "Letter Home"; *SOR*, 421, 445, 467.

27. Simon Swan, Pension File, NA; K. Jones, *When Sherman Came*, 143.

28. Hazen, *Narrative*, 345; "Letter Home."

29. "Letter Home"; Hazen, *Narrative*, 345; Logan GO 10, February 14, 1865, RG94MRR, box 620; Woodruff, *Fifteen Years*, 393–94.

30. "Letter Home."

31. *OR*, series 1, vol. 47, pt. 2, 99:1202; K. Jones, *When Sherman Came*, 150.

32. Andrew Phinney, Compiled Military Service File, NA; Campbell to Beauregard, Forno to Otey, and Forno to Booth, February 12, 1865; Griswold to Forno, February 24, 1865, *OR*, ser. 2, vol. 8, 121:210, 213, 455–57.

33. "Letter Home"; Hazen, *Narrative*, 346.

34. "Letter Home."

14. Hail Columbia, Happy Land

1. Osborn, *Fiery Trail*, 129–30; Lucas, *Burning of Columbia*, 19, 21, 27–30, 65–70, 76, 79–80, 88–93, 165; *OR*, ser. 1, vol. 47, pt. 1, 98:310; vol. 53, 111:53; Hazen, *Narrative*, 346; Griswold to Forno, February 24, 1865, *OR*, ser. 2, vol. 8, 121:456.

2. J. Jones, *Black Jack*, 250.

3. "Letter Home"; *OR*, ser. 1, vol. 47, pt. 1, 98:272,

4. "Letter Home"; *OR*, ser. 1, vol. 47, pt. 1, 98:198.

5. Hazen, *Memoirs*, 349; "Letter Home."

6. "Letter Home."

7. Ibid.

8. Ibid.

9. Winther, *With Sherman to the Sea*, 153; Hitchcock, *Marching with Sherman*, 269; *OR*, ser. 1, vol. 47, pt.1, 98:198–99, 227–28; Lucas, *Burning of Columbia*, 95; Osborn, *Fiery Trail*, 131.

10. Osborn, *Fiery Trail*, 131.

11. Hazen, *Narrative*, 346, 352–53; *OR*, ser. 1, vol. 47, pt.1, 98:199, 272–73; Lucas, *Burning of Columbia*, 117.

12. *OR*, ser. 1, vol. 47, pt. 1, 98:310; Hazen, *Narrative*, 352–53; Osborn, *Fiery Trail*, 129; February 1865 Report, RS18.

13. "Letter Home"; *AGR*, 5:299.

14. "Letter Home."

15. February 1865 Report, RS18; "Letter Home."

16. "Letter Home"; Hazen, *Memoirs*, 353.

17. "Letter Home"; Simms, *Sack and Destruction*, 36–75; *OR*, ser. 1, vol. 47, pt. 1, 98:21–22; Lucas, *Burning of Columbia*, 132–33, 164–66.

15. Leaving the Cradle

1. Johnston quoted in Cox, *Sherman's March to the Sea*, 168; Marszalek, *Soldier's Passion*, 319; Gen R. E. Lee to Pres. J. Davis, February 19, 1865, *OR*, ser. 1, vol. 53, 111:412.

2. February and March 1865 Reports, RS18; *OR*, ser. 1, vol. 47, pt. 1, 98:188, 310; Hazen, *Narrative*, 361; G. Davis, *Official Military Atlas*, plate 117.

3. Hazen, *Narrative*, 355; "Letter Home."

4. "Letter Home"; *OR*, ser. 1, vol. 47, pt. 1, 98:281, 310; Hazen, *Narrative*, 361; Microfilms, M594, Co. K.

5. "Letter Home"; Hazen, *Narrative*, 361; *OR*, ser. 1, vol. 47, pt. 1, 98:281, 310.

6. *OR*, ser. 1, vol. 47, pt. 1, 98:281, 311; G. Davis, *Official Military Atlas*, plate 79, no. 3; K. Jones, *When Sherman Came*, 245; "Letter Home."

7. "Letter Home"; *OR*, ser. 1, vol. 47, pt. 1, 98:281, 311.

8. Hazen, *Narrative*, 355–56.

9. "Letter Home"; *OR*, ser. 1, vol. 47, pt. 1, 98:311; Hazen, *Narrative*, 357.

10. Osborn, *Fiery Trail*, 159–60.

11. "Letter Home"; February and March 1865 Reports, RS18; *OR*, ser. 1, vol. 47, pt. 1, 98:311.

12. Hazen, *Narrative*, 358.

13. "Letter Home"; *OR*, ser. 1, vol. 47, pt. 1, 98:23, 202.

14. K. Jones, *When Sherman Came*, 215.

15. "Letter Home."

16. "Letter Home."

17. "Letter Home"; Sherman to Wade Hampton, February 24, 1865, *OR*, ser. 1, vol. 47, pt. 2, 99:546; Howard GFO 12, March 5, 1865, RG94MRR, box 620.

16. Touring Tarheel Country

1. Hazen, *Narrative*, 364; RG94MRR, box 620; "Letter Home."

2. "Letter Home"; Hazen, *Narrative*, 364–65; *OR*, ser. 1, vol. 47, pt. 1, 98:311.

3. "Letter Home"; *OR*, ser. 1, vol. 47, pt. 1, 98:171–72; *OR*, ser. 1, vol. 53, 111:54.

4. March 1865 Report, RS18; Hazen, *Narrative*, 365; *OR*, ser. 1, vol. 47, pt. 1, 98:253; Woods FO to 90th Illinois, March 15, 1865, RG94MRR, box 620.

5. "Letter Home."

6. Ibid.

7. Ibid.

8. Johnston, *Narrative of Military Operations*, 371, 372, 378, 383–89; Bradley, *Last Stand in the Carolinas*, 309; Howard, *Autobiography*, 147–50.

9. *OR*, ser. 1, vol. 47, pt. 1, 98:283; Hazen, *Narrative*, 366.

10. "Letter Home"; March 1865 Report, RS18.

11. Styple, *Writing and Fighting the Civil War*, 343.

12. March 1865 Report, RS18; *OR*, ser. 1, vol. 47, pt. 1, 98:284, 312.

13. "Letter Home."

14. Sherman, *Memoirs*, 806, 820.

15. *OR*, ser. 1, vol. 47, pt. 1, 98:310–11.

16. Ibid., 98:176, 189, 312.

17. French, *Biographical History*, 272–77; Redmond Sheridan and William White, Compiled Military Service Files, NA; February and March 1865 Reports, RS18; *OR*, ser. 1, vol. 47, pt. 1, 98:284.

18. French, *Biographical History*, 276; John Murphy and David Duffy, Compiled Military Service Files and Pension Files, NA; Lawrence McCarthy, Compiled Military Service File, NA; Patrick Sloan to Wife, September 1, 18, 29, and November 9, 19, 23, 28, 1864, February 15, and March 11, 1865, private collection.

19. *OR*, ser. 1, vol. 47, pt. 1, 98:312–13, 284; Stuart GO 1, April 1, 1865; Logan GO 12, March 28, 1865, RG94MRR, box 620.

20. Hazen, *Narrative*, 360, 368; Stuart to Wife, April 8, 1865, Stuart Letters, ALPL; *OR*, ser. 1, vol. 47, pt. 1, 98:284.

21. Stuart to Wife, April 8, 1865, Stuart Letters, ALPL; John McAssey, Compiled Military Service File, NA.

22. Sherman SFO 54, April 12, 1865, RG94MRR, box 621; Sherman, *Memoirs*, 832; *Story of the Fifty-Fifth Illinois*, 429; Winther, *With Sherman to the Sea*, 165–66.

23. *OR*, ser. 1, vol. 47, pt. 1, 98:313; Sherman, *Memoirs*, 832, 834–35.

24. Stuart to Wife, April 17, 1865, Stuart Letters, ALPL.

25. Sherman SFO 56, April 17, 1865, RG94MRR, box 621; Sherman, *Memoirs*, 842, 839; Hitchcock, *Marching with Sherman*, 307; Winther, *With Sherman to the Sea*, 167; Dawson, *Life of Logan*, 97.

26. Sherman, *Memoirs*, 836–42, 844–45; Johnston, *Narrative of Military Operations*, 405–7.

27. Stuart to Wife, April 21, 1865, Stuart Letters, ALPL; Oliver GO 2, April 21, 1865, RG94MRR, box 620.

28. Sherman, *Memoirs*, 852–56, 860–61; Niven, *Gideon Wells*, 500; Dana, *Recollections*, 289; Grant, *Personal Memoirs*, 569–70.

29. Winther, *With Sherman to the Sea*, 167; Henry Slocum, "Final Operations of Sherman's Army: The Way to Appomattox," in Johnson and Buel, *Way to Appomattox*, 757.

30. Sherman, *Memoirs*, 814–17, 847–48; Grant, *Personal Memoirs*, 569–70.

31. Sherman, *Memoirs*, 851, 853–54; Grant, *Personal Memoirs*, 570.

32. April 1865 Report, RS18.

17. Like the Lords of the World

1. Winther, *With Sherman to the Sea*, 168; Hazen, *Narrative*, 371–74; *OR*, ser. 1, vol. 47, pt. 1, 98:314; *Story of the Fifty-Fifth Illinois*, 431–32.

2. Hazen, *Narrative*, 373; May 1865 Report, RS18.

3. Sherman, *Memoirs*, 863.

4. Capt. David Duffy, Pension File, NA; Hazen, *Narrative*, 373–74.

5. Cram, *Soldiering with Sherman*, 168; Henry Slocum, "Final Operations of Sherman's Army: The Way to Appomattox," in Johnson and Buel, *Way to Appomattox*, 758; B. Davis, *Sherman's March*, 288.

6. Hazen, *Narrative*, 374; B. Davis, *Sherman's March*, 289.

7. Howard, *Autobiography*, 211; Hazen, *Narrative*, 375; May 1865 Report, RS18; appendix 1.

8. B. Davis, *Sherman's March*, 286, 289; Glatthaar, *March to the Sea*, 180–81; *Story of the Fifty-Fifth Illinois*, 433; Winther, *With Sherman to the Sea*, 176; "Arrival of the 'Irish Legion' at the Fair," *Chicago Times*, June 14, 1865.

9. Hazen, *Narrative*, 375; Winther, *With Sherman to the Sea*, 176; RG94MRR, box 620.

10. Patrick Sloan to Wife, May 25, 1865, private collection; Connolly, *Oxford Companion*, 200; "Arrival of the 'Irish Legion' at the Fair," *Chicago Times*, June 14, 1865.

11. Hazen, *Narrative*, 375–76; Winther, *With Sherman to the Sea*, 177–78.

12. Sherman, *Memoirs*, 865–66; Lewis, *Sherman Fighting Prophet*, 577; B. Davis, *Sherman's March*, 295; Bowman and Irwin, *Sherman and His Campaigns*, 443.

13. Slocum, "Final Operations," 758.

14. Sherman, *Memoirs*, 866–69.

15. "Review of the Armies," "The Grand Armies in Camp," *New York Times*, May 25, 27, 1865; "The Grand Review," *Evening Standard*, May 24, 1865; "The Second Day's Review," *Chicago Tribune*, May 25, 1865.

16. Lewis, *Sherman Fighting Prophet*, 576.

17. Hazen, *Narrative*, 375; May 1865 Report, RS18; Hazen GO 32, May 26, 1865, and Oliver SO 62 and 63, May 31, 1865, RG94MRR, box 620; "The Grand Armies in Camp," *New York Times*, May 27, 1865; Michael W. Murphy, Compiled Military Service File, NA.

18. Hazen, *Narrative*, 376–78; "Disorderly Conduct," *Chicago Times*, June 1, 1865; "From Washington," *Chicago Tribune*, May 30, 1865.

19. Stuart to AADC, Third Brigade, Second Div. XV A.C., May 28, 1865, Stuart Letters, ALPL; "From Washington: The Army of the Tennessee," *New York Times*, May 29, 1865.

20. "From Washington: Our Dissolving Armies," *New York Times*, June 3, 1865; *SOR*, 427, 455; front page, no title, *Chicago Tribune*, May 27, 1865; William White, Compiled Military Service File, NA.

21. "Home from the War," *Chicago Tribune*, June 12, 1865; *AGR*, 5:311; Woodruff, *Fifteen Years*, 395; Karamanski, *Rally 'Round the Flag*, 239; W. P. Shin, Supt. E. Div. Pittsburg, Fort Wayne & Chicago Railroad, June 9, 1865, Stuart Letters, ALPL.

22. "Lieut. Gen. Grant in Chicago," "General Sherman: Home from the War," *Chicago Tribune*, June 10, 12, 1865; Payette, "American Forts East, Illinois Forts, Chicago Civil War Camps"; Goodspeed and Healy, *Cook County History*, 483; "News of the Day: The Grand Sanitary Fair at Chicago," *New York Times*, May 31, 1865; "General Sherman Probably Will Arrive in Chicago Tonight," *Chicago Evening Journal*, June 7, 1865; "The Returning Veterans: Great Dissatisfaction at Camp Fry," *Chicago Times*, June 13, 1865; Asst. QM Goodman to Chief Depot QM, June 20, 1865, RG94MRR, box 620.

23. "Home from the War," "Lieut. Gen. Grant," *Chicago Tribune*, June 12, 1865.

24. "Soldiers at Camp Fry," "Our Veterans at Home," *Chicago Tribune*, June 13, 14, 1865; "Our Returned Soldiers," *Chicago Evening Journal*, June 14, 1865.

25. "Our Returning Soldiers," *Chicago Republican*, June 14, 1865.

26. "Arrival of the 'Irish Legion' at the Fair," *Chicago Times*, June 14, 1865.

27. "Our Returning Soldiers," *Chicago Republican*, June 14, 1865.

28. Ibid.; "The Irish Legion," *Chicago Tribune*, June 13, 1865.

29. "Reception of the 'Ryan Guards,'" *Galena Gazette*, June 20, 1865; Karamanski, *Rally 'Round the Flag*, 239; "Fourth of July," *Chicago Republican*, July 4, 1865.

30. *AGR*, 5:289–308.

Epilogue

1. "The Late Father Dunne," "The Death of Dr. Dunne," "The Late Dr. Dunne," *Chicago Times*, December 25, 27–28, 1868; "The Late Dr. Dunne," *Chicago Tribune*, December 27, 1868.

2. "Preparing for the Reunion," "Army Reunion: The 90th Illinois," "90th Survivors," "Civil War Flags on Verge of Perishing," *Chicago Tribune*, April 19, May 7, 1875; February 3, 1880; February 3, 2002; Henry Porter, Compiled Military Service File, NA; "A Precious Bit of a Civil War Flag," *Kansas City Star*, August 26, 1900.

3. "Veterans of the Fighting Ninetieth," "Fighting Irish Ninetieth Association," "Veterans of Two Wars Meet," "Gleanings in Local Fields: Anniversary of Missionary Ridge," "In Honor of Gen. M'Pherson," "Headquarters of Irish Legion," *Chicago Tribune*, September 23, October 14 and 27, November 17, 1890; January 22, 1891; August 28, 1900.

4. "James Dunn"; *Biographical History of Shelby and Audubon Counties, Iowa*, 308–9; Connie Snyder, "Andreas' History of the State of Nebraska"; Murphy, "Brief Sketch," 26–35; *Illustrated History of Baker, Grant, Malheur, and Harney Counties*, 309.

5. "The Final Summons," *Illinois State Journal*, August 10, 1889; Wallace, *Past and Present*.

6. William White, Manuscript, 1868, Private Collection.

7. Owen Stuart, Pension File, NA; 1870, 1880, and 1900 Federal Census; Andreas, *History of Chicago*, vol. 3, 109, 591; Edwards and Co., *Edwards' Annual Directory of the City of Chicago*.

8. Edwin S. Davis, Pension File, NA.

9. Obituaries, *Chicago Citizen*, October 24, 1885; Mulkerins, *Holy Family Parish*, 778–79.

10. Patrick Sloan, Compiled Military Service File and Patient Case File, NA; 1870 and 1880 Federal Census.

11. *History of Winnebago County, Illinois*; Patrick Flynn, Pension File and Compiled Military Service File, NA.

12. Obituary, James W. Sheahan, *New York Times*, June 18, 1883; "Heartfelt Tribute from the Members of the Press," "In Memoriam: Historical Society," *Chicago Tribune*, June 18, September 19, 1883; Andreas, *History of Chicago*, vols. 2 and 3.

13. "To the Citizens of Chicago," "Death Comes to John M. Loomis," *Chicago Tribune*, November 20, 1868, and August 3, 1900; "Loomis Chaffee School," http://www.loomis.org/about_loomis.asp?about=8 (2/2/2006); "Chicago, Oct. 8—Mrs. Mary Hunt Loomis," *Auburn (N.Y.) Daily Advertiser*, October 8, 1910.

14. RG94CMR.

15. *Memphis Bulletin*, April 1, 1863.

16. "Story of Francis Hook," *New York Times*, April 21, 1864; "Francis Hook," *Davenport Daily Republican*, March 31, 1901.

17. Blanton and Cook, *They Fought Like Demons*; RS20; *AGR*, 5:289–308.

BIBLIOGRAPHY

Primary Sources

"Camp Douglas General and Special Order Book" for October 23, 1861–November 9, 1862. Research Center, Chicago History Museum, Chicago, Ill.

Carmody, Capt. P. J. "The Battle of Collierville." *Journal of the American Irish Historical Society* 9 (1910): 466–70.

Casey, Peter. File. Research Center, Chicago History Museum, Chicago, Ill.

Chickamauga and Chattanooga National Park Commission. Map of the Battlefields of Chattanooga and Wauhatchie. 1896.

Connelly, T. W. *History of the Seventieth Ohio Regiment*. 1902. Reprint, Salem, Mass.: Higginson Book Co., n.d.

Cooley, Samuel A. *Savannah, Georgia (Vicinity). Fortifications in Front of Fort McAllister.* Civil War Glass Negative Collection. Library of Congress, Prints and Photographs Division, Washington, D.C. Call No. LC-B811-3492-4 [P&P].

Court of Claims, U.S. Congressional Jurisdiction. Case Files. National Archives, Washington, D.C.

Cox, Jacob D. *Atlanta*. Vol. 9 of *Campaigns of the Civil War*. New York: Scribner, 1882. Facsimile, Dayton, Ohio: Morningside, 1987.

———. *Sherman's March to the Sea*. New York, 1882. Reprint with new introduction, originally published as *The March to the Sea—Franklin and Nashville*, New York: Da Capo Press, 1994.

Cozzens, Peter, ed. *Battles and Leaders of the Civil War*. Vol. 5. Urbana: University of Illinois Press, 2002.

Cram, George F. *Soldiering with Sherman: The Civil War Letters of George F. Cram*. De Kalb: Northern Illinois University Press, 2000.

Dana, Charles A. *Recollections of the Civil War*. 1898. Reprint, Lincoln: University of Nebraska Press, 1996.

Davis, Maj. George B. *The Official Military Atlas of the Civil War*. 1891. Reprint, New York: Arno Press, Crown Publishers, 1978.

Dawes, Rufus Robinson. *Memoir of Rufus Dawes, in Service with the Sixth Wisconsin Volunteers*. Marietta, Ohio: E. R. Alderman and Sons, 1890.

Dupree, J. G. "The Capture of Holly Springs, Mississippi, December 20, 1862." In *Publications of the Mississippi Historical Society* 4 (1901): 49–61.

Elder, William Henry. "Diary of William Henry Elder, July, 1863." In *Civil War Diary (1862–1865) of Bishop William Henry Elder, Bishop of Natchez*. R.O. Gerow, Bishop of Natchez-Jackson, 1960. http://www.alexanderstreet4.com.proxy.library.vanderbilt.edu.

Ely, Alfred. "Memoir of Alfred Ely." In *Journal of Alfred Ely: A Prisoner of War in Richmond*. New York: D. Appleton and Co., 1862.

Federal Census of 1860, 1870, 1880, 1900. Washington, D.C.: Government Printing Office.

Ft. McAllister [map]. 1864. Library of Congress, Geography and Map Division, Washington, D.C. Call No. G3924.53.2F5S5 1864 F6 Vault: CW 183.

Fulton, Julia. "The Civil War Letters of Patrick H. Sloan." http://webpages, charter.net/julia fulton/Sloan%20Web%20Site/, moved to http://juliafulton.com/phsloan/patsloan.htm.

Grant, Ulysses S. *Personal Memoirs of U.S. Grant.* 1952. Reprint, New York: Da Capo Press, 1982.

Gray, Cordelia Lewis Scales. *"Dear Darling Loulie": Letters of Cordelia Lewis Scales to Loulie W. Irby during and after the War between the States.* Edited by Martha Nevile Lumpkin. Clarksville, Tenn.: Ben Gray Lumpkin, 1980.

Griffin, John A. Diary. Abraham Lincoln Presidential Library, Springfield, Ill.

Hazen, William B. *A Narrative of Military Service.* 1885. Reprint, Huntington, W.V.: Blue Acorn Press, 1993.

Hewett, Janet B., ed. *Supplement to the Official Records of the Union and Confederate Armies.* Part 2, vol. 13. Serial no. 25. Wilmington, N.C.: Broadfoot Publishing Company, 1995.

Hitchcock, Henry. *Marching with Sherman.* Lincoln: University of Nebraska Press, 1995.

Hogan, Sally Coplen, ed. *General Reub Williams's Memories of Civil War Times.* Westminster, Md.: Heritage Books, 2004.

Hood, Gen. John B. *Advance and Retreat: Personal Experiences in the United States and Confederate States Armies.* Philadelphia: Burk and M'Fetridge, 1880.

Howard, Oliver O. *Autobiography of Oliver Otis Howard.* Vol. 2. 1907. Reprint, Harrisburg, Pa.: The Archives Society, 1997.

Johnson, Robert Underwood, and Clarence Clough Buel, eds. *Retreat from Gettysburg.* Vol. 3 of *Battles and Leaders of the Civil War.* 1884–87. Reprint, New York: Thomas Yoseloff, 1956.

———. *The Way to Appomattox.* Vol. 4 of *Battles and Leaders of the Civil War.* 1884–87. Reprint, New York: Thomas Yoseloff, 1956.

Johnston, Joseph E. *Narrative of Military Operations during the Civil War.* 1874. Reprint, New York: Da Capo Press, 1990.

Lloyd's Map of the Southern States, 1861. David Rumsey Historical Map Collection. www.davidrumsey.com.

Loomis, John Mason. Manuscript collection. Katharine Brush Library, The Loomis Chaffee School, Windsor, Conn.

———. Manuscript M107. McCain Library and Archives, University of Southern Mississippi, Hattiesburg.

Main, Marguerite Harris. "Letter Home by Lt. William White." *ILGenWeb,* Civil War Scrapbook. http://civilwar.ilgenweb.net/scrapbk/whiteletter.html.

———. "'A Sunday in the South' by Lt. William White." *ILGenWeb,* Civil War Scrapbook. http://civilwar.ilgenweb.net/scrapbk/whitestory.html.

Manigault, Arthur A. *A Carolinian Goes to War: The Civil War Narrative of Arthur Middleton Manigault.* Columbia: University of South Carolina Press, 1983.

Map of Mission Ridge, Showing the Position Attacked by the Forces under Command of Maj. Gen. W. T. Sherman, Nov. 24th & 25th 1863. Sherman Map No. 169, Sherman Papers. Library of Congress, Washington, D.C.

Map of Tunnel Hill Area: Sherman Campaign. Archives, Accession No. 205, Catalog No. 3205, War Dept. Ph. cov. Series 7, box 1, folder 42. Chickamauga and Chattanooga National Military Park, Ga.

Medical and Surgical History of the War of the Rebellion (1861–1865). Part 3. Washington, D.C.: Government Printing Office, 1870–88.

Microfilms, M594, Roll 27, 90th Illinois Field and Staff. National Archives, Washington, D.C.

Microfilms, Regular Army Enlistments, T233. National Archives, Washington, D.C.

Milhollen, Hirst D., and Donald H. Mugridge, comps. *Civil War Photographs, 1861–1865.* Washington, D.C.: Library of Congress, 1977.

Mississippi 1860 Agricultural Census. Vol. 1. Transcribed and compiled by Linda L. Green. Westminster, Md.: Willow Bend Books, 2005.

Nichols, George Ward. *The Story of the Great March from the Diary of a Staff Officer*. 1865. Reprint, Williamstown, Mass.: Corner House Publishers, 1972.

90th Illinois File. Chickamauga and Chattanooga National Military Park, Ga.

Northwestern Mississippi 1863 Map. Mississippi State Archives, Jackson, Miss.

100th Indiana File. Chickamauga and Chattanooga National Military Park, Ga.

Osborn, Thomas Ward. *The Fiery Trail: A Union Officer's Account of Sherman's Last Campaign*. Knoxville: University of Tennessee Press, 1986.

Pension and Compiled Military Service Files. National Archives, Washington, D.C.

Record Series 301.018, 301.020, 301.023, 90th Illinois Volunteer Infantry. Illinois State Archives, Margaret Cross Norton Building, Springfield, Ill.

Records of the Adjutant General's Office, Record Group 94, 90th Illinois Volunteer Infantry. National Archives, Washington, D.C.

Report of Major General William T. Sherman. Millwood, N.Y.: Kraus Reprint Co., 1977.

Report of the Adjutant General of the State of Illinois. 9 vols. Springfield, Ill.: Phillips Bros. State Printers, 1901.

Sheridan, Redmond. Letters. Private collection.

Sherlock, E. J. *Memorabilia of the Marches and Battles in Which the One Hundredth Regiment of Indiana Infantry Volunteers Took an Active Part. War of the Rebellion, 1861–65*. Kansas City, Mo.: Gerald-Woody Printing Co., 1896.

Sherman, William Tecumseh. *Memoirs of General W. T. Sherman*. 1886. Reprint, New York: Viking Press, 1990.

Simpson, Brooks D., and Jean V. Berlin, eds. *Sherman's Civil War: Selected Correspondence of William T. Sherman. 1860–1865*. Chapel Hill: University of North Carolina Press, 1999.

Sloan, Patrick. Letters. Private collection.

Smith, William F. "An Historical Sketch of the Military Operations around Chattanooga, Tennessee, September 22 to November 27, 1863." In *Papers of the Military Historical Society of Massachusetts: The Mississippi Valley, Tennessee, Georgia and Alabama 1861–1865*. Vol. 8. 1910. Reprint, Wilmington, N.C.: Broadfoot Publishing Co., 1989.

The Story of the Fifty-Fifth Regiment Illinois Volunteer Infantry in the Civil War 1861–1865. 1887. Reprint, Huntington, W.V.: Blue Acorn Press, 1993.

Stuart, Owen. Letters. Abraham Lincoln Presidential Library, Springfield, Ill.

12th Indiana File. Chickamauga and Chattanooga National Military Park, Ga.

Urquahart, Kenneth Trist, ed. *Vicksburg: Southern City under Siege: William Lovelace Foster's Letter Describing the Defense and Surrender of the Confederate Fortress on the Mississippi*. New Orleans: The Historic New Orleans Collection, 1980.

Wallace, Maryanne. "Civil War Diary of Thomas K. Mitchell—Company C." http://www.angelfire.com/ca3/4thIllinoisCavalry/Diary.html.

Wallace-Dickey Family Papers. Abraham Lincoln Presidential Library, Springfield, Ill.

The War of the Rebellion: A Compilation of the Official Records of the Union and Confederate Armies. 128 vols. Washington, D.C.: Government Printing Office, 1880–1901.

Watkins, Sam R. *"Co. Aytch": A Sideshow of the Big Show*. 1900. Reprint, New York: Simon and Schuster, 1997.

White, Jesse. "Illinois Civil War Muster and Descriptive Rolls Database." Illinois State Archives. www.ilsos.gov/genealogy/.

White, William. Manuscripts. Private collection.

Williams, Reuben. "Memories of War Times." *Warsaw Daily Times*, 1903. *Yesteryear in Print*, Kosciusko County, Indiana. http://yesteryear.clunnette.com/index.html.

Wills, Charles W. *Army Life of an Illinois Soldier.* 1906. Reprint, Carbondale: Southern Illinois University Press, 1996.
Wilson, James H. *Under the Old Flag.* Vol. 1. New York: D. Appleton and Company, 1912.
Winther, Oscar Osburn, ed. *With Sherman to the Sea: The Journal of Theodore F. Upson.* Baton Rouge: Louisiana State University Press, 1943.
Yates Family Papers. Manuscript Collection. Abraham Lincoln Presidential Library, Springfield, Ill.

Newspapers

Auburn (N.Y.) Daily Advertiser
Boston Pilot
Chicago Citizen
Chicago Evening Journal
Chicago Post, also known as *Chicago Morning Post*
Chicago Republican
Chicago Times
Chicago Tribune
Davenport (Iowa) Daily Republican
Dawson's Daily Times and Union (Fort Wayne, Ind.)
Defiance (Ohio) Democrat
Evening Standard (Washington, D.C.)
Fort Wayne (Ind.) Evening Sentinel
Illinois State Journal (Springfield)
Kansas City Star
Memphis Appeal
Memphis Bulletin
New York Times
Northwestern Gazette, later known as *Galena (Ill.) Gazette*
Ohio Democrat (New Philadelphia, Ohio)
Ottawa (Ill.) Free Trader
Rockford (Ill.) Democrat
Rock Island (Ill.) Evening Argus
Springfield (Ill.) Sun

Secondary Sources

Andreas, A. T. *The History of Chicago.* Vols. 1–3. Chicago: A.T. Andreas, 1884–85.
Anon. "Major Daniel O'Connor." *Journal of the American-Irish Historical Society* 24 (1925): 316.
Baumann, Ken. *Arming the Suckers: 1861–1865.* Dayton, Ohio: Morningside House, 1989.
Baumgartner, Richard A., and Larry M. Strayer. *Echoes of Battle: The Struggle for Chattanooga.* Huntington, W.V.: Blue Acorn Press, 1996.
Bearss, Edwin C. *The Siege of Jackson, July 10–17.* Baltimore, Md.: Gateway Press, 1981.
———. *Unvexed to the Sea.* Vol. 3 of *The Campaign for Vicksburg.* Dayton, Ohio: Morningside House, 1986.
———. *Vicksburg Is the Key.* Vol. 1 of *The Campaign for Vicksburg.* Dayton, Ohio: Morningside House, 1985.
Bilby, Joseph G. *The Irish Brigade in the Civil War.* Cambridge, Mass.: Da Capo Press, 1997. Originally published as *Remember Fontenoy! The 69th New York and the Irish Brigade in the Civil War*, Hightstown, N.J.: Longstreet House, 1995.

Biographical History of Shelby and Audubon Counties, Iowa. Chicago: Dunbar and Co., 1889.

Black, Robert C., III. *The Railroads of the Confederacy*. Chapel Hill: University of North Carolina Press, 1952.

Blanton, DeAnne, and Lauren M. Cook. *They Fought Like Demons: Women Soldiers in the American Civil War*. Baton Rouge: Louisiana State University Press, 2002.

Bowman, Col. S. M., and Lt. Col. R. B. Irwin. *Sherman and His Campaigns: A Military Biography*. New York: Charles B. Richardson, 1865.

Bradley, Mark L. *Last Stand in the Carolinas: The Battle of Bentonville*. Campbell, Calif.: Savas Woodbury Publishers, 1996.

Bross, William. "History of Camp Douglas." In *Reminiscences of Chicago during the Civil War*. New York: Citadel Press, 1967.

Bruce, Susannah Ural. *The Harp and the Eagle: Irish Volunteers and the Union Army, 1861–1865*. New York: New York University Press, 2006.

Buck, Irving A. *Cleburne and His Command*. Dayton, Ohio: Morningside Bookshop, 1992.

Burton, William L. "The Irish Regiments." In *Melting Pot Soldiers: The Union's Ethnic Regiments*. New York: Fordham University Press, 1998.

Carman, Harry J., and Harold C. Syrett. *A History of the American People*. Vol. 1. New York: Alfred A. Knopf, 1952.

Castel, Albert. *Decision in the West: The Atlanta Campaign of 1864*. Lawrence: University Press of Kansas, 1992.

Cavanagh, Michael. *Memoirs of Gen. Thomas Francis Meagher*. Worcester, Mass.: Messenger Press, 1892.

Chesterton, Gilbert Keith. *The Ballad of the White Horse*. London: Methuen and Co., 1911.

Chicago City Directory, 1861–62. Chicago: Halpin and Bailey, 1861–62.

Christman, William. *Undaunted: The History of Fort McAllister, Georgia*. Darien, Ga.: D. N. R. Darien Printing and Graphics, 1996.

Church, Charles A. "Allen Curtis Fuller: The War Adjutant of Illinois." Paper delivered February 26, 1903, before the Chicago Historical Society. Chicago Historical Museum, Chicago, Ill.

———. "The Mulligan Guards." In *Past and Present of the City of Rockford and Winnebago County, Illinois*. Chicago: S. J. Clarke Pub. Co., 1905.

Commager, Henry Steele., ed. "XXV.7B.: Illinois State Legislature Opposes Emancipation Proclamation." In *Living History: The Civil War*. New York: Tess Press, 2000.

Connolly, S. J., ed. *The Oxford Companion to Irish History*. Oxford: Oxford University Press, 1998.

Coyle, John G. "An Unknown Hero of the Great Civil War." *Journal of the American Irish Historical Society* 15 (1916): 359–65.

Cozzens, Peter. *The Shipwreck of Their Hopes: The Battles for Chattanooga*. Urbana: University of Illinois Press, 1994.

Cunningham, John L. *Three Years with the Adirondack Regiment, 118th New York Volunteers Infantry: From the Diaries and Other Memoranda of John L. Cunningham*. Glen Falls, N.Y.: For private circulation, 1920. Quoted in B. A. Botkin, ed. "On Picket, Pat and Johnny." In *A Civil War Treasury of Tales, Legends and Folklore*. New York: Promontory Press, 1960.

Davis, Burke. *Sherman's March*. New York: Random House, 1980.

Davis, Washington. *Camp-Fire Chats of the Civil War*. Chicago: A. B. Gehman and Co., 1886.

Dawson, George Francis. *Life of Logan: The Warrior Statesman*. Chicago: Belford, Clarke and Company, 1887.

Dornbusch, C. E. *Military Bibliography of the Civil War.* Vol. 1. New York: New York Public Library, 1961.

Donald, David. *Lincoln.* London: Jonathan Cape, 1995.

Duncan, L. Wallace, and Chas. F. Scott. *History of Allen and Woodson Counties, Kansas.* Iola, Kans.: Iola Registers, Printers and Binders, 1901.

Dyer, Frederick H. *A Compendium of the War of the Rebellion.* Washington, D.C.: Gibson Brothers, Printers, 1875.

Eddy, T. M. *The Patriotism of Illinois.* Vol. 1. Chicago: Clarke and Co., 1865.

Edwards and Co. *Edwards' Annual Directory of the City of Chicago.* Chicago: Edwards and Co., 1870.

Eicher, J. H., and D. J. Eicher. *Civil War High Commands.* Stanford: Stanford University Press, 2001.

Farwell, Byron. *Ball's Bluff: A Small Battle and Its Long Shadow.* McLean, Va.: EPM Publications, 1990.

Faust, Patricia L., ed. *Historical Times Illustrated Encyclopedia of the Civil War.* New York: Harper and Row, 1986.

Ferrie, Joseph P. *Yankees Now: Immigrants in the Antebellum United States, 1840–1861.* New York: Oxford University Press, 1999.

Flanders, Michael, and Donald Swann. "Hippopotamus." *At the Drop of a Hat.* New York: Angel Recording, undated record album.

French, Charles F., ed. *Biographical History of the American Irish in Chicago.* Chicago: Chicago American Biographical Publishing Co., 1897.

Gates, Paul Wallace. *The Illinois Central Railroad and Its Colonization Work.* Cambridge: Harvard University Press, 1934.

Gibson, Charles Dana, and S. Kay Gibson. *The Army's Navy Series.* Camden, Maine: Ensign Press, 1995.

Glatthaar, Joseph T. *The March to the Sea and Beyond.* New York: New York University Press, 1985.

Goodspeed, Weston, and Daniel Healy, eds. *History of Illinois—Being a General Survey of Cook County History, Including a Condensed History of Chicago and Special Account of Districts outside the City Limits; from the Earliest Settlement to the Present Time.* Vol. 1. Chicago: Goodspeed Historical Association, 1909.

Gould, Benjamin. A. *Investigations in the Military and Anthropological Statistics of American Soldiers.* 1869. Reprint, New York: Arno Press, 1979.

Grabau, Warren E. *Ninety-Eight Days: A Geographer's View of the Vicksburg Campaign.* Knoxville: University of Tennessee Press, 2000.

Guernsey, Alfred H., and Henry M. Alden. *Harper's Pictorial History of the Civil War.* 1866. Reprint, New York: Fairfax Press, n.d.

Hallock, Judith Lee. "The Role of the Community in Civil War Desertion." *Civil War History* 29 (March 1983): 123–34.

Hernon, Joseph M., Jr. *Celts, Catholics and Copperheads: Ireland Views the American Civil War.* Columbus: Ohio State University Press, 1968.

Hicken, Victor. *Illinois in the Civil War.* Urbana: University of Illinois Press, 1991.

Hirshson, Stanley P. *The White Tecumseh: A Biography of General William T. Sherman.* New York: John Wiley and Sons, 1997.

History of Winnebago County, Illinois: Its Past and Present. Chicago: H. F. Kett and Co., 1877.

Howell, Lt. Col. William. *Officers of the Army and Navy (Volunteer).* Philadelphia: L. R. Hamersely and Co., 1893.

Hubbell, John, and James Geary. *Biographical Dictionary of the Union: Northern Leaders of the Civil War*. Westport, Conn.: Greenwood Press, 1995.

"Illinois in the Civil War." *ILGenWeb Project*. http://www.rootsweb.com/~ilcivilw/history/.

An Illustrated History of Baker, Grant, Malheur, and Harney Counties: With a Brief Outline of the Early History of the State of Oregon. Chicago: Western Historical Pub. Co., 1902.

"James Dunn." In *Biographical History of Tippecanoe, White, Jasper, Newton, Benton, Warren and Pulaski Counties, Indiana*. Vol. 1. Chicago: Lewis Publishing Company, 1899.

Johnson, Rossiter. "Minor Engagements of the First Year." In *Campfire and Battlefield*, 1894. Reprint, Slovenia: Trident Press International, 1999.

Jolly, Ellen Ryan, LL.D. *Nuns of the Battlefield*. Providence, R.I.: Providence Visitor Press, 1927.

Jones, James Pickett. *Black Jack: John A. Logan and Southern Illinois in the Civil War Era*. Carbondale: Southern Illinois University Press, 1967.

Jones, Katharine M. *When Sherman Came: Southern Women and the "Great March."* New York: Bobbs-Merrill Company, 1964.

Karamanski, Theodore J. *Rally 'Round the Flag: Chicago and the Civil War*. Chicago: Nelson Hall, 1993.

Keegan, John. *Six Armies in Normandy*. New York: Viking Press, 1982.

Kelly, Dennis. "A History of Camp Douglas, Illinois, Union Prison, 1861–1865." United States National Park Service, Southeast Regional Office, August 1989. Chicago History Museum, Chicago, Ill.

Keneally, Thomas. *The Great Shame and the Triumph of the Irish in the English-Speaking World*. New York: Doubleday, 1998.

Kennett, Lee. *Sherman: A Soldier's Life*. New York: HarperCollins Publishers, 2001.

Knight, Kevin. "Catholic Encyclopedia: The Irish." *New Advent*. http://www.newadvent.org/cathen/08132b.htm.

Kurtz, Wilbur G. *The Atlanta Cyclorama*. Atlanta: City of Atlanta, 1954.

Lawrence, Alexander A. *A Present for Mr. Lincoln: The Story of Savannah from Secession to Sherman*. Savannah, Ga.: Oglethorpe Press, 1997.

Laxton, Edward. *The Famine Ships: The Irish Exodus to America*. New York: Henry Holt, 1996.

Lewis, Lloyd. *Sherman: Fighting Prophet*. New York: Harcourt, Brace, 1932.

Long, E. B. *The Civil War Day by Day: An Almanac 1861–1865*. Garden City, N.Y.: Doubleday, 1971.

Lonn, Ella. *Desertion during the Civil War*. Lincoln: University of Nebraska Press, 1998.

———. *Foreigners in the Union Army and Navy*. Baton Rouge: Louisiana State University Press, 1951.

"Loomis Chaffee School." *Loomis.org*. http://www.loomis.org/.

Lucas, Marion B. *Sherman and the Burning of Columbia*. Columbia: University of South Carolina Press, 1976.

MacManus, Seumas. *The Story of the Irish Race*. 1921. Reprint, New York: Devin-Adair, 1968.

Marszalek, John F. *A Soldier's Passion for Order*. New York: Free Press, 1993.

McAlexander, Hubert H. *A Southern Tapestry: Marshall County, Mississippi, 1835–2000*. Virginia Beach: Donning, 2000.

McCaffrey, Lawrence J. "Preserving the Union, Shaping a New Image." In *At the Crossroads: Old Saint Patrick's and the Chicago Irish*, edited by Ellen Skerrett, 53–68. Chicago: Loyola Press, 1997.

McDonough, James Lee. *Chattanooga—A Death Grip on the Confederacy.* Knoxville: University of Tennessee Press, 1989.

McIlvaine, Mabel. *Reminiscences of Chicago during the Civil War.* New York: Citadel Press, 1967.

McPherson, James B. *Battle Cry of Freedom: The Civil War Era.* New York: Oxford University Press, 1988.

———. *For Cause and Comrades: Why Men Fought in the Civil War.* New York: Oxford University Press, 1997.

Meagher, Timothy. *The Columbia Guide to Irish American History.* New York: Columbia University Press, 2005.

Mruck, Armin E. "The Role of Railroads in the Atlanta Campaign." *Civil War History* 7 (1961): 264–71.

Mulkerins, Thomas M. *Holy Family Parish, Chicago: Priests and People.* Chicago: Universal Press, 1923.

Murphy, Rev. William. "A Brief Sketch of the Life of Captain P. S. Real." In *Proceedings and Collections of the Nebraska State Historical Society,* series 2, vol. 2, 26–35. Lincoln: State Journal Company Printers, 1898.

Nevins, Alan. *The War for the Union: War Becomes Revolution, 1862–1863.* New York: Charles Scribner's Sons, 1960.

The New Encyclopedia Britannica. Micropedia. Vol. 2. Chicago: Encyclopedia Britannica, 1980.

Niven, John. *Gideon Wells: Lincoln's Secretary of the Navy.* New York: Oxford University Press, 1973.

Northwestern Mississippi 1863 Map. Mississippi State Archives, Jackson. MA 2002.0007(b).

The Oxford Dictionary of Quotations. 3rd ed. New York: Oxford University Press, 1980.

Payette, Pete. "American Forts East, Illinois Forts, Chicago Civil War Camps." *American Forts Network.* http//www.northamericanforts.com/East/il.html.

Penniman, Major. *The Tanner-Boy and How He Became Lieutenant General.* Boston: Roberts Brothers, 1864.

Phisterer, Frederick. *New York in the War of the Rebellion, 1861–1865.* 3rd ed. Albany, N.Y.: J. B. Lyon and Company, State Printers, 1912.

———. *Statistical Record: A Treasury of Information about the U.S. Civil War.* 1883. Reprint, Carlisle, Pa.: John Kallmann, 1966.

Portrait and Biography Album, Woodford County. Chicago: Chapman Bros., 1889.

Risch, Erna. *Quartermaster Support of the Army: 1775–1939.* Washington, D.C.: United States Army Center of Military History, 1989.

Rorabaugh, W. J. "Rising Democratic Spirits: Immigrants, Temperance, and Tammany Hall, 1854–1860." *Civil War History* 22 (1976): 138–57.

Sandburg, Carl. *Abraham Lincoln: The Prairie Years and the War Years, One Volume Edition.* 1926. Reprint, New York: Galahad Books, 1993.

Saunier, Joseph A., ed. *A History of the Forty-Seventh Regiment Ohio Veteran Volunteer Infantry.* Salem, Mass.: Higginson Book Co., 1998.

Sayers, Alethea D. "La Grange, Tennessee: A Chronology of the Civil War Events." 2001. http://www.lagrangetn.com/chronology.html.

Scaife, William R. *The Campaign for Atlanta.* Atlanta: W. R. Scaife, 1985.

———. *The March to the Sea.* 2nd ed. Saline, Mich.: McNaughton and Gunn, 1993.

Secrist, Philip. *The Battle of Resaca.* Macon, Ga.: Mercer University Press, 1998.

Simms, Wm. Gilmore. *Sack and Destruction of the City of Columbia, S.C.* 2nd ed. Atlanta: Oglethorpe University Press, 1937.

Skerrett, Ellen, ed. *At the Crossroads: Old Saint Patrick's and the Chicago Irish.* Chicago: Loyola Press, 1997.

———. "The Irish in Chicago: The Catholic Dimension." In *Catholicism, Chicago Style*, edited by E. Skerrett, E. R. Kantowicz, and S. M. Avella, 29–62. Chicago: Loyola University Press, 1993.

Smith, Derek. *Civil War Savannah.* Savannah, Ga.: Frederic C. Beil, 1997.

Snyder, Connie. "Andreas' History of the State of Nebraska, Fillmore County, Part 4: Capt. P. S. Real." www.kancoll.org/books/andreas_ne/fillmore-p4.html.

Southern Historical Society Papers. Carmel: Guild Press of Indiana, 1998. CD-ROM.

Styple, William B., ed. *Writing and Fighting the Civil War: Soldier Correspondence to the* New York Sunday Mercury. Kearny, N.J.: Bell Grove, 2000.

Sword, Wiley. *Mountains Touched with Fire: Chattanooga Besieged, 1863.* New York: St. Martin's Press, 1995.

Tap, Bruce. "Race, Rhetoric, and Emancipation: The Election of 1862 in Illinois." *Civil War History* 34 (1993): 100–125.

Taylor, Thomas T. "My War: A Buckeye Warrior at Atlanta's Gates." *Civil War Times Illustrated* 39 (October 2000): 24, 26, 75–79, 81.

Tennyson, Alfred Lord. "Locksley Hall." In *The Oxford Dictionary of Quotations.* 3rd ed. New York: Oxford University Press, 1980.

Wallace, Joseph. *Past and Present of the City of Springfield and Sangamon County, Illinois.* Chicago: S. J. Clarke Publishing Co., 1904.

Warner, Ezra J. *Generals in Blue: Lives of the Union Commanders.* Baton Rouge: Louisiana State University Press, 1992.

———. *Generals in Gray: Lives of the Confederate Commanders.* Baton Rouge: Louisiana State University Press, 1999.

Welcher, Frank W. *The Union Army, 1861–1865.* Vol. 2, *The Western Theater.* Bloomington: Indiana University Press, 1993.

Wiley, Bell Irvin. *The Life of Billy Yank: The Common Soldier of the Union.* Baton Rouge: Louisiana State University Press, 2001.

Williams, David. *A People's History of the Civil War Struggle for the Meaning of Freedom.* New York: New Press, 2005.

Woodruff, George H. *Fifteen Years Ago or the Patriotism of Will County.* Joliet, Ill.: Republican Book and Job Steam Printing House, 1876.

Wright, John D., ed. *The Oxford Dictionary of Civil War Quotations.* New York: Oxford University Press, 2006.

INDEX

Page numbers in italics refer to illustrations.

A native of Illinois and lifelong student of the Civil War, **James B. Swan** is a retired professor of agronomy at Iowa State University, where he conducted research in water and solute movement in soils and served as associate director of the Leopold Center. He has published numerous scientific articles.